The Complete Elliott Wave Writings of A. Hamilton Bolton

Published by New Classics Library

The Complete Elliott Wave Writings of A. Hamilton Bolton

First Printing: January 1994

For information, address the publishers:
New Classics Library
Post Office Box 1618
Gainesville, Georgia 30503
USA

ISBN: 0-932750-22-2

ACKNOWLEDGMENTS

I would like to express my appreciation to today's editor of *The Bank Credit Analyst*, Anthony Boeckh, whom I met in 1980 at a conference hosted by the National Committee for Monetary Reform. Boeckh kindly gave New Classics Library permission to publish these works, which have been out of print for as long as forty years. He also provided photocopies of the 1955 and 1956 supplements, the only two missing from my and A. J. Frost's collections other than the still unavailable Addendum to the 1963 Supplement. Thanks are also due to Josephine Penberthy, Charles J. Collins' daughter, who supplied the photos of Collins, to Jane Estes and Karen Latvala, who produced the physical product, and to Susan Willoughby who designed the jacket.

Publisher's Note: The only publication unavailable for this volume is the Addendum to the 1963 Elliott Wave Supplement, dated November 11th of that year. If you have one, we would enjoy receiving a copy.

In order to allow the reader to have a ready reference to price action in the Dow Jones Industrial Average over the entire period of the BCA's Elliott Wave forecasts, we have included a chart on page 402.

CONTENTS

Page

This book is dedicated to

Denise Cuirot

and

Claire Chartrand.

FOREWORD

by

Robert R. Prechter, Jr.

Besides brief mentions of the subject in market letters, the first substantive material I read on the Wave Principle was Bolton's 1960 book, *The Elliott Wave Principle — A Critical Appraisal*. It not only spelled out the nuts and bolts of the Wave Principle clearly, but included one of the very few great stock market forecasts, Bolton's prediction of a major top at Dow 999, which was met in 1966 almost precisely and which remained significantly unexceeded for seventeen years. That book started me on a long and exciting journey that is still in progress. It seems fitting to repay Bolton by making his work with the Wave Principle available to all those who want to review it.

Arthur Hamilton Bolton's main publication was his monthly advisory service, *The Bank Credit Analyst*, which was published by his firm, Bolton, Tremblay & Co., at an annual subscription rate of $50. Bolton was a pioneer in the study of the relationship between bank credit availability and stock market trends. His thesis was set forth most completely in the book, *Money and Investment Profits*, which was published by Dow-Jones Irwin in January 1967. Related pamphlets published through the years included "Introduction to Bank Credit Analysis," "The Principles of Bank Credit Analysis," "The Gold Problem," "Deposit Velocity — A Speculative Indicator?" and "Inflation and Common Stocks."

Bolton was a maverick intellectually. As he stated flatly in one letter, "I couldn't care less about what the orthodox proponents of the status quo have to say." It took that kind of independence to develop his bank credit theories as well as publicly to expound upon the Wave Principle. However, he was accessible as well, being clever enough to weave, as he put it, "the current 'in' thinking" into his exposition to allow the establishment to relax enough to give his work the serious consideration it deserved. Another of Bolton's strengths was his insistence upon intellectual rigor in analytical endeavor, which is evident throughout his writings. Bolton applied both his own theories on bank credit and Elliott's concepts of market pattern with an equal measure of thoughtful analysis. A particularly forceful example of his meticulous approach is a series of personal letters he exchanged with an economist/author who had claimed a new insight into the nature and meaning of debt. Bolton dissected the theory over many pages, enumerating its flaws with a surgeon's precision. The content of the Wave Principle was certainly subject to the same intense scrutiny from Bolton and not only survived it, but profoundly engaged his intellect.

Whether it was his radicalism, accessibility or intellectual precision that played the largest part, Bolton earned and maintained the admiration of the professional community. For his participation and achievements, the Financial Analysts Federation in 1987 (a Fibonacci 34 years after he published his first Elliott Wave Supplement and 21 years after his last) posthumously granted him its most prestigious accolade, the Nicholas Molodovsky Award, which has been presented on average only once every three years since 1968.

Bolton had the rare talent to produce fascinating work in both the fundamental and technical disciplines. It is his technical work, which has been unavailable for decades, that is the focus of this book.

In 1953, four years after he started the BCA in 1949, Bolton began sending subscribers annual "supplements" consisting of market commentary based upon the Wave Principle of R. N. Elliott. Those published in the 1950s were entitled simply, "Elliott's Wave Principle"; for the 1960s, Bolton changed the title to "The Elliott Wave Principle of Stock Market Behavior." The publication of the 1960 book apparently marked a time of change for Bolton, as he not only renamed the supplements, but also had a new photo taken for the BCA.

In all, Bolton wrote thirteen annual supplements. He also wrote the 1960 book, as well as five brief updates: the 1958 Postscript, the 1960 Postscript (first printed in the October 1960 *Bank Credit Analyst*), the 1962 Addendum, the 1963 Addendum and an update in the July 1965 BCA.

Three additional Elliott Wave publications were issued by the firm following Bolton's death: the 1967, 1968 and 1970 BCA supplements. They were written by A. J. Frost (1967 and 1970) and Russell L. Hall (1968), with additional theoretical material by Walter E. White.* There was no supplement published in 1969.

Frost's recollection that Bolton wrote furiously in a short span of time is undoubtedly true, as his sentence structure is sometimes complex and, particularly in the first few supplements, was sometimes in shorthand form, undoubtedly exactly as he had written it. The contrast in writing style between the first few supplements and the later ones shows a greater editorial care given the latter. For this book, we edited those earlier publications minimally, adding occasional verbs and commas and converting some numerals to text. Otherwise, however, the work is intact.

A basic outline of the Wave Principle was included in each original supplement. Other material was occasionally repeated in subsequent supplements as a ready reference.

For this project, we reprinted repeat material only once, when it first appeared. If the material was later edited, we either used the edited version if revisions were minor, or, if the revision was material or timely, repeated the section at the time of its revision. The 1960 book, despite some repetition of earlier material, has been reprinted in its entirety. "Appendix C" from that book, a list of extracts from previous annual supplements, has been omitted for the obvious reason that the full presentation is in this book. Nevertheless, to communicate Bolton's unmatched perspective in a brief space, we present a short extract from each issue in the final pages.

This volume features a few additional treats. We start with a short biography of "Hammy" Bolton by A. J. Frost. Included later are personal letters between Bolton and Charles Collins, including a March 1967 letter that Bolton wrote a week before he died. Also included is an article that appeared in the July 1957 edition of *Investor's Future* magazine. Though credited to Bolton, it may have been a collaboration between Bolton and famed odd-lot analyst and author Garfield A. Drew, since some of the same language appeared in Drew's book, *New Methods for Profit in the Stock Market*. The article was called "The Coming Tidal Wave," and began with a simple statement that is as true today as ever: "Perhaps the most outstanding theory, based on proven record, for accurately charting the long term future movements of stock market prices is Elliott's Wave Principle." Providing what is in retrospect powerful evidence for that claim, the author commented simply, "the new bull wave that started in 1949 is of tidal proportions." In the forty-four years prior to 1949, the Dow had recorded a miserable net gain of only 60%. In the 44 years since then, the Dow has climbed over 2000%. Only the Wave Principle was able, and is able, to predict such a change in fortune for a market.

As Frost recounts, the only significant market move that Bolton missed forecasting publicly at its commencement was the 1962 drop. However, he had predicted it several times a year or so prior, and the break-of-trendline "stop" he provided in early 1962 would have kept any careful reader out of trouble. Moreover, the downside limit of "the 522 mark in the DJIA" that Bolton expressed in Chapter XII of his 1960 book was met quite precisely at the crash low of 524 in June, 1962. If this period saw a "mistake" on Bolton's part, it was such that lesser talents might have called it a success.

Most of the time, Bolton's forecasts displayed a brilliant grasp of the market's potential. For example, he targeted the Dow Jones Industrial Average with specific numbers only eight times in the thirteen years (more Fibonacci) that he wrote about the Wave Principle. Two were wrong and quickly abandoned when the market's correct course became clear. A third, which was based only on pattern, called for a decline in 1957 to 400; the actual bottom occurred at 419, a good forecast by most standards. However, from 1960 forward, he was nearly perfect in the five other forecasts (the last as refined by A. J. Frost). He called the downside limit of the 1962 decline to within two points. His forecast for a Dow top at 999 was precise to within 1%, six years in advance. One might disregard his comment that Dow 777, which was indicated by a Fibonacci relationship, was of secondary importance for a future high, but that level not coincidentally marked precisely the August 12, 1982 low at 776.92, the orthodox end of wave IV. His mention in early 1966 that important support lay at Dow 740 pinpointed that year's low to the dollar. As Collins summed up the outlook in early 1966, weeks from top tick in a 24 year advance, "Might not the A wave of [the bear market] carry to the 770-710 area, the C wave to around 524, with a sizeable intervening B wave?", a near perfect forecast of the 1966-1974 period. Indeed, Bolton and Collins' call for the ultimate wave IV low to occur "around 524" was based only on pattern, the 1962 low having occurred at 524. After Hammy's death, A. J. Frost in the 1970 Supplement refined the forecast using the Fibonacci ratio and called for a low at Dow 572, which was also hit precisely to the dollar, on December 9, 1974 at an hourly reading of 572.20.

Bolton used Dow numbers less specifically once, on June 28, 1965. He had concluded prematurely that the bull market was over and listed support levels at "800-830" and "710-750." The hourly low occurred the next day at 835.54, and after the February 1966 top, the 1966 low occurred at 740. Despite the imperfect market call, it was obvious that he knew how to apply the Wave Principle to determine support levels.

Specific forecasts are one thing; perspective is another, and the Wave Principle has no peer in providing a good one. Bolton's commentary throughout the 1950s continually stressed the Wave Principle's message for the multi-year outlook, that prices were "on the low side for some years to come... with lots of time and bullish amplitude ahead ...." His forecast graphics show that he was projecting a DJIA peak of approximately "1000 in 1965" at least as far back as 1953. Bolton's perspective, and particularly his steadfastness, stood in clear contrast to the recurring fear of crash and depression among many investors and the continually hedged and changeable views of the majority of economists and analysts.

Perhaps equally significant is that Bolton also continually recognized what the market was *not* going to do. He often stated that certain levels would not be exceeded on the downside, contrary to the views of many market watchers. For instance, he said in 1957, "It does not look under any circumstances we will drop below 400." In 1959, probably in response to numerous published forecasts calling for a repeat of the 1929-1932 experience, he commented that "any idea of returning to the 50 or 100 level DJIA would be pure fantasy." In his first Elliott Wave Supplement in 1953, he stated, with more reliability and accuracy than economists can even imagine, "no major depression of the 1929-32 variety is in the cards in our life-time." Knowing for certain what the market is not going to do is another great luxury provided by Elliott Wave analysis.

If Bolton had been asked to acknowledge a peer in market acumen, he undoubtedly would have named Charles J. Collins, money manager, editor of *Investment Letters* and writer of R. N. Elliott's first book. (For more on Collins, see the Foreword to *Elliott Wave Principle* by Frost and Prechter and the biography of R. N. Elliott in *The Major Works of R. N. Elliott.*) Bolton and Collins exchanged some 120 personal letters over a dozen years, from April 27, 1955 to March 29, 1967, an almost monthly correspondence. The two men met at least six times. The first meeting was in Montreal in August 1955; the last was in Detroit in February 1963, two months after Collins' "semi-retirement" in December 1962. Their relationship was one of professional independence and mutual respect, Bolton occasionally contrasting their discussions to input from the general crowd of "Elliott buffs." They often had the same wave counts for market moves, yet freely explained and discussed differences when they arose. Indeed, it was Collins' labeling of the Supercycle's components that eventually prevailed over Bolton's 21-year triangle idea. The 1966 Supplement contains a section by Collins that straightforwardly presented the correct long term stock market interpretation from 1932, which Bolton had then come to accept. That meeting of the minds set the stage for the continued success of the Wave Principle through the bear market of the 1970s, as analyzed by A. J. Frost, Russ Hall and Richard Russell.*

Skeptics should consider that each of Bolton's forecasts represented only one of countless outcomes which would have been possible if the market were walking randomly and if turning points were made by chance. Keep in mind also that the Wave Principle's forecasting success during this period was achieved despite stock splits, changes in the Dow's components and divisor, the assassination of one president and the resignation of another, the Vietnam War and a million other events. That the Dow qua Dow is patterned makes sense only in terms of social psychology. The precision in those patterns makes sense only if the

Wave Principle indeed governs the movements of the market.

Given the remarkable body of evidence herein, one must accept either that Bolton was the luckiest forecaster ever to have lived, or that he understood a profound truth about markets, and thus of human behavior. To this observer, the correct conclusion is inescapable. A. Hamilton Bolton knew what he was talking about, and he knew it because he understood the Wave Principle.

—Robert R. Prechter, Jr., 1993

---

*Walter White's treatise is available in an Appendix to *Elliott Wave Principle* by Frost and Prechter. The final three BCA Supplements and Richard Russell's writings will be included in our companion volume, *The Elliott Wave Writings of A. J. Frost.*

THE HAMILTON BOLTON STORY

by

A. J. Frost

Hamilton Bolton, called Hammy by his friends, was a genius. When Bolton wrote his high school matriculation examination, he attained the highest marks in mathematics that had ever been attained in the Province of Quebec. He studied economics and mathematics at McGill University and then took the MBA course at Harvard. He then joined Wood Gundy, doing analysis and writing reports for that firm.

One of Wood Gundy's top salesman was Maurice Tremblay, who recognized Hammy's genius. After a brief acquaintanceship, Tremblay suggested the two men go into business together as investment consultants and portfolio managers, with Tremblay soliciting the accounts for Bolton to manage. Bolton agreed, and in 1946 the firm of Bolton Tremblay, Inc., was formed in Montreal, with Bolton as its president. Bolton's main occupation was as editor-in-chief of the Bolton-Tremblay *Bank Credit Analyst*, a monthly commentary on market trends and forces that soon won the respect of the financial community.

A few years earlier, R. N. Elliott had published a series of articles in *Financial World* magazine. A connection between the Wave Principle and the Fibonacci sequence of numbers was soon after introduced to Elliott by Bolton's friend, Charles J. Collins of Detroit. The combination of these ideas struck a responsive chord with Bolton. After confirming these ideas empirically, he began publishing his own Elliott Wave analysis in an annual supplement to his publication, *The Bank Credit Analyst.*

As far as I know, Bolton met R. N. Elliott only once, briefly, just prior to Elliott's death. The meeting was not very productive, as Elliott was very ill by this time and only moderately responsive.

I had the good fortune to be one of Hammy's partners for about two and a half years, but left the firm in late 1966. During this period, we spent many hours together discussing "Elliott" both in the office and at his home.

I have often been asked, what kind of a man was Bolton? To say the least, he was natural and friendly, but inclined to be somewhat of a recluse. He loved to be alone to listen to good music and his inner self. He enjoyed silence, and had no difficulty in shutting out the world. He also had a sense of humor. When a female analyst asked him one day what one thing he would most desire on a desert island, Bolton replied, "*Barron's.*"

Bolton had remarkable self control. On one occasion while traveling back from Bermuda in the spring of 1961, he wrote out longhand the entire text of the next BCA publication in three and a half hours. His writing was fast and furious and difficult to read, but his secretary, Claire Chartrand, faithfully transcribed it. When Bolton proofread her typed copy, he did not have to change a single word. It seemed to me he was virtually in a trance when he was writing about the market. His absorption and concentration were unbelievable.

Hammy was not religious in the orthodox sense of that word, but was fascinated by nature and its law. He felt that the market had its law, which he said was inexorable in its action. I found Bolton's interest in nature and the stock market a revelation. Hammy often said privately that the market's and the economy's cycles of optimism and pessimism reflected the Fibonacci ratio, which in turn related to "the spirit of nature." He once said, "if you keep the Law, you will be kept by the Law, and there is no third person between yourself and the Law." I once asked him if he felt Man was predestined to grow according to this Law. He said yes, and the challenge was to *know it*. He never felt that acceptance of the Law was just a one time opportunity, but that it was always with us, providing the opportunity whenever we got around to recognizing it. Law and order were the cornerstone of Hammy's philosophy of life.

Bolton had many friends and contacts worldwide, especially in the United States, and was very active professionally. He was a Founding Director of the Montreal Institute of Investment Analysts and President of the National Federation of Financial Analysts Societies (known later as the Financial Analysts Federation, or FAF) in 1959-1960 (its 13th year), serving as a director for years thereafter. Bolton was also an associate editor of *The Financial Analysts Journal* and a regent of the Beloit Financial Analysts Seminars. *Fortune* magazine rated him as one of the world's greatest analysts, and his firm ultimately managed upwards of three hundred million dollars. Although his main work was with bank credit statistics, invariably after a 45 minute speech the first question from the audience would be about "Elliott."

Hammy targeted the market three times within a few points years in advance and caught all major turns except for the 1962 debacle. Actually, he called the decline a year or two in advance and marked the word "PANIC" on one of his charts, but when the turns came, he was busy traveling on FAF business and missed it. That miss almost broke Bolton's spirit, especially as he had seen it coming well in advance of the event.

For such a short career, Bolton achieved a great deal. In the field of fundamental analysis, he invented the debit/loan ratio and pioneered the study of the relationship between bank credit measures and the stock market. In the field of technical analysis, he kept the Elliott Wave Principle alive. He didn't get the Wave Principle "out there," as that great achievement became Robert Prechter's contribution to financial analysts worldwide. However, Bolton showed great courage in championing a technical approach to the market during a time when such approaches were considered nonsense by most of the financial establishment.

In the spring of 1967, Bolton visited me at my home at Manotick, Ontario for a long weekend. He was ill, but I did not perceive the extent of his illness. I did, however, get the feeling that he was being pressured by one of his associates to stick to bank credit analysis and "fundamentals," and forget about Elliott. Bolton cheerfully ignored this advice, and discussed the Wave Principle with his usual enthusiasm during those two and a half days we spent together. In fact, as he related in the March 29, 1967 letter he wrote to Collins (which Bob has included in this book), he had just become keen on forming a group of Elliott Wave intellectuals to research and refine the theory into more of a science.

Unfortunately, those were Bolton's last days. He flew to Bermuda the following weekend, and on April 5th, at the young age of 53, he died.

—A. J. Frost, 1993

A. Hamilton Bolton

WHAT THE Bolton-Tremblay BANK CREDIT ANALYST OFFERS YOU

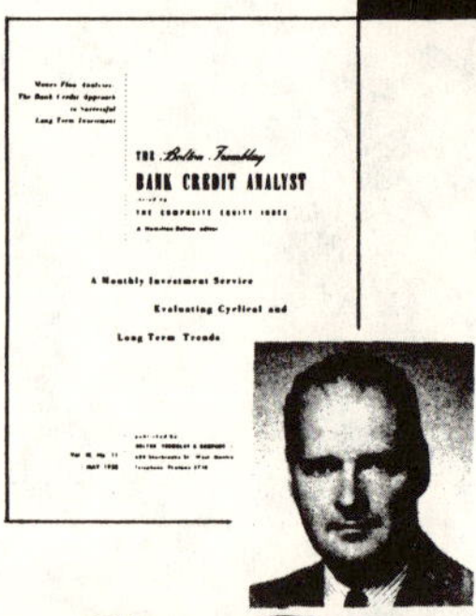

THE Bolton-Tremblay BANK CREDIT ANALYST
680 SHERBROOKE ST., WEST,
MONTREAL 2, Canada

BASIS

A fundamental investment service devoted to the study of changes from week to week in banking and credit trends, evolving a method of analysis from banking data both timely and comprehensive which provides advance information on probable future trends, of immense value to professional and private investors.

SOURCE OF DATA

Federal Reserve System's
Weekly Condition Statements

EDITOR

A. Hamilton Bolton,
B.A. (McGill), M.B.A. (Harvard)

PUBLISHERS

Bolton, Tremblay & Company,
Investment Consultants, Montreal.

Registered with the Securities and Exchange Commission, Washington, D.C.

RATES

$100.00 for 12 months
$ 60.00 for 6 months

TIME OF PUBLICATION

Friday closest to first of month.

DELIVERY

Overnight service, incl. airmail
(no extra charge) throughout the world.

TYPE OF CLIENTELE

Professional, institutional and sophisticated private investors.

GENERALLY

A unique investment service . . .

. . . that analyses the Money Forces behind investments and projects the DIRECTION of the major cyclical trend;

. . . that evaluates what "Money" will mean to investment values in terms of APPRECIATION or DEPRECIATION;

. . . that is not only a dependable guide to stock market trends, but that provides guidance well AHEAD of THE TURN in the trends themselves.

A combination of Research with Judgment resulting in lucid and straightforward analytical appraisals of the American investment weather.

SPECIFICALLY

1 — **Monthly** — a 20 page monthly bulletin made up of :

A) Latest summary of bank credit indices in tabular form;

B) Several regular charts brought up-to-date each month and presenting these facts and figures in graphic form;

C) A complete analytical study (text portion) of the changes in these figures and charts with definite and clear-cut conclusions as to what the investment trend really is.

II — **Periodically** (as required) — a special supplement of charts, data and indices not regularly included in the monthly bulletin.

III — **Occasionally** — special timely studies are published from time to time and distributed without charge to subscribers. Among them are :

A) a comprehensive handbook on bank credit analysis;

B) a yearly review of the Elliott's Wave Principle, of which our Editor is recognized as "one of the most discerning students";

C) a review of Newsprint, an important sensitive and economic investment barometer (as circumstances warrant).

AN ESSAY ON INVESTING

by

A. Hamilton Bolton

(Excerpted from advertising material for *The Bank Credit Analyst*)

Research and judgment are the two cornerstones upon which the art of successful investment is built, but of the two there is little question that *judgment* is the more important. *The Bank Credit Analyst* in its monthly appraisals of the forces at work toward higher or lower prices attempts to combine both research and judgment. The monthly bulletins therefore enable the long-term investor to keep on top of research in a complex field, and in addition to benefit from the judgment factor on the part of experts in interpreting and evaluating the meaning of change and its probable effect on the investment outlook.

The ideal barometer does not and never will exist; one can only reach for it. Let us nevertheless look at the qualities of the ideal barometer as a theoretical concept:

1) direction of the next move;
2) its amplitude;
3) length of time;
4) fairly constant lead in terms of time on the downside as well as on the upside from cycle to cycle, even though these lead times need not be the same for up or for down.

Now, from the very moment of its conception, the "ideal" barometer will cease to be ideal. Given a perfect indicator, investors will tend to discount its signals simply on the principle of musical chairs, i.e., that not everyone can wait till the last moment, else there will be no one to sell to or to buy from. Gradually, if the ideal barometer continued to be ideal, its signals would become almost reversed. Since so many people had sold in anticipation of the down signal, it would prove better to buy at the time of the signal, or vice versa to sell at the up signal.

It is much better, therefore, for the few who really stand to gain, first, that the signals' indications be less than clear as to timing and amplitude and, second, that there be a good deal of controversy about their validity.

The first purpose of a cyclical indicator is to determine the area where major buying can be made with little risk and at prices likely to show substantial gains later. The second purpose of an indicator, or a series of indicators, is to alert us to such dangers to the favorable economic trend so as to make moves out of stocks into reserves well worthwhile.

For much more time than not, one will want to remain as fully equity-invested as possible since the secular trend is up. However, there are cyclical periods when it is much better to be out of the market altogether. Our barometer should therefore point out in advance the investment impact of these periods and the degree of severity of the economic deterioration.

Many times one may be warned of the potentially dangerous economic period ahead; yet there is, because of the bullish bias, a definite reluctance to "lose one's position." This is primarily a psychological attitude based on one's missed opportunities of the past. It overlooks the fact that, even in a bullishly biased [inflationary] economy, equities will not react equally to that inflation, with the result that the average portfolio gets oriented into some good and some not-so-good equity vehicles. Consequently, when a modicum of monetary deflation is felt, the wrong vehicles suffer greater-than-average losses, and these losses are often in relation to the excessive bullishness of the prior period.

Even if, in retrospect, it should turn out that one did not gain too much in selling out for the one-to-three year period, the bank credit approach affords this great advantage: that when one gets to buying again, one takes an entirely new look at the various groups and individual stocks instead of being hamstrung by holdings acquired in a previous investment cycle. If adhered to strictly, the bank credit signals force selling at the end of an old cycle and, consequently, allow buying later without the bias of having to take sometimes large losses.

A Brief Introduction to Elliott's Wave Principle

by

A. Hamilton Bolton

The first page of this essay is excerpted from the Foreword to Hamilton Bolton's 1960 Book, *The Elliott Wave Principle — A Critical Appraisal.* The remainder first appeared in the 1957 Supplement and was repeated in numerous supplements thereafter. For extensions of this presentation, see Bolton's 1960 book, as well as his 1964, 1965 and 1966 Supplements.

INTRODUCTION

This book is about a technical tool for stock market analysis and forecasting known as *Elliott's Wave Principle.* It is not a well-known tool, but it deserves to be better understood. The excuse that I have in writing this book is that while my basic interest in recent years in the analysis of the economy and the stock market has been by way of my firm's extensive studies of bank credit trends, as edited by us in the Bolton-Tremblay *Bank Credit Analyst,* nevertheless I have been impressed with (as well as critical of) the truths behind Elliott's hypothesis as set forth some twenty years ago in a little known and now out-of-print monograph entitled *The Wave Principle.*

As we have advanced through some of the most unpredictable economic climate imaginable, covering depression, major war, and postwar reconstruction and boom, I have noted how well Elliott's Wave Principle has fitted into the facts of life as they have developed, and have accordingly gained more confidence that this Principle has a good quotient of basic value.

It is extremely difficult, of course, to accept any modicum of determinism in our thinking with regard to values and price trends. Nevertheless, it is becoming increasingly apparent that emotions are greatly responsible for price fluctuations, and these emotions not only follow laws of action and reaction, but also adhere to more complicated laws, the surface of the knowledge of which has but barely been scratched.

To suggest that the Elliott Wave Principle can give us the answer is to overstate grossly the case. Nevertheless, I believe that it offers, especially if combined with other studies, an excellent tool that should be studied with some care.

HOW THE WAVE PRINCIPLE WAS BORN

During an illness in the middle thirties, R. N. Elliott discovered the basic rhythm of what he called "The Wave Principle" (later he changed the name to "Nature's Law"). This consisted of a series of waves in the direction of the main trend which could always be subdivided into smaller waves and subdivided again into smaller waves, still within the framework of certain empirical rules.

WAVE THEORY VS. DOW THEORY

During the last 40 years, the Dow Theory has become a household word in the world of the investor and investment manager. It is, as one commentator remarked, "a triumph of advertising," having been publicized and backed by one of the most important financial weeklies in the U.S. Because of its wide following, its signals (which incidentally do no forecasting other than on the proposition that a trend once started is not likely to reverse immediately) in recent years have been of less value to the investor in providing useful buying and selling junctures.

For every 100 investors who have heard of the Dow Theory, there is probably not one who knows about Elliott's Wave Principle. The late R. N. Elliott was a remarkable man. The writer knew him personally and corresponded with him at intervals over the period 1938-1947. Elliott lacked the backing of an organization which could give his "Principle" a wide interest. Further, he was so meticulous as to details that in his writings he often seemed to put the trees before the forest. Nevertheless, he developed his principle into a rational method of stock market analysis on a scale never before attempted.

ELLIOTT AND THE CYCLE THEORISTS

Elliott alone among the cycle theorists (despite the fact he died in 1947, while others lived) provided a basic background of cycle theory compatible with what actually happened in the post-war period (at least to date).

According to orthodox cycle approaches, the years 1951-1953 were to produce somewhat of a holocaust in the securities and commodity markets, with depression centering in this period. That the pattern did not work out as anticipated is probably a good thing, as it is quite doubtful if the free world could have survived a decline that was scheduled to be almost as devastating as 1929-32.

Elliott's Wave Principle differs from other cycle theories in that it does not hinge upon periodicity of recurring cycles. Within the framework of the Principle, waves may extend or contract in time over very considerable periods. Thus, the potential minor patterns are far more flexible than under orthodox cycle theories.

ELLIOTT AND BANK CREDIT

One of the interesting facets to Elliott's Wave Principle is the fact that the whole concept is one of *growth*. The main direction can be considered as always upward, the downward waves always being corrections. Thus, in the stock market, one starts a new Cycle of waves on a small scale, and these then become parts of larger waves in set patterns. No corrective wave should ever exceed the amplitude of the wave it is supposed to correct, otherwise it is not a real corrective wave, or again it is not correcting just one wave, but a series.

Now it is a fact that all through history, *money* has acted in the same way. Always money and credit expand; always the money unit depreciates. Any in-between appreciations (declines) are simply corrections of a previous larger upward trend. There seems to be no period in history where there has been a trend in the opposite direction that was not preceded by a previous greater trend in the main direction, upwards.

During the period covered by Elliott's Super Cycles III, IV and now V (1857-1928, 1928-49 and 1949 to date), we find that money supply per capita has generally been in a long-upward trend (for reference, see chart I, page 9, in our "Inflation and Common Stocks"[1]). It is perhaps significant that modern capitalism took birth in the late 1700s, and it would appear that Super Cycle I must have started sometime around that time. This was the time of Adam Smith and his *Wealth of Nations*. It is also significant that in 1837 we had a collapse of bank credit comparable to that of 1929, and that in between the periods of bank credit deflation have been less severe.

Thus, in the wave pattern of a long-term secular growth in common stocks, we see the influence of a slowly rising money supply. The relationship of money and stock prices is not necessarily close over any five to ten year period, but as we pointed out in "Inflation and Common Stocks," the long-term relationship is solid. Stock prices depend in the final analysis on the public's evaluation of earning power. Earning power is expressed in terms of the dollar, and its long-term trend adjusts itself inevitably to the slow change in the value of the dollar. Long-term inflation points to the inevitability of a slow depreciation in purchasing power, and this depreciation is an important ingredient in the long rise in stock prices. Waves in between reflect the vagaries of public opinion and human nature.

Why the waves break down into set patterns is, of course, a major mystery. Perhaps we could as well ask why the human being has five fingers.

WAVE DEGREES

Before getting down to details, it is as well to have a general idea of Elliott's terminology. The main point where Elliott terminology differs from others is in the concept that *each completed wave becomes a subwave of a larger wave of the next degree* (amplitude). The degree of a wave should, and with rare exceptions does, bear some relationship to both time and amplitude, but unlike other cycle theories, there is no firm concept of periodicity. (This may be considered by some too strong a statement, since Elliott did use a periodicity pattern known as the Fibonacci series, 1, 2, 3, 5, 8, 13, 21, 34, 55, 89, 144, etc., each number of which is obtained by adding the last two numbers of the series at any point.)

The main patterns that Elliott's waves take are shown graphically in the chart on the next page.[2] These patterns apply to any wave of any degree. Elliott classified the degrees as follows, in order of ascending magnitude.

Subminuette
Minuette
Minute
Minor
Intermediate
Primary
Cycle
Super Cycle
Grand Super Cycle

Thus, on the chart, the whole wave (under I, The Main Trend, Up) from 1 to 5 might be of any degree, but supposing it were of Primary degree, each of the waves marked 1, 2, 3, 4, and 5 would then be Intermediates, and each of the lettered waves a, b, c, d, e would then be Minors.

It is doubtful if the waves of the lower degrees are of much practical value. Since we are interested in the broad sweep, we will generally only talk of waves of Intermediate degree and up.

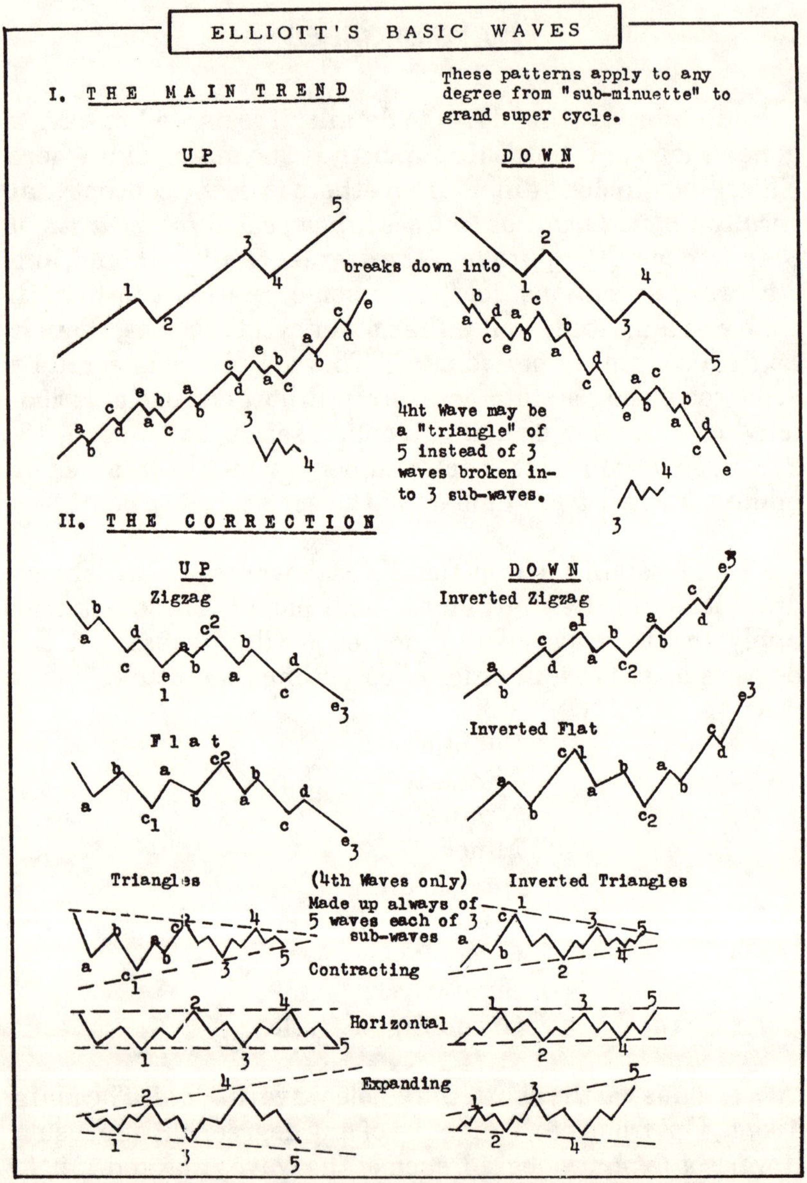

THE MAIN TREND AND THE CORRECTION

The main trend may be up or down, and that depends entirely on what degrees of waves you are talking about. Thus, assuming a Cycle wave up, there will be Primaries within that Cycle wave, some of which will be up, and some of which will be down. The subdivision of the waves will be as follows:

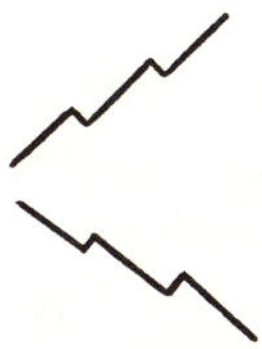

The main trend (up or down) will always consist of five waves: three in the direction of the trend (nos. 1, 3, 5) and two as corrections (nos. 2, 4).

The correction (up or down) will consist normally of three waves: waves 1 and 3 in the direction of the correction, with wave 2 a counter move in between.

The corollary of this is that if a wave of any degree cannot be subdivided into five waves within the rules laid down by Elliott, it must be a corrective wave either up or down, and this will then govern the interpretation to be placed on the next larger set of waves.

In Elliott's later work, he elaborated on the possible types of corrections and pointed out that in addition to the zigzag, flat and triangle type corrections, there could be other more complex corrections. Thus, one can have a "single 3" of three waves, a "double 3" of seven waves and a "triple 3" of eleven waves.

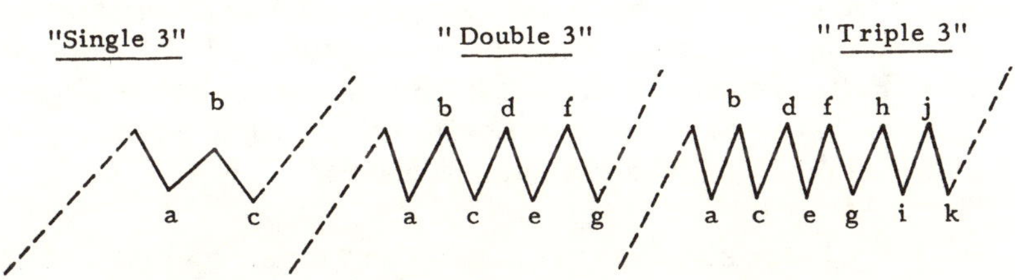

SOURCE OF BACKGROUND INFORMATION

Very little literature is currently disseminated on the position of Elliott's Wave Principle. Probably the biggest publicity it has ever had was in Garfield Drew's *New Methods for Profit in the Stock Market*, published in 1948.[3] Elliott's monographs and "educational letters" are long since out of print.[4] There are, so far as this writer knows, no commentators analyzing from day to day the market along Elliott's lines. Garfield Drew, however, in his Odd Lot service occasionally outlines the apparent current position. We are indebted to Mr. Drew for his published ideas on the subject, and we have on one or two occasions discussed the position with him since Elliott's death. We have also had from time to time correspondence with other wave students, whose work has helped clarify difficult points. However, the projections herein of Elliott's thinking are based on a restudy of a great deal of Elliott's personal literature, which we happen to have in our files.

FOOTNOTES

1 This was one of Bolton's BCA publications.

2 Bolton makes a rare error here. Despite his depiction near the bottom of this chart, there is no specific triangle named "horizontal." Elliott described two basic types of triangles, diagonal (impulsive) and horizontal (corrective). There are four types of horizontal triangles: ascending, descending, contracting and expanding. Bolton adds "horizontal" as an additional type when in fact it is merely an inclusive term for any corrective triangle. This diagram he shows is somewhat suggestive of triple threes, which have a roughly rectangular structure. Diagonal triangles, which Bolton never mentions, occur occasionally as fifth impulse waves. Bolton later says, in the 1956 Supplement, that he did not display all patterns on this chart because "the other types may be considered modifications of the main waves."

3 Later supplements added the words, "and revised in 1954."

4 See *R. N. Elliott's Market Letters, 1938-1946* (New Classics Library).

ELLIOTT'S WAVE PRINCIPLE

1953

The Bolton-Tremblay

BANK CREDIT ANALYST

A. Hamilton Bolton, editor

ELLIOTT'S WAVE PRINCIPLE 1953 [1]

The late R. N. Elliott in 1941[2] projected a pattern of future stock market behaviour which has not varied in fundamentals from his original outline years ago.

His thesis has certain features which parallel markedly the action of bank credit in the 100 years prior to 1941 and in the dozen years since.

In view of the recent indications of (a) a probable turn to the favourable side of the Composite Equity Index and (b) our newly created "Trade and Money Trend," Elliott's Wave Principle provides an interesting hypothesis at this juncture.

Elliott's Wave Principle first appeared in the *Financial World* in the summer and fall months of 1938 in a series of installments. At about the same time,[3] he published a monograph outlining the law behind the Principle, which monograph was revised in late 1945. At the time of the first monograph, Elliott stated that according to his Principle, March 31, 1938 represented the end of the first wave of the bear market from the March 1937 top, which would encompass three major waves, the first down, the second up (actually later shown as March 1938 to September 1939) and the third down again. It will be seen from a glance at any stock market chart that the major bear market of 1937-1942 fitted exactly this pattern projection as outlined by Elliott four years in advance of the end of the bear market.

SUPER-CYCLE STARTED IN 1942

It is impossible at this time to attempt to cover the detailed principles making up his over-all "Wave Principle." Suffice to say that he analyzed stock prices on a daily, weekly and monthly basis for as far back as stock prices of any kind were available. He concluded that 1929 represented the peak of a "Super Cycle" starting in 1857, which was broken down into 5 smaller Cycle waves, 3 up and 2 down, each of which again could be broken down into smaller waves (Primaries, Intermediates, etc.), the forward moving ones into 3 up and 2 down, and the reversal waves into 2 down with 1 up in between, and so on, breaking down each wave so discovered into its components, either 3-2, or 2-1 on a successively smaller scale. He later, in 1941, concluded that when the then-current bear market would be over (actually terminated May 1942), the whole period 1929-42 would qualify as a giant "triangle" correction from which a bull market would start, comparable to the 1857-1929 Super Cycle bull market.

ELLIOTT'S LONG TERM ANALYSIS
AND 1941 PROJECTION

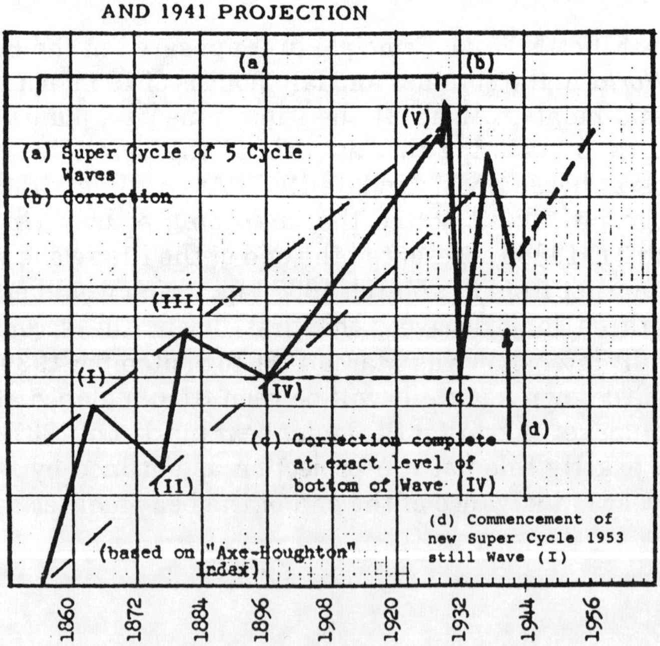

This last prediction, or hypothesis, is vitally important, because if Elliott is right, we will not see again probably in this century stock prices as low "in dollar price" as they were in 1942. Of course, inflation will take care of a great deal of that hypothesis anyway, but it does mean that no major depression of the 1929-32 variety is in the cards in our life-time (although there may well be 1921s, 1896s, 1873s again within this span). Further, it is as well to keep the background in perspective; Elliott's projection was made at a time when deflation and not inflation was the current fear.[4]

Elliott further went on in early 1946 to call the first wave of a bull market starting in 1942 as finished, with a correction pending, which, however, he did not think would go very deep, nor take very long. In this he was correct on amplitude but a little out on time, as the correction to wave 1 took three years to be accomplished.

Elliott's death in 1947[5] did not allow him to complete his analysis of the 1946-49 correction. A cursory glance at any stock market chart, however, shows the typical correction pattern in 3 waves, 2 down (1946-47 and 1948-49) with 1 up in between (1947-48). The last wave (1948-49) further has a very clear-cut 5 sub-wave break-down, which is typical of the end of all moves according to Elliott.

The significance of Elliott's projection should now become more apparent.

(1) Elliott's hypothesis calls for a series of bull markets from 1942 similar in degree to those between 1857 and 1929, in the pattern of 5 waves, 3 up and 2 down in between, followed by 3 down (2 down and 1 up), all moving on to successively higher levels.

(2) Wave I of the first Cycle bull market was completed in 1946 (Elliott's analysis), and its correction (wave II) was completed in June 1949.

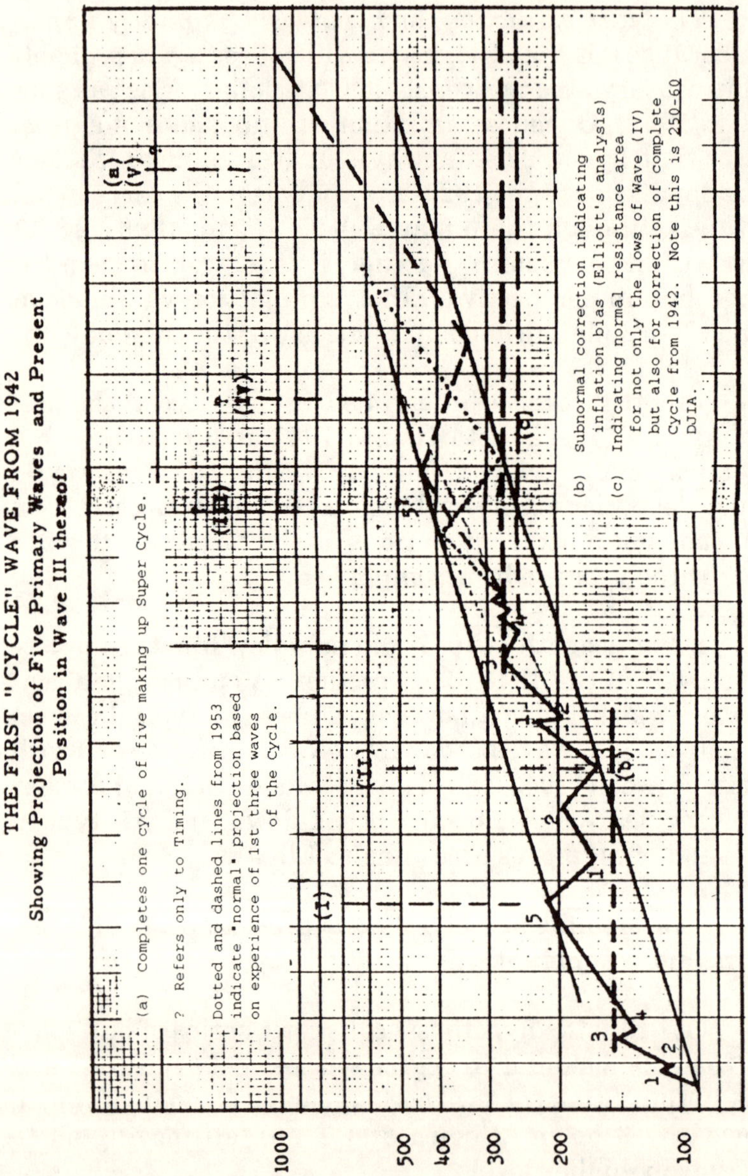

(3) Because of both the time element (a third wave according to Elliott is never shorter in time than the first wave)[6] and amplitude indicated, we must now still be in wave III of the 1942 - ? bull market (one Cycle wave).

(4) Following completion of wave III (not likely before 1954 because of time and amplitude elements), there should be a correction (wave IV) on the order of 1946-49, which, however, should not break the base line of the 1942-1949 lows, according to one of Elliott's tenets. (This is a normal expectation only and might in an extreme case be violated slightly.)

(5) Following wave IV, wave V should close out the first upward Cycle from 1942.[7] Because of the time element again, it looks like the '60s before we face a correction to the whole rise from 1942 and anything approaching a major depression in stock prices.

CURRENT JUNCTURE

Analyzing the current juncture, several factors are worthy of note. If Elliott's hypothesis is correct:

(1) We are now in wave III of the Cycle from 1942. (These waves in Elliott's language are "Primaries.") This wave commenced in June 1949.

(2) Since according to Elliott, wave III is never shorter than wave I, wave III will probably not be completed till 1954 or 1955 or later (wave I took 4 years, 1942-46).

(3) Within wave III, four distinct waves are now apparent: wave 1 (June 1949 to June 1950); wave 2 (correction, short in time but heavy volume, June 1950 to July 1950); wave 3 (July 1950 to September 1951 -- also visible in five distinct sub-waves); wave 4 (September 1951 to May 1952); wave 5 (May 1952 to date and on into 1954 probably, since a fifth wave is often longer than either the first or third wave).

(4) Another interpretation of wave 4 is that it runs from September 1951 to October 1952 in the form of a "triangle," which Elliott noted as an irregular type of correction.

(5) At all events, *since at least October 1952, and possibly since May 1952, we have been in wave 5 of the Primary bull market from 1949, which is wave III of the Cycle from 1942.*

(6) At the end of wave 5 of wave III, we should expect a correction (perhaps two years in duration) of 1949-5? similar to 1946-49, which corrected 1942-46 (wave 1). Thereafter, the market should continue up with Primary wave V of the Cycle from 1942. Then, and only then, should we expect a depression of considerable depth in amplitude and time.

In the chart herewith, we have graphically reproduced Elliott's break-down of the Super Cycles from 1857 to 1941 and his general projection beyond, plus our own break-down of the Cycle wave now in force since 1942, carrying forward Elliott's lines of analysis. On the graph, we have put a number of notes as to channels, etc., which were outlined by Elliott as aids in gauging amplitude. Some factors might be noted as *tentative* conclusions.

1. The correction of the 1942-46 bull market only brought the market back to a level not as low as the top of wave III. This was sub-normal in amplitude and suggests there is a marked "inflation" bias to the present Cycle wave. (Elliott so stated.)

2. If the market keeps in the channel bounded by the 1942/1949 lows and 1946 highs in parallel (a normal expectation), then the culmination of wave III of the Cycle since 1942 in 1954-5 (a guess on our part based on (a) the length of the first wave, 1942-46, four years and (b) the nine year cycle of stock prices, which has shown up in the past in 1919, 1928/1929, 1937 and 1946) might hit around 360-420 in the DJIA.

BREAKDOWN OF THIRD PRIMARY
and Tentative Projection

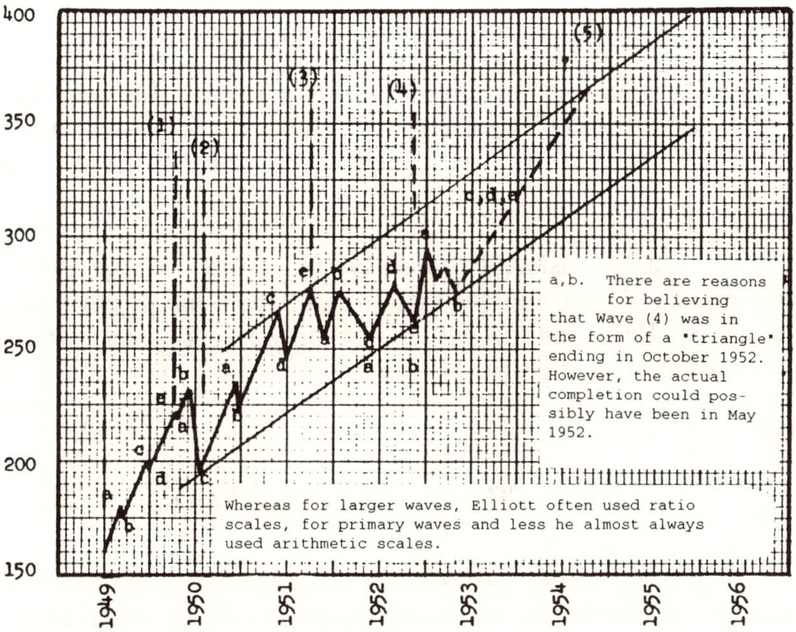

3. If this channel is maintained, then the correction (wave IV) following the 1949-5? bull market should not carry down much below 280 DJIA, or about to present levels. Further, after wave V, completed say in the 1960s, the correction of the whole 1942-196? advance should not drop too far below present levels.

4. Thus, while the market as a whole seems high historically, if *Elliott's hypothesis is correct, we may not see average prices much lower than the present for a number of years to come.*

At first sight, Elliott's Wave Principle smacks of a considerable determinism, which may mitigate against its public acceptance. Nevertheless, it is important to keep in mind certain points. First, the waves adapt themselves to momentary news, reflected by changes in amplitude and timing, without a break-up of the essential patterns. Second, despite economic events and forecasts, World War II, post-war and Korea, the pattern of stock prices has in all respects kept to the broad blueprint first outlined by Elliott in 1938, later in 1941, and later still in 1946. Third, while Elliott's predictions as to the time when a wave would be complete were sometimes off base, there has not been any variation in overall pattern in the twelve years which have elapsed since 1941.

It is interesting to note that while 1951-52 had all the ear-marks of a possible starting point for a major reversal, the Wave Principle indicated that any corrections would be of Intermediate significance only.

BANK CREDIT CONFIRMATION?

Strangely enough, when Elliott's analysis of the stock market showed that the last Super Cycle ran from 1857-1929, he was unwittingly confirmed by our later analysis of bank credit expansion and contraction. *Only in the period 1837-57 did bank credit contract on a scale comparable to that following 1929.*[8] (See our 100 year chart last published in the April 1952 issue.)

It is also interesting to note that the Wave Principle confirmed in all respects our own recently completed Trade and Money Trend, *which throughout 1951-2 has shown no signs of a recession even as important as 1946-49.*

CONCLUSION

If Elliott's hypothesis is correct, then we are in a generally expanding stock market economy, and are not too close either to the top of the Primary bull market which started in 1949 nor to the Cycle bull market which started in 1942.

Further, while the market seems historically high, and a great deal of current comment is emphasizing this point, it may well be that current levels generally are on the low side for some years to come. Such a possibility was foreseen to some extent also in our September 1952 issue under the title, "Is the Market 100 Points Too High?"

CANADIAN MARKET OFFERS FIELD FOR FURTHER STUDY

For those who study the Canadian market, it is unfortunate that the Wave Principle applied thereto is by no means so clear-cut in its indications. Further, any study of the Canadian market would lack some authenticity owing to the fact that Elliott himself never mentioned it. Nevertheless, while Canadian and American markets may vary widely at times in amplitude, the basic trends have always been reasonably similar, except in such specialty markets as mining and oil.

February 22nd, 1953

FOOTNOTES

[1] Bolton used this form of title through 1959, then changed it in 1961.

[2] See Interpretive Letter No. 17 in *R. N. Elliott's Market Letters*.

[3] The *Financial World* articles were actually published in 1939. His first monograph, *The Wave Principle*, was published on August 31, 1938.

[4] These paragraphs are an awesome display of the long term perspective that the Wave Principle provides.

[5] Actually January 1948.

[6] More precisely, he said that the third wave is never shorter than the first wave *and* shorter than the fifth wave, which Bolton later clarifies.

[7] Note that even this early, Bolton's chart projects the Dow to top at 1000 by January 1965. It peaked at 1000 in February 1966.

[8] That was Supercycle wave (II). The next credit contraction will be larger than either of these.

ELLIOTT'S WAVE PRINCIPLE

1954

The Bolton-Tremblay

BANK CREDIT ANALYST

A. Hamilton Bolton, editor

FOREWORD

Due to the evidence of interest in Elliott's Wave Principle accumulated in the last year by various subscribers and readers of the Composite Equity Index as a result of a study we published in February 1953, we have thought it opportune to bring it up to date at this time.

In this study, we have attempted to bring to light a number of alternative comments and criticisms. It will be seen that, while Elliott's basic pattern is apparently still in force, there are some of us who feel that certain modifications, not of basic principles but of interpretation in the light of seven years since Elliott's death, may be in order.

The author wishes to acknowledge the very considerable help vouchsafed by interested readers and students all over the North American continent. This study would not have been possible without the correspondence which the original study provoked.

ELLIOTT'S WAVE PRINCIPLE 1954

INTERPRETING THE WAVES

In interpreting the waves, it has been the author's experience that most of the difficulty arises from not being able *at the time* to distinguish with perfect certainty whether a wave is really of one degree or of the next smaller or larger degree. Obviously, elapsed time is one check on degree, but often corrective waves which seem to have terminated will continue on through another set of waves or even more, apparently waiting for the necessary impetus of events or psychology to implement the unfolding of the next wave in the direction of the major trend.

The Wave Principle applies (according to Elliott) to all forms of life, to all data such as production, price series, etc., and to individual stocks. It follows, therefore, that in interpreting an average such as the Dow Jones Industrials, if various stocks in that average are in different cycles either of time or degree, the average will often have to "wait," usually in the form of a correction, until the majority of stocks again start to get in gear with the main trend.

This also provides a complication in that the writer has often had difficulty in getting the exact number of Minor waves to fit into the pattern.

1951-53, AN APPARENT EXAMPLE

In our study last year, from a short term point of view, we fell into the trap of insisting that either May 1952 or October 1952 was the end of the correction from September 1951. As usual in such interpretations, no sooner does such an interpretation appear in print than events prove it wrong. This tends to give a temporary "black eye" not only to the basic principle but also (less important, perhaps) to the interpreter.

From the vantage point of 310 in the Dow Jones Averages, after having plumbed to 255 in September, it appears, quite reasonably, that September 1953 marked the bottom of the corrective wave which began in September 1951, instead of the assumed May 1952 or October 1952. The waves now appear to fit the pattern required, as follows:

Wave a: September 1951-May 1952
Wave b: May 1952 to January 1953
Wave c: January 1953 to September 1953.

Thus, the pattern that we visualize as *probable* at the present time is that starting in September 1953, we commenced wave 5 upward of the Primary wave which started in June 1949. (See chart in the 1953 study for comparison with the chart herewith.)[1]

5TH WAVE COULD BE LONG AND HIGH

How long wave V will last and to what extremes it may eventually take the market is anybody's guess, but there are several pointers to indicate that it may be both long and high:

BREAK-DOWN OF PRIMARY FROM 1949
DOW JONES INDUSTRIALS

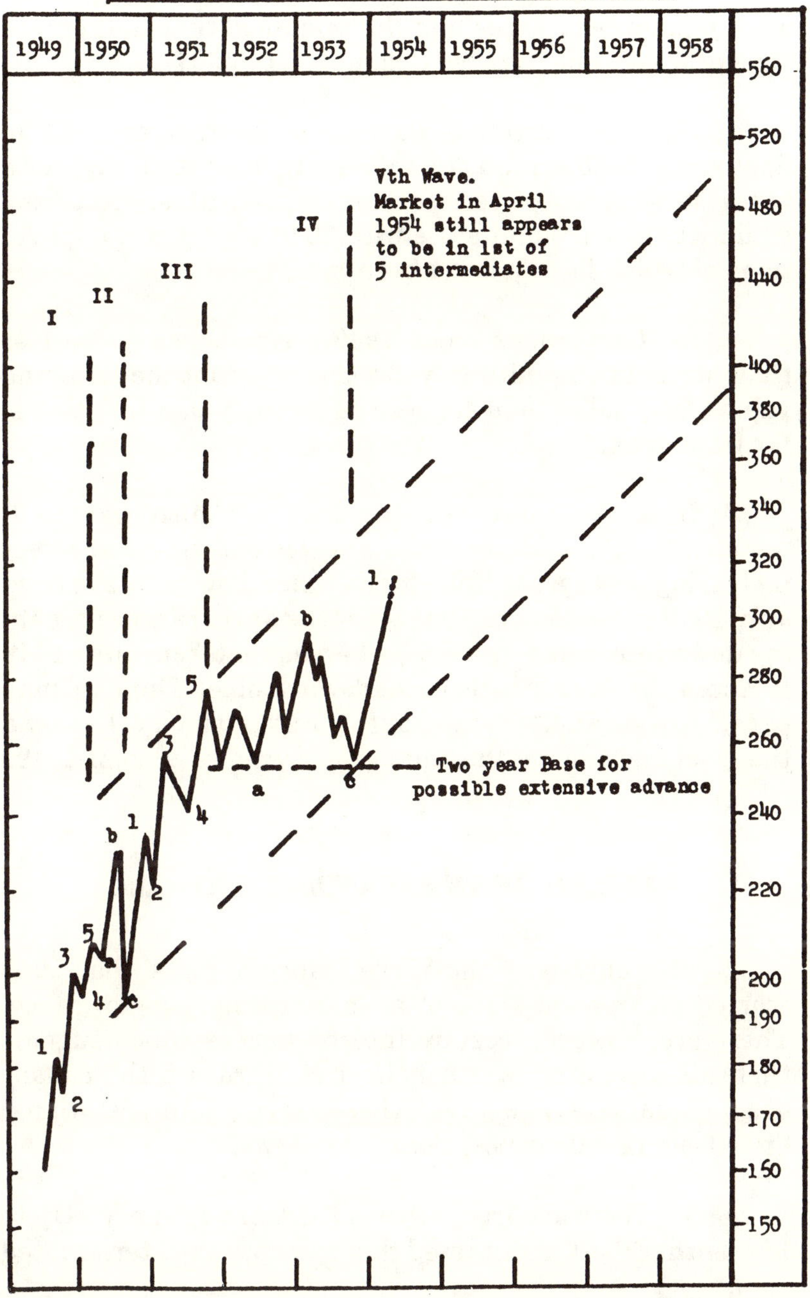

(1) The first and third waves were approximately of equal amplitude. Under these circumstances often in the past, the next upward wave has been considerably greater, often equalling or exceeding the combined time and amplitude of waves one to three (example: 1932-37).

(2) The corrective wave from September 1951 to September 1953 spread out sufficiently long as to suggest a big base for both price rise and elapsed time. Note the similarity on a smaller scale with 1946-49, the full implications of which have not yet been met.

(3) Corrections since 1942 have tended to be less than normal in amplitude, reflecting no doubt the changing value of the dollar, and suggesting strongly that inflation is far from dead.

It is also quite possible that this fifth wave will "extend," i.e., break down into a series of 5 waves of seemingly a higher degree. Note, for instance, how the wave from July 1950 to September 1951 gives the appearance of breaking down into well defined 5s, whereas that from June 1949 to Korea shows very little breakdown visible. Thus, we may be facing a gradual "fanning-out" of waves which will extend the level and time of the end of the Cycle wave from 1949.

PATTERN OF AN EXPANDING ECONOMY

All analysts of the Wave Principle agree that 1949 started an upward wave of at least Primary significance. There are, however, certain interpretations which suggest that this wave may be either the first, third or fifth Primary of a bull market Cycle wave. These varying interpretations[2] arise from certain conceptions, as follows:

1. The wave from 1949 is the third Primary. Up to his death, Elliott maintained this concept. 1942 terminated

his 13 year triangle, and therefore 1942-46 was Primary I. 1946-49 would be classified as Primary II and 1949 - ? as Primary III.

2. One commentator, Mr. Carroll Gianni, a partner of Asher & Gianni (60 Beaver St., New York 4, N.Y.), feels that 1951 to 1953 is an Elliott Wave made up of five 3s, which automatically places it as wave 4 from 1949. Mr. Gianni has therefore suggested that we are still in Primary I, with 1942-46 as waves 1, 2 and 3 thereof. 1946-49 is a "triangular" correction to wave 3, and 1949 to date is part of the fifth wave of the Primary, not yet complete. This does not change the basic interpretation in any way.

3. The writer has long felt that Elliott's 13 year triangle violated his own rules, and is not in fact correct. All triangle waves, according to Elliott, must break down into 3; one of his, from March 1937 to March 1938, is a clear-cut 5. Further, the termination of his triangle sub-waves are not at the logical points of major tops and bottoms. Instead, the writer offers his own 21-year triangle, 1928-49, as conforming perfectly to all Elliott's rules. For a chart and a more extended analysis, see Appendix A. Should this be correct, then June 1949 started Primary I of the bull market cycle which could be expected to carry on well into the '60s. (Mr. Gianni in recent correspondence with the writer now rather favours this interpretation of a 21-year triangle correction.)

4. Alternatively, and this is not yet beyond the realm of possibility, we may still be in a corrective wave of very large dimensions correcting the Super Cycle wave from 1857-1929. The implications here, while probably not so bullish as those of conditions 1 to 3 above, do suggest 400 for the Dow-Jones before a major set-back.

Basically, at this point, it does not greatly matter which of the four interpretations is correct. No matter how you look at it, the basic interpretation must be that we are in a large-size upside cycle at present and that we have nowhere near reached the apex. Time and continuing inflation will take care of the rest.

GENERAL CONCLUSION

This analysis makes no attempt to break down the Intermediate and Minor waves starting in September 1953. The writer has found that it is usually only well after a wave is completed that one can be sure of the exact pattern. The idea that one can be absolutely sure of the manner in which the waves will unfold is extremely dangerous. Waves have a habit of accommodating themselves to events or basic impulses. This is also especially so at this stage of the investment cycle when some stock groups are in quite different stages of advance from a Wave Principle point of view.

The Intermediate wave that started in September 1953 has all the earmarks of similar waves starting in 1934, 1942 and 1949. The writer assumes that we are still in the first Intermediate of the fifth Primary from 1949. Thus, when this first wave is completed, we should see four other waves before the fifth Primary closes out, which close-out would terminate the first Cycle wave from 1949. Obviously, if this interpretation is correct, there is lots of time and bullish amplitude ahead.

The value of Elliott's Wave Principle is one which has stood the test of time since first he started to write about it in 1938. During his lifetime, he modified considerably his interpretations, yet at no time has his basic theory that we were in a series of advancing bull markets from 1942 been proven false. Regardless of modifications of interpretations which the writer and other students have come forward with, the fact remains that Elliott's Principles have proven sound as a basis for long-term investment, and there is every assurance that they will continue so in the foreseeable future.

APPENDIX "A"
A TWENTY ONE YEAR TRIANGLE?
1928 - 1949

In 1941, Elliott set out what he thought was a triangle wave correction of the Super Cycle wave 1857-1928. His reasoning was that 1857-1928 was wave III of a Grand Super Cycle, with two waves prior to 1857 and two waves yet to come after 1928. The triangle wave (a type which is always the fourth wave, so far as is known) would run from 1928-42, and would then occasion an upward thrust from 1942, as wave V of the Super Cycle got underway, to carry on in all probability into the 21st century.

The writer has long had a technical objection to Elliott's 13 year triangle:

All triangle waves according to Elliott should subdivide into subwaves of 3. Elliott's third wave of the triangle violates this principle by being a 5, since he listed this wave as running from March 10, 1937 to March 31, 1938, which Elliott had always analysed as a 5 down and continued to do so after his 13 year triangle theory was formulated. (See bottom diagram for instance, on page 31 of *Nature's Law*, wherein he outlines how his 5 waves break down. Also, page 32, paragraph 4.)

The chart herewith shows the break-down of the 13 year triangle according to Elliott.

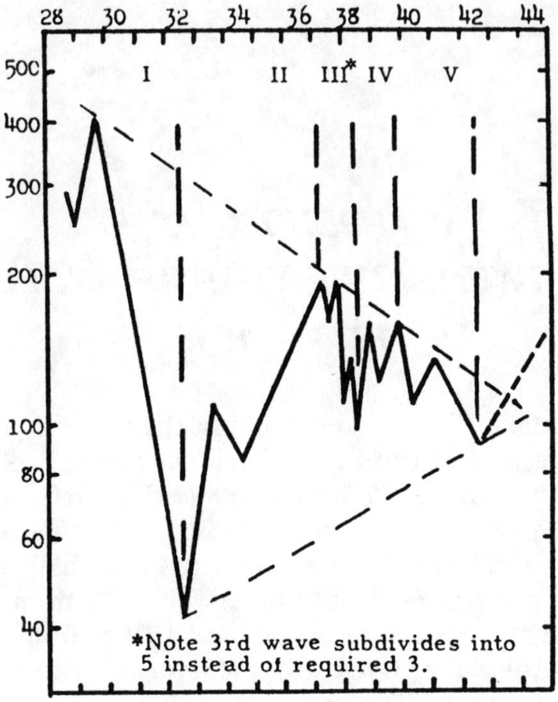

BREAKDOWN OF ELLIOTT 13-YEAR TRIANGLE

In early 1953, the writer evolved the possibility that in effect there was no "Wave Principle" triangle 1928-1942, but there could easily be a "Wave Principle" triangle 1928-49. (Students will recognize the 21 year period as fitting into the Fibonacci series, which Elliott thought was one of the bases of the Wave Principle: 1, 2, 3, 5, 8, 13, **21**, 34.)

So far as is known, it having been checked by other students, there are no technical objections to the 21 year triangle based on Elliott's own Wave Principle. The graph herewith shows the break-down of the triangle into 5 waves, each made up of orthodox 3 corrective type subwaves. It is also believed that each of the subwaves (fifteen in all) can be broken down into the proper sequences of 5s and 3s.

Until a better interpretation comes along, the writer is prepared to accept 1949 as the beginning of a new series of five Cycle waves rather than 1942.

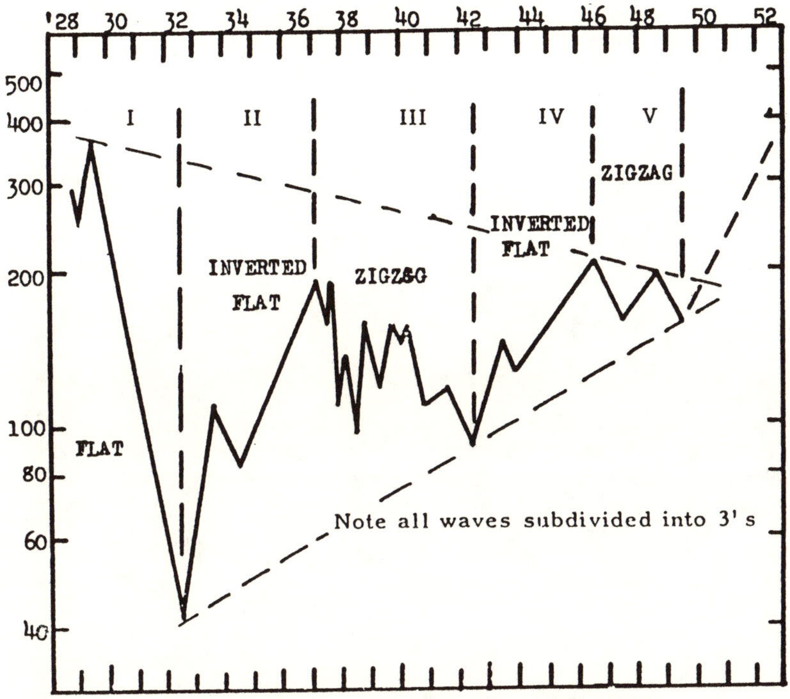

THE TWENTY-ONE YEAR TRIANGLE

FOOTNOTES

[1] In a later republication of this chart in the 1957 Supplement, Bolton attached this comment: "Note: this chart was published by us in April 1954, an excellent example of the value of the Wave Principle at certain times. Note also, our latest interpretation reclassifies wave I, II, III into I, and waves IV and V to II and III respectively."

[2] Elliott's triangle interpretation is discussed in detail in the footnotes of *The Major Works of R. N. Elliott* and *R. N. Elliott's Market Letters*. Gianni's interpretation was incorrect. Bolton's interpretation was correct for the *inflation adjusted* DJIA, as he argues in the 1955 Supplement, and as *The Elliott Wave Theorist* has illustrated in detail. The interpretation that was ultimately proved correct for the "current dollar" DJIA was Collins', which is described brilliantly in Chapter X of Bolton's 1960 book as well as in the 1966 Supplement to *The Bank Credit Analyst*. See Footnote 2 of the 1955 Supplement.

ELLIOTT'S WAVE PRINCIPLE

1955

The Bolton-Tremblay

BANK CREDIT ANALYST

A. Hamilton Bolton, editor

FOREWORD

This study represents the third supplement published by us on Elliott's Wave Principle. The first appeared in February 1953, the second in April 1954. Both of these were combined in the 1954 edition. This third supplement should be considered in the light of the two previous; a limited supply is still available for the benefit of any subscribers to the Composite Equity Index who may not have received or may have mislaid their copies.

Since the publication of the second supplement last year, we have had a substantial correspondence with a number of students of the Wave Principle. Many of these had intimate personal connections with Elliott during his lifetime. They have passed on bits of information and personal interpretations which have been greatly helpful to the author of these monographs.

In many ways, the present juncture is more interesting than any in recent years. While 1953 offered the prospect that there was only one way the market could go (up), 1955 may see some divergence of opinion developing once the current market phase has terminated. This supplement outlines some of the apparent possibilities for future years.

March 1955

ELLIOTT'S WAVE PRINCIPLE
1955

1949: A MAJOR STARTING POINT

It has long been the writer's contention that any interpretation of the waves should accept the obvious outlines. In other words, when you look at a stock market chart, you see some very obvious things, such as [the trend changes in] 1929, 1932, 1937, 1942, 1946 and 1949. The Wave Principle interpretation should accept these vital turning points, even if in doing so it becomes difficult to define each wave down to the last possible subdivision. It must be obvious to anyone that the last major starting point was 1949, and that the 1953 starting point is not of the same magnitude. Thus, 1949 appears to us as the starting point of the latest primary cyclical move.

Three major possibilities of the significance of 1949 were put forth in the April 1954 study:

(1) *Elliott's theory*: After completion of the 1928-42 "triangle," 1942-46 was Primary I of a "thrust" which should encompass five such Primaries: I, III and V upward, and II and IV, corrections in between. This would place II as 1946-49 (note the generally apparent 3 pattern) and III as 1949 to date, not yet completed.

(2) *The Twenty-One Year Triangle*: Developed by the author as a probable sequence. (See Appendix A of the April 1954 study.) Wave I of the "thrust" from the 21 year triangle should coincide exactly with Elliott's Primary III. This would eventually be followed by Primaries II, III, IV and V, and would probably carry on into the '60s before a major correction of the magnitude of 1937-42, say, would appear.

(3) *Super correction to the 1857-1929 Super Cycle*: We could still be in a large correctionary cycle. It might imply a double top with 1929 (corrected for inflation of the dollar), followed by, after a long series of years, a double bottom with 1932 (again corrected for change in the value of the dollar). There are only two technical factors in favour of this interpretation: (a) the time factor (it being hard to visualize a complete correction of a rise lasting 70 years taking only at most 21 years), and (b) the pattern since 1929 looks at all stages like a series of 3s. rather than 5's. Pending evidence of a more cataclysmic nature, we are inclined to discard this possibility; it does not seem to fit into the obvious pattern of an expanding economy.

One criticism of the 21 year triangle might be that the 1929, 1932, 1937, 1942, 1946 and 1949 apexes do not fit exactly into a triangle. In other words, the 1937 high was not high enough.[1] (See the second chart in Appendix A of the 1954 Supplement.) The same criticism applies to Elliott's 13 year triangle: the 1938 low is not low enough. These difficulties are resolved in the case of the 21 year triangle when stock prices are adjusted for the changing value of the dollar. By dividing the averages by an appropriate price level index, the pattern becomes considerably more exact.[2]

THE PRIMARY SINCE 1949

The Primary since 1949 [is wave] number I according to our twenty-one year triangle, number III according to

Elliott on information available to him prior to his death in 1947. We are now fairly clearly in the last wave of that Primary. This fifth wave commenced in September 1953. Because of developments to be discussed below, it may have yet some way to go.

The apparent breakdown of the Primary since 1949 is indicated on the next chart. This is simply an extension of the chart which was published in the analysis of last April. A word of caution: this is one man's interpretation based on an incomplete cycle. To quote last year's bulletin:

> "The writer has found that it is usually only well after a wave is completed that one can be sure of the exact pattern."

To show how this can work, consider the writer's interpretation last year, when he said, "...The writer assumes that we are still in the first Intermediate of the fifth (wave of the) Primary from 1949."

Actually, the writer was expecting that a series of well-defined waves would materialize, somewhat on the pattern of July 1950 to September 1951. Instead, the pattern is much more like that of 1934-37, wherein the break-down into five waves, particularly on the monthly charts, is hardly discussable.

In retrospect, it now appears that we may have completed the fifth Intermediate of the fifth wave of the Primary from 1949, i.e., of the wave from 1953.

AN "EXTENSION" IN THE MAKING?

That this wave from 1953 has developed more momentum than any other wave since 1927-28 can be seen by the fact that the market is now above the upper parallel on tops and bottoms since 1949, when graphed on a semi log, or

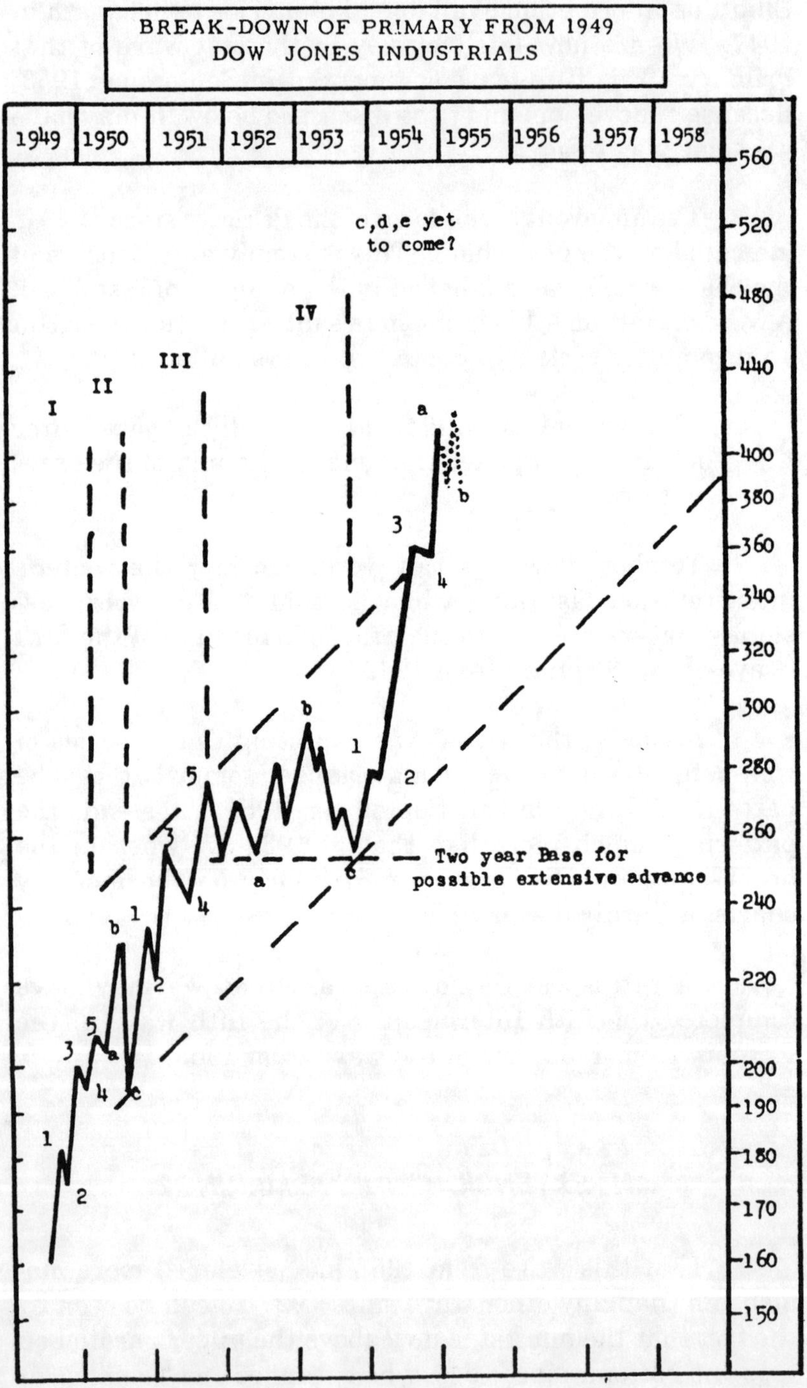
BREAK-DOWN OF PRIMARY FROM 1949
DOW JONES INDUSTRIALS
1949
1950
1951
1952
1953
1954
1955
1956
1957
1958
c,d,e yet
to come?
I
II
III
IV
Two year Base for
possible extensive advance
560
520
480
440
400
380
360
340
320
300
280
260
240
220
200
190
180
170
160
150

ratio, scale. Elliott would have termed this a highly inflationary characteristic, and one which resembles an "end-of-move" wave of some importance. Taken at face value, this would indicate that we are close to the end. However, there seems to be the possibility that this fifth wave, which we calculate may have started at election time 1954, will break down into what is known as an extension. I.e., instead of stopping where it should (say, last December 1954), this fifth wave becomes wave 1 of an extended fifth wave which could conceivably carry up another 100 points or more in the averages.[3] The evidence at the moment is admittedly slim, but we suggest a review of a few main points:

(1) The whole pattern since 1949 is one of rising tops and bottoms, indicating inflation.

(2) Corrections have been subnormal, limited usually to 20% of the wave in question.

(3) No extension of this degree has been seen since the late 1920s.

(4) The stock pattern is breaking through upper channels on ratio paper, on heavy momentum.

Again, however, we must caution that this is a very tentative conclusion.

AFTERMATH

Accepting the possibility of the extension now developing, one rule of Elliott's may prove useful. Extended waves always "double retrace." The fifth wave from 1953 ran from about 350 at the elections in 1954 to about 410 in late December 1954. The correction carried back to about 385 in January, and to a double bottom at the same level in March. The extension, if such it be, starts from this point. When the whole move is finished, therefore, the correction should come back to about this level before carrying on in a new Cycle. Thus, some sign-post may be given by this figure as to the extent of the major corrections to the 1953-? rise. Since, however, any corrections of the 1953-? rise will also probably be the first wave of a 3 wave correction of the whole 1949-5? rise, it is conceivable, in line with reaction history since 1938, that this level would also mark the approximate level of a later double bottom terminating the whole correction.

This would be a considerably more bullish development than that of the theoretically possible correction level of 255-85 given in our 1953 bulletin as the probable ground floor level for any correction in the next 10 years.

OR AN "IRREGULAR" TOP?

Failing the "extension," another possibility suggests itself to this writer — that of an irregular top formation. Assuming that January 1955 represented the end of the orthodox fifth wave from 1953, sheer momentum suggests the possibility that the ensuing corrective wave (A,B,C) will be subnormal and such as to make wave B of the correction higher than the fifth wave top.

The most famous irregular top in history was in 1929. Here the orthodox waves from 1921 ended in late 1928, to be followed by a consolidation in the spring of 1929 and a rise to 386 in September. All in all, some 90 points were added from the orthodox top in 1928 to the final top in 1929.

(No further parallel with the subsequent history of 1929 exists, however. According to Elliott, the whole 1921-29 rise was an "extension," which under a retracement rule required that the subsequent correction return to the 1896 base area, or around 40 in the Dow Jones Industrials.)

FOR THE FUTURE

The general bullish prediction of basic Elliott theory is still intact. We are, however, nearer to a crossroads of some importance than we have been in the whole period since 1949. That important turning point, comparable perhaps to 1946-49, could arrive by late 1955 or by 1956. The present degree of momentum suggests, however, that any consolidation of this kind should be from considerably higher levels.

The pattern after this turning point may do much to reconcile some of the minor divergent views concerning which Primary wave we are really in, in the Super Cycle following the [correction of the] 1857-1929 [advance].

When we review Elliott in 1956, it should prove an interesting study.

March 25th, 1955

FOOTNOTES

[1] That's one of the two big problems with the interpretation.

[2] It does indeed, and this is the correct interpretation for the inflation adjusted DJIA. The triangle was followed by a classic "short, sharp" thrust up to a peak in 1966, which has not been exceeded to this day. See Footnote 2 of the 1954 Supplement.

[3] In the 1956 Supplement, Bolton repeated this and the next section, but, since his forecast had succeeded, he omitted the next sentence and inserted, "... from the point of its commencement."

ELLIOTT'S WAVE PRINCIPLE

1956

The Bolton-Tremblay

BANK CREDIT ANALYST

A. Hamilton Bolton, editor

FOREWORD AND CONCLUSION

It has been our policy every year to review Elliott's Wave Principle in the light of the previous year's progress. No attempt is made to "forecast" what the market will do; rather, an attempt is made to see how the market has done within the framework of the overall design.

So far, it appears that the general outline presented last year has held reasonably firm. Further, the bull market from 1949 gives every indication of still being intact. There is, however, a definite possibility that 1956 will see the end of this bull market, to be followed by a major consolidation of some duration (possibly two to three years or more). But the timing cannot be envisaged with any degree of certainty.

If either the original Elliott thesis of 1942 as a starting point or the Twenty-One Year Triangle thesis (see Appendix A of the 1954 Supplement) is correct, any consolidation around present levels should not represent the start of a major depression in stock prices. While theoretically such a consolidation could come back to around the 285 level in the DJIA, the history of postwar inflationary influences suggests a more likely target not much below the 350-400 level. In the meantime, there would certainly still seem to be some leeway on the upside before the current 1953-56 wave is terminated.

March 1956

ELLIOTT'S WAVE PRINCIPLE
1956

GENERAL BACKGROUND

A continuing interest has developed in "Elliott's Wave Principle," that remarkable story of market movements first published in 1938, and subsequently brought up to date by Elliott in 1945. A theory of patterns in the market,[1] which, in Elliott's language, is its own forecaster, this Principle has stood the tests of time and a changing economic environment.

Briefly, Elliott's forecast was that 1942 started a series of developing bull markets fitting into certain fairly well defined patterns which should carry on perhaps throughout the whole of the 20th century before we would have another "1929-32."

The basic rhythm is as follows: a series of waves in the direction of the main trend which can be subdivided into smaller waves and again re-subdivided into smaller waves still, within the framework of certain empirical rules:

The Main Trend (up or down): Always 5 waves; three in the direction of the trend (1, 3 and 5) and two as corrections (2 and 4).

The Correction (down or up): Normally 3 waves; 1 and 3 in the direction of the correction, and wave 2 a countermove in between.

Elliott's basic waves are shown graphically on the inside back cover to this Supplement [see page 32 — Ed.]. This presentation is not all inclusive, there being a number of other types of waves which may be considered modifications of the main waves.

FURTHER CONFIRMATION IN 1955

The extension theory (see chart), first proposed in March 1955, now a year later seems to be more likely. The rise from March 1955 to September 1955 is clearly a five wave affair, and should therefore be the c wave indicated on the chart. The Eisenhower correction and the ensuing seesaw in recent months may well be the fourth, or d wave. It is possible, but by no means yet sure, that the current wave into new high ground is the beginning of wave e.

This wave should logically carry us into the middle 500s of the DJIA. However, this is no assurance that this wave will not itself end up in a further extension.

Thus, while the action of the market in 1955 has tended to confirm the theory of an extension propounded in March 1955, there is no sure yardstick as to how high it may go.

FOR THE FUTURE

The general bullish prediction of basic Elliott theory is still intact. We are, however, nearer to a crossroads of some importance than we have been in the whole period since 1949. That important turning point, comparable perhaps to 1946-49, could arrive in 1956. The present degree of momentum suggests, however, that any consolidation of this kind should be from considerably higher levels.

BREAK-DOWN OF PRIMARY FROM 1949
DOW JONES INDUSTRIALS

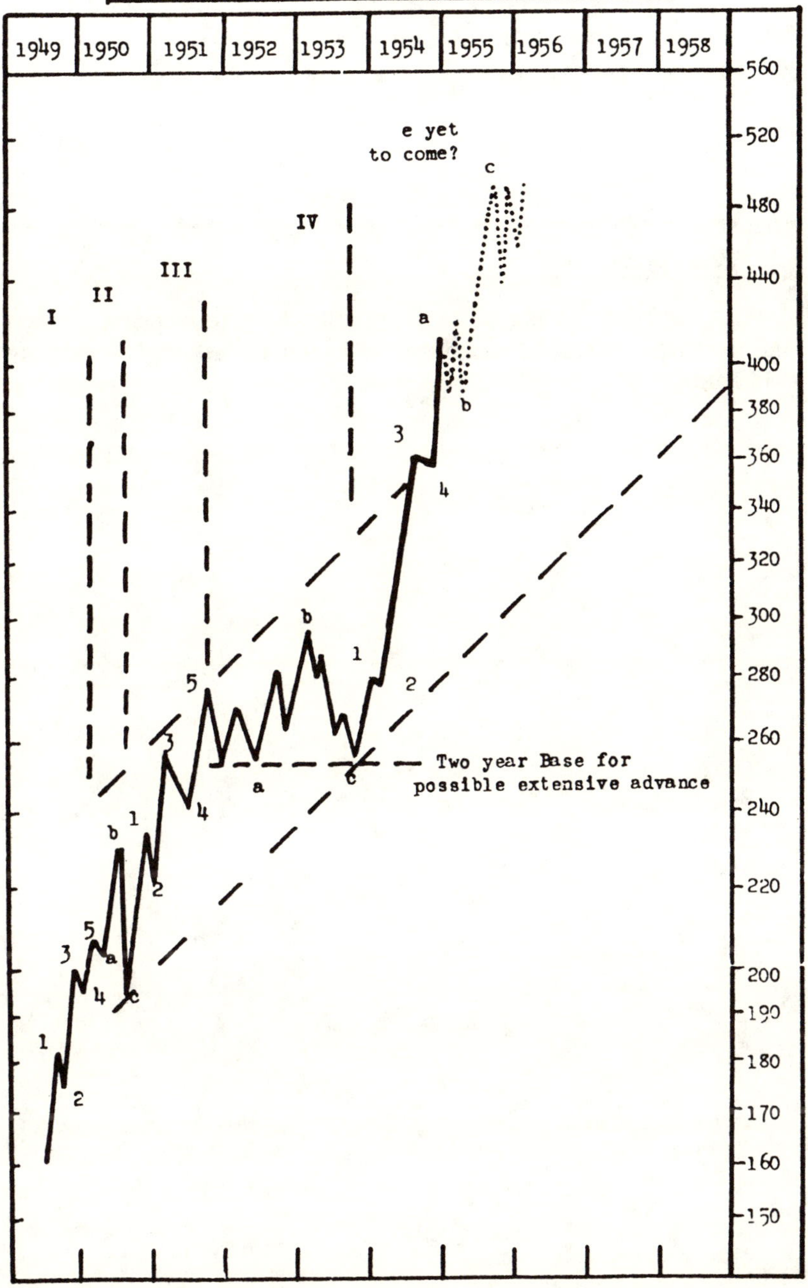

The pattern after this turning point may do much to reconcile some of the minor divergent views concerning which Primary wave we are really in, in the Super Cycle following the [correction of the] 1857-1929 [advance].

March 20th, 1956

FOOTNOTES

[1] This phrase originally read, "A cycle forecast...", and had an indecipherable meaning, so I took the liberty of making this change.

ELLIOTT'S WAVE PRINCIPLE

1957

The Bolton-Tremblay

BANK CREDIT ANALYST

A. Hamilton Bolton, editor

INTRODUCTION

The present booklet, repeating our practice of publishing an annual review, has been substantially rewritten. It attempts to place Elliott's Wave Principle in the focus of today's economic and stock market climate. At the same time, it covers the history of the last 100 years as set out by leading stock market averages. It also points to probabilities for the future. Finally, it is not an attempt to forecast the market, but it may be used as another tool to confirm or otherwise one's findings from other sources.

Elliott's Wave Principle in fact should be considered more as a philosophy than as a precise forecasting instrument. It is true there have been precise forecasts of great accuracy by Elliott and his students, but there have also been miserable failures. The main philosophy is simply this: in an expanding economic climate, the stock market will tend to advance in a series of waves with corrections in between. When a certain number of these have been realized, the whole series of waves becomes one big wave, and this in its turn has to be corrected. Naturally, the correction of the big wave will tend to be larger in time and amplitude than the correction of the smaller series of waves. And so on: a series of big waves makes one bigger wave followed by its correction.

The great advantage of the Elliott philosophy is that where before one could only view the stock market as patternless in the broad sense, now the pattern becomes meaningful.

Finally, we would like to state that this booklet is not written with the idea of being a textbook on the subject. Rather, it is hoped it will engender interest in a very useful stock market concept.

The periodic annual analyses of Elliott's Wave Principle that we publish make an interesting complement to our monthly service analyzing bank credit changes — *The Bank Credit Analyst*.

It will be noted from prior Reviews that we made no attempt to "forecast" precise timing and amplitude. Rather, we let the wave develop until such time as it appeared we were fairly close to the end of the move. As we said in March 1956, at Dow 490:

> "The general bullish prediction of basic Elliott theory is still intact. We are, however, nearer to a crossroads of some importance that we have been in the whole period since 1949. That important turning point, comparable perhaps to 1946-49, could arrive in 1956. The present degree of momentum suggests, however, that any consolidation of this kind should be from considerably higher levels."

In actual fact, the move, according to our chart, petered out in April 1956 at 522 in the DJIA. Since that time, we have been in a corrective type phase, which may last some time yet.[1]

April 15th, 1957

ELLIOTT'S WAVE PRINCIPLE 1957

THE PATTERN OF A HUNDRED YEARS

According to Elliott, we have been in a Grand Super Cycle for over 100 years, and we will continue in this Grand Super Cycle for many, many more years, probably into the 21st century. This, then, is of somewhat academic interest. Of more interest is the fact that Elliott, before he died in 1947, placed us in the fifth (of five) Super Cycles which make up the Grand Super Cycle, and therefore in a rising type wave of large dimensions.

Elliott's study of stock prices back to 1854 using the Axe-Houghton Index led him to the following breakdown:

GRAND SUPER CYCLE

Consisting of five waves of Super Cycle magnitude from sometime prior to 1854 to sometime in the future.

SUPER CYCLES

Two of those were recognizable: 1857-1928, subdivided into five waves of Cycle magnitude; and in Elliott's analysis, 1928-1942, a triangle wave in five waves of Cycle magnitude. Our research since Elliott's death suggests that the second of these Cycle waves was actually from 1928 to 1949 instead of from 1928 to 1942, also in the form of a triangle.

Elliott placed these two Super Cycle waves as numbers 3 and 4 of the Grand Super Cycle. His reason: that a wave in triangle formation is always wave 4, in any degree, so 1928-42 (or as we now feel, 1928-49) is wave 4, and therefore 1857-1928 is wave 3.

CYCLES

Taking the known completed Super Cycles, 1857-1928 and 1928-49, the breakdown into Cycle waves according to Elliott in the former, and ourselves in the latter, is as follows:

Super Cycle III		Super Cycle IV	
Cycle I	1857-64	Cycle I	1928-32
Cycle II	1864-77	Cycle II	1932-37
Cycle III	1877-81	Cycle III	1937-42
Cycle IV	1881-96	Cycle IV	1942-46
Cycle V	1896-1928	Cycle V	1946-49

The next chart shows the broad perspective of 100 years.

The implications of this are not too hard to imagine. The last forward Super Cycle (III) lasted some 70 years. This gives some idea of the possible magnitude of the new bull wave which started in 1949. *It is of tidal proportions.*

This tidal wave, of course, will be interrupted from time to time. For instance, we calculate we are still in the first Cycle of the Super Cycle, with after that four more to come. We also calculate that we are only in the fourth Primary of this Cycle wave, with the fifth and possibly the most dynamic yet to come.

A HUNDRED YEARS' PERSPECTIVE

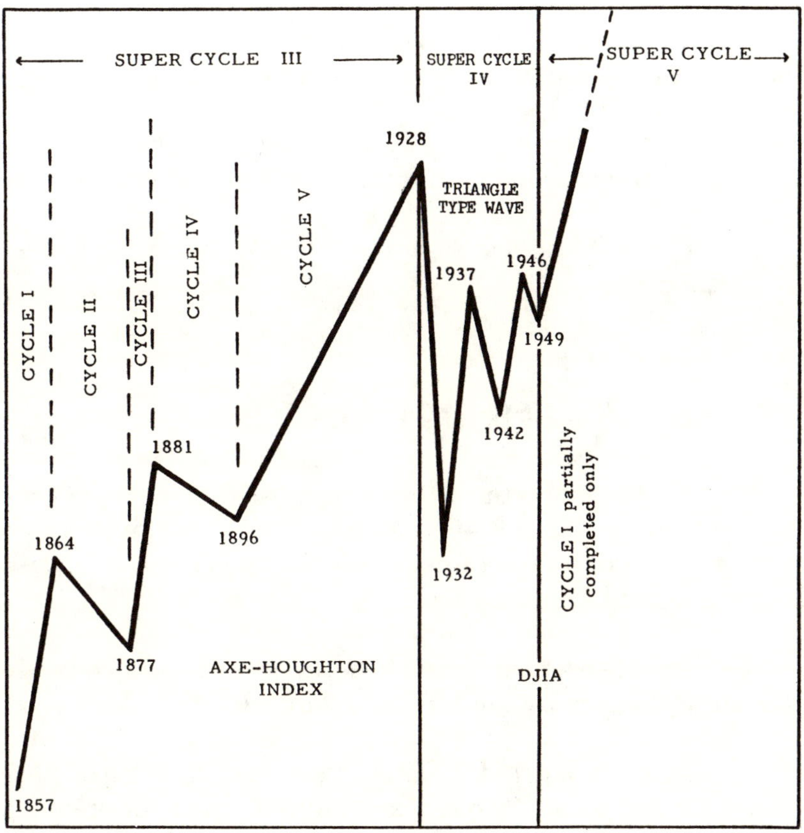

"THRUST"

The characteristics of the market since 1949 are interesting. They spell out the term "thrust," which Elliott used in all cases of a pull-out from a "triangle" formation. A "thrust" is a speedy movement following the triangle in the direction of the trend. *And the corrections on the way in this thrust tend to be subnormal.*

The 1928-49 triangle calls for a "thrust" in the upward direction. The "thrust" wave is the first Cycle wave, since we are dealing with this order of magnitude, the preceding triangle having consisted of five Cycle waves. This

Cycle wave is now in force, and its record so far points to the validity of the concept of subnormal corrections.

In late 1952, when writing about the future market possibilities as indicated by the Wave Principle at that time, we said:

> "...we may not see average prices much lower than the present for a number of years to come."

The DJIA was then around 280; 255 was the lowest it touched!

THE NEW CYCLE 1949 TO DATE

As we have stated, we calculate that a new Cycle wave started in June 1949, the first of five such waves which will go to make up the Super Cycle which of itself will close out the Grand Super Cycle.

The theoretical characteristics of a "thrust" have so far amply been borne out, as noted above.

We consider that the first Cycle wave starting in 1949 is not yet complete. We have carefully gone over our previous count of the Primary waves since 1949 and have revised them. Readers who have our last year's and previous years' studies will note that up till then we felt that September 1953 to 1956 was the *fifth* Primary. We now place this wave as *only the third* Primary, which means that currently we are in the fourth Primary, which itself will be followed by the fifth Primary, then concluding the first Cycle of the Super Cycle.

Our reasons for this are fairly simple, and may be accepted or not as the reader sees fit. (Essentially, however, it is not likely to make a great deal of difference in market movements).

BREAKDOWN OF DJIA FROM 1949

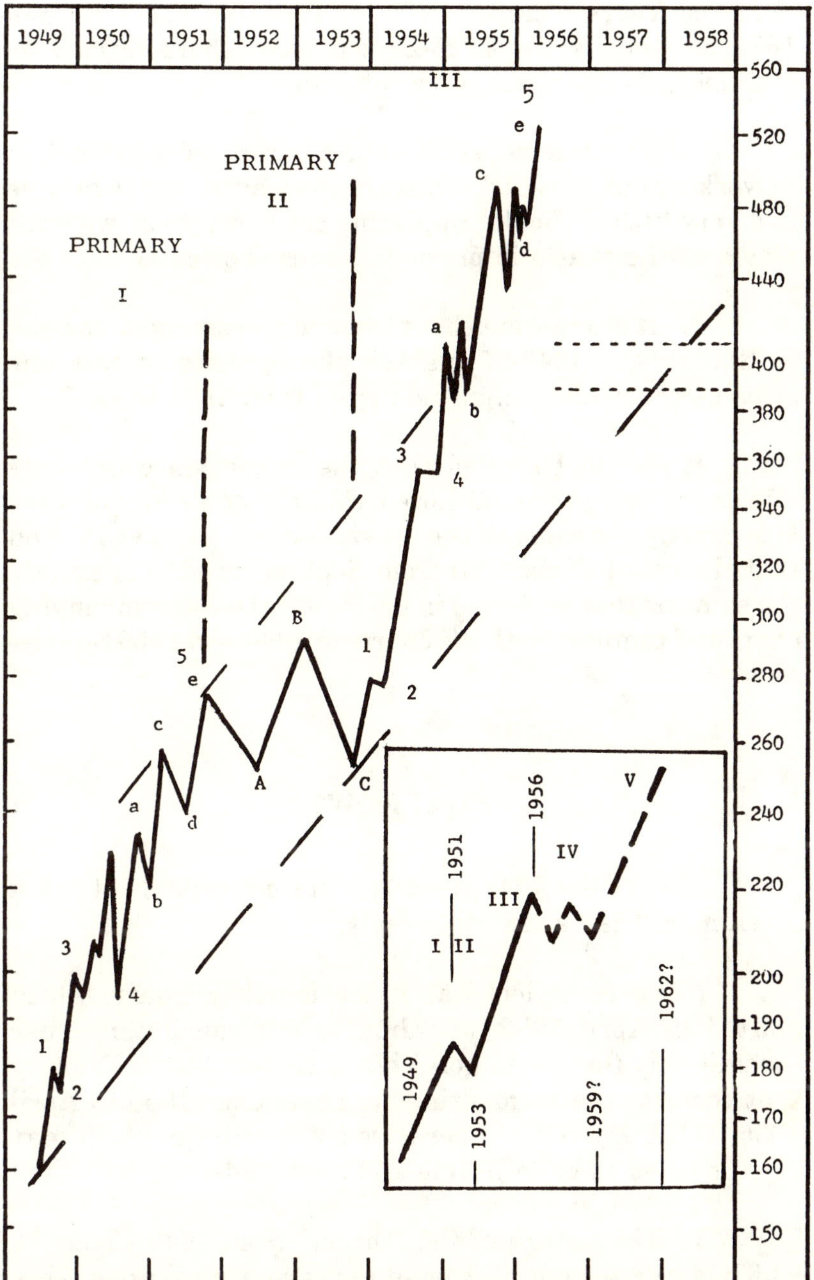

1. The characteristics of rampant speculation were missing from the 1956 top. If we look back at recorded market history in Super Cycle III (see chart entitled, "A Hundred Years' Perspective"), we find that the 1864 and 1881 as well as the 1928-29 top were characterized by extremely frothy types of speculation.

2. There do not seem to be any technical difficulties in working out the subdivisions of the waves, and in fact we had very little difficulty in placing these waves as we went along, as the charts in previous issues showed.

3. It is apparent that this count "looks right" to date, in that in the 1949-56 market phase, there is only one sizeable consolidation, in the period from 1951 to 1953.

It should be noted that the change in count only affects the period around Korea, that the new count of wave II is exactly the same as the previous count in wave IV, and that the count of wave III from September 1953 is exactly the same as that projected in prior years (see accompanying chart and compare with the charts in 1954 and 1956 Supplements).

WHAT NOW?

Always the $\$64^2$ question, and not capable of being given more than a tentative reply.

However, it looks as if the fourth Primary, which started in April 1956 according to our calculations, has considerably further to go. This is the corrective Primary that corrects the third Primary, September 1953 to April 1956 (DJIA 255-522). There are some criteria which may give us clues as to both time and amplitude:

1. The nature of the "thrust" from 1949 (Cycle I), which is still in force, does point to the continued probability

of subnormal corrections. A normal correction might be anywhere from 35-50% in the averages. Subnormal ones may run only 10-25%.

2. This fourth Primary should be expected to take up about as much, if not somewhat more, time than the second Primary. This second Primary lasted exactly two years. This would place the termination of the fourth Primary probably not earlier than the spring of 1958.

3. It would be quite possible for the fourth Primary to break down into three Intermediates, the second of which could theoretically be even higher than the top of the third Primary (i.e., 522 DJIA). In favour of this would be the experience in 1951-53, when the second Intermediate closed out at a figure higher than the end of the first Primary (295 in January 1953 versus 275 in September 1951).

4. Because we have had what appears to be an extension (marked a, b, c, d, 5e on the chart), we should follow the rule of extensions, which is that they are retraced before the move continues in the main direction again. In other words, sometime in the period ahead, during which the fourth Primary is working itself out, we should come down into the approximate area 410-390 DJIA.

5. It is usual for the fourth wave of any degree, and in particular in larger degrees, to break through the trend line, in this case the rising line on the chart which passes through the bottoms of June 1949 and September 1953. It would be unusual if it did not.

TENTATIVE CONCLUSIONS

Any conclusions as to the probable immediate direction are extremely tentative. However, there are no indications that the present corrective Primary is completed. The time element is too short, unless of course our whole calculation of the wave since 1953 is wrong. We need a good two years of consolidation to build up the technical strength to enable the fifth Primary to have the force it should.

Still, it would be technically possible for the market to exceed the April 1956 high (522 DJIA)[3] and then consolidate further in 1958-59, say. Sometime in this whole period we should get down to around the 400 level or a little lower. It does not look under any circumstances as if we are likely to get much below this.

The power-house that will be building up if the market consolidates for another year or so along orthodox lines, it seems to us, will offer the probability that Primary V could be quite sensational, taking the DJIA to 1000 or more in a wave of great speculation.

The insert on the chart gives some idea of what to expect. As we said, the second Intermediate of Primary IV could top the end of III and still not violate the pattern.

To sum up — this is a very strong *long-term* pattern. Each time of course that the market takes a major step forward, as from 1953-56, in excess of the improvement in fundamentals (price-earnings ratios increasing, as has been the successive history since 1949), the vulnerability to set-back also increases. But viewed from the broad point of view, any decline to somewhat below 400 should not be considered calamitous by any means. With the later prospect of perhaps 1000 DJIA in the early '60s, there need be no excess of long-term pessimism.

FOOTNOTES

[1] This last paragraph originally appeared in the back of the booklet, following quoted excerpts from the 1953, 1954, 1955 and 1956 Supplements.

[2] Actually $64,000!

[3] I.e., in an expanded, or "irregular," flat.

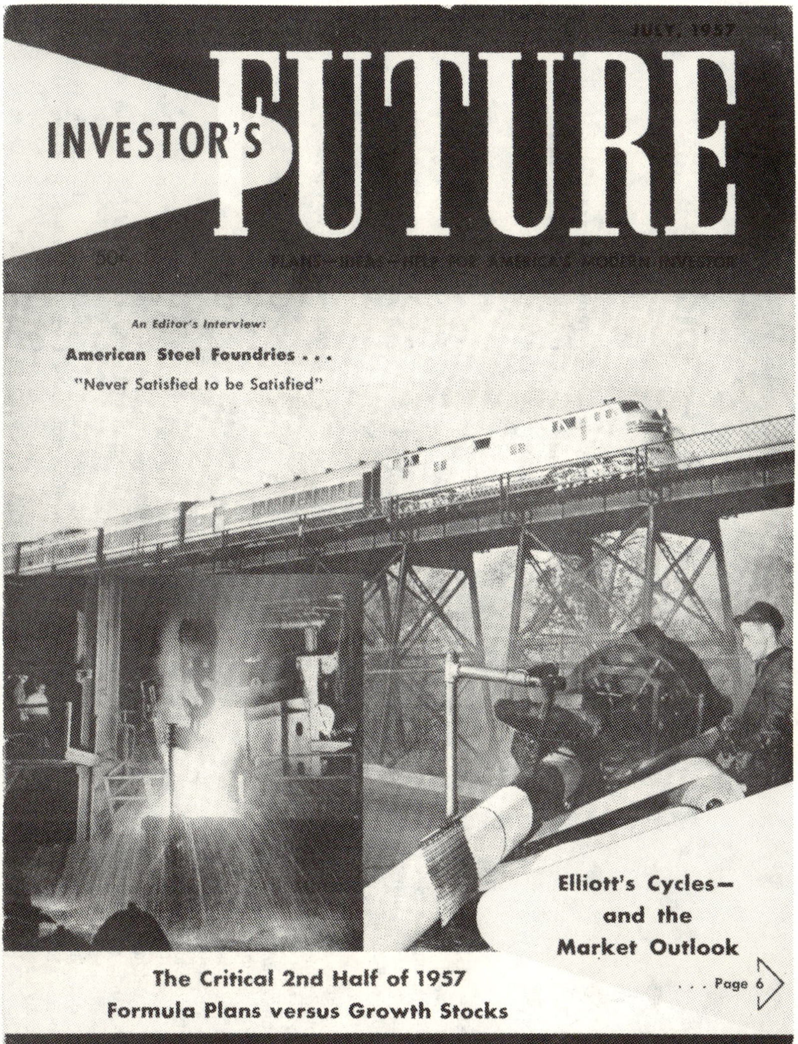
JULY, 1957
INVESTOR'S FUTURE
An Editor's Interview:
American Steel Foundries . . .
"Never Satisfied to be Satisfied"
Elliott's Cycles—
and the
Market Outlook
. . . Page 6
The Critical 2nd Half of 1957
Formula Plans versus Growth Stocks

The Coming Tidal Wave

Elliott's Cycles — and The Market Outlook

"The last forward Super Cycle lasted some 70 years. This gives some idea of the possible magnitude of the new bull wave which started in 1949. It is of tidal proportions."

PERHAPS THE MOST outstanding theory, based on proven record, for accurately charting the *long-term future* movements of stock market prices is *Elliott's Wave Principle.*

R. N. Elliott alone among the cycle theorists (despite the fact that he died in 1947, while others lived) provided a basic background of cycle theory compatible with *what actually happened in the post-war period to date.*

We have discussed Elliott's theory several times throughout the years — since his principle is a proven and valuable guide for intermediate and long-term planning . . . although it does not "pinpoint" the timing of market movements.

*Mr. Hamilton Bolton**, foremost exponent of the principle today, recently has interpreted Elliott's theory in the focus of today's economic and stock mar-

<u>The Main Trend</u>
(Up or Down)

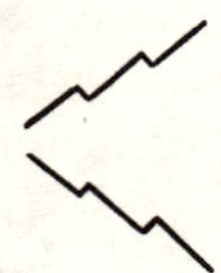

Always 5 waves
3 in the direction of the Trend i. e. the first, third and fifth and 2 as corrections (i. e. the second and fourth).

<u>The Correction</u>
(Down & Up)

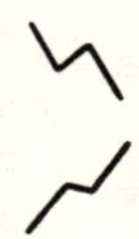

Normally 3 waves.
The first and third in the direction of the correction and the second as counter-move in between.

A look at Chart I shows that the *overall* trend from 1857 to 1929 was up-up-up . . . but there were fluctuations up and down between those years. Remember, this "super cycle" covered 72 years — so there was plenty of time for the smaller cycles.

according to Elliott and Mr. Bolton is as follows:

Super Cycle III		*Super Cycle IV*	
Cycle I	1857-64	Cycle I	1928-32
Cycle II	1864-81	Cycle II	1932-37
Cycle III	1877-81	Cycle III	1937-42
Cycle IV	1881-96	Cycle IV	1942-46
Cycle V	1896-28	Cycle V	1946-49

ket climate. In view of the amazing accuracy of Elliott's theory so far, it strikes us as very worthwhile for any investor to study Mr. Bolton's "up-to-date" analysis of the theory . . . . even though, of necessity, some of the points must be quite technical.

During the Middle . . .

Thirties, R. N. Elliott analysed stock prices on a daily, weekly and monthly basis as far back as they were available. By doing this, he discovered the basic rhythm of what he called the *Wave Principle.*

This consisted of a series of waves in the direction of the main trend which could always be subdivided into smaller waves and sub-subdivided again into smaller waves still within the framework of certain empirical rules.

He also found that the period from 1857 to 1929 represents one big "super cycle" — with its peak in 1929. This "super cycle" was broken down into five smaller cycles (or waves) . . . *three of which showed prices moving up,* and *two which showed prices moving down.* And each of the five smaller cycles broke down again into smaller waves.

The subdivision of the waves is as follows:

Also, Elliott's calculations showed that this "super cycle" was part of a "grand super cycle". And, just as the "super cycle" was broken down into five smaller cycles, the "grand super cycle" would break down into five "super cycles".

According to Elliott, we have been in a "grand super cycle" for over 100 years, and we will continue in the "grand super cycle" for many, many more years . . . *probably into the 21st century.*

From the Peak . . .

of the "super cycle" in 1929, Mr. Elliott concluded that there would be a correction that would last until 1942 (changed to 1949 by Mr. Bolton after Elliott's death). And then, when this correction reached a bottom, he judged (based on charts of the past) *a new basic uptrend in stock prices would start that would be comparable to the "super cycle" from 1857 to 1929.*

Elliott placed the two "super cycle" waves of 1857-1928 and 1928-1949 as numbers 3 and 4 of the "grand super cycle". His reason — that a wave in triangle formation (a correction in the main trend) is always number 4.

So — taking the known completed "super cycles", 1857-1928 and 1928-1949, the breakdown into cycle waves

The Implications of . . .

this are not too hard to imagine. The last upward "super cycle" (III) lasted some 70 years. This gives some idea of the possible magnitude of the new bull wave which started in 1949. *It is of tidal proportions.*

This tidal wave, of course, will be interrupted from time to time. For instance, Mr. Bolton calculates we are still in the first cycle of the "super cycle" — *with four more to come after that.* He also calculates that we are only in the fourth primary of this first cycle wave — with the fifth *and possibly the most dynamic yet to come.*

Also, the market since 1949 "spells out" the term *"thrust"* — which Elliott used in all cases of a pull-out from a "triangle" formation (a corrective cycle). A "thrust" is a speedy movement in the direction of the trend . . . *and the corrections on the way in this thrust tend to be subnormal.* In other words, while we will have corrections to the overall upward trend we are experiencing — they probably will be of subnormal size.

What Now?

This is always the $64,000 question — and no more than a tentative reply can be given. Mr. Bolton's conclusions follow.

***Senior Partner of Bolton Tremblay & Company, Investment Consultants, 680 Sherbrooke St., West, Montreal, Canada**

It looks as if the fourth primary, which started in April, 1956, has considerably further to go. This is the *corrective* primary that corrects the third primary of September, 1953 to April, 1956 (DJIA 255-522).

There are some criteria which may give us clues as to both time and amplitude:

(1) The nature of the "thrust" from 1949 (Cycle I), which is still in force, does point to the continued probability of subnormal corrections. A normal correction might be anywhere from 35-50% in the averages. Subnormal ones may run only 10-25%.

(2) This fourth primary should be expected to take up about as much, if not somewhat more, time than the second primary. This second primary lasted exactly two years. This would place the termination of the fourth primary *probably not earlier than the Spring of 1958.*

(3) It would be quite possible that the fourth primary breakdown into three intermediates (corrective primaries have 3 waves) could have a second wave which could theoretically be even higher than the top of the third primary (i.e. 522 DJIA).

A look at Chart 2 will show that this is what happened in 1951-53, when the second intermediate closed out at a figure higher than the end of the first primary (295 in January, 1953, versus 275 in September, 1951).

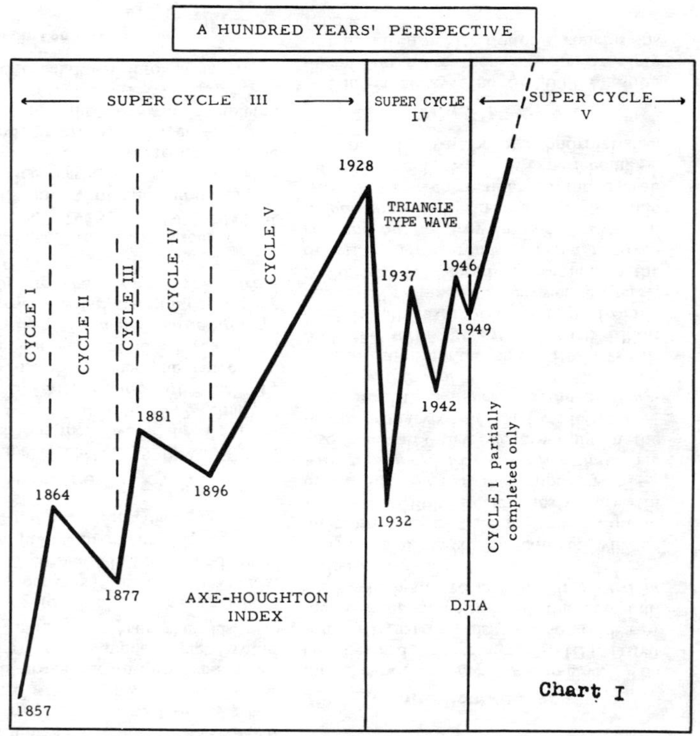

Chart Showing Super Cycles III, IV, and V — Covering 100 Years

(4) Because we have had what appears to be an extension (marked a,b,c, d,5e, on Chart 2), we should follow the rule of extensions — which is that they are retraced before the move continues in the main direction again.

In other words, sometime in the period ahead, during which the fourth primary is working itself out, we should come down into the approximate area 410-390 DJIA.

(5) It is usual for the fourth wave of any degree, and in particular in larger degrees, to break through the trend line (the rising line on chart 2 which passes through the bottom of June, 1949, and September, 1953). It would be unusual if it did not.

Any Conclusions . . .

as to the probable immediate direction are extremely tentative. However, there are no indications that the present corrective primary is completed.

The time element is too short. *We need a good two years of consolidation to build up the technical strength to enable the fifth primary to have the force it should.*

Still, it would be technically possible for the market to exceed the April, 1956 high (522 DJIA) and then consolidate further in 1958-59, say.

Sometime in this whole period we should get down to around the 400 level — or a little lower. It does not look as if, under any circumstances, are we likely to get much below this.

The power-house that will be building up if the market consolidates for another year or so along orthodox lines, according to Mr. Bolton, *will offer the probability that primary V could be quite sensational . . . taking DJIA to 1000 or more in a wave of great speculation.*

The insert on Chart 2 gives some idea of what to expect.

To Sum Up . . .

this is a very strong *long-term* pattern.

Each time, of course, that the market takes a major step forward as from 1953-56, in excess of the improvement in fundamentals (price-earnings ratios increasing as has been the successive history since 1949), the vulnerability to set back also increases.

But, viewed from the broad point of view, any decline to somewhat below 400 should not be considered calamitous by any means. *With the later prospect of perhaps 1000 DJIA in the early 60's, there need be no excess of long-term pessimism.*

END

Chart Showing Three Primaries of Super Cycle V and Projection of Fourth and Fifth Primaries

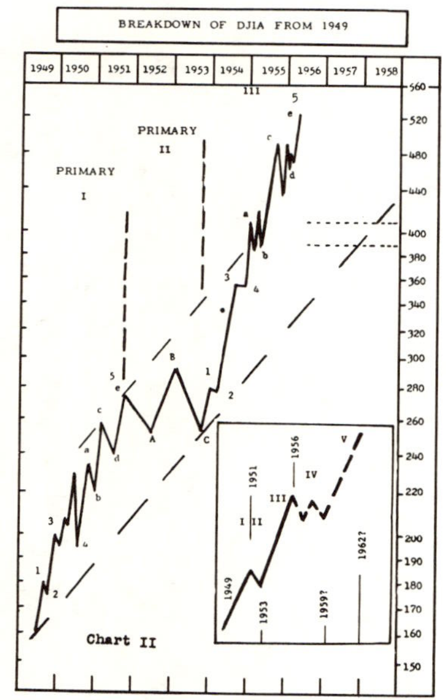

ELLIOTT'S WAVE PRINCIPLE

1958

The Bolton-Tremblay

BANK CREDIT ANALYST

A. Hamilton Bolton, editor

ELLIOTT'S WAVE PRINCIPLE
1958

INTRODUCTION

In 1957, after a number of annual editions, we substantially rewrote our annual review of the Elliott's Wave Principle, giving a considerable amount more of broad background material. The 1958 edition is substantially the same as the revised 1957 edition, with the exception that Section V, "The New Cycle 1949 To Date," has been completely rewritten and brought up-to-date to show how the counts of last fall have neatly fitted into the Elliott pattern.

The booklet therefore gives us a 100 year sweep to consider. It also answers a basic number of hypothetical questions on the future, outlining in a sense a basic philosophy of investment, which is consistent with events as they are unfolding.

April 25th, 1958

THE NEW CYCLE 1949 TO DATE

As we have stated, we calculate that a new wave of Cycle dimensions started in June 1949. It is only partly completed. There should be five of these to complete the Super Cycle (1949-?). And as can be seen from the chart, this Super Cycle should complete the Grand Super Cycle. Thus, the pattern points to a generally rising stock market from now, punctured by occasional consolidations and bear markets, but none of the magnitude of the Great Depression 1929-32, nor probably of the magnitude of the 1937-38 decline percentage-wise.

In the 1957 review, we ran the chart only up to our top in April 1956, the subsequent moves being too small to make an interpretation possible. However, the decline in late 1957 has made it possible to fill in some details, and it now looks as though the wave from April 1956 to October 1957 classifies as Intermediate "A" of Primary IV. So we are marking it on our chart.

WHAT NOW?

The major probability ahead, taking into consideration time and amplitude, is that we are still in the corrective wave from 1956, that we will stay in it for some time before resuming the bull market, and that any declines should be relatively small in terms of the overall. Thus, while we have sky-rocketed up from 160 in the DJIA since 1949, all indications seem to point to the likelihood that the correction or consolidation is likely to be of restrained amplitude, perhaps with a final floor not lower than 386, the old 1929 top.

Observe the lower insert on the chart. This was published in early 1956, and represents the best estimate we can still make of probabilities. We judge that the fall of 1957 saw the completion of the *first* of the three waves shown in the insert as comprising IV. We judge that we are currently in the *second* of three waves. This second should last longer than the subwave from February 1957 to July 1957 (5 months). If so, we will not see a final topping out in the current recovery before early summer 1958. (It might of course take months longer than this.) In other words, the February 1958 highs will probably be broken on the upside (above 460).

After termination of this second wave at somewhere below the 520 mark as a good probability, we should then see a third wave downward to "test" and possibly "break" the 1957 lows of 416. Unless there is a virulent and irresponsible outpouring of monetary inflation, we should anticipate at least a double bottom around the 420 level or else a break-through to somewhat below the 400 level, as mentioned above.

BREAKDOWN OF DJIA FROM 1949

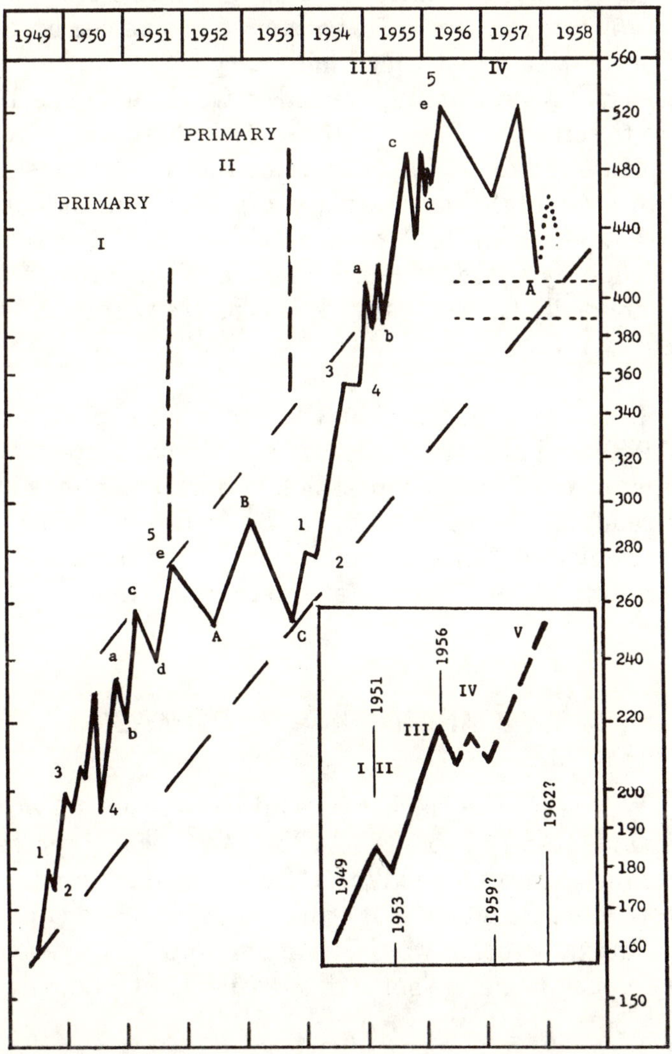

In sum, the "Elliott" outlook is not too bearish for the next year or two, and ultimately we should push up to new highs way above the levels of 1956.

INFLATION VS. NORMALCY

Each of the Cycle waves of the Super Cycle from 1857 about doubled or more than doubled the peaks of the previous Cycles (see long term chart, "A Hundred Years' Perspective," in the 1957 Supplement). This occurred in a period up to the 1920s of relatively restrained monetary inflation, i.e., monetary normalcy. Assuming normalcy, we should expect this pattern to continue. Twice 386, the 1929 high, calls for 772 DJIA. If we make any allowance for the tremendous monetary inflation of the last twenty years, plus what it looks as if we can expect in the future, then this level of 772 will surely be exceeded by a wide margin. Levels of upwards of 1000 DJIA can easily be rationalized as possible within the next ten years.

It is our thought that the recurrence particularly since 1949, and also since 1942, of subnormal corrections is tantamount to a market expression of the tremendous inflation already built in and what in the future is bound to be further activated. This, in our opinion, is the basic message of the Elliott Wave Principle at the present time.

SOME ARGUMENTS BY OTHERS

Whenever the market gets into a bear phase, we find correspondents who think that "Elliott" can be interpreted to justify much lower prices. While "Elliott" can be interpreted with considerable latitude, it still cannot be twisted entirely out of context. In other words, as in amateur vs. professional hockey, you can change some of the rules, but basically you must stick to the ground rules, or else you are in danger of creating a new game.

In order to show how "Elliott" is a disciplined form of technical analysis, we are putting forth certain hypothetical questions, with our answers.

Q. Why could not 1942-56 be a completed Cycle Wave, which would mean (a) we should expect a correction perhaps back to the 212 level (top in 1946) before we start a new bull market?

A. To get a completed Cycle wave 1942-56, it must break down into 5, either counted:

(a) 1942-46, 1946-49, 1949-51, 1951-53, 1953-56, or
(b) 1942-43, 1943, 1943-46, 1946-49, 1949-56.

The pattern (a) violates one of Elliott's rules: the third wave must not be shorter than both the first and the fifth wave. Pattern (b) falls down in that 1942-3 cannot be subdivided into a 5 subwave, as it must if it is to be part of the main movement.

Thus, if you are counting from 1942, then 1942-56 can only be three waves or part of three waves out of a total of five (1942-46, 1946-49, 1949-56).

Q. You object to considering 1928-1932 as the full correction for 1857-1928. Could not 1932 be the real start of the Super Cycle? If so, where are we now?

A. The objection is on one ground only. Corrections should conform to both amplitude and time. Assuming that 1928-32 is an ample correction amplitude-wise, it is terribly inadequate time-wise. Thus, we discarded it in favor of the 21 year correction. If we accept it, however, then 1932-37 is Cycle I (5 waves up), 1937-42 is Cycle II (3 waves down) and we are still only halfway through Cycle III, having completed perhaps three Primaries of the five required from 1942.[1] (See answer to preceding question.)

Q. How about the thought that 21 years is not adequate time-wise for a 70 year previous Super-Cycle? If so, could not 1928-32 have been simply the first wave only of three of a super-correction? This would mean 1932-56 would be the completed second wave, and now we go back down in a third wave pretty close to the old depression lows.

A. Our answer to that is, Why try to twist an obviously bad interpretation? To get this, you have to assume a philosophy which is completely at odds with the American growth pattern of the last 15 years. It won't sell. But if you insist, then you still come up with the same stumbling block, i.e., 1956 cannot be the top because to get this pattern completed by 1956 you have to have three waves up from 1932 (i.e., 1932-37, 1937-42, 1942-56). The first of these *can* be a 5 or a 3, the second *must* be a 3, but the wave 1942-56 *must* be breakable down into five waves, with the following subwaves: 5-3-5-3-5. As above, you can only get three waves so far from 1942. So the 1932-? wave before the great downward cataclysm when we head back to 1932 levels (which this interpretation calls for) is not yet complete and probably won't be till the 1960s at some figure much higher than today's levels. By this time, the averages will probably have been up close to 1,000, and any idea of returning to the 50 or 100 level DJIA would be pure fantasy.

April 25th, 1958

FOOTNOTES

[1] This is the correct count. Time is secondary to amplitude. See the section entitled, "Alternative Interpretation" in the 1959 Supplement.

ELLIOTT'S WAVE PRINCIPLE

October 1958 Postscript

(For insertion into
"Elliott's Wave Principle 1958")

Our conclusions in "What Now?", written in April of this year, may now need modification. The course of the market since last spring suggests that the fall of 1957 may well have concluded wave IV of the Cycle which started in June 1949.

According to our calculations, this wave IV started in April 1956 and may well have been completed in December 1957 with a 5 sub-wave formation downward from July 1957. Wave IV qualifies as a full correction in amplitude, but is a little short in time. However, this has happened in the past, notably in 1926. It is virtually a quickening up process, which may now be underway.

Accepting this as possible, we would now expect the stock market to follow the pattern indicated in the insert on the chart labeled "Breakdown of DJIA" by completing wave V of the Cycle from 1949.

ELLIOTT'S WAVE PRINCIPLE

1959

The Bolton-Tremblay

BANK CREDIT ANALYST

A. Hamilton Bolton, editor

ELLIOTT'S WAVE PRINCIPLE 1959

INTRODUCTION

"Elliott's Wave Principle 1959" has been expanded somewhat from previous editions. The reason is that 1958 has produced a situation which is somewhat less clear-cut than many of the previous reviews. In view of this, we feel that a somewhat expanded section of the possible current alternatives is justified.

In essence, we have two schools of thought: first, that December 1958 completed wave IV from 1949, and that we are now well away in the final wave V; two, that we are still in the corrective wave which started in 1956 (or 1957, depending on who does the counting) and which we numbered in 1956 wave IV from 1949.

The implications, of course, of these two interpretations are somewhat different, and may well lead to different conclusions. We happen to subscribe to the first, i.e., that we are now fairly entrenched in wave V, which should be the last upward wave in the Cycle from 1949. It could last a year, two years, or even five years. It could also end in 1959. Because of our bank credit studies, as well as our various breadth and momentum studies, we are not inclined to think it will end in 1959. Nevertheless, we issue this "caveat": We are no longer on the firm ground of 1952-53, when we could say, "...we may not see average prices much lower than the present for a number of years to come."

*****

The order of material in this year's edition has been modified slightly into what we believe is a better arrangement.

More amplification has been given to certain alternative interpretations, since it has been found that many students have decided views, which in many cases will hold water. Attention, however, is directed to the series of questions and answers which categorically eliminate a number of interpretations on the grounds that they break the rules.

Again, we emphasize that the Wave Principle is more of a philosophy than a forecasting tool. However, if viewed broadly and flexibly it can be useful in stock market trend analysis.

March 1959

ALTERNATIVE INTERPRETATION

The reasoning behind the twenty one year triangle correction (1928-49) and why we believe that Super Cycle V started in 1949 is explained in Appendix A of the 1954 Supplement. We might say, however, that it has been contested in some circles. Alternatively, as we mention in the next section, "The New Cycle 1949 To Date," another interpretation is feasible. This is that 1928-32 was an adequate correction for Super Cycle III, and that therefore Super Cycle V began in 1932 rather than 1949.

This interpretation is perfectly tenable. (Note: Elliott's original 13 year triangle 1928-42 is not tenable under Elliott's own rules, as can be seen from the discussion and the first chart in Appendix A of the 1954 Supplement. However, it does look a little odd to correct in three years what it took 71 years to build up, especially as each of the corrections within Super Cycle III took no less than 13 years!

Having decided on this interpretation, at what stage in Super Cycle V are we now? The following is one suggested interpretation:

1932-37	Cycle I	5 waves
1937-42	Cycle II	3 waves
1942-	Cycle III	3 or possibly 4 waves only so far completed

1942-46	Primary I	
1946-49	Primary II	
1949-56	Primary III	
1956-58	Primary IV	) Maybe only still
1958-	Primary V	) Primary IV

THE NEW CYCLE 1949 TO DATE

As we stated, we calculate that a new wave of Cycle dimensions started in June 1949. It is now nearing completion. Altogether, there should be five of these to complete the Super Cycle (1949-?). And as can be seen from the next chart, this Super Cycle should complete the Grand Super Cycle. Thus, the pattern points to a generally rising stock market punctuated by occasional consolidations and bear markets, but none of the magnitude of the Great Depression, 1929-32.

WHAT NOW?

In the 1958 Review, we classified the top of the market in April 1956 to the bottom of the market in late 1957 as wave A (one of three, A, B and C, or possibly five, a triangle A, B, C, D, E) of wave IV (the fourth Primary since 1949). Later in the fall of 1958, we expressed the view that it was more likely that April 1956 to late 1957 had completed the whole of wave IV (short in time but adequate in ampli-

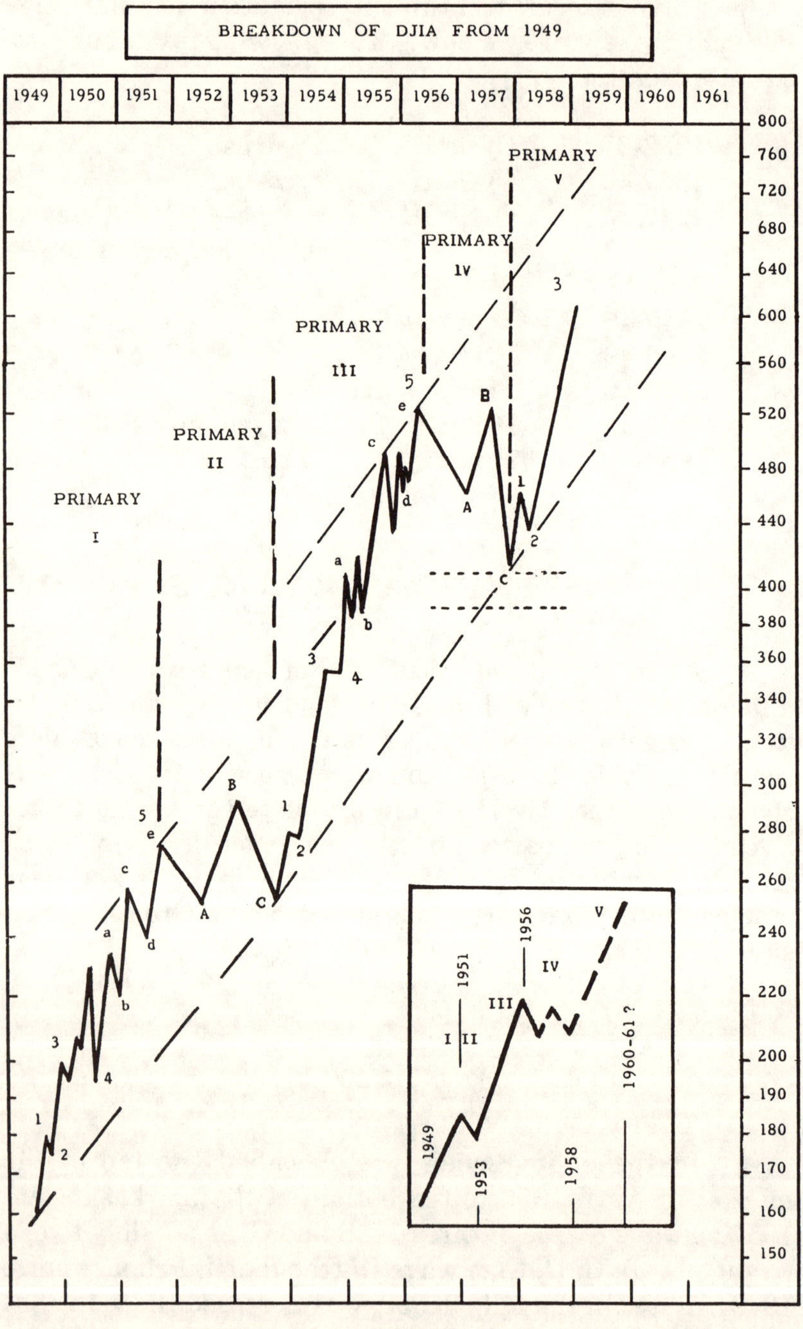
BREAKDOWN OF DJIA FROM 1949
1949
1950
1951
1952
1953
1954
1955
1956
1957
1958
1959
1960
1961
PRIMARY I
PRIMARY II
PRIMARY III
PRIMARY IV
PRIMARY V
800
760
720
680
640
600
560
520
480
440
400
380
360
340
320
300
280
260
240
220
200
190
180
170
160
150
I
II
III
IV
V
1949
1951
1953
1956
1958
1960-61 ?

tude), and that *we are now well along in Primary wave V, which will complete the Cycle wave from 1949.*

As we watch the market action in conjunction with our bank credit and other technical studies, we become more convinced that this view is probably correct, and have so marked the graph. It will be noted that we consider now that we are in and close to the end of Intermediate wave 3 of Primary V, with only probably waves 4 and 5 still left to go. However, this is no assurance that the bull market since 1949 is nearing its end either in time or price, but it does offer a substantial warning that from now on, the market may well be on "borrowed time," just as the 1921-29 market was on "borrowed money" from 1927 on.

Tentatively and with diffidence, we close up the time limit, with the suggestion that the bull market top may well be seen in 1960 or 1961.

Having got off ground in 1958 much faster than might normally have been expected, the question now is: Where do we go from here?

It would seem that we face a major problem in interpretation. In theory, waves 4 and 5 of Primary V could easily be completed in 1959. In practice, they may be, or, more likely, we think the whole fifth Primary wave will tend to broaden out, with the result that the Primary may not be completed till 1960 or 1961. So far, we are still waiting for the corrective wave 4. This could well develop this spring and last for several months. Depending on how long it lasted, wave 5 of the Primary could be longer or shorter. If wave 4 takes several months to complete, the implications would be that wave 5 could expand in time and amplitude.

But regardless of the exact top of wave 5 of Primary V, there is no assurance at all that this will necessarily be followed immediately by a major decline. More likely, perhaps, is a broad see-saw type of market similar to that from

1956 to summer 1957. Because the correction following the orthodox top of wave 5 of Primary V is of a larger degree than any since 1946-49, it would be logical for it to exceed in time and amplitude the correction of 1951-53, which was essentially sidewise in the averages, as well as that of 1956-57, which though more serious, was in the light of hindsight extremely moderate as far as bear markets go.

CONCLUSION

We seem to be well along in the 1949-? bull market. Where the market may go is indicated broadly by the channels on the chart. If waves 4 and 5 develop quickly, the orthodox top will probably be lower than if wave 4 and wave 5 (of Primary V) spread out.

Following the top of Primary V, an A, B, C correction is called for of some time and magnitude. However, assuming a top in 1959, '60 or '61, there is nothing to prevent a higher top later within the A, B, C corrective wave.

From a practical point of view, what this amounts to then, is, as time goes on, an increasingly selective market.[1] At the present time, practically all stock groups are advancing. Gradually, a minority of stock groups will have passed their long-term peaks. Thereafter, a sufficient number of these groups will be falling to make larger corrective waves in the averages. We may well, at over 600 DJIA, be within 25-30% of a major top. Portfolio profits will become increasingly more difficult to pin down. Without necessarily reverting to old fashioned bear markets, many investors will find the going tougher and tougher. Eventually, something approaching a major bear market may well emerge.

For the time being, however, the line of least resistance still seems up.

MINORITY VIEW

There is a minority view which feels that the rise from the late fall of 1957 is still only wave 3 of an A, B, C, A being the wave ending in December 1957, and B being the 3 wave formation into 1959. This view now calls for wave C (in five subwaves) downward to form a new base for a bull market. As we have noted above, while admitting this possibility, we feel it adds a rather odd interpretation that seems somewhat out of place in view of (a) bank credit trends and (b) technical momentum studies.

FOOTNOTES

1 Bolton shows an excellent knowledge of breadth behavior.

A. HAMILTON BOLTON
Editor-in-chief

THE *Bolton-Tremblay*
BANK CREDIT ANALYST
680 SHERBROOKE ST. WEST, MONTREAL 2 - CANADA

A. HAMILTON BOLTON, Editor,
B.A. (McGill), M.B.A. (Harvard)

April 29th, 1960

ELLIOTT'S WAVE PRINCIPLE

Dear Subscriber:

Our annual revision of the Elliott Wave Principle - which is usually released around this time - will be replaced this year by a much more comprehensive and detailed study, presented in a better format, augmented and, of course, brought up-to-date as regards interpretation.

We are confident that this new book will be ready for release by the end of May to all regular subscribers on our books at the time of publication.

Sincerely,

Jules L. Tremblay
Business Manager

JLT:dc

THE ELLIOTT WAVE PRINCIPLE

A Critical Appraisal

[1960]

A. Hamilton Bolton

FOREWORD

This book is about a technical tool for stock market analysis and forecasting known as Elliott's Wave Principle. It is not a well-known tool, but it deserves to be better understood. The excuse that I have in writing this book is that while my basic interest in recent years in the analysis of the economy and the stock market has been by way of my firm's extensive studies of bank credit trends, as edited by us in the *Bolton-Tremblay Credit Analyst,* nevertheless I have been impressed with (as well as critical of) the truths behind Elliott's hypothesis as set forth some twenty years ago in a little known and now out-of-print monograph entitled "The Wave Principle."

As we have advanced through some of the most unpredictable economic climate imaginable, covering depression, major war, and postwar reconstruction and boom, I have noted how well Elliott's Wave Principle has fitted into the facts of life as they have developed, and have accordingly gained more confidence that this Principle has a good quotient of basic value.

It is extremely difficult, of course, to accept any modicum of determinism in our thinking with regard to values and price trends. Nevertheless, it is becoming increasingly apparent that emotions are greatly responsible for price fluctuations, and these emotions not only follow laws of action and reaction, but also adhere to more complicated laws, the surface of the knowledge of which has but barely been scratched.

In the last few years, because of duties in other spheres, I have travelled fairly extensively over the North

American continent. I have fortunately been exposed in these wanderings to many keen minds. To name them all would be quite impossible, but I would like to mention a few — as prototypes of what I have in mind — to whom I would like to dedicate this book, men who by their encouragement in all fields of investment analysis (certainly not limited in any way to this present study, since many of them have no basic interest at all in "Elliott") have given me a great deal of courage to develop new ideas, and who by their judgment have greatly sharpened my own.

First, perhaps I should mention Humphrey Neill of Saxtons River, Vermont, whom I met for the first time just ten years ago this year and through whom I later met such thinkers as Jacques Coe of Jacques Coe & Company, New York, and Jeff Drew, the well-known odd-lot analyst of Boston. Then in the technical field, there are such gentlemen as Harry Comer of Paine, Webber, Jackson & Curtis, New York, Ed Tabell of Waiston & Company and Jimmy Hughes of Auchincloss, Parker & Redpath, who all have left an indelible mark on Wall Street in the present generation.

But apart from the well-known names, there are many others who have remained behind the scenes, including Ed Johnson of Fidelity Fund, Inc. in Boston, George Morey of R. W. Presspritch & Company (whose encouragement has been more than intangible), as well as Charles Eddy of the Chemical Bank New York Trust, Jim Miller of Cooke & Bieler, Inc., of Philadelphia, Bill Berger of Centennial Fund, Inc. in Denver, Colorado, Herb Drake of Crocker-Anglo National Bank, Herb Turrell, Jr., of Turrell Hunter in San Francisco, John Westcott of Greene & Ladd of Springfield, Ohio, and Bill Swartz of Goodbody & Company, New York. My list should certainly include such "elder statesmen" as Bob Warren (late of Keystone Company of Boston), Charles J. Collins of Detroit and Everett Dominick of Greenwich, Connecticut.

To go on would be endless. To stop at any point is not to do justice to those omitted. I may say that I have not asked these gentlemen's permission to have this book dedicated to them. They are, willy-nilly, caught in the web of my making. The main object, however, is to suggest, in the words of my partner, Maurice Tremblay, that "He who sees one sun, sees one light," and that in the words of another of my associates[1] "there is a little truth in everything." It only remains to sort the wheat from the chaff.

Since 1956, investment thinking has been divided as seldom before into two camps. On the one hand, common stocks have become admittedly overvalued. On the other hand, trends in the economy in the subsequent period have been favorable to rising stock prices. Where do we go from here? Can we live with serenity with stocks at least twenty-five to thirty-five percent higher than sound levels of central value? Are we doomed to another 1929? Can we prevent another 1932-3? These and many other questions are constantly plaguing us.

To suggest that the Elliott Wave Principle can give us the answer is to overstate grossly the case. Nevertheless, I believe that it offers, especially if combined with other studies, an excellent tool. While this book is dedicated to those who over the years have been of great help to me and my thinking, I especially commend its study to the technical analyst who is intrigued by something new, something different. My suggestion is that, in the coming years, every available tool will be required to survive in the investment jungle, and that accordingly Elliott's Wave Principle, despite some of its inconsistencies, which our Critical Survey will certainly bring to light, should be studied with some care.

A. Hamilton Bolton

FOOTNOTES

1 This is A. J. Frost.

CHAPTER I
HOW THIS BOOK GOT STARTED

A number of years ago, in 1953 to be exact, the author decided to put out a small pamphlet on what he thought the Elliott Wave Principle was saying so far as the stock market was concerned. We need bear in mind that Elliott had been dead since 1947 and none of his intimate students had seen fit to carry on his work. The author was not one of his more intimate friends; nevertheless, he had originally become intrigued with the possibilities of the Wave Principle when he first came across a series of articles by Elliott in the *Financial World* in 1938. After Elliott's death in 1947, only one or two students were willing to discuss the Wave Principle, including Garfield Drew, who spent some time on Elliott's theories in his *New Methods for Profit in the Stock Market,* published in 1948 and 1954.

It is perhaps interesting to go back to that bulletin of February 1953, as it throws light on the value of the Wave Principle at certain confusing market periods. Eisenhower had been elected President in November 1952, and the stock market enjoyed a post-election celebration in rising to a peak of 295 in the Dow Jones Industrials at the end of 1952. By early 1953, uncertainties loomed high. The Federal Reserve was accused of following a too tight monetary policy and the market subsequently went into a tailspin that was eventually (Dow Theory wise) classified as a major bear market by September of that year. However, the bear market theory of that time was untenable under any interpretation of the *Elliott Wave Principle* known to this writer. We quote directly from our bulletin of that time:

"Further, while the market seems historically high and a great deal of comment is emphasizing this point, *it may well be that current levels generally are on the low side for some years to come.*"

The Dow Jones Industrials were then 284. They dropped about 10% by September and have never seen these levels since.

Throughout the subsequent years, our *Bank Credit Analyst* (a monthly service analyzing trends in bank credit and forecasting stock market weather) made a practice each spring of publishing a new review of the Elliott Wave Principle, and up until recently at least (including the 1956-57 recession in stock prices), has pointed out that no major bear market was indicated by a reasonable reading of Elliott's Wave Principle.

At some time in the near future, however (within say the next two to four years), it does appear that a more extended decline in stock prices is feasible and even likely, but it does also seem quite unlikely still that we face a cataclysmic decline in stocks from current levels. Instead, this is more likely to be a very broad consolidatory movement with perhaps a limit of a 30-35% decline from any final high registered.[1] This may of course be attempting to "call" the market too closely, but it does suggest that certain market predictions currently (spring 1960) in vogue of a drop to say 400 or lower in the Dow Jones Industrials are not likely to be realized, barring some untoward outside happening such as war,[2] which could upset the momentum and indicated amplitude of the stock market flow since the late 1940s.

Since 1949, three orthodox Dow Theory bear market signals have been given: September 1953, February 1957 (re-confirmed in the fall of 1957) and recently in February 1960. These signals have been out of step with the Elliott Wave Principle. It will be extremely interesting to see how this battle of Goliath versus David will work out.

It seemed to the author appropriate then, here in early 1960, to develop the Elliott theme on a broader scale than heretofore and to produce in fact a handbook on the Wave Principle that will attempt to give Elliott its proper place in technical analysis, at the same time applying a critical eye to the whole problem of finite prediction for which Elliott himself claimed near infallibility. If this book aids market technicians in understanding some of the facts and foibles of Elliott's work, it will have accomplished its purpose.

FOOTNOTES

[1] The 1962 drop was 28.5%.

[2] Since social events are a *consequence* of social mood as reflected by stocks, such events cannot disrupt or change a pattern. They are its results.

CHAPTER II
ELLIOTT'S BROAD CONCEPT

Perhaps the simplest way to introduce the Elliott Wave Principle to the reader is to say that in the middle 1930s, after a great deal of detailed research, Elliott developed the following long-term pattern:

(1) Great tidal wave bull markets develop in series of five upward waves. These are followed by corrections in waves of three.

(2) In 1857, at the bottom of the panic and depression of that era, began a series of tidal waves which lasted to 1929. The wave pattern conformed to the pattern indicated as shown in Figure 1.

(3) Each great tidal wave of this magnitude can be divided into subwaves of 5 in the direction of the main trend (i.e., waves (I), (III) and (V) in Figure 1).

(4) Each great tidal wave involves corrective waves (i.e., (II) and (IV)), and these are subdivided into subwaves of 3.

(5) As an example of the subdivision process, the (V) wave can be subdivided into five waves as indicated (waves I, II, III, IV and V).

(6) Similarly wave V can be subdivided into five waves of smaller degree, as indicated (waves 1, 2, 3, 4 and 5).

(7) After any upward wave of any degree *in the main stream,* a correction of the same degree will follow, and this

wave will be in three waves of lesser degree.

As we develop the Elliott theme, it will be seen how the various pieces fit into the Elliott Wave Principle pattern.

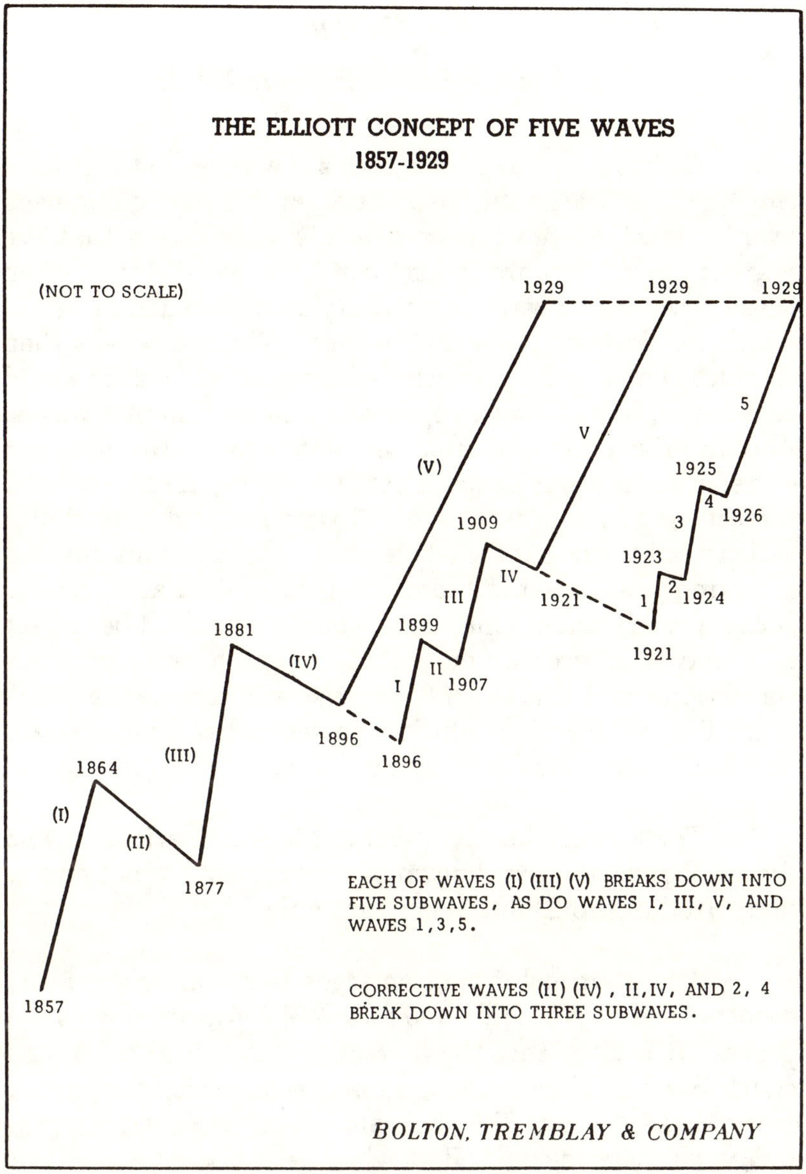

Figure 1

CHAPTER III
WHAT IS THE WAVE PRINCIPLE?

Elliott pointed out in a series of articles in the *Financial World* in 1939 that observation on his part going back over at least 80 years proved to his satisfaction that the market moved forward in series of 5 waves, and that when these 5 waves forward were completed, a reaction set in which would take place in 3 waves. These 8 waves then completed a cycle from which a new series of 5 waves would commence, to be followed by another correction in 3 waves. And finally, after the first set of 5 waves, the set of 3 correcting waves, the second set of 5 waves, and its set of 3 correcting waves, a final set of 5 waves would materialize which would close out the whole phase. At this point, instead of having another set of 3 corrective waves similar to the two series already undergone, there would now come about a set of 3 waves of greater magnitude than the two previous corrections, and this set of 3 waves would correct the whole of the 5 upward waves, which themselves had broken into 5 and 3 smaller waves each along the way.

The idea can best be seen in a diagrammatic form, and Figure 2 gives the breakdown of the "perfect" round trip as visualized in the Elliott Wave Principle.

The main point that emerges from this elementary concept is that we now have *form*. With form now comes *degree*. It is clear that the corrective waves marked on the chart "B" and "D" are of the same *degree* as the forward waves marked "A", "C" and "E". It is also clear, however, that the corrective wave marked "BB" (which is composed of A, B and C) is of a higher, or larger, degree and may be considered to

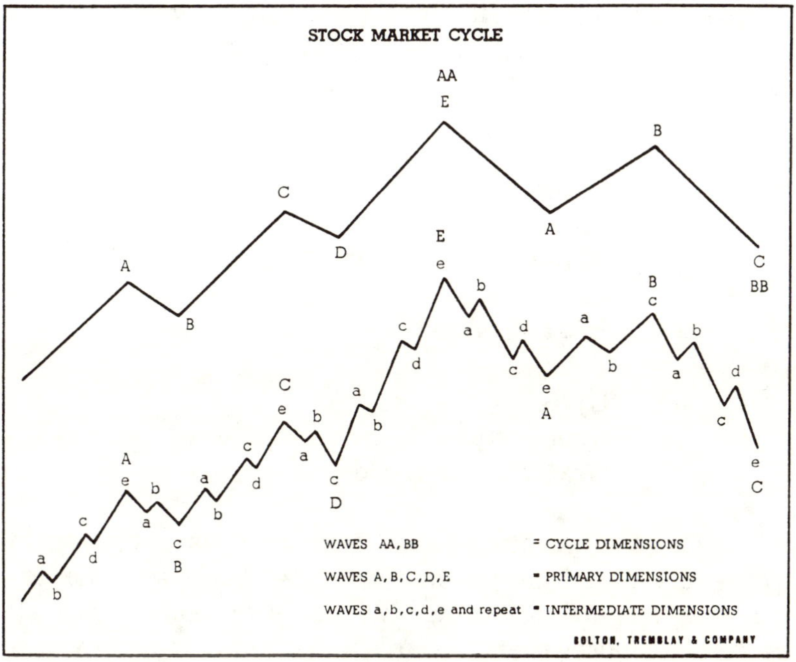

Figure 2

be of the same degree as the five wave pattern marked "AA," which is the wave made up of the five smaller waves A, B, C, D, and E.

If the reader has followed the line of argument so far, the *implications* begin to appear. Given a recognizable 5-wave pattern, it should be possible to break down each of the 5 waves into 5 and 3 waves of smaller degree. Or, conversely, given a series of smaller 5 and 3 waves, one should be able to predict the continuation of the 5-3 pattern until a wave of larger degree is completed, which would of necessity have 5 subdivisions, for a total of 21 sub-subdivisions (5 plus 3 plus 5 plus 3 plus 5).

Having worked this out in theory on an empirical basis, Elliott then went back over stock prices from 1854 using the Axe-Houghton Index and satisfied himself that this was true, or at least essentially true. It then became necessary to classify all these waves into *degrees* and to cudgel up names for all the varying degrees. Elliott showed considerable imagination in this regard, and called them in order of rising magnitude:

Subminuette
Minuette
Minute
Minor
Intermediate
Primary
Cycle
Super Cycle
Grand Super Cycle

These classifications of degrees apparently would cover everything from the smallest imaginable wave formation to a formation lasting 200 years or more. For all practical purposes then, we have here the ultimate in work-a-day stock market sequences.

Figure 2, however, only shows those degrees of waves which we shall call Cycle, Primary and Intermediate. They could just as well be called any other three consecutive degrees listed above, but in stock market day-to-day history, perhaps the three noted degrees are most valuable to the analyst.

What sets the Wave Principle in theory aside and ahead of other technical approaches is primarily this characteristic of *design* or *form*. The waves take shape; they can theoretically be defined with precision; given any one degree of wave recognizable, it becomes possible in theory to put these waves into a context of waves of a larger degree. A pattern emerges which allows one to judge the probable impact of future amplitude and time with some degree of accuracy. Thus, if one has defined accurately the first Primary wave of a new Cycle, and one has now completed the second (corrective) wave of Primary degree, one *knows* that the next series of waves will make up the third Primary wave and that this wave should be comparable in degree with the first Primary and should break down into five Intermediate waves. It becomes clear that toward the beginning of this new (third) Primary there should be no dangers of a major reversal, and therefore investment positions can be taken with equanimity.

The only hitch of course is: Does one always *know* at what exact spot one is in the wave formation? And it is here that one may disagree with the attempted *precision* that Elliott insisted upon. So far as he was concerned, all i's had to be dotted and all t's crossed without any room for argument. As we shall see, this is not so at all, and the farther along in any wave of any degree one gets, the more subject to possible variations does one's interpretation become.

In conclusion then, at this stage, Elliott's Principle says that the stock market expands and contracts in line with a set pattern. Forward (upward) waves start developing from a final point of correction in a series of 5 waves followed thereafter by correction of 3 waves, and so on alternating until each degree formation of 5 waves becomes one wave of the next higher degree, and itself has its 3 waves correction followed by another 5 waves of the same greater degree. Corrections take place in 3 waves (with one exception which will be noted later), but as we shall see, the make-up of these 3 waves is subject to considerable variation and *alternation*.

It can be seen already that the Principle is tending to get more complicated as we go along. No wonder, then, that many students have given up in despair!

CHAPTER IV
FROM SIMPLICITY TO COMPLEXITY

When the writer first came across the Wave Principle in the series of articles in the *Financial World*, it occurred to him that here was something extremely simple to understand. One had a 5-3 pattern forever. One could draw trend lines to help indicate changes in degree. There was no doubt about it; if one looked at any graph of stock prices in the last 20 years, the Wave Principle was very clear.

Figure 3 shows the market history from 1921 to late 1949.

Take 1921 to 1929, for instance. Obviously, this was 5 waves up: 1921-23, 1923-24, 1924-25, 1925-26 and 1926-1929. Quite as obviously, 1929 to 1932 was a 3 wave pattern down, 1929, 1929-30, 1930-32. So far so good; as we shall see, however, there actually were certain *irregularities* in this pattern which only came to light when one tried to break down all the waves into waves of smaller degree and still come out with a subdivided pattern which meets Elliott's 5-3-5-3-5 rules.

Again, 1932-37 (remember we are looking at this from the hindsight of 1938-39, having just read Elliott's *Financial World* articles) is clearly a five upward wave affair:

June - Sept. 1932
Sept. 1932 - March 1933
March - July 1933
July 1933 - Nov. 1934
Nov. 1934 - March 1937

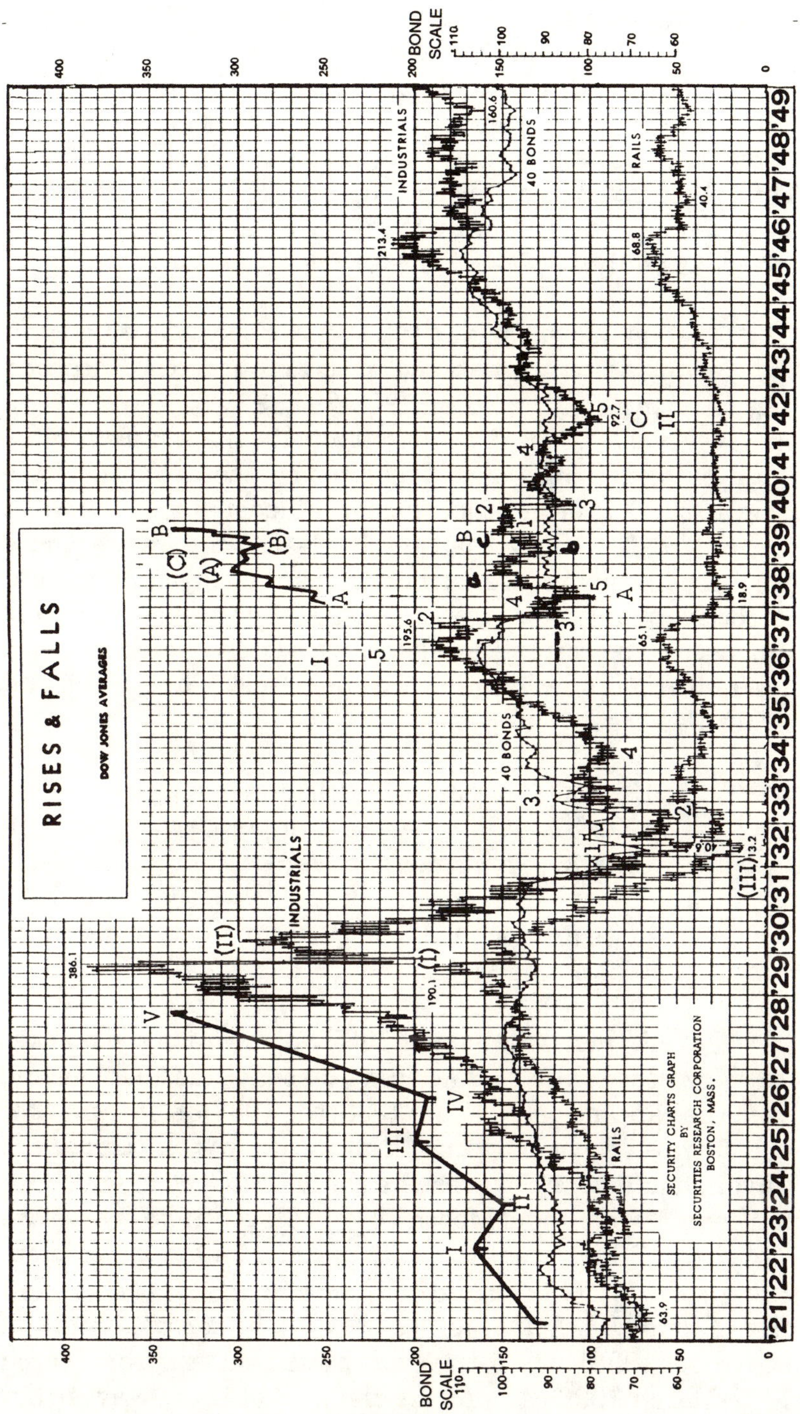
RISES & FALLS
DOW JONES AVERAGES
INDUSTRIALS
40 BONDS
RAILS
BOND SCALE
SECURITY CHARTS GRAPH
BY
SECURITIES RESEARCH CORPORATION
BOSTON, MASS.

Figure 3

But what strikes one in examining the 1932-37 series of five waves in comparison with the 1921-29 series of waves is that they *surely cannot be of the same degree*. 1932-37 is much shorter in time and in amplitude. Further, the corrections along the way are much deeper than those of 1921-29. This, then, gives us a clue as to *degree*. If 1921-29 is a wave of *Cycle* magnitude (simply to give it a name) then 1932-37 is perhaps only a wave of Primary magnitude.[1]

Again, as we look at 1929-32, we see that its magnitude is considerably greater so far as amplitude is concerned (but shorter as to time) than 1921-29. 1929-32 starts where our Cycle wave 1921-29 leaves off and declines to *well below* the starting point of 1921. Must it not be, then, that the wave from 1929-32 is either the whole or at least a part of a wave of even greater degree than our 1921-29 Cycle wave? There can be no other answer, since we cannot logically have a corrective type wave correcting more than the wave that it is supposed to be correcting. Thus, we perforce must give it a new and greater designation of Super Cycle. Thus, the grand pattern emerges:

1921-29	A wave of Cycle dimension
1929-32	All or part of a Super Cycle
1932-37	A Primary wave?

Or so we are inclined to argue at a point "some time" in the 1938-39 period.

Well, then, what about 1937-38, in which the market lost 50% of its value? How do we classify this? Obviously, from the vantage point of late 1938, the 1937-38 bear market is a 5-wave down pattern. But we know that corrective waves should be in 3 waves and there is no way in which we can get a 3-wave out of March 1937 to March 1938. So we are forced (as Elliott was) to another unfortunate concession. *The correction of the 1932-37 bull market, if this is classified as a Primary bull market, cannot yet be completed* (as of December 1938). The 5-wave downward pattern from March 1937-March 1938 can only be the *first* of three waves that will make up the full 3-wave correction of the 1932-37 advance. From the vantage point of, say, 150 in the DJIA in late 1938, this was valuable information and would at least have prepared one for another major decline in stock prices which should at least equal and probably break the lows of 1938. This forecast alone was worth its weight in gold.

As we shall later see as we get into *refinements* of the various types of corrections, we could also come to another conclusion in late 1938. Since the first wave of the correction starting in March 1937 was in the form of a 5-wave down, the whole correction would have to be what is known as a *zigzag* and not a *flat*. Zigzags *always* are made up of three waves of the 5-3-5 variety. Flats are made up of 3-3-5. The diagrams below show the essential difference.

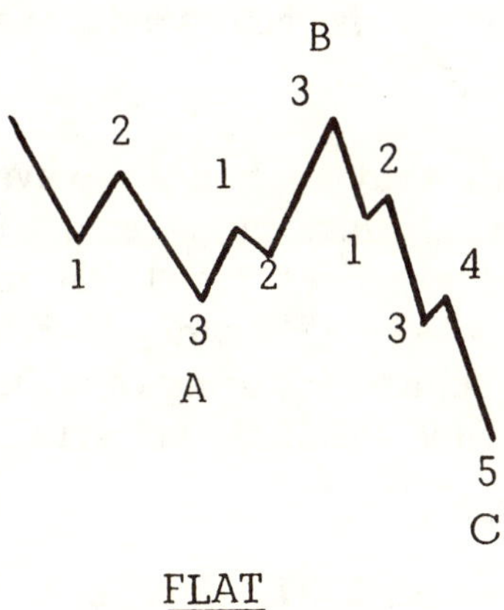

Figure 4

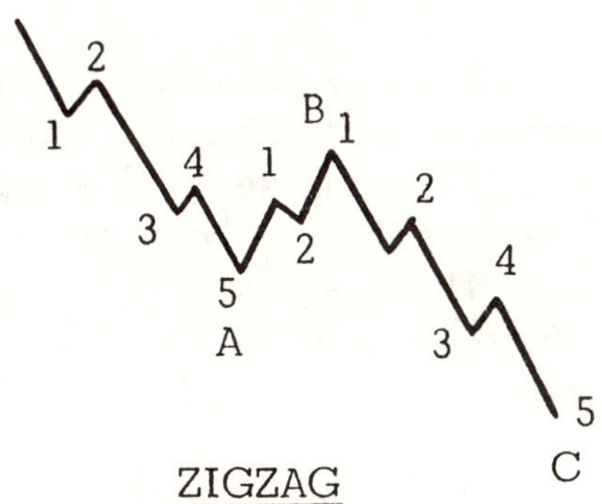

Figure 5

We note that the flat correction tends to bring wave "B" back to close to, or even higher than, the start of the correction, whereas by definition the "B" of the zigzag is almost certain to be lower than the start of the correction.

Thus, it can be seen that from the point of view of late 1938, we "know" several things:

(1) If 1932-37 is classified as wave I of Primary degree, then corrective wave II has to be in three downward waves, either flat or zigzag.

(2) The fact that wave 1 of wave II is a 5 tells us several things:

(a) The correction is *not* over at March 31st, 1938.
(b) It must be a zigzag correction, i.e., 5-3-5.
(c) The "B" wave will be a 3-formation.
(d) The "C" wave will be a 5-formation, and
(e) The top of the "B" wave is not likely to go back to equal or exceed the beginning of the wave at 195 DJIA.

As we said, this was *valuable information*. An almost foolproof forecast could be made: at 150 DJIA in late 1938, the odds in favor of substantial further rise before a decline to or below 98 DJIA were extremely small.

But it was indeed fortunate that we had a 5-wave down so clearly delineated. What would have happened if, let us say, the market had stopped at about 112 DJIA in November 1937, and *not broken this level in February-March 1938?* This is a good question, and one which brings out the *lack of precision* in the *Elliott Wave Principle* at certain times.

First, let us look at it in December 1937. (Cover up the balance of the stock picture in Figure 3). *There was no way of knowing whether the correction was over with three waves down.* In fact, the presumption was that it was, and Elliott forecast it as completed as of that time.[2]

Now, this correction would certainly have been ample in terms of price to serve as a full correction of the 1932-37 rise. It would have brought one down exactly to the top of wave 3 of the 1932-37 rise, a logical stopping point. In point of view of time, of course, it would have been short. If one had hung one's hat on the inadequacy of the time element, one would then expect that March 1937 - November 1937 was wave "A" of the correction, that this would make the whole correction a *flat* (three waves to start with), that wave "B" should bring the market up to close to or above the March 1937 top, and that wave "C" would then be a 5-down eventually breaking the lows of 1937. At 125 DJIA, say, in December 1937, the outlook would have been for considerable capital gain possibilities (back perhaps to 195 DJIA) before the final bear market onslaught began.

Unfortunately, the experience by February-March 1938 would have been very disturbing and discouraging. Instead of three waves completing wave "A" of the correction as of November 1937, we got five waves carrying the market down to 98 DJIA as of March 1938. And instead of an indication of a possible double top at 195, the zigzag formation suggested we would have to settle for a lot less.

Now let us take the next step forward. Looking at Figure 3 again in, say, November-December 1938, what would be our view of the future? From March 31, 1938, we find a clear-cut 5 up to November 1938. Because this is a 5 instead of a 3, we "know" that wave "B" of our correction starting April 1938 is *not* complete. Applying the same reasoning as on the downside, the 5 up pattern points to this as being only the first of 3 waves up from March 1938, and now we look for an *upward zigzag* of the 5-3-5 (A-B-C) pattern, of which March-November 1938 is "A."

November to April 1939 is, of course, a clear-cut three waves for b, so now we are all set for a 5 up starting April 1939 at about 120 in the DJIA. If all works out according to Hoyle, wave "c" should terminate somewhere above 158 and somewhere in the area of 175-185, sometime perhaps in the first half of 1940. (This estimate could be made by extending trend lines using March 1938 and April 1939 as the line of bottoms, November 1938 as the parallel line of tops, and keeping in mind the large supply area between 165 and 195 and the fact that the downward zigzag wave "A" from 1937 does *not* call for a double top around 195, but something quite short of this figure).

Unfortunately for our sanity, something happened to truncate the advance of wave "c" from March 1938. No adequate explanation of this was given at the time except that the preparation for, and the outbreak of, World War II in September 1939 caused all the waves of wave "c" to be subnormal, with the result that our objective of, say, 185 was never reached, and in fact the market made only 155 or slightly less than the old top of wave "A" in November 1938.

Up to this point, everything seemed so simple. 1932-37 came along in 5 waves. 1937-38, while a disappointment to those who thought the correction over in November 1937, at least acted quite normally up to April 1938. Then came our second disappointment, and one which was considerably more difficult to analyze at the time.

Elliott in his writings up to this point had been pretty sure of his position (too sure in fact). From this point on, his interpretations became quite ragged, and it wasn't till several years later that he got back on the track. Thus, 1942 came and went and he misinterpreted the length of the decline, insisting that we were still in the downward cycle from 1937 well into and beyond 1943. The fact that we were in a new bull market from May 1942 was not recognized at the time until we were at least half way through it, and this result, we are sure, was responsible for a great deal of skepticism concerning the validity of his theory, with the result that it fell into disrepute. We should keep in mind, however, that his "public" at this point was quite meager.

What was wrong, of course, was not so much the Principle itself but the *interpretation* thereof. And this, in our opinion, will be the major fault in the Wave Principle as we move away from the points of fulcrum of the Principle, which in the writer's opinion were the dates 1929, 1932, 1937, 1942, 1946 and 1949. We will discuss the importance of these terminal dates in later pages of this book as we come to discuss the varying interpretations of where we stand now in the *Elliott Wave Principle* delineation of the market environment.

FOOTNOTES

[1] This discussion is inaccurate. 1921-1929 was a 6x multiple and 1932-1937 was a 5x multiple, *quite* close in size. In fact, they are the same degree (Cycle). The rest of Bolton's analysis is correct and well argued.

[2] While there is no direct evidence of this fact, Elliott suggests it in *The Wave Principle* by referring to the fifth wave down as a "supplementary cycle." His market letters' first reference to the 1937-1938 decline, however, labels it correctly as a "five."

CHAPTER V
WAVE SEQUENCES

By this time, our reader, we hope, has given up the idea that the *Elliott Wave Principle* is any simple means of getting from rags to riches in no time flat. We have pointed out indirectly the difficulties of determining wave degrees by inference, and we have pointed out that *events* can sometimes influence the magnitude of the waves to the point that it is difficult to maintain a proper perspective. World War II was typical of this.

What must also be clear to the analyst is the point that history is always right, and that if one's analysis of the waves does not agree with history as it subsequently unfolds, then the analysis and not history is at fault. It's a bit like the old saw about the man being killed in accident maintaining his right of way, or the cliche about the doctor whose operation was a tremendous success but the patient died.

Elliott's major research was applied to market averages, in particular those of the Dow Jones Company. The great advantage of these averages over any others available at the time was that the daily range of average prices was inaugurated in 1928 and the hourly averages commenced in 1932. These were necessary, he claimed, to be able to distinguish the waves, particularly of smaller degree and in fast moving markets.

But we must not forget that an average is just that. The Dow Jones Industrials have been pointed to as a highly unscientific average. This point is of less import than many think. However, if we average 30 different stocks, each of which is going through a different market cycle, it must be clear that it would be highly unlikely that the resultant average would follow the Elliott Wave pattern exactly according to the book in all details. But it is surprising nevertheless how closely the patterns have been followed over recorded history.

Having learnt to our sorrow perhaps that "all that glistens is not gold," let us take some time out to see how Elliott finally broke down the wave pattern into possible sequences. In this connection, Elliott's monograph, *The Wave Principle,* published by him in 1938, is a simple document compared to the later complexities of his 1946 *Nature's Law*.

Figure 6 depicts Elliott's Basic Wave Sequences.[1] This chart serves to portray most of the important wave formations that Elliott discovered in his study of stock prices from at least as far back as 1854.

What is not perhaps clear from this diagram, but which we pointed out in Chapter III, is that a 5-wave in the direction of the *main trend* is followed by a *correction*. Thus, a completed *bull market cannot consist of three waves, it must consist of five waves.* Thus, if one finds a 3-wave upward pattern of sufficient size to qualify as a bull market — as for instance March 1938 to October 1939 — then this is not a bull market as such, but really two bull markets. And the two bull markets are part of a correction within a correction in the opposite direction, in this case.

This may sound like pure semantics, but it is important. We have to think continually in terms of Elliott's concepts. Likewise, *bear markets* are 3-wave formations in the Elliott context. We may speak of the 1937-38 bear market in ordinary conversation, but it is *not* a completed bear market in the Elliott sense, since it has five waves. It can only be *one* of three waves of the completed bear market, which in Elliott's parlance encompasses the period 1937-42.

The 5-wave upward pattern allows for very little

flexibility so far as the waves in the main direction are concerned. It's five, and that is it. When it comes to corrections, however, we do have a considerable variety, and it is extremely difficult to know what degree we are talking about at times, as well as to know which of the many possible formations are to be expected.

BASIC WAVE SEQUENCES

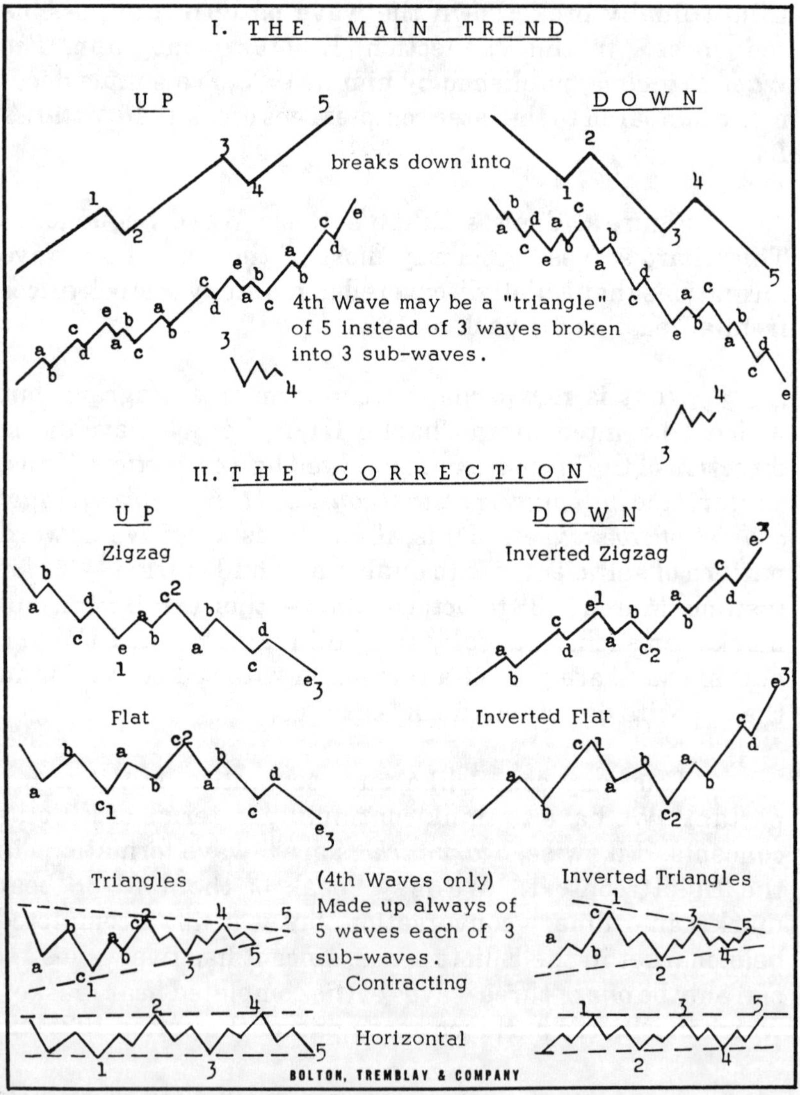

Figure 6

Elliott outlined in his 1946 monograph a number of variations which do not appear in Figure 6. To give the reader some idea of what can happen in the way of corrections, let us look at the 3 major forms first: *zigzags, flats* and *triangles*.

The *zigzag* may be single or double:

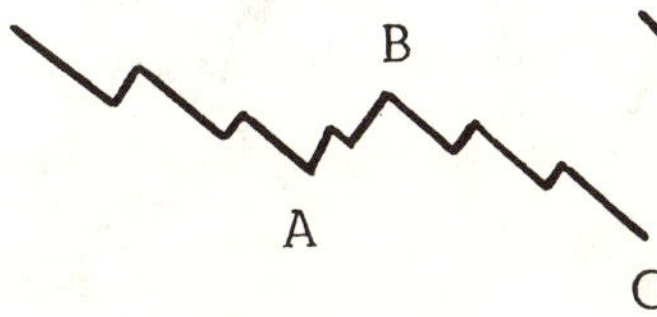

Figure 7

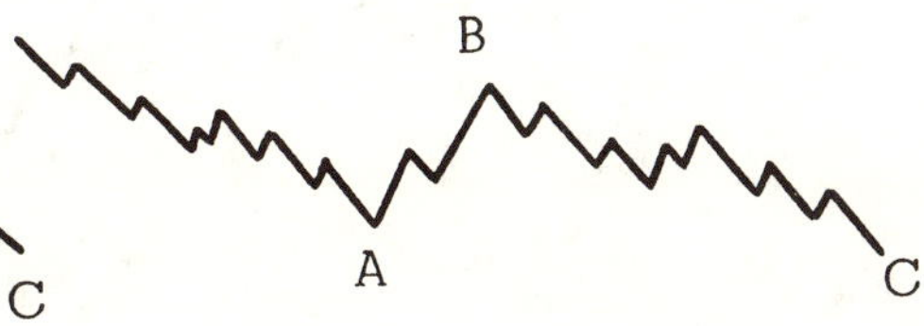

Figure 8

The double zigzag was not mentioned as a possible form of corrective wave in Elliott's first monograph. In a sense, this is a form of double 3, and tends to be an exception to the general principle that the third wave of any correction (either up or down) always ends in a 5 sub-wave formation. It is the general rule of the 5 sub-wave ending which often gives the analyst a clue that the move is over.

Of course, the zigzag also can be a correction of a downtrend, in which case its appearance is as follows:

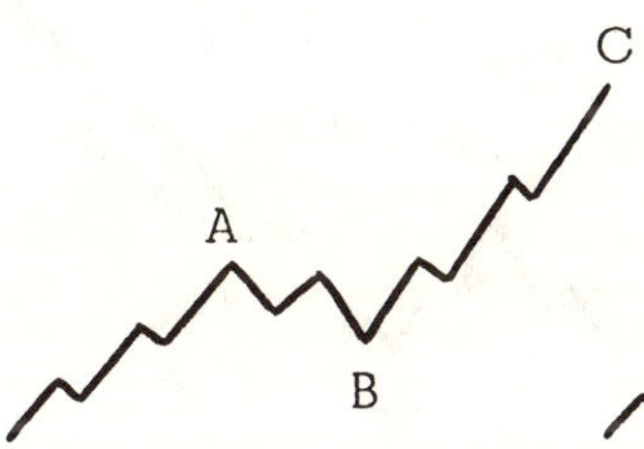

Figure 9

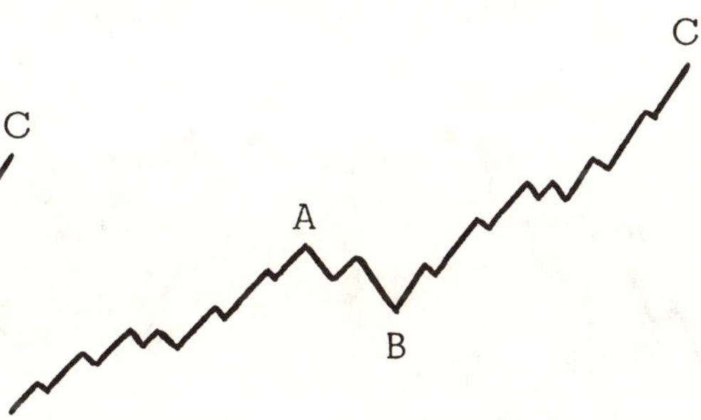

Figure 10

The downward zigzag correction pattern is called simply a zigzag correction. The upward form is called an *inverted zigzag* (double or single as the case may be).

The *flat* correction is so-called because it has a more or less flat appearance, although it may slope up or down a bit. The flat may take several forms:

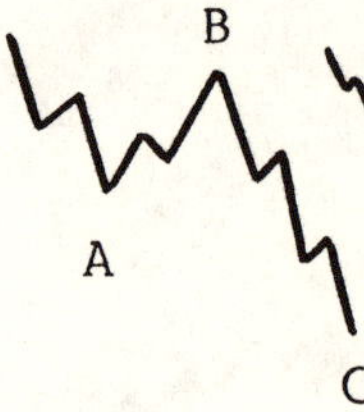

Figure 11

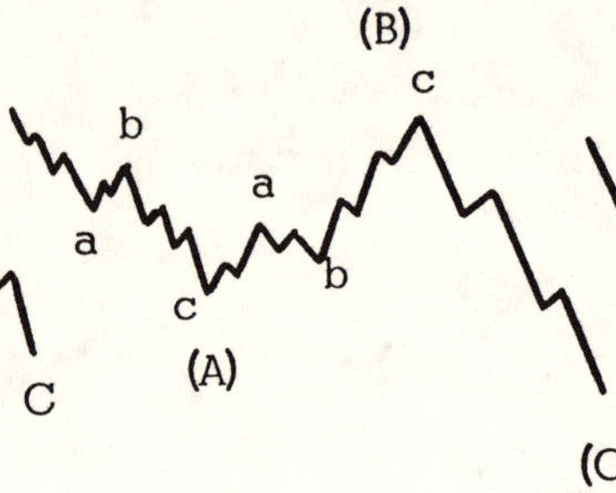

Figure 12

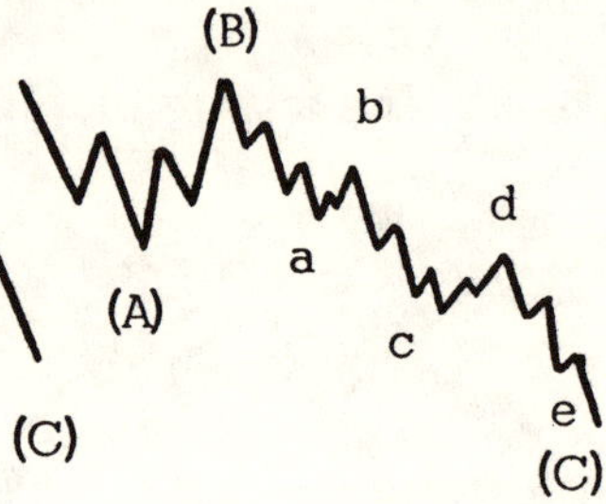

Figure 13

It is noted that the main theme here which distinguishes the *flat* from the *zigzag* is (a) the "A" wave of the flat must break down into a 3, (b) the "B" wave breaks down into a 3 of which the first, and second, are again subdivided into 3s,[2] and the last is subdivided into 5 (never 3).

Inverted flats are the same, but in the opposite direction, and are corrections to previous and subsequent waves in a *downward* direction.

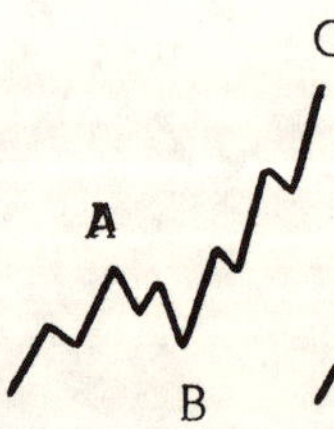

Figure 14

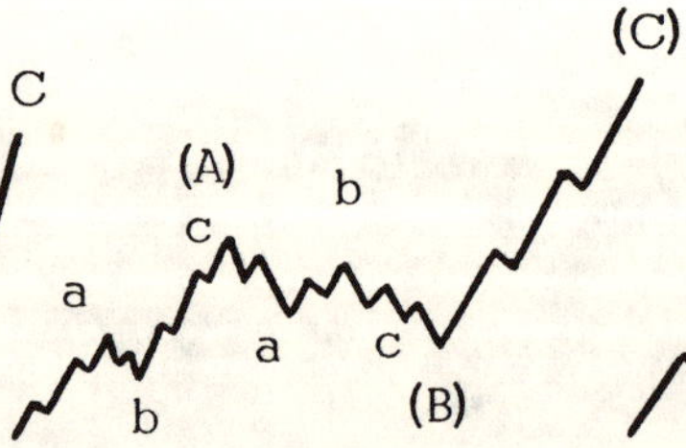

Figure 15

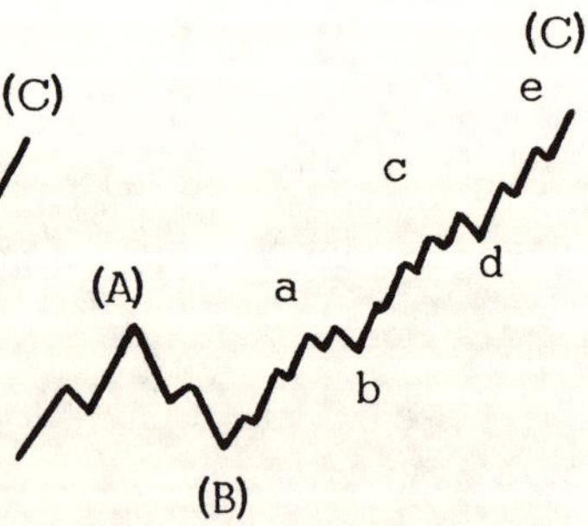

Figure 16

In order to complete the survey of corrective waves in subdivisions of 3, we now need to look at *complex corrective waves*. Just as the zigzag can broaden out into a *double zigzag*, so too one can find *double threes* and *triple threes*.

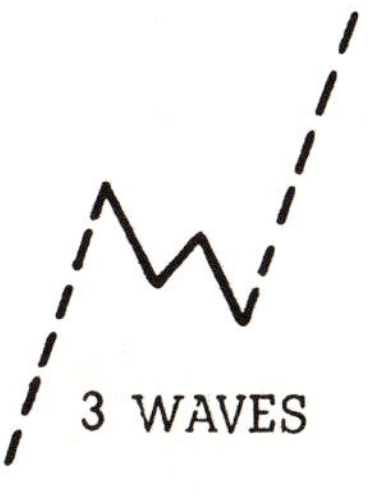

Figure 17

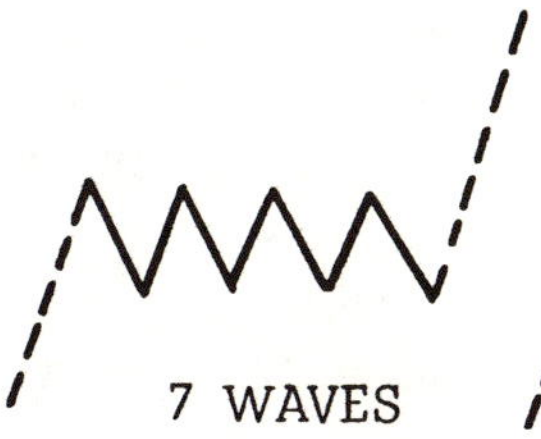

Figure 18

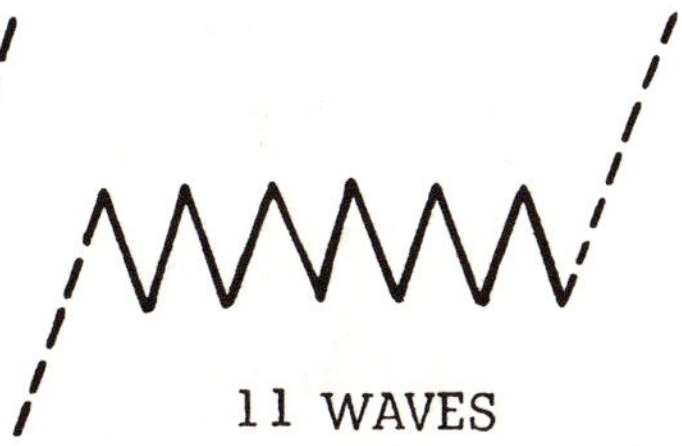

Figure 19

The same can be found in the opposite direction, i.e., *inverted single threes, inverted double threes and inverted triple threes.*

It becomes apparent that with all this variety of corrective waves, it can become extremely difficult for any analyst to be sure what may be expected. Generally speaking, however, double and triple threes would not be expected in large formations or degrees, but only in smaller formations of Minor or Intermediate size.[3]

To top the whole question of corrections, we still have the *triangle,* and this instead of a 3 formation is a 5 formation. Elliott claims, and this is borne out by the author's own experience, that triangles are fairly rare, and so far as is known, they only come as wave 4 of any five wave movement. This eliminates a lot of trouble, since they can only appear in the fourth position of any 5 wave up or down and cannot therefore appear in a 3 wave of the various sorts mentioned above.[4]

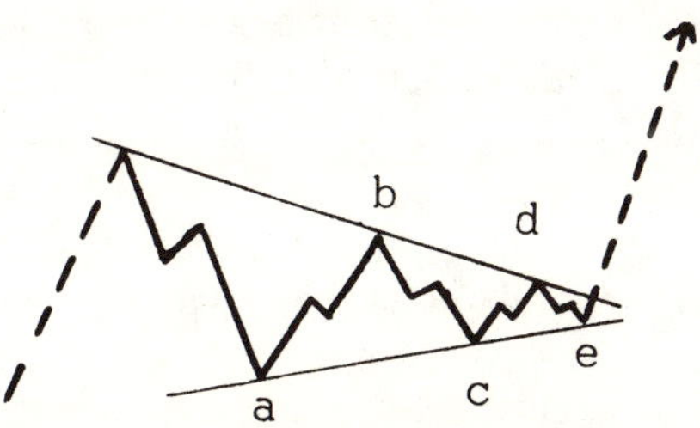

Figure 20

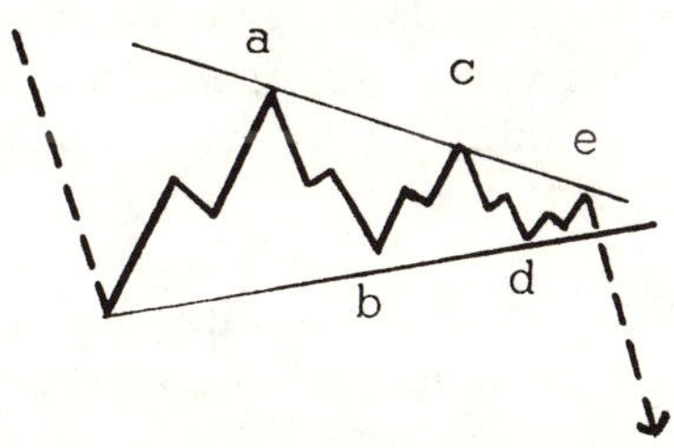

Figure 21

Elliott in his first monograph (1938) thought that triangles could be of the expanding or the contracting type. However, in his 1946 monograph, he only refers to the contracting triangle.[5]

Expanding triangles, after all, can always be classified as *double threes.*[6] This is the kind we picture above where the waves grow smaller and smaller and the apex of the triangle becomes a sort of springboard which causes a *thrust* in the direction of the *main trend* (either up or down). The fourth wave of the 5-wave downwards market cycle from March 1937 to March 1938 was a triangle, and the largest that had thus appeared. It confirmed that *each of the five waves of a triangle are threes (not fives at any point).*

This is an important rule according to Elliott, and it needs to be kept in mind in any consideration of larger triangles that have subsequently appeared since 1938.

In conclusion, the complexities of *corrective waves* are quite profuse. Oh! for the simplicity of the basic *main trend* 5-3-5-3-5 wave. But this again only points up the difficulties from a practical point of view of using Elliott's Wave Principle as a forecasting device.

FOOTNOTES

[1] See Footnote 2 on page 34. Note that this figure has been changed from the 1957 original, shown on page 32. Since Bolton does not mention "horizontal triangles" in his text, he may be depicting a triple three, as illustrated in his Figure 19, to stand for both double and triple threes, which are sideways corrections. He apparently meant the bottom illustration also to include expanding triangles, as he implies in his upcoming discussion of triangles.

[2] The "first," i.e., a of (B), need not be three waves; it can be five, as part of a zigzag.

3 Not so. The distribution appears equal across degrees, as is fitting for a fractal process.

4 The rule is more accurately stated, "Triangles never occur as second waves." In fact, triangles can and do appear as wave "B" in an A-B-C or as the second half of a double three.

5 Expanding triangles are rare, but they do exist.

6 They might be classified as "*triple* threes," but their shape is clearly different, triangular rather than rectangular.

CHAPTER VI
FURTHER COMPLEXITIES

As if not to be satisfied with a baker's dozen or more of different *correction patterns*, let us now look at a seeming batch of irregularities that add further complexities to Wave Principle interpretation.

Among the first irregularities to consider should be the *extension*. The extension is where *one* of waves 1, 3 or 5 extends out by breaking down into a further five waves. The effect of this is to elongate one of the three waves in the direction of the five wave trend. The diagrams herewith show the idea.

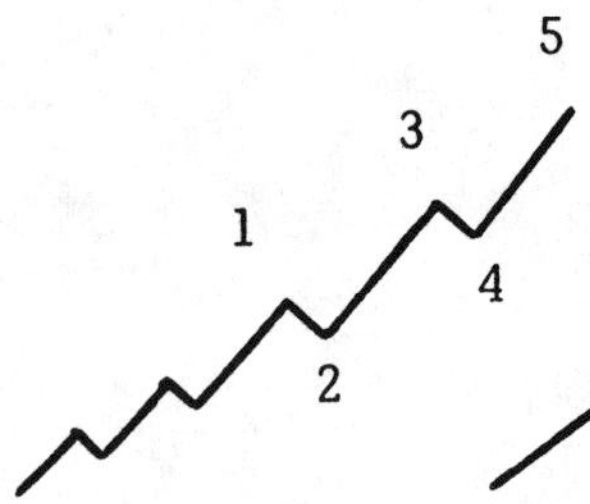

Figure 22

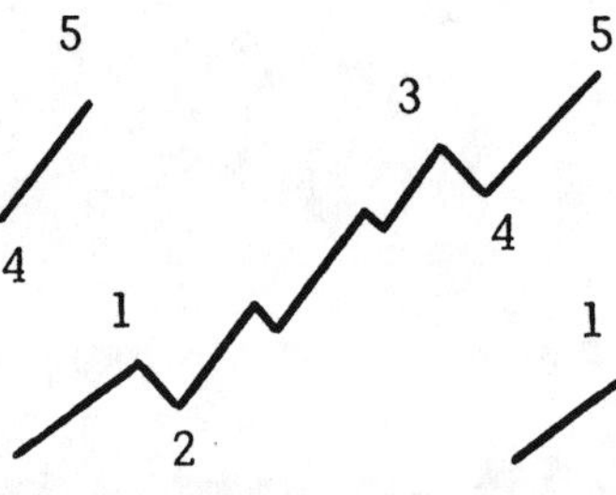

Figure 23

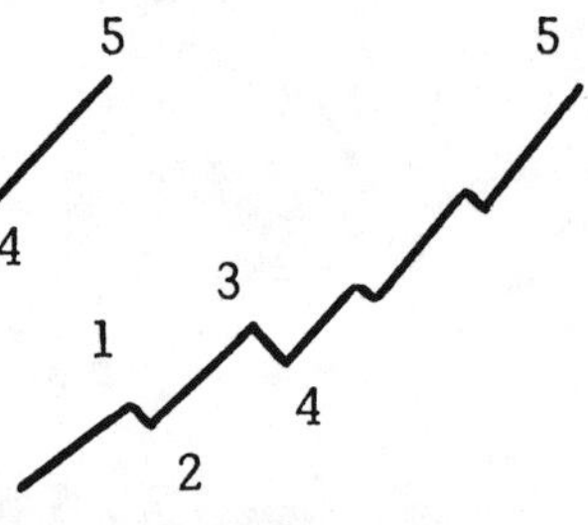

Figure 24

The effect is to make the 5-wave pattern into *nine waves*. Sometimes it is impossible to tell which of the waves really is the extended one.

Extensions do not occur in a corrective type wave. When an extension occurs in a fifth wave, Elliott formulated a rule called "double-retracement." That is that the subsequent correction will come back at least to the *top* of the wave that was the first of the 5-wave extension and would then retrace again in the opposite direction [see Figure 25].

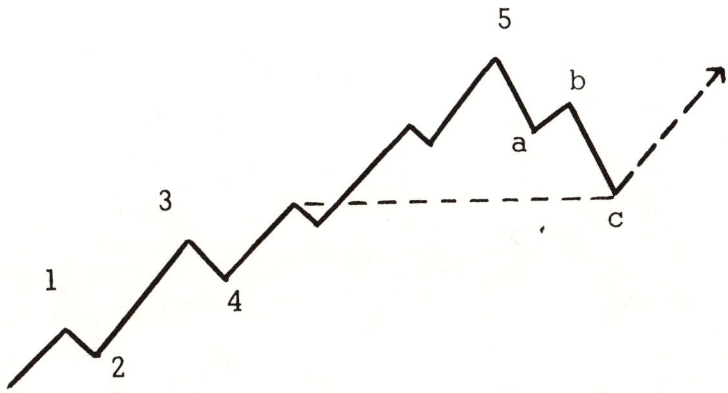

Figure 25

We have never considered this double retracement as particularly unusual, since this is bound to happen in the normal course.

The whole concept of *extensions* so far as this rule is concerned is a difficult one, but they do happen from time to time. A typical one was pointed out in our bulletins covering the extension in the fifth wave up from September 1953 to April 1956. This called for a retracement to 410 in the DJIA, and this was reached within a few points when in late 1957, 416 was touched on the downside.

Of more importance are *irregular tops*. These tops are caused when after five waves up, the ABC correction results in the "B" wave terminating higher in level than the end of wave 5. This happens quite often and perhaps most fatuously in the 1929 bull market [see Figure 26].

Presumably, this could also happen in an irregular bottom, but a little thought will show that it could only happen in a "B" wave of an ABC correction [see Figure 27].

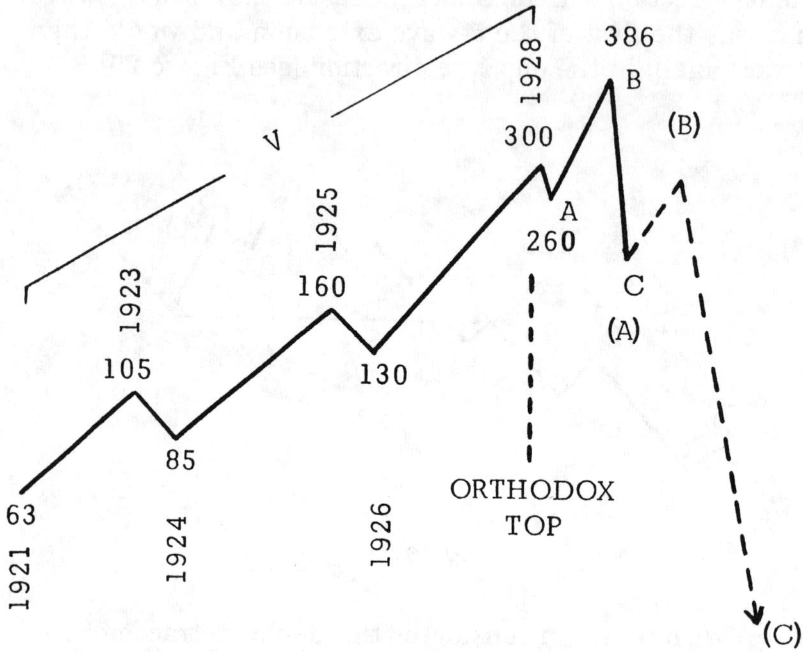

Figure 26

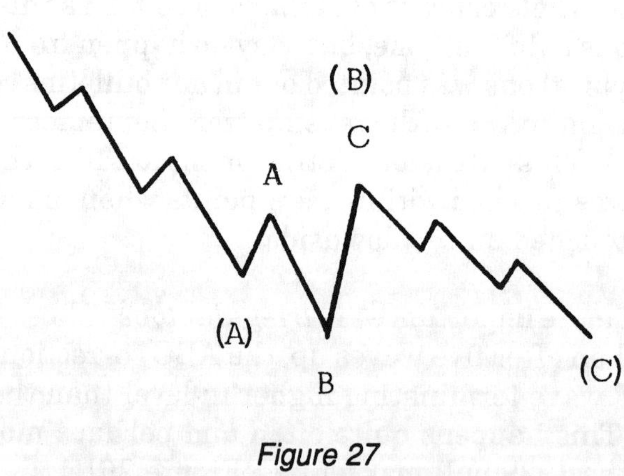

Figure 27

Distinguishing waves and degrees of waves can become quite a complex task, and in many cases in the light of hindsight, the analyst has to readjust his count to the facts of life. This has led to the complaint that the Wave Principle is of no value anyway since it can be twisted to fit any situation. There is, of course, something to this accusation and it accounts for the fact that different analysts come up with different interpretations of wave breakdown from time to time.

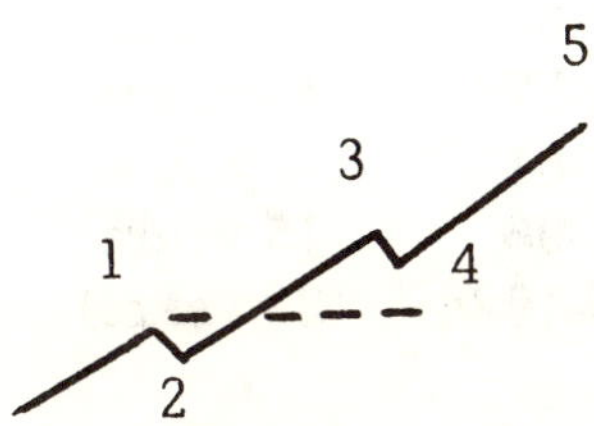

Figure 28

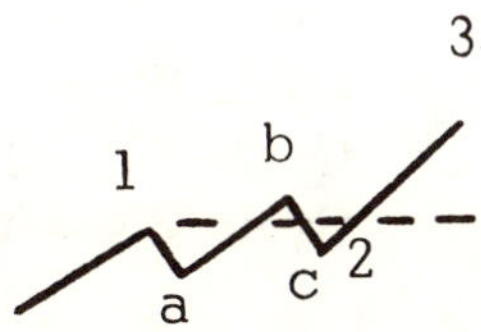

Figure 29

Nevertheless, Elliott did produce some common sense rules for telling where one is in the normal case. Thus, take the two examples side-by-side above.

Figure 28 depicts a true 5 up. But because in Figure 29 wave "c" drops below the top of 1, this is an indication that what one might have classified as wave 3 is part of a corrective wave 2. Wave 4 should not ordinarily drop below wave 1, otherwise the second wave is still in force, and wave 4 would only be subwave "c" of wave 2.

Some of Elliott's writings, however, were somewhat obscure, as for instance the famous statement in his 1946 monograph wherein he states that wave 3 can never be shorter than both waves 1 and 5. This statement has caused more call for clarification than any other statement that he made. He then goes on to say that if wave 3 appears to be shorter than either wave 1 or wave 5, it is necessary to classify the so-called wave 3 into an "a-b" wave as indicated in the chart above. He clearly states that wave 4 should not overlap wave 1, i.e., go below the top of wave 1, but he does not solve two problems which often arise, which are (1) was Elliott talking in terms of *amplitude* or size of the wave — in points say — or (2) was he talking in terms of *time*?

After going through all Elliott's work, the writer is pretty well convinced that he was talking in terms of *amplitude,* and *not time*. The reason for this conclusion is based on Elliott's own classification of the Super Cycle from 1857 to 1928, wherein he classifies the waves as follows:

Cycle Wave I	1857-64	(7 years)
Cycle Wave II	1864-77	(13 years)
Cycle Wave III	1877-81	(4 years)
Cycle Wave IV	1881-96	(15 years)
Cycle Wave V	1896-1928	(32 years)

This pretty well establishes that what Elliott had in mind by this statement was that price was involved, not time. If this criterion is given then as measured by the Axe-Houghton index, the following results are obtained:

Cycle Wave I	About 30 points
Cycle Wave II	About 40 points
Cycle Wave III	About 250 points

It is also interesting to note that Cycle wave IV, which terminated in 1896, did not go as low as the top of Cycle wave I, which ended in 1864, thus proving Elliott's point above.

Even here, however, we find further obscurity. Wave III in this case is greater than wave I, but it is obviously less than wave V. Thus, Elliott's wording using "either" or "both" is really incorrect. What he meant was that wave III must not be smaller than both waves I and V taken individually, but may be shorter than one of them.

In establishing wave terminations, Elliott also made good use of *parallel trend channels*. It appears that in larger formations, Elliott used almost exclusively *ratio* or *logarithmic charts*, whereas in smaller formations *arithmetic scales* were used. Actually Elliott called for arithmetic scales as standard until it was clear that upward trend lines were being broken, at which point the prices should be recharted on logarithmic scale. The examples below show what happens when arithmetic and logarithmic scales are used for the same data [see Figures 30-35].

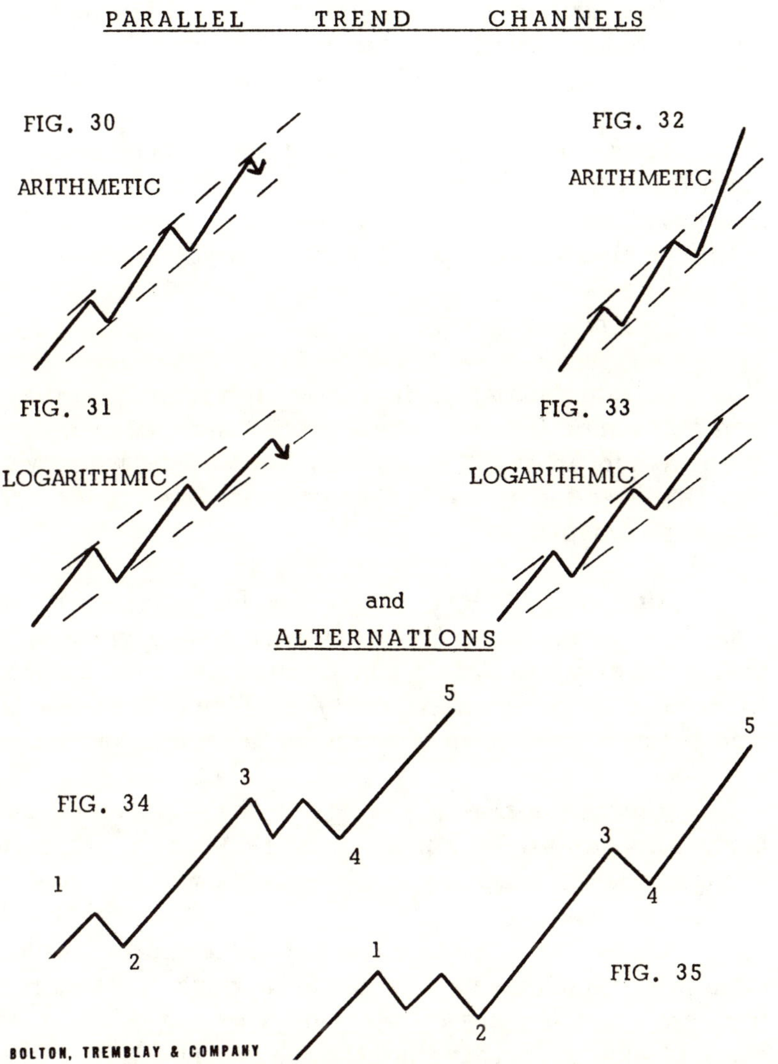

Figures 30 - 35

Elliott pointed out that the need to use *logarithmic* scales in order to have parallel trend channels come out properly was an *indication of inflation.* Thus, the fact that the Super Cycle 1857 to 1928 had to be drawn on logarithmic scales if parallel trend channels were to apply was prima facie evidence of the *inflation* which characterized this 70 year period.

One further complexity that Elliott developed, particularly in his second (1946) monograph, was the principle of *alternation*. This worked in several different ways.

Thus, bull markets alternate with bear markets. Main trend movements of five waves alternate with corrective movements of three waves. Corrective waves, according to Elliott, alternate in *size*. Thus, if the first corrective wave within a 5 (wave 2) is a *simple* wave, the second (wave 4) will be *complex, or vice versa*.

One implication of the pattern in Figure 35 is that *it is quite feasible to have wave 4 shorter than wave 2.* This happened, for instance, in the 1921-29 episode, when wave 4 in 1926 was considerably shorter in both *time* and *amplitude* than wave 2.

Alternation in larger corrective formations will take place in different ways. If the first corrective wave is a *flat*, the second may be a *zigzag*. Thus, wave "A" may be a *zigzag,* with wave "B" being an inverted *flat.* Wave "C" will be the traditional 5-wave down to complete the whole correction.

Alternation also takes effect in the sequence of regular and irregular tops. For instance, 1919 was a *regular* top formation, 1929 *irregular*, 1937 *regular*, etc.[1]

The writer is *not* convinced that alternation is *inevitable* in types of waves in larger formations, but there are frequent enough cases of alternation to suggest that one should look for it rather than the contrary.

FOOTNOTES

1 Despite Elliott's commentary on the alternation of tops, it just isn't true. Alternation is confined to corrections of the same degree within the same larger wave.

CHAPTER VII
APPLICATION TO STOCK MARKET, 1857 TO 1929

So far, we have considered the way in which the waves of the stock market break down. Basic, of course, is the pattern of five waves in bull markets followed by three wave corrections.

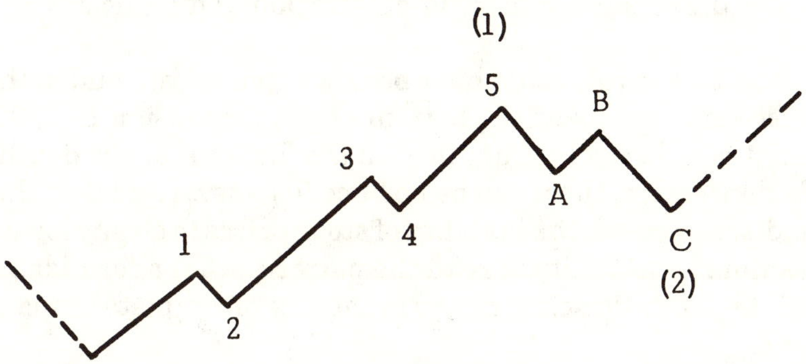

Figure 36

The net result of this pattern is that point "C" inevitably historically must be higher than the beginning of the previous bull market. And as these patterns are continued, a set of five larger waves begins to take appearance. In the diagram above, we have designated the first of these larger waves as (1), which corresponds to the end of 5, and (2) as the end of "C," and so on.

In classifying the stock market in his studies in the mid-1930s, Elliott used the Axe-Houghton-Burgess Index from 1854 to 1929, and then used various other indexes such as the Dow Jones Industrials, which were currently more easily available. Whether he went back much further in stock prices than 1854 by looking at other indices is not clear. Suffice to say that 1857 was obviously a major low of very great importance, and one which appears to be of comparable dimension with the historic low of this century of 1932. To substantiate this, we quote in part from the October 10th issue of *Harper's Weekly* 1857:

> "...It is a gloomy moment in history. Not for many years — not in the lifetime of most men who read this paper — has there been so much grave and deep apprehension; never has the future seemed so incalculable as at this time. In our country there is universal commercial prostration and panic...."

This surely could have been written as well and in the exact same words at the bottom of the depression in 1932. And it is indeed a commentary on the fact that at the depths of a depression, there can be no hope in general and that this condition leads to the inability of stock prices to go any lower. Assuming the ability to read the pattern, what a formidable tool the Wave Principle can be in the face of complete despair.

In any event, Figure 37 outlines Elliott's breakdown of the Axe-Houghton Index from 1857 to 1932 as shown in Elliott's 1946 monograph *Nature's Law*, and covers the *complete* Super Cycle from 1857 to 1928 and the *irregular corrective wave* which Elliott originally in 1938 considered as a second Super Cycle, but which later he modified to the view that it was only wave "A" of a *correcting triangle* formation. We shall examine these two interpretations later and will also suggest a third possibility, which only became possible of analysis after 1949, or considerably after Elliott's death.

Figure 38 depicts Elliott's 1946 breakdown of the Cycle wave 1896 to 1928, which Cycle wave is the *fifth wave* of the Super Cycle 1857-1928. Figure 39 depicts the 1938 interpretation.

In looking at these two breakdowns, one is of course impressed with the fact that they abide by rules, generally of five waves in each case, but other things may be noted which add to rather than detract from the complexities of a running analysis in contemporary times.

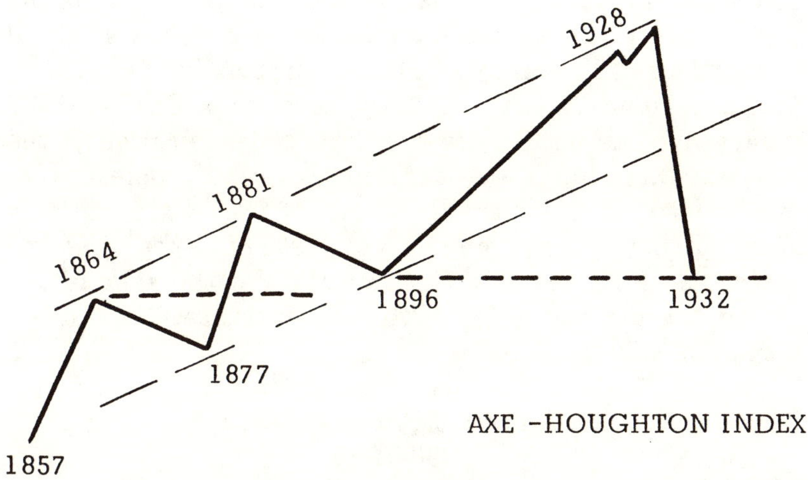

Figure 37

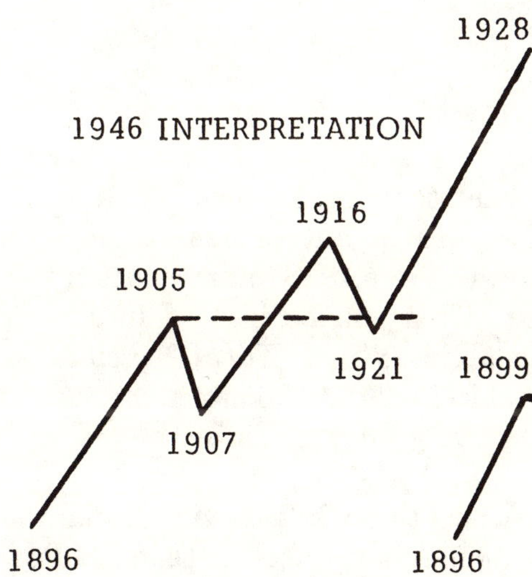

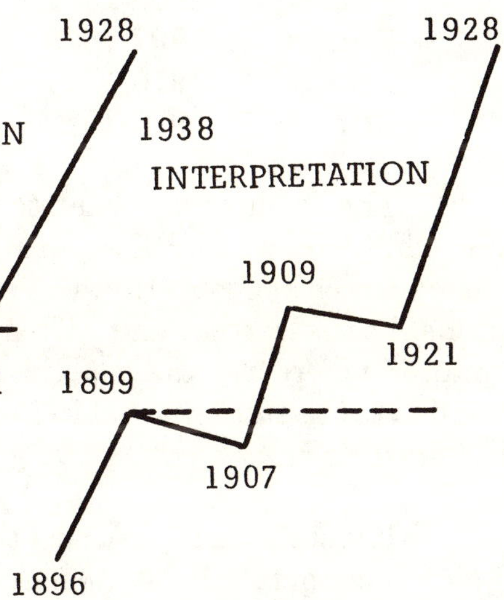

Figure 38 *Figure 39*

First, the bull markets of Cycle dimension, with the exception of the fifth Cycle, are *short* in time as compared to the corrections (Cycle waves two and four), whereas the Primary bull markets of the fifth Cycle are much longer in time than their corrections. Further, one may note that the fourth Primary of the 1896-1928 Cycle violates slightly the rule that this wave 4, 1916-21, should *not* be lower than the top of wave 1. This violation, however, is a relatively small one, and perhaps we may give Elliott the benefit of the doubt. It is still somewhat of a mystery, because in Elliott's 1938 monograph, he used quite a different classification of the Axe-Houghton Index waves (Figure 39), which instead were much closer in the over-all pattern of 1857-1928, with its short bull markets and long corrections. This is the broad one indicated as Figure 1 in Chapter II. For the sake of the record, we put the dates of the two interpretations down herewith, side-by-side.

Breakdown of Fifth Cycle Wave
1896-1928

	1946 Interpretation	1938 Interpretation
Primary 1:	1896-1905	1896-1899
Primary 2:	1905-1907	1899-1907
Primary 3:	1907-1916	1907-1909
Primary 4:	1916-1921	1909-1921
Primary 5:	1921-1928	1921-1928

The reader may want to draw his own conclusions. For what it is worth, however, the author has developed a theory which suggests that Elliott's 1938 interpretation was probably the correct one. This will be treated in a later chapter where we discuss the *Elliott Wave Principle* as applied to the stock market in the light of historic changes in the *nation's bank credit*.

It is sufficient to say here that while the Axe-Houghton Index is not generally available, if one uses instead the Dow Jones Industrials or Standard & Poor's Cowles Commission Index, it is apparent that the 1946 interpretation, if broken down further into Intermediate waves within each Primary, shows the same fault of having the 4th Intermediate *overlap* the top of wave 1, which again is a point in favor of returning to Elliott's first interpretation of the Cycle wave from 1896 to 1928.

As a final thought on the Super Cycle 1857-1928 and its subdivision into *five cycles*, let us reiterate the theme that we have mentioned in other discussions before: there is bound to be a great deal of *interpretation* in any analysis of the wave pattern. If Elliott, with all the advantages of hindsight (1946 vs. 1938 editions), could drastically change the count of his waves covering the period 1896-1921, it must be clear that we mortals who have to deal with the *future* as well as present and past may be forgiven for changing the pattern of the past from time to time as the future indicates such advisability.

In passing, it is also the writer's opinion that as the events of the late 1930s and the war period came along, Elliott became less secure in his analyses, and the general quality of his perspective tended to deteriorate. But this should not take away from the immense value of the tool that he left posterity, despite its obvious defects.

Let us take a look now at the fifth Primary of the fifth Cycle of the Super Cycle 1857-1928. This ran from 1921 to 1928, as follows, according to Elliott:

Wave One	June 1921 to March 1923
Wave Two	March 1923 to May 1924
Wave Three	May 1924 to November 1925
Wave Four	November 1925 to March 1926
Wave Five	March 1926 to November 1928

See Figure 3 in Chapter IV.

In passing, we might note Elliott's *alternation* principle in the corrective waves 1923-24 and 1925-26. Wave 2 (1923-24) is a double three, whereas wave 4 (1925-26) is a simple correction. This makes the second correction shorter in *time* than the first. Also, we may note that wave 3 is larger in *amplitude* than wave 1 (1921-23), thus fulfilling Elliott's apparent requirement that wave 3 should not be shorter in distance (points covered) than *both* waves 1 and 5 taken separately. It can be larger than either wave 1 or wave 5, but it must not be shorter than both.

As a matter of *logic*, it has always seemed desirable to expect wave 4 to be more extensive in amplitude than wave 2, since in effect wave 2 is simply correcting wave 1, whereas wave 4 may be thought of as correcting not only wave 3 but also all that came before.[1] However, the facts are that logic does not always win in the Wave Principle any more than in any other examples of human behavior.[2]

FOOTNOTES

[1] As a matter of logic, actually wave 4 corrects only wave 3.

[2] Logic *always* applies, if your premises are correct and knowledge sufficient.

CHAPTER VIII
THE STOCK MARKET, 1928 TO 1932

As we have noted to date, the Super Cycle which started in the depths of the depression of 1857 came to an official end in November 1928. At this point were completed:

5 waves of Cycle dimension from 1857,
the last of which comprised

5 waves of Primary dimension from 1921,
the last of which comprised

5 waves of Intermediate dimension from May 1926,
the last of which comprised

5 waves of Minor dimension from August 1927.

According to Elliott, two of these wave dimensions were extensions (i.e., elongations of one wave into five sub-divisions). These were the whole Primary from 1921, and the last wave of the Intermediate from 1926, i.e., the whole of the Minor wave from August 1927 to November 10th, 1928.

November 10th, 1928 was, then, the *orthodox top* from which began a huge *corrective wave* of *irregular outline*. This wave took the form of the usual A-B-C formation, but with the "B" wave terminating at the top of the market on September 3rd, 1929, and wave "C" terminating on November 12th, 1929. Figure 40 shows the breakdown of the waves from November 1928 to November 1929, as well as the further development of the corrective wave into 1932. It will be noted that we break down the corrective wave from 1928 to 1932 into 3 waves, which are further sub-divided into 3, 3 and 5.

The first of these waves we have labelled as wave (A). The second, which runs from November 13th, 1929, to April 12th, 1930, we label (B), and the third wave from April 1930 to July 1932, we label (C). The subdivision of wave (A) is indicated at A, B and C, that of (B) similarly and that of (C) as A, B, C, D and E. (Incidentally, this breakdown is our own and is somewhat different from that shown by Elliott in his 1938 monograph, but it works out to essentially the same result.)[1]

The waves (A) and (B) also show up the principle of *alternation*, and wave (A) is an irregular *flat* top, i.e., (3-3-5), and wave (B) is a regular *zigzag*, i.e., 5-3-5. Wave (C), of course, is a 5.

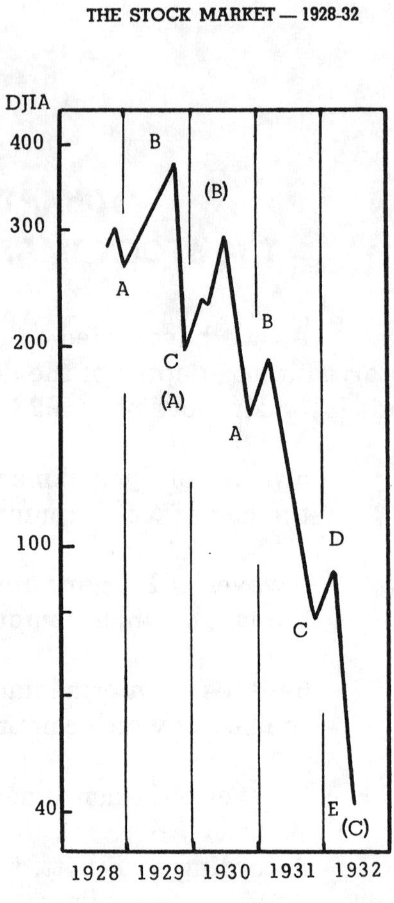

Figure 40

The wave correction from 1928 to 1932 also complies with Elliott's rule about extensions, i.e., that the ensuing correction would go back to at least the point from which the extension started. The 1921-28 extension started after the first wave of the Primary, i.e., after the 1921-23 wave (see Figure 3). Thus, the correction should *retrace* at least to this point, i.e., about 110 in the Dow Jones Industrials. It is interesting to note that wave (A) of the correction fully retraced the Minor wave extension which started in August 1927 when it hit 195 in November 1928, but the correction at this point had *not* retraced the 1921-28 extension. Thus, one could anticipate that the whole correction was not finished at the November 1929 bottom.

In the longer term pattern, it can be seen that, using the Axe-Houghton Index as the base, the decline into 1932 took the market back exactly to the bottom of wave IV from 1857 in 1896 (see Figure 37). The fact that the market went *below* the lows of 1921, of course, indicated that the correction pattern of the 1928-32 waves was of *greater magnitude* or *degree* than the 1921-28 wave. It was thus a corrective wave to the whole Super Cycle from 1857 to 1928, rather than simply to the Cycle from 1921.

It may be as well to leave our study of Elliott as applied to the stock market at this point, July 1932, and take a look more closely at what Elliott found out about the recurrence of waves in set fashion and its relation to natural design. The reason for doing so is to study some of the factors that led Elliott into a consideration of *time periods* as well as wave subdivision. These studies of Elliott are perhaps the most *controversial* aspects of his whole theory, and it is the writer's opinion that he put far too much emphasis on the *immutability* of what he called *Nature's Law*, with the result that he gave the Wave Principle a *quasi-cyclical* basis, which it may have, but not to the extent imagined by him.

After developing in very elementary form what Elliott's thinking was on the *causes* of the Wave Principle, we will be able to take up the threads of analysis of the stock market starting from 1932.

It will then be apparent that this opens up *three alternative interpretations,* of which *two* are *technically correct* and *one* (Elliott's as expounded by him in his 1946 monograph) is *technically incorrect* and must be abandoned in the light of present day facts.

FOOTNOTES

[1] 1929-1932 is much better counted a simple 5-3-5 zigzag, exactly as Bolton's (and Elliott's) (A)-(B)-(C), but starting at the 1929 high.

CHAPTER IX
ELLIOTT AND CYCLE THEORIES

The Elliott Wave Principle is *not* a true cycle theory. True cycles are observed repetitions of events at stated intervals. Well known cycles, for instance, are the 9 year cycle and the Decennial Pattern in stock prices. Elliott did *not* originally attempt to work on any theory of periodicity. Rather, the waves would unfold somewhat *regardless of the time element*, with the proviso, however, that waves did bear certain *degrees of time* due to their *degrees of amplitude* inherent in whatever position in the "wave cycle" that they held.

Thus, in Elliott's first monograph (1938) on the Wave Principle, no mention is made of any basis for the 5-3-5-3-5 pattern that he found in the stock market. However, in Elliott's 1946 monograph, a great deal of space was used in developing the basis for the 5/3 breakdown pattern.

In Chapter I of the 1946 monograph, *Nature's Law*, Elliott mentions research from measurements of the Great Pyramid of Gizeh, which many interested in the occult have claimed has a divine message of revelation. Among the measurements mentioned is the fact that the elevation of the Pyramid to its base is 61.8% and the number of inches of its height is exactly 5813, all numbers of the Fibonacci series mentioned below. (Ancient Egyptians used the present day inch as their basic measure as well as developing the 12 system, which is standard in English-speaking countries today).

It is recorded that a famous Italian mathematician of the 13th Century (Fibonacci, known also as Leonardo de

Pisa) visited Egypt and came back with a summation series which bears his name:

1, 2, 3, 5, 8, 13, 21, 34, 55, 89, 144, etc.

This series has a number of interesting properties:

(1) The sum of any two consecutive numbers forms the number above it. Thus, 3 plus 5 equals 8, 5 plus 8 equals 13, 8 plus 13 equals 21, etc.

(2) The ratio of any number to its next higher is 61.8 to 100 (after the very early numbers, which of course are rounded).

(3) The ratio of any number to its next below is 161.8 to 100.

(4) The ratio of each number to the second below is always 261.8 to 100 (note: 2 plus .618).

(5) Each number divided into the second above it goes 2 times, with a left-over of the exact number below it. Thus, 34 goes into 89 twice with 21 left over, and 5 goes into 13 twice with 3 left over, etc.

(6) This summation series has been classified as being related, each number to the number before, by the formula

$$\tfrac{1}{2}(\sqrt{5} + 1) \qquad (1.618),$$

and each number is related to the number above by the formula

$$\tfrac{1}{2}(\sqrt{5} - 1) \qquad (0.618).$$

It is most interesting that the square root of the number 5 (2.236) is the dominant factor in the formula.

(7) The ratio 1.618 multiplied by the ratio 0.618 equals 1.

(8) It may be of interest that the number 5813 (the height of the Great pyramid in inches) is intimately connected with the number of days exactly in a year since the radius of a circle of 58.13 inches produces a circumference exactly of 365.242 inches — the exact length of a year in days. This brings in the mathematical factor of π.

(9) It may also be of interest that the angle of the "Ascending Passage" in the Great pyramid is 26°18', thus conforming to the pattern mentioned above in a different sphere.

The Fibonacci Summation Series is also prevalent in plant life. Elliott quotes from Jay Hambidge's *Practical Application of Dynamic Symmetry* to the effect the sun flower has 89 curves, 55 winding in one direction and 34 in the opposite direction. Below the apex flower of the stalk, there are usually secondary smaller flowers, with 34 curving in one direction and 21 in the other. Similarly, lower down there may be a third row, in which case there will be 34 curves, 21 in one direction and 13 in the other.

The stock market waves follow the Fibonacci Series. Thus, in a bull market, there are 5 waves; in a correction, 3. Breaking down the 5 waves into 5-3-5-3-5, we get 21 waves of lower degree; in a correction, 5-3-5, or 13 waves. Each of these, of course, is a Fibonacci number. In a bull market of greater detail, we have 21-13-21-13-21, which totals 89 waves, and the correction is 21-13-21, for a total of 55. The perfect bull and bear cycle will comprise 5 plus 3, which equals 8 waves. Of next lower degree, the total will be 21 plus 13, or 34, and the next lower degree will be 89 plus 55, which equals 144, and so on ad infinitum.

Elliott also points to the pattern of 5s and 3s in human life. The human body has 5 extremities: 2 arms, 2 legs, and a head, total 5. Five fingers, five toes. In music, we find the octave made up of 13 keys, 8 white and 5 black on the piano.

Without pushing too far, it certainly would appear

that the 5-3 relationship of the Wave Principle, which Elliott first discovered in the stock market, is well established in much of life itself.

Having established the basis of the Wave Principle, Elliott began to apply the series to see if *time* as well as *amplitude* conformed to the numbers pattern. He found many coincidences which suggested that there might be some important law of time at work as well. For instance, the 1921 bottom in stocks is 21 years away from the 1942 bottom. Similarly, the 1928 orthodox top is 21 years from the 1949 bottom. 1932 to 1937 is 5 years, as is 1937 to 1942. Other periods are 1946 to 1949, 3 years (and about 34 months), and 1921 to 1929, which was 8 years, as was 1949 to 1957. The bear market of 1937 lasted 13 months, whereas the bear market from 1929 to 1932 lasted 34 months. From 1927 to the orthodox top in 1928 was 89 months. Etc., etc. More recent examples are September 1953 to August 1956, 34 months, and April 1956 to December 1957, 21 months.

Many other examples of Fibonacci time periods exist, but unfortunately there does not seem to be any sure way that these can be used for forecasting purposes. In other words, the coincidences are *interesting,* but hardly of sufficient use or accuracy to become the basis for forecasting.

Another interesting facet of the numbers in the series is their relation to 12, which is an important factor in our system of time, navigation, astronomy, etc. (12 months to the year, 60 minutes to the hour, 60 seconds to the minute, 24 hours to the day, 360° in a circle, etc.). This is that multiples of 12 will often have a left over, or a left under, when divided into a number of the Fibonacci series, which is a number of the series itself. Thus, 3 years is 21 months plus 3 months, 5 years is 55 months plus 5 months, 7 years is 89 months less 5 months, etc.

The ratio of 61.8 to 100 and 100 to 161.8 became a central part of Elliott's theories in regard to both *time* and *amplitude*. Thus, Elliott pointed out a number of other coincidences. For instance, the number of points from 1921 to 1926 (i.e., the first three waves) was 61.8% of the number of points of the last wave from 1926 to 1928 (the orthodox top). Likewise in the five waves up from 1932 to 1937. Again, the wave from the top in 1930 (297 DJIA) to the bottom in 1932 (40 DJIA) is 1.618 times the wave from 40 to 195 (1932 to 1937). Also, the decline from 1937 to 1938 was 61.8% of the advance from 1932-37 in DJIA points.

Should the 1949 market to date adhere to this formula, then the advance from 1949 to 1956 (361 points in the DJIA) should be complete when 583 points (161.8% of the 361 points) have been added to the 1957 low of 416, or a total of 999 DJIA.

Alternately, 361 points over 416 would call for 777 in the DJIA.

All these and many more coincidences led Elliott to put considerable stock in the importance of the time periods. However, experience shows that while these periods turn up with frequent recurrence in actual fact, as with the price movement, it is extremely difficult to use such time periods as a basis for forecasting, because there are no indications whether these periods will produce tops to bottoms, tops to tops, bottoms to bottoms, or bottoms to tops. The permutations tend to become infinite.

Figure 41 herewith projects various Fibonacci time periods into the future from important timing points in the past. These suggest that 1962 and 1963 may be important stock market years, but they do not give any clues as to the nature of the importance.

It can now be seen that by way of the Fibonacci Series, while Elliott's Wave Principle has not taken on the aspects of a cycle theory, it has presented somewhat of a *bridge* between technical analysis and cycle theory. It has in fact suggested that *periodicity* will exist (i.e., within the framework of the 3-5-8-13-21, etc., series), but that this periodicity will not necessarily be of such a sort as to be predictive.

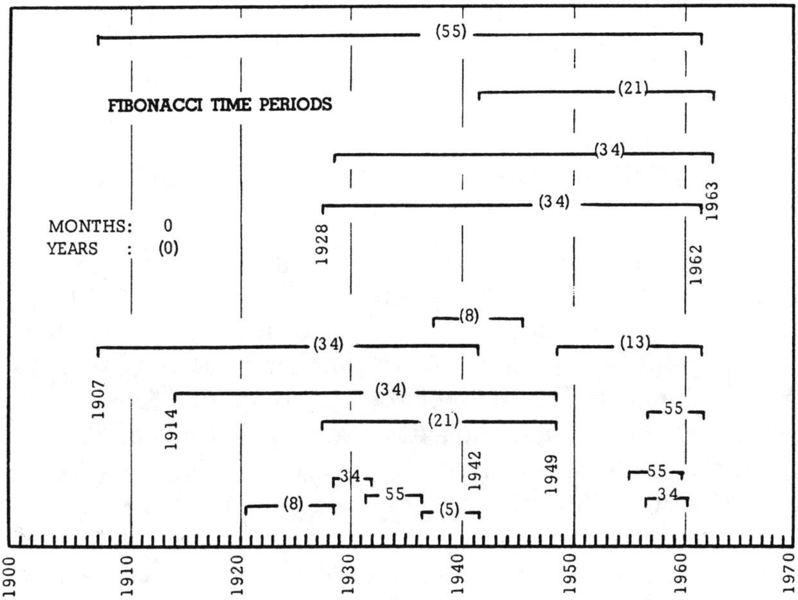
FIBONACCI TIME PERIODS
MONTHS: 0
YEARS : (0)
(55)
(21)
(34)
(34)
1963
1928
1962
(8)
(34)
(13)
1907
(34)
1914
55
(21)
1942
1949
34
55
55
34
(8)
(5)
1900
1910
1920
1930
1940
1950
1960
1970

Figure 41

(The following extension of the commentary in Chapter IX was published as an appendix to the 1963 Supplement.)

FURTHER NOTES ON FIBONACCI NUMBERS

By way of addendum to "Mathematical Basis Of Wave Theory" in the extracts above taken from the 1960 edition of *The Elliott Wave Principle*, there are a number of additional properties of Fibonacci numbers which may be of interest to the mathematically inclined of our readers. These are contained and discussed in a little book recently published in a translation from Russian: N. N. Vorobev, *Fibonacci Numbers*, Braisdell Publishing Company, New York, 1961.

(1) The sum of the squares of any consecutive series of Fibonacci numbers from 1 will always equal the last of the series chosen times the next higher number. For instance:

$$1^2 + 1^2 + 2^2 + 3^2 = 3 \times 5;$$
$$1^2 + 1^2 + 2^2 + 3^2 + 5^2 + 8^2 = 8 \times 13, \text{ etc.}$$

(2) The square of a Fibonacci number less the square of the second number below it in the series always is a Fibonacci number. For example:

$$8^2 - 3^2 = 55;$$
$$13^2 - 5^2 = 144, \text{ etc.}$$

(3) The square of any Fibonacci number is equal to the number in the series before it multiplied by the number in the series after it, + or - 1. Thus:

$$5^2 = (3 \times 8) + 1,$$
$$8^2 = (5 \times 13) - 1,$$
$$13^2 = (8 \times 21) + 1,$$

and the plus and minus 1 always alternate.

CHAPTER X
THE AFTERMATH OF THE GREAT DEPRESSION

The year 1932 represented the low point in the stock market for a generation back and so far for a generation forward. It is logical, therefore, that it should represent the termination of a wave of large degree and the beginning of a new wave of a similar large degree. And so Elliott classified it in his monograph of 1938: July 8th, 1932, ended a Super Cycle which was the full corrective wave of the previous Super Cycle from 1957 to 1928. Logically, a new wave of the 5-3-5-3-5 variety should begin. And so it did, as can be seen from Figure 42.

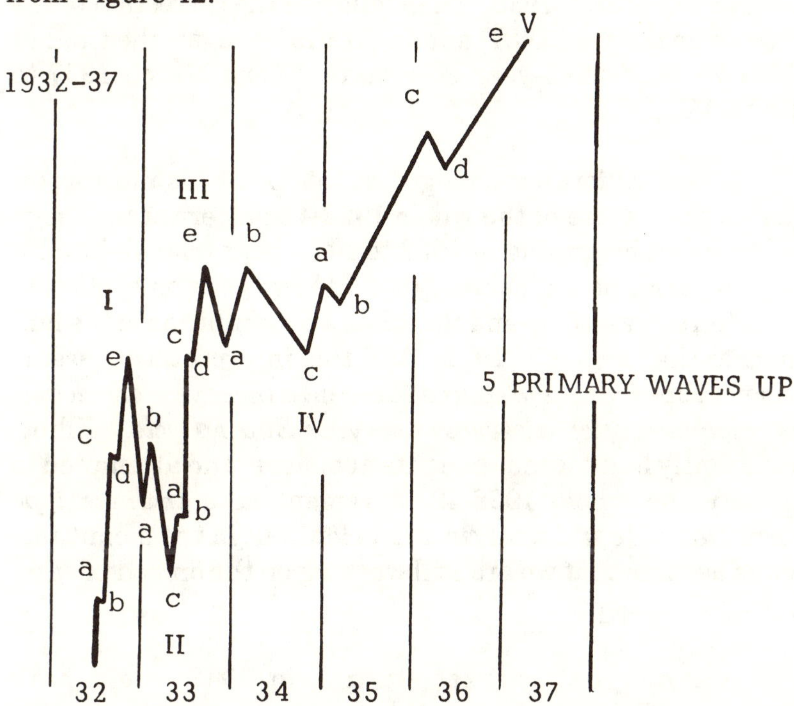

Figure 42

Each of these waves fulfilled the essential characteristics as laid down by Elliott. The waves in the main direction of the move, i.e., those numbered I, III and V, clearly subdivided into five of lesser degree. The first corrective wave II was classified as a *zigzag*, whereas wave IV was a *flat*, thus developing the principle of *alternation*.

The whole pattern from July 1932 to March 1937 in the Dow Jones Industrials was extremely *regular* as compared to the *irregular top* of 1929, again developing *alternation*.

The 1937 bear market came and went in entirely orthodox fashion, and Elliott classified this 13-month market decline as wave "A" of the bear market. Since it was a 5 down, it *had to be* either the first or third of a 3-wave pattern, and of course as it came immediately after the preceding bull market, it had to be the first. The bear market could not be *complete* in March 1938. Then followed the correction of the 5-wave down from 1937, and in late 1939 began the final or third wave of the 5-year bear market from March 1937 to May 1942.

Had Elliott not changed at this point his interpretation of the nature of the whole 1928-42 pattern from a new bull market beginning in 1932 to a "13-year triangle" (actually 14 years) he undoubtedly would have gone on to classify 1942 to 1946 as a 5 up and therefore a continuation of the bull market that began in 1932. And this interpretation seems a logical one *if one is prepared to accept a three year correction as adequate after a seventy-one year Super Cycle*. Elliott apparently had second thoughts about this and attempted to classify the whole 1928-42 movement as a *triangle type correction*. We will analyze this below, but in the meantime, let us assume that we are still working on the orthodox *"pre-triangle"* concept.

A new bull market starting in 1942 would have completed five waves upward by 1946. On the charts, this looks more like a 3 than a 5, but it can be classified as a 5 on the daily charts. As will be seen later, we believe this is really a 3 rather than a 5. Refer to Figure 3 in Chapter IV.

But having completed five waves by 1946, a bear market could now be expected, and it came on schedule from 1946 to 1949 in three easily discernible waves, as it should. *But,* this 1942-46 wave could not possibly be of the same degree as the 1932 to 1937 wave for several reasons. First, the correction of a third wave (classifying 1942-46 as a third wave after 1932-37 and 1937-42) should not overlap the top of the first wave by any great margin. Further, the 1946 high was barely higher than the 1937 top (212 vs 195 DJIA).

Again, it is most unusual for the amplitude of a third wave to be less than a first wave, and this one obviously is (92 to 212 DJIA vs 40-195 DJIA in 1932-37).

If, then, this five wave up is not of the same degree as 1932-37, this implies that wave 3 beginning in 1942 was only *partly completed*, i.e., wave 1 of five had taken place by 1946. So we see that *wave three* of the new Super Cycle that began in 1932 was bound to be a long affair and, so far as our counting along these lines is concerned, is still only in the *middle* of the five waves expected from 1942, and approaching the end of the *middle or third* wave of the five, as suggested diagrammatically in Figure 43.[1]

It was this failure of the 1942-46 market to develop sufficient magnitude to classify as a counterpart of 1932-37 that tripped up wave analysts who thought that 1956 was the *big top. Under no interpretation known to this writer was it possible to arrive at 1956 or 1957 as the big top.* This was stated at the time, and proved to be the correct interpretation.

From the point of view of the late 1930s, Elliott's predictions made considerable sense. From 1932, quite clearly a new set of waves had set in, and equally clearly, 1932-37 had all the earmarks of a 5 up. This was, from 1938 on, to be followed by a 3-down correction, of which 1937-38 was the first wave, and as subsequently worked out, 1939-42 was the third and final downward wave.

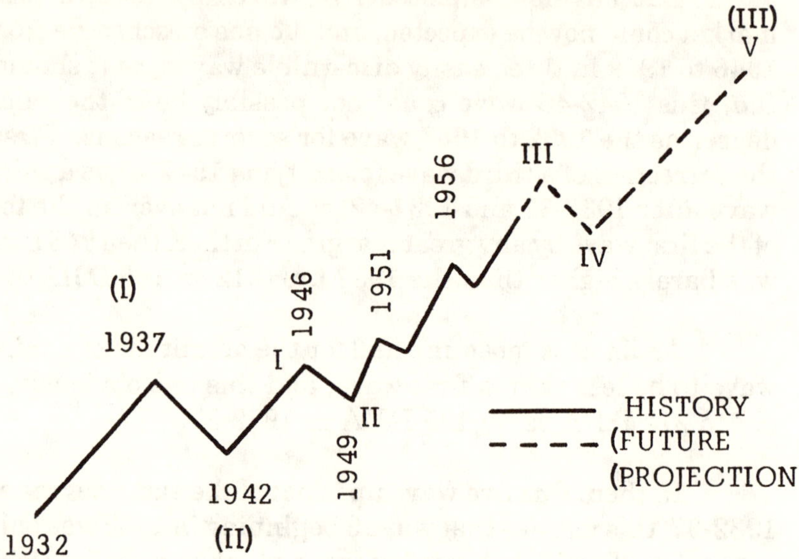

Figure 43

The main reservation that one might have would be simply: *Can* 1929-32 be sufficient to correct the whole advance from 1857 to 1929? From several points of view, this could be justified. Thus, the 1929-32 decline took stock prices back to the lows of 1896 (Axe-Houghton Index), a logical expectation for so large a correction. But *time-wise,* the period seemed, and still does, quite inadequate. We must realize, of course, that Elliott put no stock in time necessarily matching amplitude as a function of the Wave Principle. Thus, waves would take their own time to develop and could not be expected to fit into neat cubicles.

However, that Elliott began to itch about the time element is clear when he began to look for a larger correction than simply 1929-32. Thus, somewhere along in the 1940s, he began to conceive of the whole pattern from 1928 as being all part of a larger *triangle* formation.

Elliott's vision at the time looked to a large 13-year triangle (1929-42) which would provide a platform for a *thrust* in an upward direction. The largest triangle up to that time was a triangle fourth wave in the bear market of 1937-38, from November 1937 to February 1938. This wave had proven his theory that triangle waves are divided into 5, which further are subdivided into 3, making 15 waves in all. It further backed up his theory that triangle waves only appeared as a fourth wave in a series of five waves (either up or down).

If Elliott's 13-year triangle (1929-42) were true, then this suggested a further thought of some significance, i.e., that 1857-1928 was one Super Cycle, but being followed by a triangle (1929-42), this latter would have to be Super Cycle *four*, thus 1857-1928 would be Super Cycle *three*, and anything following 1942 would be Super Cycle *five*. Elliott projected this as likely to last well into the 21st century.

Thus, we now have two interpretations:

(1) That a new set of Super Cycle waves started in 1932. 1932-37 was the *first* Cycle, 1937-42 was wave *two*, and 1942 on is wave *three*.

(2) That the Super Cycle was completed between 1929 and 1942, leading to a new set of waves starting in 1942. Thus, 1942-46 was the first Cycle in this thinking.

The construction of the 1928-42 triangle, according to Elliott, would take the form of five waves, as follows:

(a) 1928-32
(b) 1932-37
(c) 1937-38
(d) 1938-39
(e) 1939-42.

Of the two interpretations, this looked in retrospect to be more sensible. It involved a recount of certain of the waves. For instance, in particular, whereas the "1932 is a new Super Cycle" school figured that 1932-37 was a 5-wave pattern, now of course it was clearly not a 5 up, but really a 3.[2] Thus, 1932-33 was a three (5-3-5, or *inverted zigzag*), followed by a correction (in 3) to November 1934, and followed thereafter by a 5 up to March 1937. Thus, the whole rise from 1932 to 1937 became an *inverted flat*, i.e., a 3-3-5 combination, as compared to the original thinking of it being a 5-3-5-3-5.

Figure 44 shows the recounted waves from 1932-37, which should be compared with Figure 42.

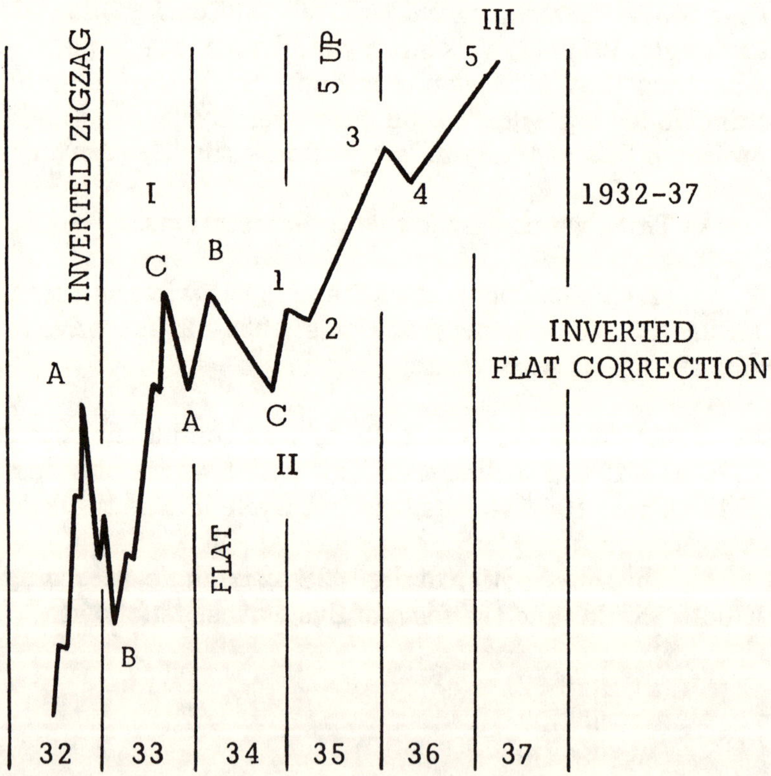

Figure 44

Unfortunately, Elliott found that in order to get his five waves to come out at 1942, his triangle had to be:

1928-32, 1932-37, 1937-38, 1938-39, 1939-42.

All these were clearly divisible into three subwaves *except* 1937-38, which was clearly an unalterable 5-wave downward. Thus, either the whole theory of triangles as five waves subdivided into three had to go by the wayside, or else it had to be juggled in different ways. Elliott proceeded to try to fit various odd-looking 3s into the pattern, such as calling 1928-38 a *flat*, 1938-39 a *zigzag* and 1939-42 a flat, all of which was an attempt to make a real Elliott triangle out of something that could not be made into such a configuration without changing the rules.

This had led the author to discard the 1928-42 correction as a possible Elliott triangle and to go back to the original theory of 1938. In the early '50s, however, it did appear that a 21-year triangle had developed. As compared to the only other interpretation possible, i.e., starting a new Super Cycle in 1932, and as compared to the problem of trying to make a 1928-42 triangle work out technically, the 21-year triangle does have certain advantages:

(1) All waves of the 21-year triangle are easily divisible into 3s. Further, they follow the principle of *alternation* that Elliott expounded.

(2) The time element of 21 years of correction to a Super Cycle of some 70 years' duration (1857-1928) seems more appropriate than a mere 3-4 years (1928-32).

(3) 1949 in pure terms probably represented the high water mark of security undervaluation.[3]

(4) 1949 was clearly the beginning of the reversion to free enterprise after the experiences of depression socialism and war finance.

(5) The whole pattern since 1949 has conformed to the concept of a *rapid thrust* in the direction of the trend which Elliott hypothesized as the action to be expected after

a descending triangle of the sort suggested by such a triangle.[4]

At all events, one is clearly left with one of two possible interpretations. Either one accepts the 1929-32 correction as adequate for 70 years of back history, in which case a new Super Cycle began in 1932. Or, one accepts the 21-year triangle (note the Fibonacci numbers involved) as a correction, from which the new Super Cycle started in June 1949.

Appendix "A" sets out the arguments in favor of the 21-year triangle over the 13-year triangle. This is taken from our previous monograph, "Elliott's Wave Principle 1959." As they say in other circles, "you pays your money and you takes your choice."

Given the choice of these two interpretations, it is extremely interesting to see how they work out side by side. Thus, Figure 45 and Figure 46 show a comparison between the two interpretations. In actual fact, the results are not far different. Assuming the count since 1949 as correct, it is apparent that wave I of the 21-year triangle theory coincides with wave III of wave (III) of the *original* theory. This seems entirely logical, since it is a well-known fact that the first wave of any series is likely to be smaller in amplitude and time than later waves.

From a practical point of view, of course, the differences are not too material. In both interpretations, the current wave from 1949 is still incomplete, and probably should be expected to coincide more completely as the current upward market develops. The correction of wave I of the 21-year triangle could well be extensive, perhaps lasting as much as 5 years, but the same can also be said of wave III of (III), which also could last five years, considering that wave II of (III) lasted three years, from 1946-49.

All told then, we can reasonably be happy that the two "correct" interpretations, i.e., (1) a new Super Cycle started

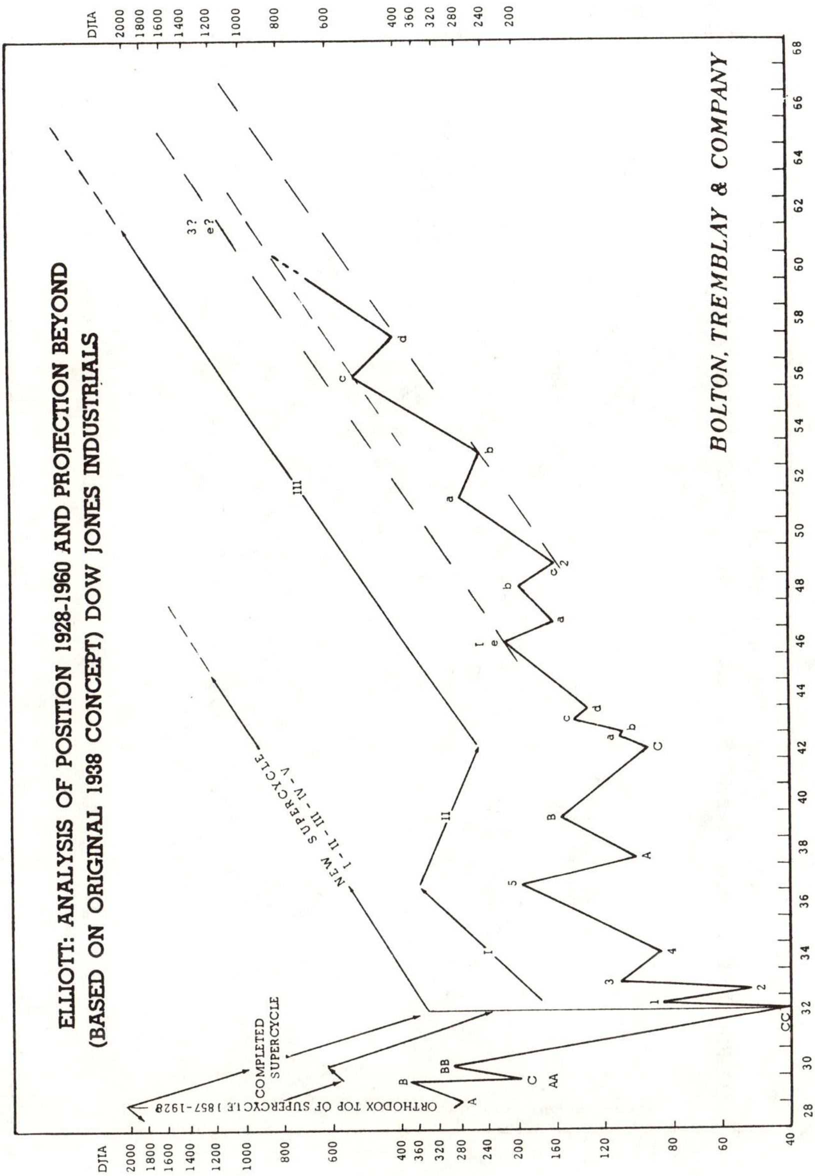

Figure 45

in 1932 and (2) a new Super Cycle started in 1949, can live together without producing any anachronistic or irreconcilable attributes.

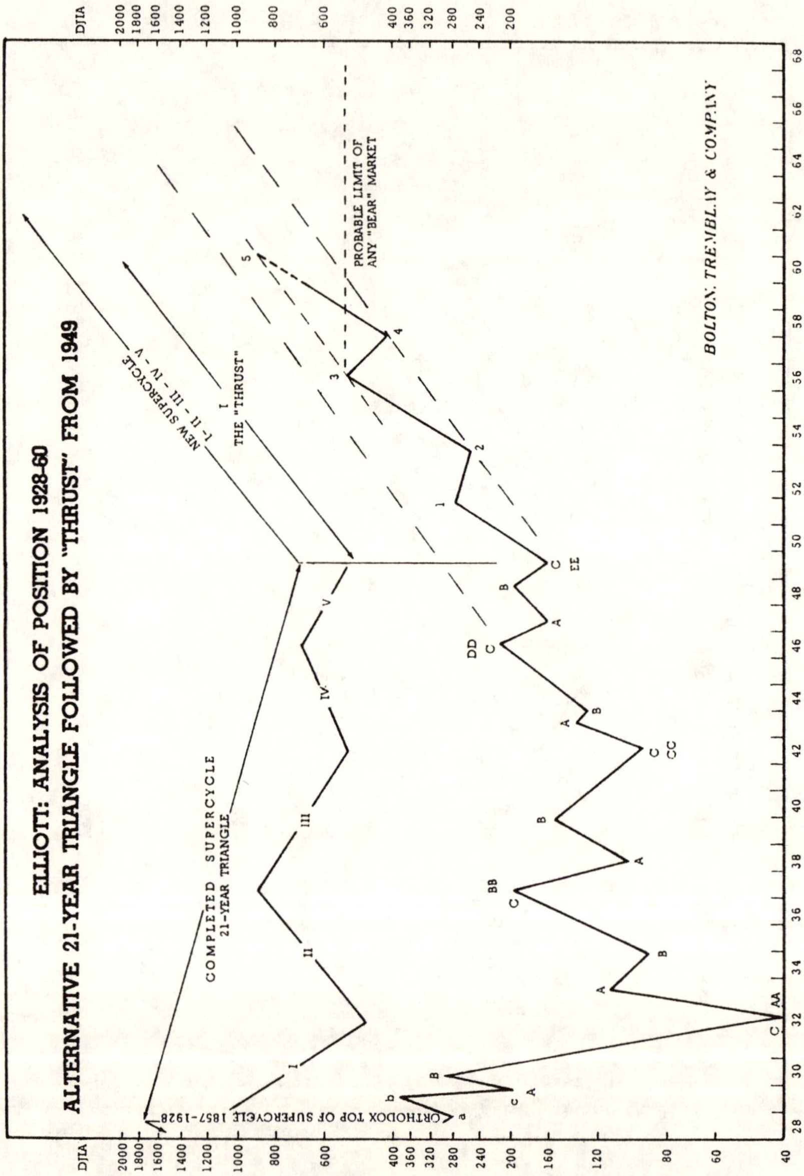

Figure 46

The next question that might be asked would be: Accepting the above, how can the two different interpretations arrive at a common ending? In other words, how do Cycle V of Interpretation (1) and Cycle V of Interpretation (2) ever arrive to produce a high top comparable in magnitude and definitely with, say, 1929?

The answer is frankly that we do not know the future, but we might nevertheless simply consider the "stylized" chart set forth in Figure 47.

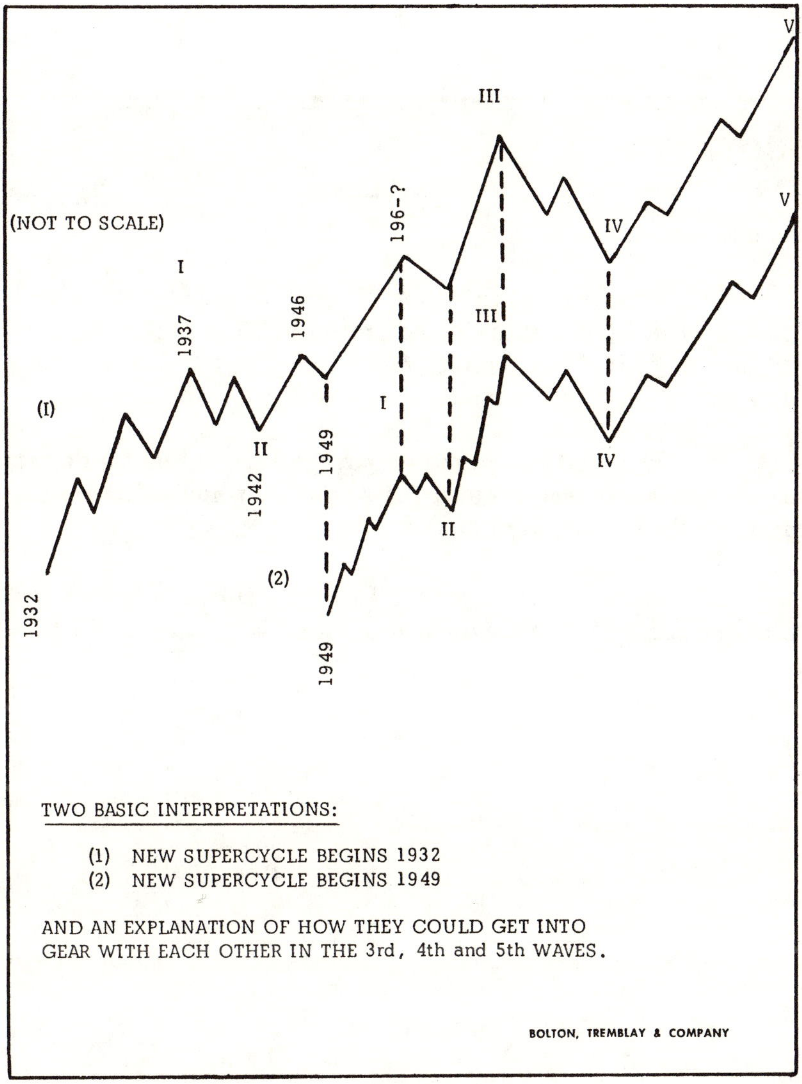

Figure 47

This chart brings up the whole problem that haunts Elliott students to this day: What is the real determination of *degree* in Elliott wave theory? Again, we are faced with the confession that we really cannot be absolutely sure -- at the time. This gives Elliott's wave theory an indefiniteness which precludes it from a truly scientific approach to stock market interpretation, despite Elliott's protestations otherwise.

FOOTNOTES

1 This is an excellent description of the exact position of the market.

2 As explained in *Elliott Wave Principle* by Frost and Prechter, this kind of thinking destroys the Wave Principle, as it can turn any "five" into a phony 3-3-5 flat. The problem with the supposed "flat" is that it isn't!

3 This and the next two paragraphs brilliantly depict the underlying corrective nature of the period, which is the correct count for the constant dollar Dow.

4 In the constant dollar Dow, the thrust followed the rules and peaked in 1966, a top which has not been exceeded to this day.

CHAPTER XI
THE POSTWAR STOCK MARKET

By all accounts, the great Postwar stock market began in June 1949. This was the time of the greatest undervaluation in history. Prices were lower in 1932, but there was no earning power to substantiate values. Prices were lower in 1942 in actual terms, but the question arose as to what the future of the American economy would be. War-time regimentation precluded any prediction of how earning power could develop. Excess profit taxes precluded any firm view of what the shareholder could expect out of his investment. In 1949, however, all war-time controls had been relinquished. There was great fear of course of the *inevitable postwar depression*. Yet, this fear was mostly on the part of investors. Industry was paying no attention. Plans for capital expenditure were going ahead unhampered by investor thinking.

During this period, the Dow Jones Industrials touched its lowest level — *terms of earning power* — in history.

From these beginnings began *the greatest bull market in history*. In 1960, eleven years later this bull market is still with us. If we accept Elliott's theories as valid, this basic bull market on the broadest scale will continue probably throughout this century.

Figure 48 herewith brings up-to-date to the spring of 1960 a chart of our interpretation of the breakdown of the waves since 1949. This suggests that the decline from July 1959 to April 1960 (684 to 597 DJIA) constitutes Intermediate 4 of the fifth Primary since June 1949. One possibility, however, which must not be overlooked, is that July 1959 to

BREAKDOWN OF DJIA FROM 1949

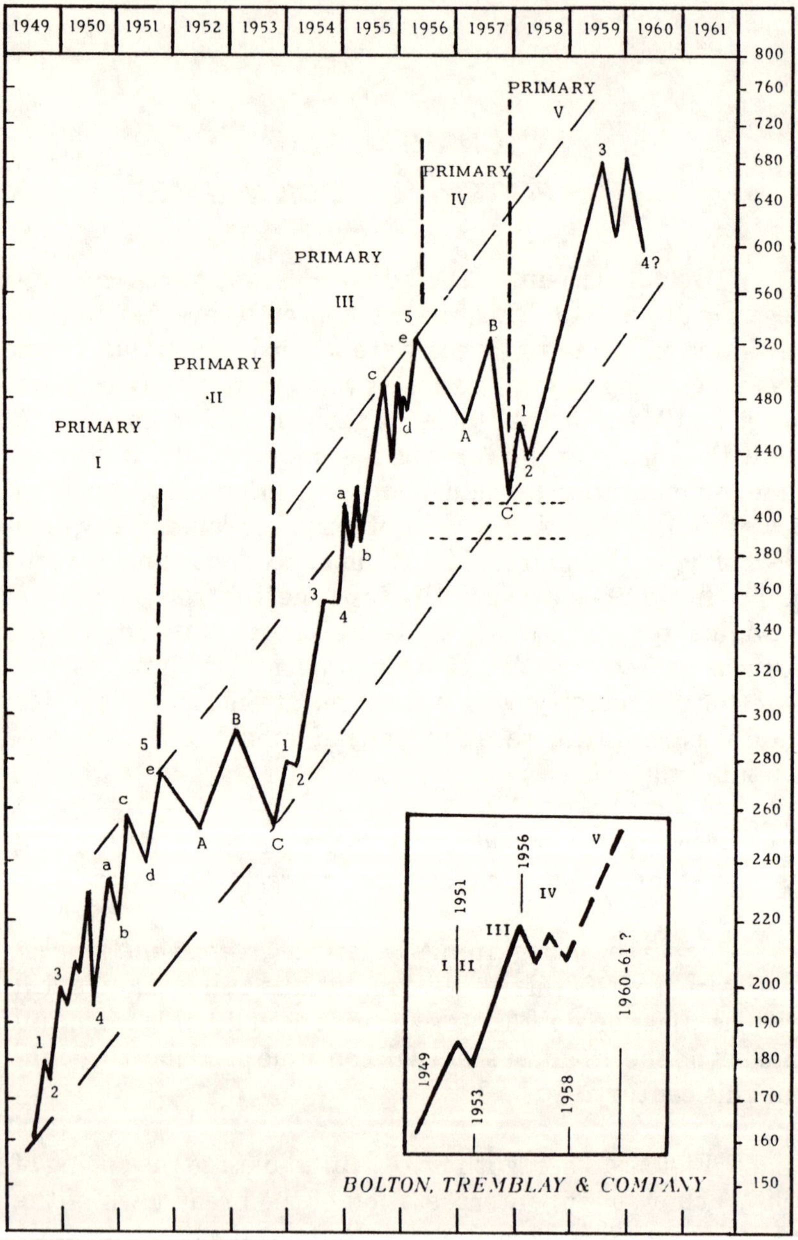

Figure 48

April 1960 could be only wave "A" of a total correction which could take wave "B" up to, and perhaps considerably higher than wave "A", and which could be followed by a bear market in traditional terms of some considerable extent.

As we advance in the stock market cycle from 1949, it becomes apparent that the possible future permutations and combinations tend to advance toward the infinite. It also becomes increasingly apparent that it is extremely doubtful that Elliott Wave theory can provide us with the answer on a day-to-day basis. As an example of the possible permutations at this point, we submit Figures 49, 50 and 51. And these are only the beginning.

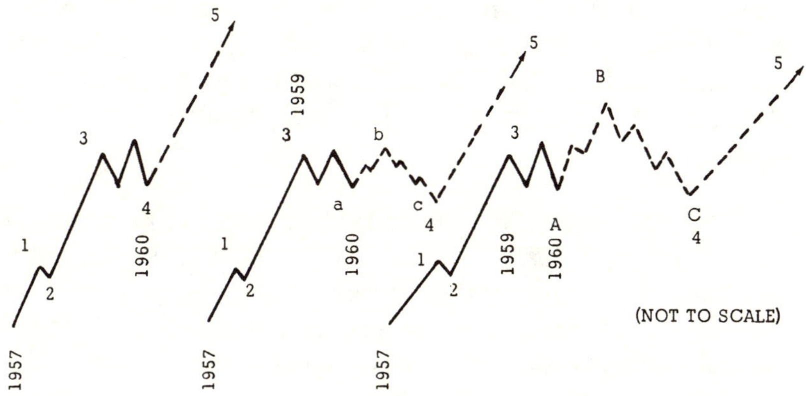

Figure 49 *Figure 50* *Figure 51*

All of these interpretations are possible at this point, and in fact there are a myriad of other subtleties which could take place from now on. Who knows?

We may well ask ourselves: How can we reconcile the implications of the Wave Principle with the *obvious facts of life* in which the American economy is beset on all sides by competition not only from the Russian economy but also from every other member of the greatly increasingly powerful British and European economic systems?

The obvious facts of life, of course, have been apparent for a number of years and represent concepts which may have a long-term significance but which in any time period fail to make an important impact. Thus, the market is created not by facts, but by the sum total of what people think about these facts. How else can one explain the obvious *undervaluation* of such a period as 1948-50? Or yet again, the overvaluation of 1928-29, and its counterpart today? Obviously, we get cycles of mental aberration during which it is quite possible to have an extended period of *gross undervaluation* of security prices, followed in due course (perhaps a decade or more or less) by a period of *gross overvaluation*. The fundamentalists deplore today's overvaluation of security prices. Yet it is doubtful that they were more comfortable in yesteryear's undervaluation. How was one to justify the purchase of a stock which on value proceeded to decline 50% after a careful analysis suggested its sterling qualities? And this a few years ago was "par for the course."

As we enter 1960, the market atmosphere has changed radically from "tongue-in-cheek" bullishness to skepticism as to what the basis for further increases in security prices may be. Views, however, are not yet clearly defined: It is not possible today to say that everyone is bullish or everyone is bearish. Such contrasts are simply not possible. Certainly, there is no rampant bullishness on hand. Nor yet is there that overweening bearishness which characterized mid-1949, 1953 and late 1957. One remains in a *quandary*. Yet the facts are — if our interpretation of the Elliott Wave Principle is correct or even near correct — that we have *not yet* seen the final phase of the great 1949-? bull market. Will it be put off several years or are we due to complete it in the next year or so? These remain unanswered questions.

CHAPTER XII
CHARACTERISTICS SINCE 1949

The characteristics of the stock market since 1949 conform extremely well to the idea of a *thrust*, such as one should have after an Elliott triangle. Figure 52 depicts the Dow Jones Industrials since the bottom in 1949. This bottom is variously:

> the beginning of wave I after a 21-year triangle,
> or
> the beginning of wave III of wave (III) from the 1932 bottom.

In order properly to be a *thrust,* it must exhibit extraordinary strength. This, in fact, it continues to do *even eleven years after* its commencement. In support of this, we suggest that the following factors be noted:

(1) All charting in Figure 52 is on a logarithmic scale, indicating a high *inflation factor,* indicative of a *thrust.*

(2) The base line from 1949 through the 1953 low was not broken in 1957, nor to date.

(3) The bottoms of waves 4 of each of Primaries I and III were substantially above the tops of waves 1.

(4) The fourth wave of the whole Cycle, i.e., the bottom of Primary IV in late 1957, was far above the top of the first wave of the Cycle, i.e., the top of Primary I in September 1951.

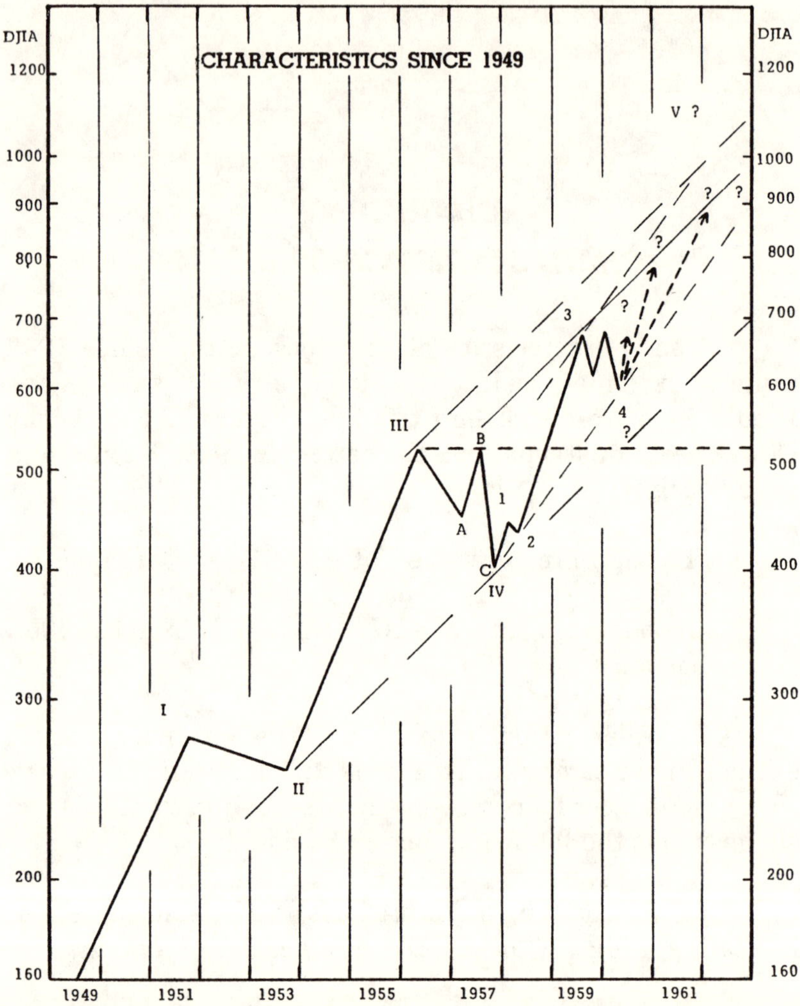

Figure 52

Markets tend to change their habits slowly. There is great concern in early 1960 that we may be in a *major bear market*. Some Dow Theorists claim with some reference to hindsight that mid-1959 closed out the whole bull market from 1949. This is based on the confirmation of the Rail Average and the Industrial Average in the spring of 1960, when both went to new lows under the lows of September 1959. The action of the market, however, in Elliott's terms and as interpreted by Elliott's thinking as best it can be projected in his absence, seems to be at time of the writing (May 1960) that a new bear market has not yet begun. This is supported by the following factors.

(1) It does not seem possible to develop a 5 count for the market since the fall of 1957. Thus, Primary V seems incomplete.

(2) Our count suggests that the highs in 1959 completed only wave 3 of Primary V. Wave 4 may still be in progress, but there is a possibility that the lows of April 1960 completed the whole of wave 4 of Primary V.

(3) Confirmation is heightened by the fact that the January to April decline can be classified into 5 downward waves, the last wave of which also developed a clear-cut 5 subwave pattern. (The Rail average also has a clear-cut 5 subwave pattern, often a sign, when both in gear, of the end of the move.)

If this should prove to be correct, we would expect either:

(1) Wave 5 of Primary V will now develop quickly, in which case new highs would probably be expected by late 1960.

(2) April 1960 will prove to be simply wave "A" of wave 4 of Primary V. This would call for a swift A-B-C formation, with "B" probably a triple top (as in 1957) and "C" a probable 5 down into new low ground, somewhere perhaps around 570 DJIA. All this would, of course, take perhaps six months to a year, or more.

(3) It is possible that wave 4 of Primary V is still not complete in the short term sense. Thus, there might develop a downward impetus to the Minor wave which began downward in April 1960. If so, it must do so practically immediately, as time and the season, as well as momentum, seem to be running out.

What conclusions can we come to then? It is always extremely dangerous to be dogmatic. The evidence as we see it points to the incompletion of Primary V since 1949. Based on past proven momentum and projected trend channels, and depending on the time element, the DJIA *could* complete the orthodox top of Primary V of Cycle I (21-year triangle interpretation) in late 1960 or the spring of 1961 at somewhere in the area 760-800.

Given this possibility, and assuming it happened, would this be the final top for some years to come? *Not necessarily,* for the simple reason that the whole *inflationary characteristic of the upward thrust* since 1949 is replete with examples of where wave "B" of the A-B-C correction formation is *higher* than the top of the previous 5 wave.

Thus, again assuming our hypothesis of a top in late 1960 or early 1961 should pan out, we would expect then a very substantial set-back, perhaps in the order of 15%, completing wave (A) followed by another rapid run up into new high ground above whatever the previous top finally came out to be and completing wave (B), followed by perhaps a rather disastrous decline in five smaller waves, completing wave (C).[1]

The *time* and *amplitude*? Anybody's guess. Wave (B) might be completed by 1963, and wave (C) by 1965-66. There would be a strong presumption because of past history of the *thrust* since 1949 that the 522[2] mark DJIA would be about as low as one could expect the market to go. (In no case in the bull markets since 1949 did the correction of any whole 5 waves go lower than the top of wave 3. There is also a presumption that the 1949-53-57 base line on the logarithmic chart *would* be broken. In waves of this degree in the past, it always has.)

So ends our *guessing game* as of May 1960.[3] It could be off-base, but it might prove quite correct.

FOOTNOTES

[1] This is a near-perfect description of what ensued from this time through 1962.

[2] The 1962 intraday low was 524.55.

[3] In a later edition of the book, Bolton appended this footnote here: "The above was written before Khrushchev sounded off in Paris about spies and spying. Subsequent history suggests that wave 4 was completed in April 1960."

CHAPTER XIII
IS "ELLIOTT" AN EXACT SCIENCE?

Regardless of the outcome of the current Cycle wave and its position so far as the Primaries are concerned, we may take a look at some important generalities. Earlier in this book, we said that instead of becoming more and more specific in Elliott forecasts, it was much more likely that the further we get away from 1932 to 1949, the more different interpretations it will be possible to develop.[1] Let us theorize about this for the moment.

Given a specific starting point, proved by history, a 1929, a 1932, a 1949, etc., Elliott's waves will commence to develop. The faster up (or down) one goes, the larger will be the corrections along the way. This is entirely logical. Averages, of course, are made up of a combination of different stocks, but each stock does not necessarily follow or conform to the averages. The fact that the Averages do conform to an over-all pattern is interesting, but should not be considered entirely fatalistic. The further one gets away from a *terminal point,* the more likely it will be that the interpreter will miss the forest for the trees. For this reason, the writer believes that Elliott is useful for developing broad lines of directional impulses, but that it is futile to quibble about minor wave completions or lack thereof. The stock market price of an individual stock takes on many of the characteristics of a *living organism*. The averages, however, are less so. Nevertheless, averages such as Standard and Poor's, Dow Jones, etc., with their predecessors spliced together, *do* give a sweep of history that is not available in individual stocks.

Elliott is *not an exact science*. It never will be. The two great *terminal dates* of the century are obviously 1929 and 1932. We are getting further away from them. If the implications of Elliott that we have discussed come to pass, there will be a much greater interest in interpreting Elliott. New students will try their hand at it. There won't be any one expert, but several, just as today there are several Dow Theory experts, some of whom do not agree with one another.

The times are ripe for this sort of thing to develop. A great deal more research will be made into the finer points of Elliott. It will not necessarily, however, produce a greater amount of truth. The writer suggests that the student try at all times to *keep it simple*. Elliott in a vacuum, however, will not work. It should be related to economics and to other technical market studies. In particular, it needs to be studied along with changes in bank credit.

FOOTNOTES

[1] This is true, but only for awhile. The Wave Principle has a remarkable way of bringing the analyst from a state of uncertainty to one of *total clarity* at the time that a wave is completed. The reason is that "Elliott" is a study of patterns, and when a *completed* pattern is staring you in the face, it is hard to mistake it.

CHAPTER XIV
BANK CREDIT AND THE WAVE THEORY

The writer has not had time to do any extended research into the possibilities of cycles (periodicity) in bank credit. Nor has any attempt been made to see if the *Elliott Wave Principle* can be applied effectively to bank credit expansion and contraction. Inasmuch as expansion and contraction of bank credit are fundamental to our economic capitalist system, it does seem highly likely that these changes take place in waves which could be classified in accordance with Elliott's rules.

Regardless of this point, we may draw certain analogies between the behavior of bank credit and that of stock prices over the last 130 years.[1]

Elliott used the Axe-Houghton-Burgess Index of stock prices from 1854 to 1929 for his analysis of the waves in the previous century. If one splices onto this index the Ayres index of common stock prices, which covers the period from 1831 to 1870, i.e., use this index from 1831 to 1854 and link it to the Axe-Houghton index, it becomes clear that a *major bear market* took place from 1836 to 1857 (21 years). As we have mentioned in previous reviews of the Elliott Wave Principle, the United States had a collapse of bank credit following the land boom of the early 1830s on a scale comparable to the collapse of bank credit following the stock market credit boom of the late 1920s. Further, no collapse of bank credit of a comparable scale happened between the 1835-45 period and the 1930-40 period.

One characteristic we would like to point out, however, is that regardless of which stock index one uses, whether

Axe-Houghton-Burgess or Cowles Commission linked to the Ayres index, the great bull markets of the last century, and generally up to 1914 or so, were *short* and *fast* followed by *long corrections*, whereas the bull markets since about World War I have been *long* followed by *short corrections*.

We refer you back to Chapter VI, wherein we showed that Elliott's count of Super Cycle (III) was:

		Short	Long
Cycle I	1857-64	7 years	
Cycle II	1864-77		13 years
Cycle III	1877-81	4 years	
Cycle IV	1881-96		15 years
Cycle V	1896-1928		32 years

Only Cycle V was long in relation to the corrections that followed, and one may say that the transition from short orthodox bull markets and long corrections took place basically around World War I.

We may perhaps blame World War I, the Depression and World War II for this change, but actually the change in character is due primarily to the *change in banking system* which took place when the Federal Reserve System was formed in 1914.

Prior to the Federal Reserve was the National Banking System. This system was highly inflexible and was one of the reasons why stock market collapses in the 19th and early part of the 20th century were often so severe. What used to happen was essentially this: at the end of a depression, money became very easy and credit became available. Since business did not need the money, speculators sensing the changing times started buying securities on bank credit. Stock prices would rise rapidly from the depths of the depression. But after a very few years of this, credit would again be needed by business and industry. As there were very finite limits to possible credit expansion due to the highly developed International Gold Standard which was in full

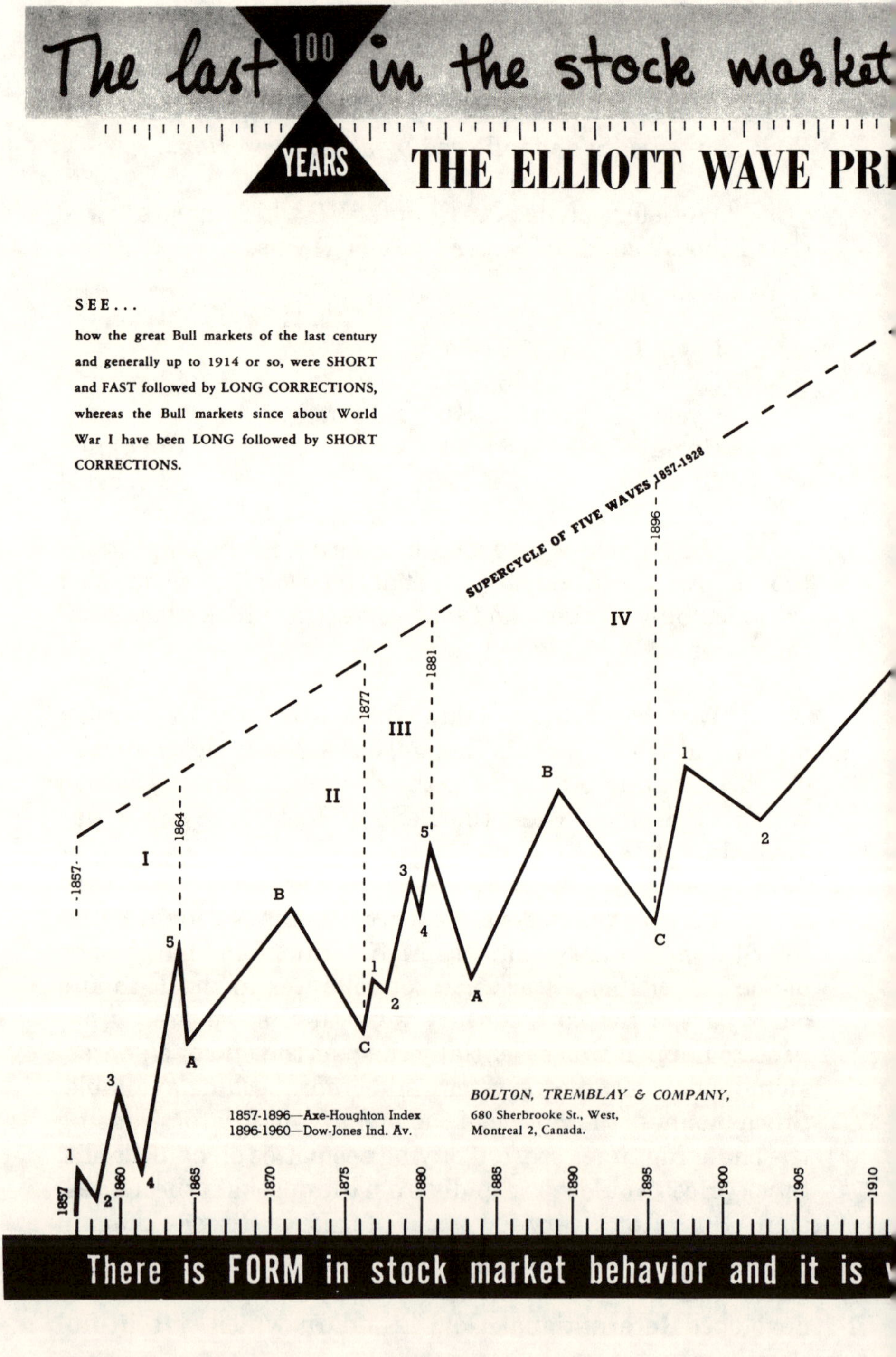

The last 100 YEARS in the stock market
THE ELLIOTT WAVE PR
SEE...
how the great Bull markets of the last century and generally up to 1914 or so, were SHORT and FAST followed by LONG CORRECTIONS, whereas the Bull markets since about World War I have been LONG followed by SHORT CORRECTIONS.
SUPERCYCLE OF FIVE WAVES 1857-1928
1857
1864
1877
1881
1896
I
II
III
IV
1
2
3
4
5
A
B
C
1857-1896—Axe-Houghton Index
1896-1960—Dow-Jones Ind. Av.
BOLTON, TREMBLAY & COMPANY,
680 Sherbrooke St., West,
Montreal 2, Canada.
1857
1860
1865
1870
1875
1880
1885
1890
1895
1900
1905
1910
There is FORM in stock market behavior and it is

...ng the lines of

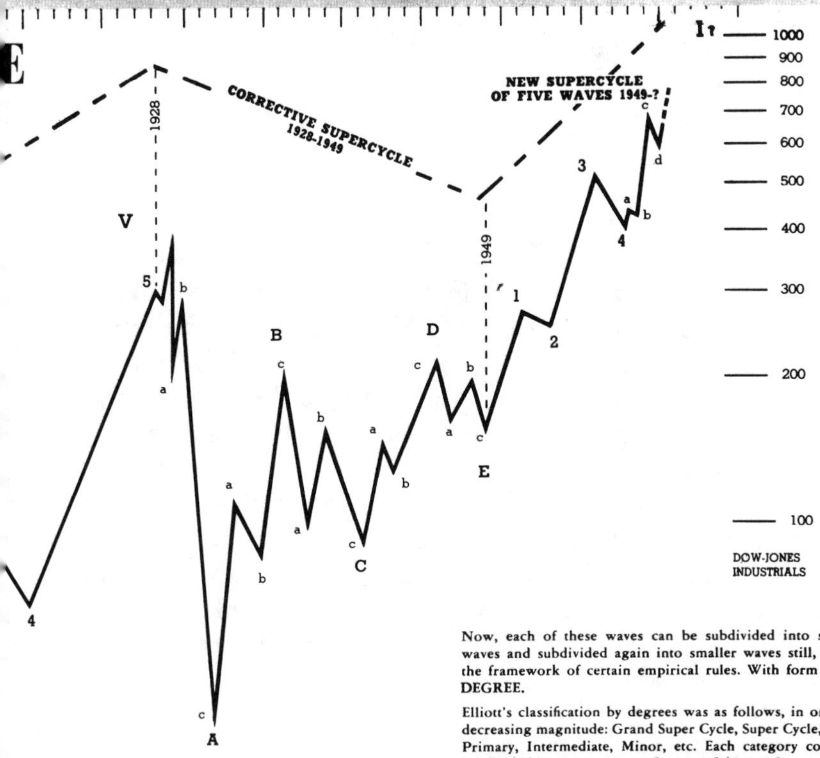

Now, each of these waves can be subdivided into smaller waves and subdivided again into smaller waves still, within the framework of certain empirical rules. With form comes DEGREE.

Elliott's classification by degrees was as follows, in order of decreasing magnitude: Grand Super Cycle, Super Cycle, Cycle, Primary, Intermediate, Minor, etc. Each category could be subdivided into set patterns of waves of the next lesser degree. For instance, the 1857-1928 Super Cycle can be broken down into 5 Cycles (1857-64, 1864-77, 1877-81, 1881-96, 1896-1928), and each of the 5 Cycles can be broken down into either 5 or 3 Primaries in accordance with Elliott's law.

During an illness in the middle 1930's, the late R. N. Elliott discovered the basic rhythm in the Stock Market and elsewhere which he called the "Wave Principle" and, later, "Nature's Law".

In a series of articles in the Financial World in 1938-39, Elliott pointed out that observation on his part — going back over at least 80 years — proved to his satisfaction that, generally speaking, the market moved in cycles of 21 waves: 5 up, 3 down, 5 up, 3 down and 5 up. To qualify, only waves 1, 3 and 5 of the UP series are up; 2 and 4 being actually down (corrective) waves. Likewise, only waves A and C of the DOWN series are down; wave B being actually up (corrective). The concept which emerges from this elementary description is one of FORM.

Elliott's Wave Principle differs from other cycle theories in that it does not hinge upon periodicity of recurring cycles. Within the framework of the Principle, waves may extend or contract in time over very considerable periods. Thus the patterns are far more flexible than under orthodox cycle theories.

One of the interesting facets to Elliott's Wave Principle is the fact that the whole concept is one of GROWTH. The main direction can be considered as always upward, the downward waves always being corrections. Thus in the stock market, one starts a new cycle of waves on a small scale, and these then become parts of larger waves in set patterns.

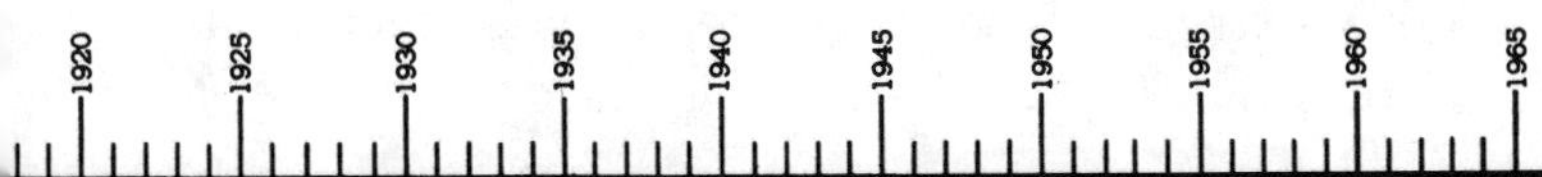

...KNOW WHERE WE ARE IN THE INVESTMENT CYCLE.

sway from 1875 to 1914, when business credit began to expand, speculative credit had to be restricted. Thus it was, that in those days stock market peaks tended to *precede* by a wide margin peaks in industry and business. All the rush upward in stock prices took place in a short period and from then on for long periods would follow bear markets followed by bull markets, but overall not getting very far. These so-called bull and bear markets invariably under Elliott's rules took the form of long corrective patterns (i.e., threes instead of five).

With the coming of the Federal Reserve, however, in 1914, and in particular with the final collapse of the full gold standard in 1933 in the U.S., the way was paved for *almost infinite* expansion of bank credit, which would mean in the future that there would not be for a long time at least the type of bank credit collapses that were prevalent in the period between 1836 and 1933. This fact was further greatly strengthened in reliability of forecast by the tremendous collapse in bank credit from 1929 to 1933, and by the characteristic of the credit expansion of World War II whereby it was almost entirely in the form of government rather than private sector bank credit.

The expansion of government sector bank credit in World War II and the extremely low level of private sector bank credit in 1945 assured the economy that there would be no economic collapse in the immediate postwar period. In fact, it assured the economy that there would be ample funds in the banking system for an almost endless time ahead, and that on this base could be built a tremendous boom in business and presumably in stock prices.

The nature, then, of the situation in 1949 when the postwar boom in stock prices really began was such as to produce long bull markets and short corrections based on:

(a) Extremely low valuation of stock prices.

(b) Extremely low amount of private sector bank credit.

(c) Extremely large reservoir (greatest in history) of idle money in the form of deposits created by bank monetized government debt.

(d) A political environment, unhemmed in by the old shackles of the international and domestic gold standard, which after the depression of the '30s became *inflation-minded,* and which still despite the efforts of the Federal Reserve Board to tone down the more virulent inflationists in Congress may be considered to be much more favorably inclined toward monetary inflation and deficit financing than to the stricter medicine of budgetary control and gradual deflation of the money supply.

Nor is there at this date any reason to believe that a deflationary bank credit policy will be tolerated in the United States. Only one automatic restraint is now left, and this is the rather tenuous link still existing between Federal Reserve deposits and currency outstanding and the gold supply whereby, by law, the latter must at least equal 25% of the two former items combined (the current ratio is around 40%).[2]

The credit ingredients cooked up by the World War II credit monetization brew are unique in United States history. Already they have resulted in a boom in stock prices since 1949 of about four times in terms of leading averages such as Dow Jones Industrials, Standard and Poor's, etc., in a space of 11 years. But considering the expansion of private sector bank credit that has taken place, and the fact that there are still important reserves left for future expansion, it appears likely that the postwar pattern of long periods of rising prices and shorter and subnormal periods of stock market corrections, Elliott-wise, will be the prevalent trend as compared to the rapid uprush and long periods of relative stagnation which were the trends in the 19th and early 20th centuries.

Nevertheless, the present stock market boom (the Cycle starting in 1949) is now 11 years old. We have indicated our belief that it has not yet completed the fifth stage (Primary V). There are obvious elements missing. After so much infusion of bank credit into the economy, we should expect a final all-out speculative phase. This has not yet appeared. It may well do so.

It is perhaps significant that the peak of the capital boom (expansion of capital goods) was reached in 1956-57. It is generally considered unlikely that we will have so strong a relative surge in the remainder of this business cycle. Funds which are available for promotion of capital expansion can easily be transferred into other uses. The Federal Reserve has a tight control on stock market margins (currently 90% in May 1960). Nevertheless, these regulations can be side-stepped by the provision of funds from outside the control of the banking stream.[3] Thus, if money is available and idle, it can be used to foster what increases in bank credit might also foster. What happens is that money begins to be used more rapidly. There is no control possible on the part of the banking system over how fast the public will choose to turn over its own banking resources. Banking policy can only limit the expansion of new credit or perhaps even deflate some existing credit, but it cannot control how fast money will be used.

The ingredients for a speculative boom are here: tremendous increase in private bank credit, whetting of the appetite through rising interest rates of getting money to work, the spectacle of rising stock prices and falling bond prices, labor's inflationary cost push, the obvious political bias towards inflation, or at least no deflation (nobody will tolerate a policy of deflation such as we had in the early 1930s — see author's booklet, "1929 and Now"), and the fact that we have a new generation to whom 1929 and its aftermath are simply recorded history rather than live experience.

Will such a boom come about in the period ahead? The ingredients are there, and the *pattern of the cycle wave* since 1949 *seems still to be incomplete*. No firm prediction can be made; nevertheless, the odds seem to be balanced in favor.

Some thoughts on the time and amplitude elements may be noted from the point of view of Elliott's theories:

(1) Many important time periods from key dates in the past point to 1962 and 1963 as key periods. (Check various Fibonacci series numbers, i.e., 3, 5, 8, 13, 21, 34, 55, etc., against key Elliott turning points in the past such as 1928, 1929, 1942, 1949, etc.). There is no indication of whether tops or bottoms are expected, but no matter how looked at, the confluence of time series indicating these years as *terminal* in some way is worthy of continuous study.

(2) The nature of the *thrust* since 1949 and the economic credit background, as well as the count of Primary and Intermediate waves since 1949, point to the probability that either the top of Primary V or the subsequent top of an irregular wave "B" of the correction Cycle should reach one or more of the upper parallels to the 1949-53-57 base line (see Figure 48 in Chapter XI). The pattern (to scale) is summarized in Figure 52 in Chapter XII.

Depending on the length of the time element, we may project the height of the Average. Elliott used this technique of base lines and parallels throughout his work as possible targets for wave completions at all stages and degrees.

A *corollary,* however, to this seeming boom culmination is the suggestion that the stock market decline thereafter may well be of considerably greater magnitude than anything seen in the whole postwar period:

(1) The whole Cycle from 1949 will have been completed. This calls for Cycle II from 1949.

(2) Cycle II obviously should be of greater amplitude and time than Primaries II and IV of Cycle I.

(3) We have suggested that owing to the character of a *thrust,* it is unlikely that Cycle II would go lower than the

top of Primary III of Cycle I. Nevertheless, if any of the targets suggested by Figure 52 are reached, such a drop would constitute a decline in the Average of somewhere between 30 and 40%, thus confirming our surmise of a *major stock market decline* for the first time in the postwar period.[4]

(4) The bank credit background suggests that for the first time in the postwar period, we may in the next few years be running into a *monetary crisis* (see our continuing studies of this interesting trend in the Bolton-Tremblay *Bank Credit Analyst*), as, if and when bank reserves finally become depleted toward the danger point.

This, then, seems to be the combined message of both the Elliott Wave theory and the Bolton-Tremblay Bank Credit studies: further stock market boom ahead, followed by the most severe decline in stocks since the period 1937-42.

FOOTNOTES

[1] The accompanying chart, "The last 100 years in the stock market along the lines of the Elliott Wave Principle," actually appeared in the 1961 Supplement, but it was created to illustrate this discussion, so we have moved it to this part of the book.

[2] This restraint has long gone by the wayside.

[3] Or by a change in the rules, which is what happened.

[4] This forecast refers to the upcoming 1966-1974 bear market.

CHAPTER XV
"ELLIOTT" APPLICABLE TO INDIVIDUAL STOCKS

The problem of applying the Wave Principle to individual stocks is the obvious fact that each stock has a history of its own. A stock like U.S. Steel obviously has a longer market history than, say, General Motors and the latter a longer history than, say, Minneapolis Honeywell. Theoretically, therefore, each is in a different position at different times as to Primaries, Intermediates, Cycle degrees, etc.

The history of an individual stock can best be seen marketwise by use of a graph — usually of the bar graph type, with price range on the vertical axis and time (days, weeks, months, etc.) on the horizontal axis. A number of investment services provide such a background history.

Examples of the use of the Elliott Wave Principle are legion. In Figures 53 and 54, we give two examples simply as an illustration. In individual stocks, one cannot develop a broad picture such as that of the Super Cycle from 1854 to 1928, thus one does not have the advantage of long-term perspective. Perhaps the most significant use of Elliott in individual stocks is the appearance of the *five-wave* pattern. The author has found that when one sees a clear-cut 5-wave pattern developing and being completed, one is almost sure that it is the *end of the move*. This can be useful particularly in preventing investment in a stock which is obviously *well advanced in its fifth wave*.

Of course, the degree of the wave as indicated by the amplitude of what has gone before is most important. Investing in the fifth wave of a stock in which five waves have carried it from 20 to 150 is likely to be far more dangerous than investing in a minor fifth wave in a move of a stock from 20 to 30.

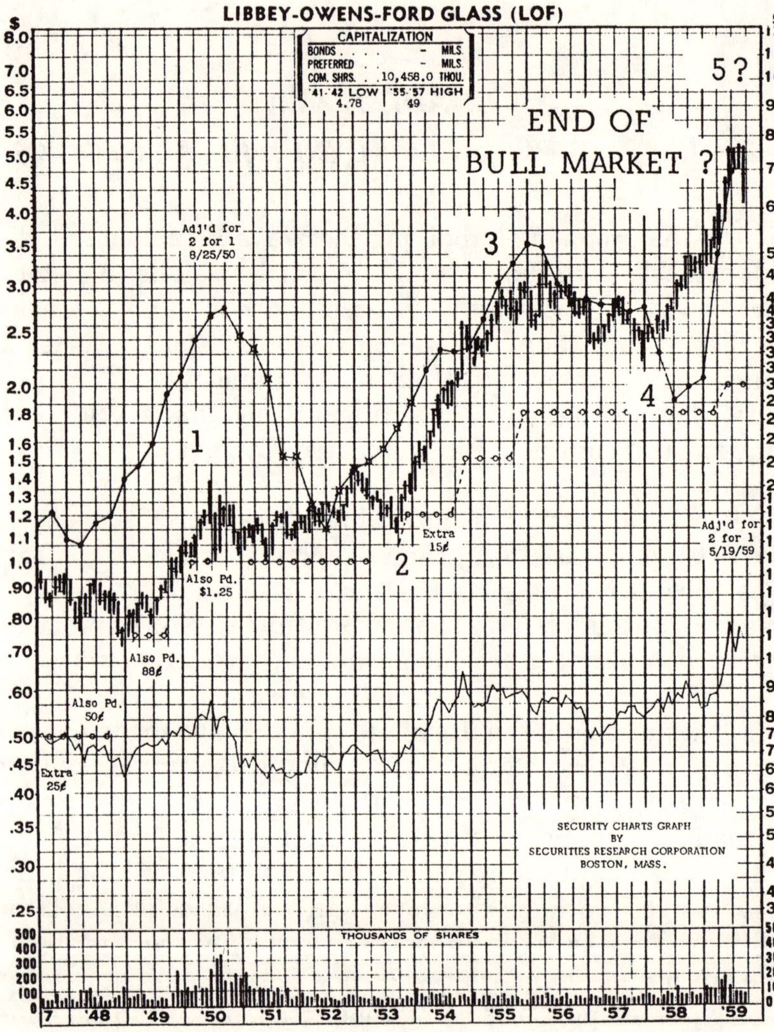

Figure 53

A great deal of further research needs to be done in the application of the Wave Principle to individual stocks. Elliott was always careful to suggest that if one wished to apply the Wave principle to individual stock investment, one should be careful to select stocks which perform like the averages.

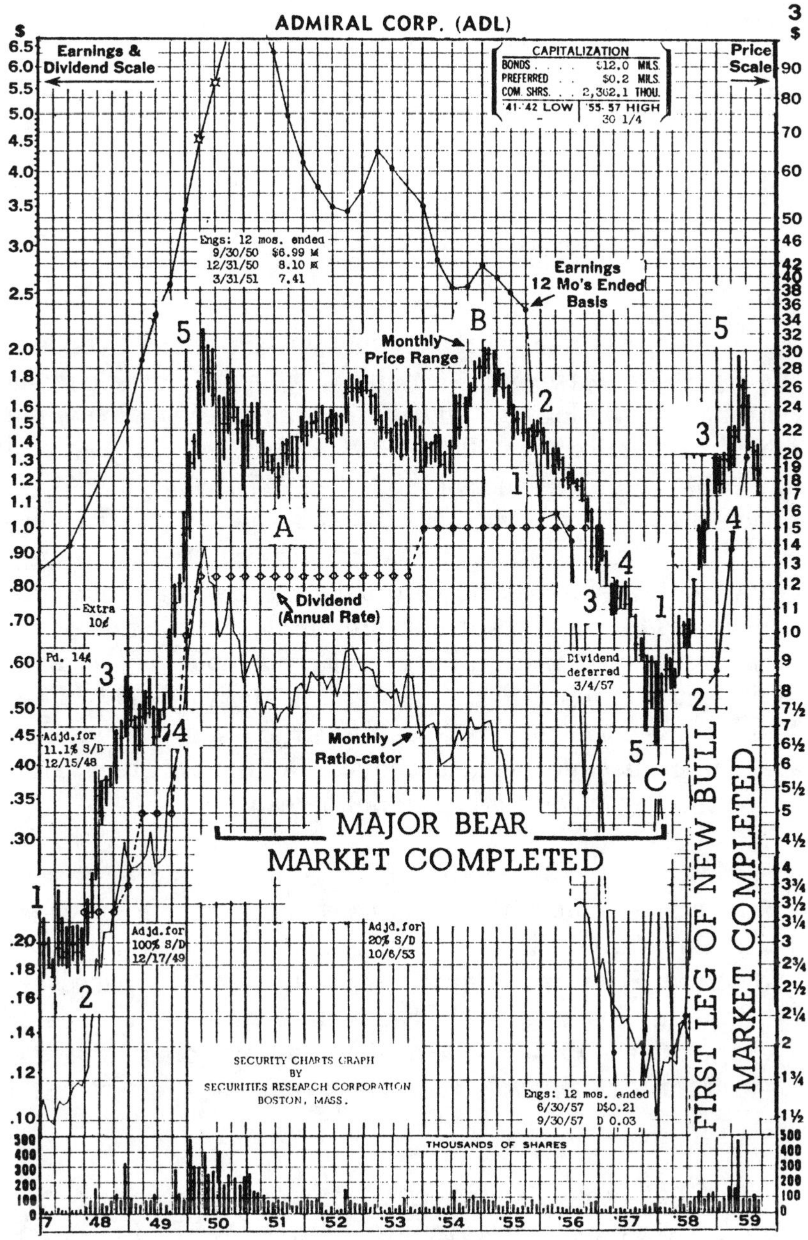

Figure 54

One further suggestion would be to study the Wave Principle in relation to *closed-end investment companies.*

CHAPTER XVI
ELLIOTT: FACT OR FANCY?

In any summary of this kind, we are bound to do less than justice to the job at hand. To have developed as complicated, yet logical, a mechanism as the Wave Principle must have meant that Elliott, in roughly the dozen years he had to work on his theory (1935(?) - 1947), must have done little else but look at waves, subdivide them, classify them, etc., etc. That his Principle is the *ultimate truth* we may fairly doubt. Yet having said this and having made due allowances for an overenthusiasm for the cosmic influence, we may perhaps assess Elliott's work as a model of precision in comparison with, let us say, the modern school of Dow Theorists, whose continual qualifications and virtual disagreements between various cliques offer little of great value to the intelligent and professional investor.

Elliott, in the middle '30s, when his basic work took shape, started out with an *empirical theory*. He provided stock market analysis with a sense of *form* which it had never had before. His work, enquiring into the past, was necessarily limited. Prior to 1928, there were no daily ranges of average prices. Prior to 1897, with the Dow Jones Industrials and Rails as the only consistent vehicles, there were no daily prices.

Of all economic data available, stock prices were the best, but they were nevertheless scanty. We had the Axe-Houghton-Burgess Index of industrial stock prices, 1854 to date. After 1938, by which time Elliott had developed his Principle, we obtained the Cowles Commission indices of stock prices which literally carried back the Standard &

Poor's indices from 1919 to 1871, but this was a later development. The Federal Reserve Bank of New York developed the Dow Jones Industrial Average also back into the 1870s. And finally, Col. Ayres of the Cleveland Trust Company developed a comprehensive index of stocks (banks, canal stocks, rails, industrials, etc.) which he spliced onto the Cowles Commission Index and onto Standard and Poor's Index in 1919 to make a long-term *monthly* index of stock prices covering the period 1831 to date.

Such an index cannot be expected to bring out the finer points of the Elliott Wave Principle. Yet this was the background upon which Elliott had to work up his theory. Needless to say that if we had today the information for byegone days that we can produce for the last generation, we would undoubtedly be able to come to a better set of ground rules than we have.

(We may mention in passing that no other set of economic data offered even a fraction of the opportunity for analysis that stock prices do in point of view of quantity of data available.)

Elliott's theories are plausible. We are beginning to realize as time goes on that there is something to cycle theories. In the 1930s, when Elliott put forth his Principle, and particularly in 1945, when his second monograph, *Nature's Law,* attempted to probe into the causes of the Wave Principle phenomenon, the idea that such "occult" factors as sunspots could affect human behavior were "pooh-poohed." They still are, yet not perhaps so vehemently as heretofore. Nelson of Radio Corporation of America shook the world in the early 1950s when he proved that he could predict radio reception clarity within 80 to 95% accuracy by reference to astronomical cycle analysis and its effect on the sun, which is the turbine that keeps all earth life going. Edgar Lawrence Smith's more recent *Common Stocks and Business Cycles* probes even deeper into the causes of changes in mass behavior and into his well-known Decennial Pattern, as well as the nine-year cycle in stock prices. Work done by Edward

Dewey at the Foundation for the Study of Cycles is beginning to bear fruit. What these various themes have to do with Elliott's Wave Principle may well be a moot point. Yet it is clear that all cycle theories, including Elliott's, depend on the principle that there is *form* in the world we live in and in the universe around us.

It is, of course, easy from any set of statistics to prove that it is or it is not. The National Bureau of Economic Research under Wesley Mitchell and Arthur Burns refuse to have any truck with any thoughts about periodicity or form. Perhaps they are right. Perhaps all changes in the economic scene are due to accidental impulses which when totalled up come to a net of plus or minus factors without rhyme or reason. On the other hand, nothing in nature suggests that life is formless. If life has form, then it is a logical assumption that economics (which is a form of life) have form as well.

Elliott's theory has something to offer. It certainly is not the precise instrument that he hoped it would be. And as we have explained in previous chapters, so far as the stock market is concerned, as we move away from the major terminal dates of the century, i.e., 1929 and 1932, its use will tend to become even more tentative.

Most of us, when we discuss the Elliott Wave Principle, do so with a certain "tongue-in-cheek" attitude. If sometimes it does not work, well, we probably can find a reason in retrospect. The trouble is, however, that it has had a rather unique habit in recent years of coming up with the right answer. Provided we do not try to make it do something that it is not supposed to, i.e., provided we use it solely as a tool rather than a system for "beating the market," we see no reason why it should not be extremely valuable over the coming years. No doubt it will tend to produce increasing controversy, but it may also prove to be quite a solid crutch to the investor who has an open mind.

In sum: Fact or Fancy? In the belief that coincidence can be carried too far, and based on our own use of the Wave

Principle as set forth in our annual bulletins since 1953, the batting average in its favor seems good. Often we become confused as to detail. Seldom, if ever, however, have we made a basically incorrect analysis. Without form, life becomes meaningless. Elliott's Wave Principle provides some sense of form to investment and market analysis.

We suspect that the Elliott Wave Principle has more fact than fancy.

May 1960

APPENDIX "A"
DATA AND BIBLIOGRAPHY

R. N. Elliott, the discoverer of the Wave Principle, during an illness in the 1930s, formulated the theory of waves which bears his name. Elliott died in 1947. There has been very little written on the Wave Principle. However, the following source material has been used by the author:

R. N. Elliott (1) *The Wave Principle*
monograph (1938),

(2) *Nature's Law*
monograph (1946),

(3) *Special Letters* (1938-47),
Interpretive Letters (1938-47),
Forecast Letters (1946).
These letters were issued from time to time as events warranted.

In addition to the above was the series of articles in the *Financial World* in 1939, but the author has not had recent access to them, nor as he recalls it did the articles throw any new light on the subject which could not be found in the 1938 monograph.

All these sources are out of print. However, they can probably be found in the New York Public Library. Also, book dealers dealing in second hand financial books might be a help in locating copies.

Other source material includes the 1948 and 1954 editions of Garfield Drew's *New Methods for Profit in the Stock Market*, wherein several pages are devoted to Elliott in the context of contemporary thought.

In addition, Bolton, Tremblay & Company each year since 1953, in the spring, have put out an annual review, attempting to interpret the then current position. Extracts from these bulletins appear in Appendix "C,"[1] and much of the material previously presented in these bulletins has been incorporated in greater detail in the current *critical survey*.

May 1960

FOOTNOTES

1 Extracts from previous annual "Elliott" reviews can be found at the end of this book.

APPENDIX "B"

THE TWENTY-ONE YEAR TRIANGLE

1928 - 1949

[For the full text with charts, see the 1959 Review]

THE ELLIOTT WAVE PRINCIPLE — A CRITICAL APPRAISAL

Postscript to the First Edition

[The following is excerpted from the October 1960 issue of *The Bank Credit Analyst*]

It is not our custom to comment on the Elliott Wave Principle except in our annual reviews. However, in view of our recent book on the subject and the thought expressed that the correction from July 1959 may have been completed on May 2nd, 1960, perhaps some further comment is in order.

Since May 2nd, we have had a further test of this approximate level (596 Dow Jones Industrials) in July and a break through in September to, at time of writing, about 570 in the Average. How does this fit in with the premises?

First, let us reiterate what we were very emphatic in pointing out, that we never (or rarely) know the full story till "after the fact."

Secondly, the premise is that from 1949 we have encompassed the good part of five Primary waves, and that the fifth Primary began in late 1957. Again, we have stipulated that there is no count of the waves that will bring a termination of the fifth sub-wave of this fifth Primary in either July 1959 or January 1960. This has been checked with various students who keep track of the waves in accordance with Elliott's rules. Our calculation is that July 1959 completed only wave 3 of the fifth Primary. There was no count in the rise from September 1959 to January 1960 which could terminate the Primary at that later date. Thus, we assume that all that has happened since is part of wave 4 of the fifth Primary. (For a review of this, simply see Figure 48, "Breakdown of the DJIA from 1949.")

Fourth waves of any degree may well be *triangles*. There is justification for suggesting that the current fourth wave is a triangle made up of 5 waves, all of 3 sub-waves. This is indicated by the fact that all the waves since July 1959 can clearly be divided into 3s, as per the attached diagram.[1]

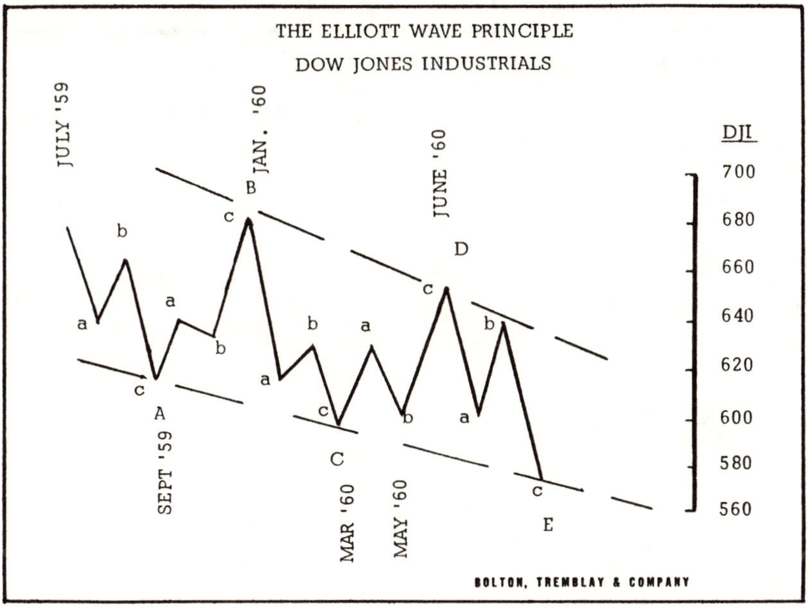

It is interesting that the May 2nd bottom now appears to be the bottom of the 2nd wave of D. This was confusing at the time, because it was clear that the sub-wave "c" of wave D was a 5 up. At the time, this looked like the beginning of a new Minor wave up of the final fifth wave of the Primary. However, waves "a" and "b" of D were 3s. Thus, wave D took shape as an inverted flat (3-3-5). Similarly, waves "a" and "b" of E were 3s. If wave "c" of E should turn out to be a Minor 5 down, as appears likely on the hourly chart, point E could finish the triangle at or near the lower trend line, as indicated.

Alternatively, of course, the correction from July 1959 could continue in the form of a 7 wave affair (see Figure 18 for the prototype). The fact, however, that this is a fourth wave and that 5 waves of 3 subdivisions each have now appeared suggests that the correction will shortly terminate.

September 28th, 1960

FOOTNOTES

[1] This is not a legitimate triangle, as both trendlines are downsloping. It's a triple zigzag.

THE ELLIOTT WAVE PRINCIPLE OF STOCK MARKET BEHAVIOR

1961

The Bolton-Tremblay

BANK CREDIT ANALYST

A. Hamilton Bolton, editor-in-chief

THE ELLIOTT WAVE PRINCIPLE OF STOCK MARKET BEHAVIOR 1961 SUPPLEMENT

THE CURRENT STATUS

In order to outline the current status of the stock market so far as the Elliott Wave Principle is concerned, we need to review the stock market since the last terminal point of major significance, which is June 1949.

Since June 1949, according to Elliott Wave theory, we have been in a major bull market of Cycle dimension. Further, according to one interpretation, which we favor, June 1949 is also the beginning of a Super Cycle, which will be composed of five Cycle waves. The term Cycle should neither be confused with "cyclical," as used in ordinary business parlance, nor with "cycles," meaning ups and downs measuring fixed time periods (e.g., the 10-year cycle or Decennial Pattern in stock prices).

Cycle waves under Elliott's definitions are broken down into Primaries. Thus, the Cycle wave from 1949 will be made up of 5 Primaries, 3 up and 2 consolidating in between. In turn, Primaries will be broken down into Intermediates. Each upward Primary will have 5 Intermediates. The first downward Primary (wave 2) will have 3 Intermediates, and the second downward Primary (wave 4) may have either 3 or 5 (a triangle) Intermediates.

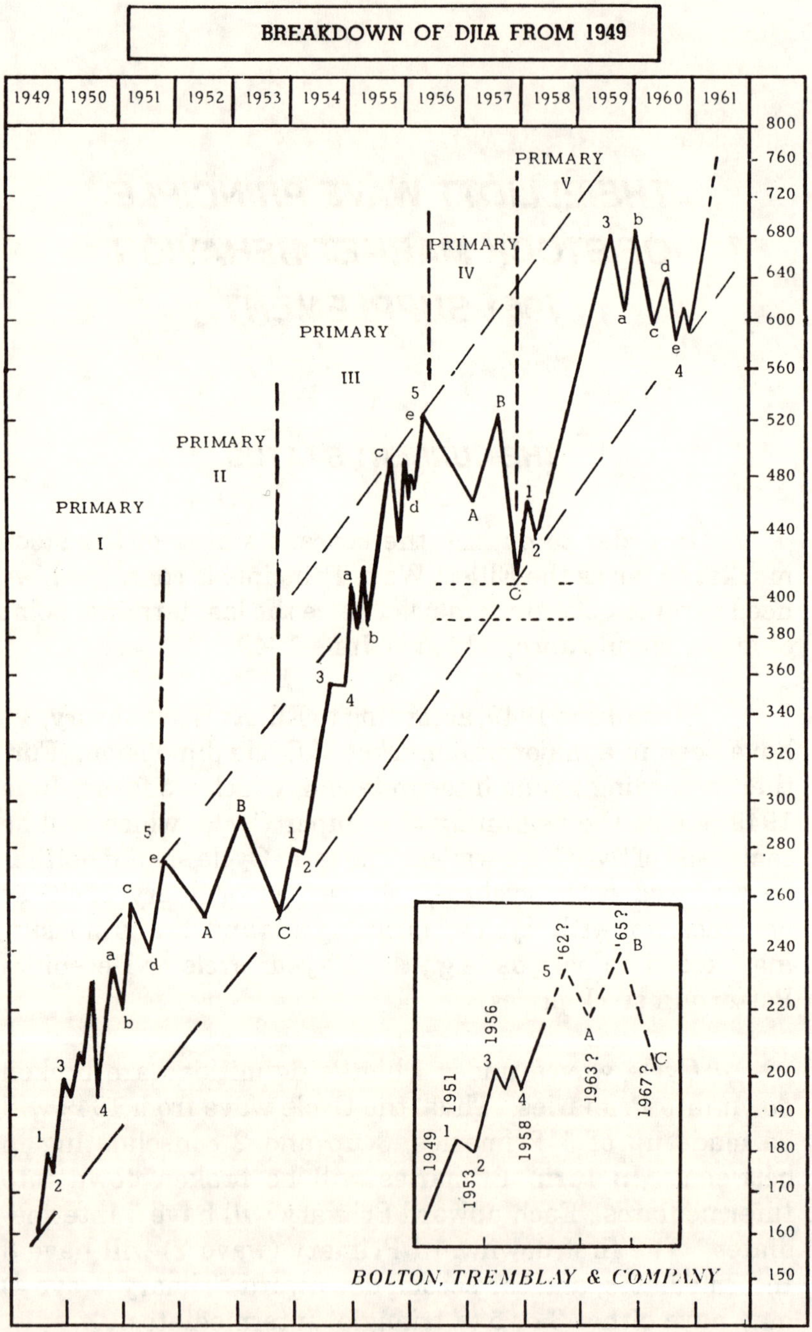
BREAKDOWN OF DJIA FROM 1949
1949
1950
1951
1952
1953
1954
1955
1956
1957
1958
1959
1960
1961
PRIMARY
I
PRIMARY
II
PRIMARY
III
PRIMARY
IV
PRIMARY
V
BOLTON, TREMBLAY & COMPANY

Figure 48

The progress of the bull market is illustrated by the chart on the previous page, which updates Figure 48 from the 1960 edition of *The Elliott Wave Principle*. If this chart is now compared with that of the book published this time last year, it will be seen that whereas we had a 4? on the wave termination in late April 1960, we now have the 4 definitely placed against the October 24th 1960 bottom and we are now in the fifth and final wave of Primary 5[1] from 1949. On completion of this fifth Primary, which may be expected probably by sometime perhaps in 1962, this will also complete the *first Cycle* from 1949. A major correction will then be due.

Because this correction would be of the whole bull market from 1949, i.e., perhaps 13 years of time and 600 odd points in the Dow Jones Industrials, one would expect a minimum retrenchment of one third (200 Dow Jones Industrial points),[2] and more likely a 40% retrenchment. In point of view of time, one could logically expect that the correction could stretch out to 5 years. This means not that one would have a 5-year continuous bear market, but that one could possibly have two major bear markets with a bull market in between.

In view of the nature of the market rise from 1949, in which the first Cycle wave becomes the "thrust" from undervalued territory, in connection with the bull market intervening between the orthodox peak of Primary 5 of Cycle I and the bottom of Primary 3 of Cycle II that we may hypothesize as terminating 1967 (5 years from our hypothesized peak in 1962, and a Fibonacci number to match the 13-year hypothesized rise from 1949 — all pure guess-work of course), it would not be at all surprising if this intervening bull market carried prices above the peak of Primary 5. This can be illustrated as a possibility by the insert in the lower left hand corner of the chart, "Breakdown of the DJIA from 1949."[3]

As we mentioned, however, in the 1960 edition of *The Elliott Wave Principle,* the possible permutations and combinations of what the general market might do from here on are becoming greater and greater. One thing seems reasonably clear: The long logarithmic trend line from the 1949, 1953, 1957 and 1960 bottoms should be decisively broken. Assuming that the Dow Jones Industrials eventually work up into the 800-1000 level, either at the end of Primary 5 or alternatively at the top of wave B (see preceding chart), then a logical area to expect the bottom of the ensuing bear market would be about the 520 level, which was the top area in 1956-57. It should be kept in mind that while 520 does not seem far in relation to 565 reached in October 1960, it will seem well-nigh calamitous in relation to a figure, say, of 900. The present generation will not have seen a market decline of anywhere near this magnitude. Thus, there could be much "wailing and gnashing of teeth."

This, then, is the pattern that we see unfolding as indicated by the Elliott Wave Principle in the spring of 1961: Further rises ahead followed by bear markets of greater amplitude and duration than we have seen in the postwar period.

THE FIFTH WAVE

One concept that is bandied about quite a bit these days amongst the more knowledgeable Dow Theorists is that of the *third phase*. Charles Dow apparently never spoke of the third phase, the expression being an invention of William Peter Hamilton. The third phase is the speculative phase. This is when the public takes the stock market and whips it up into a frenzy which carries prices way beyond realistic values. Investors become speculators simply because the only reason they buy a stock is in order to sell it to someone else at a higher price. All emphasis is on capital gain at any cost, and no consideration is given to the income that capital will produce.

Now, investing for capital gain is a perfectly legitimate avocation, but if one is to keep one's perspective, it must be to produce a rising capital which ultimately will produce a growing return. Investing simply to pass on a stock to someone else at a higher price is pure speculation, and this is what happens in all third or final phases.

It should be clear that Elliott's *fifth wave* should correspond to Dow Theorists' third or final phase, except that Elliott was able to be much more specific in delineating the fifth wave than most Dow Theorists have been.

For instance, because of the gathering speculation in 1955-56, some Dow Theorists were certain that the speculative markets of 1956-57 were a real third phase and that the bear market signals of 1957 meant real business. Not so Elliott. It was clear at that time that the 1956 top was only completing the *third wave* of five, and that no major bear market could develop from this situation.

Similarly in 1959-60, when in the spring of 1960 (confirmed again in the fall of that year) a Dow Theory sell signal was given, this was taken as a sign in some quarters that the bull market was over, that the third phase had been completed as of the previous July and that a major bear market was ahead. As in 1956-57, the bear market signal was reconfirmed in September 1960 when the Industrials broke the 596 level, within about 5% of the ultimate bottom at 565. A collapse in prices was generally anticipated, but a major bull market then developed. Again, these bear signals lacked precision as well as forecasting ability and needless to say did not agree with the Elliott Wave Principle.[4]

In 1956, the market from 1949 was completing only the third Primary of the whole Cycle. In July 1959, while the market was in the fifth and final Primary of the Cycle, it was only, according to our interpretations at the time and subsequently confirmed, in the third Intermediate of that Primary. It makes a great deal of difference, and shows how added precision can be given to general market interpretation by using the basic principles of the Elliott Wave theory.

Now, in early 1961, we are beginning to see what a real "third phase" looks like, and there seems little doubt that what some Dow Theorists mistook as third phase characteristics respectively in 1951, in 1956, and again in 1959, were only parts of an incompleted Elliott wave of Cycle dimensions.

The Elliott reading that we have consistently given is that the fourth Primary ended in December 1957, and the *fifth* Primary began at this date. Up to the spring of 1960, it had completed three out of five Intermediates. Thus, the peak in the market in July 1959 marked the completion of the third Intermediate, and the start of the fourth Intermediate, which in our Elliott book we thought might have been completed by early May 1960. In actual fact, however, this proved erroneous, and the whole fourth wave Intermediate was not completed till October 24, 1960.

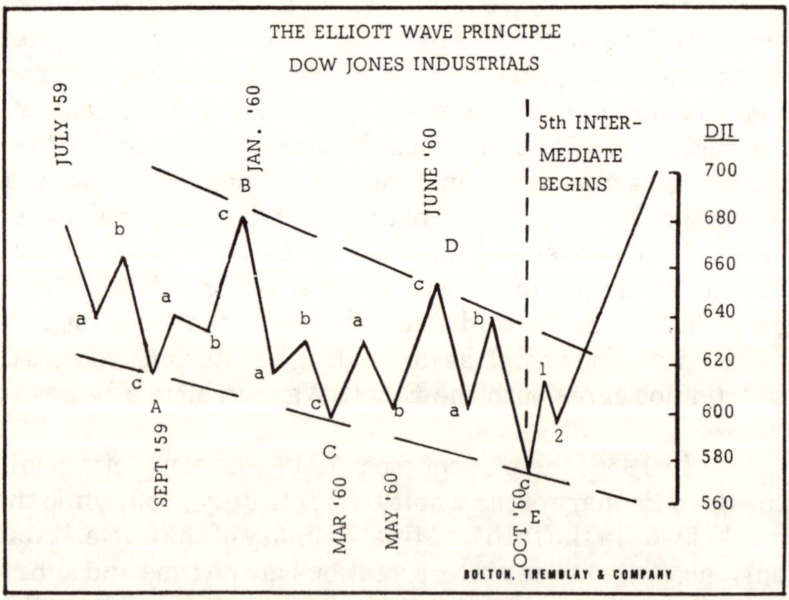

We reproduce above an updated chart of the one that appeared in our October issue of *The Bank Credit Analyst*. October 24th completed Intermediate 4 (in the form of a triangle which only appears as a 4th wave) and from this date began what now appears to be the real *third phase.*

One may legitimately ask why the 1958-59 market cannot be considered a real third phase. The answer is clear, that that market phase had few characteristics that were not simply a repeat of 1955-56. Market volume, which is a key factor, never rose to heights much greater than 1955. Four million share days were a rarity, and generally speaking, three million was the norm.

Now, however, we see the market from October 1960 emerging from the 1959-60 consolidation and building up volume on the rise to 6-7 million share days, i.e., almost twice the peak volume in 1955-56 and in 1958, just as a good third phase should. In addition, all the characteristics of forward momentum building up have also appeared, and leading averages, including Standard & Poor's and the Dow Jones Industrials, have recently moved on to new all time highs.

The next question that naturally comes to mind is, how far are we up the fifth Intermediate of the fifth Primary of the Cycle wave from 1949?

Based on the use of daily and hourly charts of the Dow Jones Industrials, it is clear that the first Minor wave of the fifth Intermediate was completed in November 1960 at 612, from which the second Minor took us back to 592 in late November. From this date appears to have begun the third Minor of the fifth Primary, and this wave is apparently still in force. This means, then, that we may be about half-way or perhaps a little more through the fifth Intermediate of the fifth Primary. It is our guess, then, that probably by mid-1962, this fifth Primary may well have been completed. At the earliest, we do not see much possibility of completing this fifth wave before the late fall of 1961, and it could expand out into 1963.

This, then, is the message: we are now well entrenched in the fifth wave, and this corresponds in fact to the

Dow Theorists' third phase. This should be a period of great activity and speculation, and may well be followed by an important market crash. There seems very little likelihood of this arriving, however, before the period mid-1962[2] to mid-1963.

FOOTNOTES

1 The text refers to Primary waves with Arabic numerals and Cycle waves with Roman numerals, but the chart depicts Primary waves with Roman numerals.

2 Once again, a near-perfect forecast of the 1962 drop.

3 In this and the next two paragraphs, although Bolton is working from a false conclusion (that Cycle wave I is ending), his outline of ensuing action is remarkably accurate.

4 The 1962 Supplement reprinted most of this section, which repetition we have omitted from the 1962 chapter. Bolton's only additional comment here was this one: "It should be noted that the view expressed in the paragraph above is *not* based on hindsight. The 1960 edition of *The Elliott Wave Principle*, published in the summer of 1960, had this to say: '...Since 1949, three orthodox Dow Theory bear market signals have been given: September 1953, February 1957 (reconfirmed in the fall of 1957), and recently in February 1960. These signals have been out of step with the Elliott Wave Principle. It will be extremely interesting to see how this battle of Goliath versus David will work out.' "

THE ELLIOTT WAVE PRINCIPLE OF STOCK MARKET BEHAVIOR

1962

A SUPPLEMENT TO

The Bolton-Tremblay

BANK CREDIT ANALYST

A. Hamilton Bolton, editor-in-chief

THE ELLIOTT WAVE PRINCIPLE OF STOCK MARKET BEHAVIOR 1962 SUPPLEMENT

INTRODUCTION

It has been the custom of our firm each year in the late spring to publish a supplement on the Elliott Wave Principle. This custom was started in 1953, and has been carried forward each year since. The object of the supplement has been to familiarize a growing public with the rather relatively unknown technical stock market tool of that name.

In June 1960, we decided to publish a book of over 100 pages devoted entirely to the Wave Principle. This book seemed necessary because of the paucity of information available from original sources. Its title, *The Elliott Wave Principle — A Critical Appraisal*, indicated the nature of the work. This book, which is still in print and available from our organization, is to our knowledge the only authentic critique of the Elliott Wave Principle in existence. Its contents and scope are listed on the outside back cover, and for anyone attempting to become familiar with Elliott, it is (if we do say so) a must to study this book.

The present supplement attempts to bring Elliott up to date in the second quarter of 1962. It follows up on the various thoughts that were expressed in the then current situation (May 1960) as well as in the 1961 Supplement (May 1961) as to what was likely to happen in the stock market.

In time, it also suggests projections of what may result as we move through in the fifth and last wave of the long bull market since 1949. It points out the possibility that 1962 and 1963 may prove to be critical and exciting years for the market, and it also presents what may be a dilemma, say, a year from now.

In order to provide some background to the broad principles of the Elliott Theory, extensive use is made in the supplement of short extracts from the 1960 book. It is hoped that these excerpts will enable the reader to follow at least the rudiments of Elliott theory.

Finally, a word of warning is necessary. The Elliott Wave Principle has had an excellent record in the postwar years. At no time has it been possible to proclaim the imminence of a major bear market. This position is now changing. In Elliott parlance, we appear to be well into the "fifth wave of the fifth wave." While the sky is currently apparently the limit, a day of atonement is probably due sometime in the not-too-distant future. When it arrives, nevertheless, we expect it will come from considerably higher levels.

April 27th, 1962

THE STATUS SINCE 1949

The progress of the bull market is illustrated by the next chart, which updates Figure 48 from the 1960 edition of *The Elliott Wave Principle*. On completion of this fifth Primary, this will also complete the *first Cycle* from 1949. A major correction will then be due.

Because this correction would be of the whole bull market from 1949, i.e., perhaps 13 years of time and 600 odd

BREAKDOWN OF DJIA FROM 1949

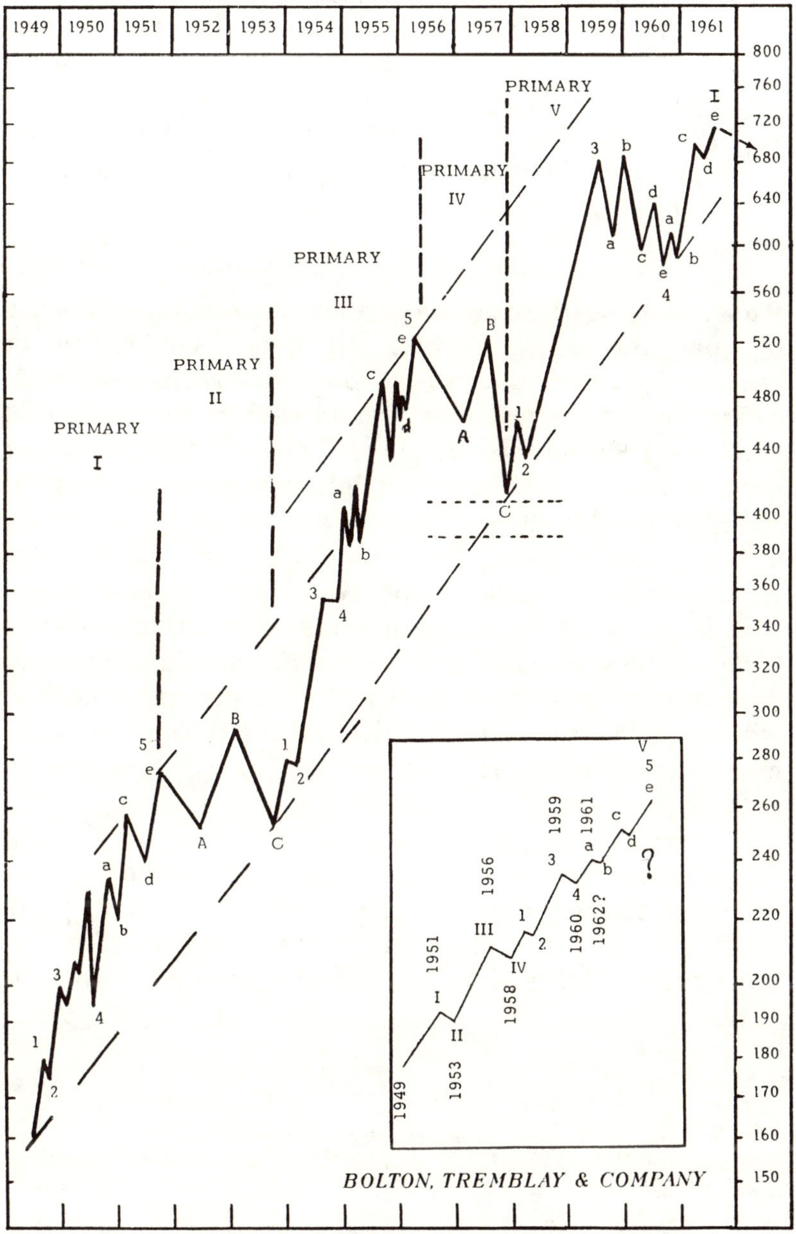

An update of Figure 48 from
The Elliott Wave Principle — A Critical Appraisal

points in the Dow Jones Industrials, one would expect a minimum retrenchment of one third of 200 Dow Jones Industrial points, and more likely a 40% retrenchment. In point of view of time, one could logically expect that the correction could stretch out to 5 years. This means not that one would have a 5-year continuous bear market, but that one could possibly have two major bear markets with a bull market in between.

As we mentioned in the 1960 edition of *The Elliott Wave Principle,* the possible permutations and combinations of what the general market might do from here on are becoming greater and greater. One thing seems reasonably clear: The long logarithmic trend line from the 1949, 1953, 1957 and 1960 bottoms should be decisively broken. Assuming that the Dow Jones Industrials eventually work up into the 800-1000 level, then a logical area to expect the bottom of the ensuing bear market would be about the 520 level, which was the top area in 1956-57. It should be kept in mind that while 520 does not seem too far in relation to current levels of the stock market, it will seem well-nigh calamitous in relation to a figure, say, of 900. The present generation will not have seen a market decline of anywhere near this magnitude. Thus there could be much "wailing and gnashing of teeth."

This, then, is the pattern that we see unfolding as indicated by the Elliott Wave Principle in the spring of 1962: further rises ahead followed by bear markets of greater amplitude and duration than we have seen in the postwar period.

THE FIFTH WAVE

We reproduce on the previous page an updated chart of the one that appeared in our October 1960 issue of *The Bank Credit Analyst*. October 24th completed Intermediate 4 (in the form of a triangle, which only appears as a fourth wave), and from this date began what now appears to be the real *third phase*. It appears still to have a long way to go.

THE ELLIOTT WAVE PRINCIPLE
DOW JONES INDUSTRIALS

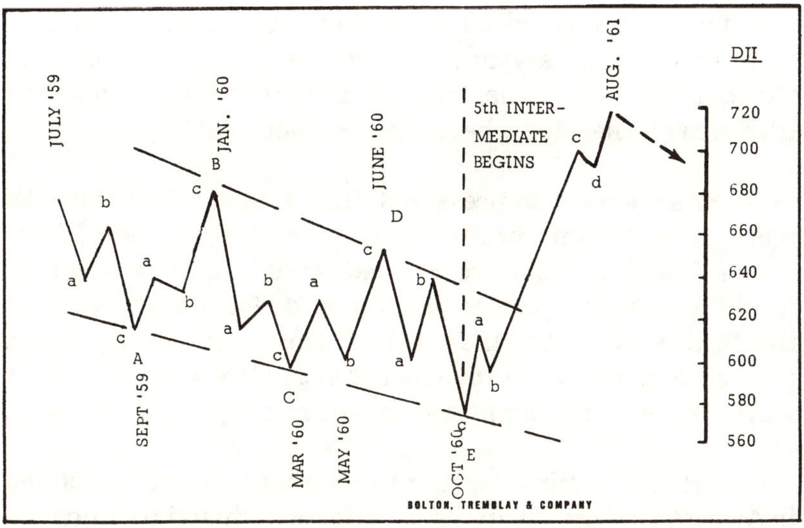

THE FIFTH WAVE OF THE FIFTH WAVE

The interpretation of Elliott that we like the best is that 1949 started a new series of Cycle waves. This Cycle from 1949 could be the first of a large Super Cycle, which began in June of that year. Some analysts of Elliott's theories prefer to date the start of the Super Cycle from 1932. Others prefer to take 1942 as a starting point, since this was Elliott's own interpretation prior to his death. These various differences have been covered in some detail in the 1960 edition of *The Elliott Wave Principle*. From a practical point of view, it makes very little difference at this stage. In Figure 47 of the book will be found a reconciliation of how the two major interpretations of starting points of the new Super Cycle (1932 and 1949) can very well mesh in later years.

As noted earlier in this supplement, we have consistently followed the view that October 24, 1960 was the beginning of the fifth wave. However, some clarification is necessary. This is the fifth wave of the fifth wave.

The fifth Primary of the first Cycle began in late 1957. It had completed three Intermediate waves up to July 1959. The fourth Intermediate was complete in the form of a triangle (some analysts have considered it a double 3) in October 1960. The final Intermediate (the fifth wave of the fifth wave), therefore, began in October 1960.

As we went to press last year with the 1961 Supplement, it was then our view that we had completed Minor waves 1 and 2 and were well advanced in wave 3, which would have meant 4 (a correction) and 5 to come to wind up the "fifth wave of the fifth wave." However, subsequent to publication, it became apparent that the five so-called Minor waves were being completed rather rapidly.

It is now our view that five waves up were completed in August 1961 at 726 in the Dow Jones Industrials, and that what has been happening since August 1961 is a correction of the advance from October 1960. (One analyst whose views we greatly respect feels that the five waves were completed in May 1961, and that what we have been seeing since is a correction. The differences in interpretation are not too important, especially as we both seem to agree on the basic unfolding of the final wave.)

The question that will naturally arise from the paragraph above is: Having completed five waves up from October 1960 in August (or, if you prefer, May 1961), does this terminate the "fifth wave of the fifth wave"? In our view, the answer is *no*.

To understand why, we must refer to the preceding chart entitled, "Breakdown of the DJIA from 1949," which is an update of the chart which appeared as Figure 48 in *The Elliott Wave Principle,* 1960 edition. Subscribers may find it interesting to compare the two, since what is involved is a two-year evolution of the market since this chart was published at that time.

It will be at once apparent from this chart that if August 1961 is the termination of the "fifth wave of the fifth wave," the whole pattern is one of a mouse, whereas what we are looking for is the pattern of a lion!

It reminds the author a bit of the 1946 situation. At that time, some analysts were trying to put the 1942-46 wave into the same degree pattern as 1932-37. However, in 1946 the market (at 212 Dow Jones Industrials) was barely higher than the 1937 top of 195. Obviously, what we were seeing then was a wave (1942-46) of a *different degree,* or size, to that of 1932-37. (Bear in mind that nobody had then evolved the idea of a 1928-49 triangle, as explained in Appendix B of *The Elliott Wave Principle.*) Similarly, the top in August 1961 at 726 is barely higher than the top of the third wave (of the fifth wave) in July 1959 (681).

The only conclusion that we can come to at this point is that the *five waves up to August 1961 completed the first Minor*[1] *of the fifth Intermediate* (which began in October 1960) *of the fifth Primary* (which began in late 1957) *of the Cycle* (which began in June 1949).

Since August 1961, we have had a sidewise consolidation of stock prices, all of which seems to fall into a pattern of 3's. The difficulty with all corrections is that it is impossible to know for sure how long they will go on. To quote from the 1960 edition of *The Elliott Wave Principle:*

> "...In conclusion, the complexities of *corrective waves* are quite profuse. Oh! for the simplicity of the basic *maintrend* 5-3-5-3-5 wave."

Each year as the Elliott patterns advance, we have to try to adjust our thinking to the facts as they develop. We make no apology for this. We have no crystal ball which will tell us exactly what is going to happen. However, a knowledge of the wave theory does produce a certain sense of fitness in interpretation within the framework of the broad principles which were laid down by Elliott in his two monographs, *The Wave Principle* (1938) and *Nature's Law* (1946), as well as in his various *Interpretative* and *Forecasting Letters*, which he issued in the period 1938-47.

Back to the current scene, what is in store? Taking the final Intermediate commencing October 24, 1960, it now looks as if we have completed the first Minor (August 1961) and possibly the second Minor (January-April 1962). The third of five Minors, therefore, should now be developing, or at most within the next two or three months. A logical expectation would be that the Dow Jones Industrials should not break the rising trend line (see next chart).

Minor wave 1 ran from 565 Dow Jones Industrials to 730 (August 1961) or alternatively 715 (May 1961), a total of 150-165 points.

Under Elliott's rule, the third wave should not be appreciably less than the first wave (see *The Elliott Wave Principle* for an attempt to clarify this obscurity). Thus, depending on where Minor wave 3 begins, one should expect that it would build up about 150-plus points. If so, and assuming 685 as the beginning point, the third wave should build up to well into the 800s in the Dow Jones.

But this would be *only wave three*. Obviously, if this count since the fall of 1960 is correct, it will take a great deal of time to complete the last Intermediate (1960 to date) of the last Primary (1957 to date) of the first Cycle (1949 to date). Our guess now is that five Minors from the fall of 1960 *cannot be completed in either 1962 or 1963*.

This is where, then, we begin to get a better perspective as compared to our analysis of last year (1961 Supplement). At that time, it looked as if the whole five waves up from October 1960 could have been completed by say late

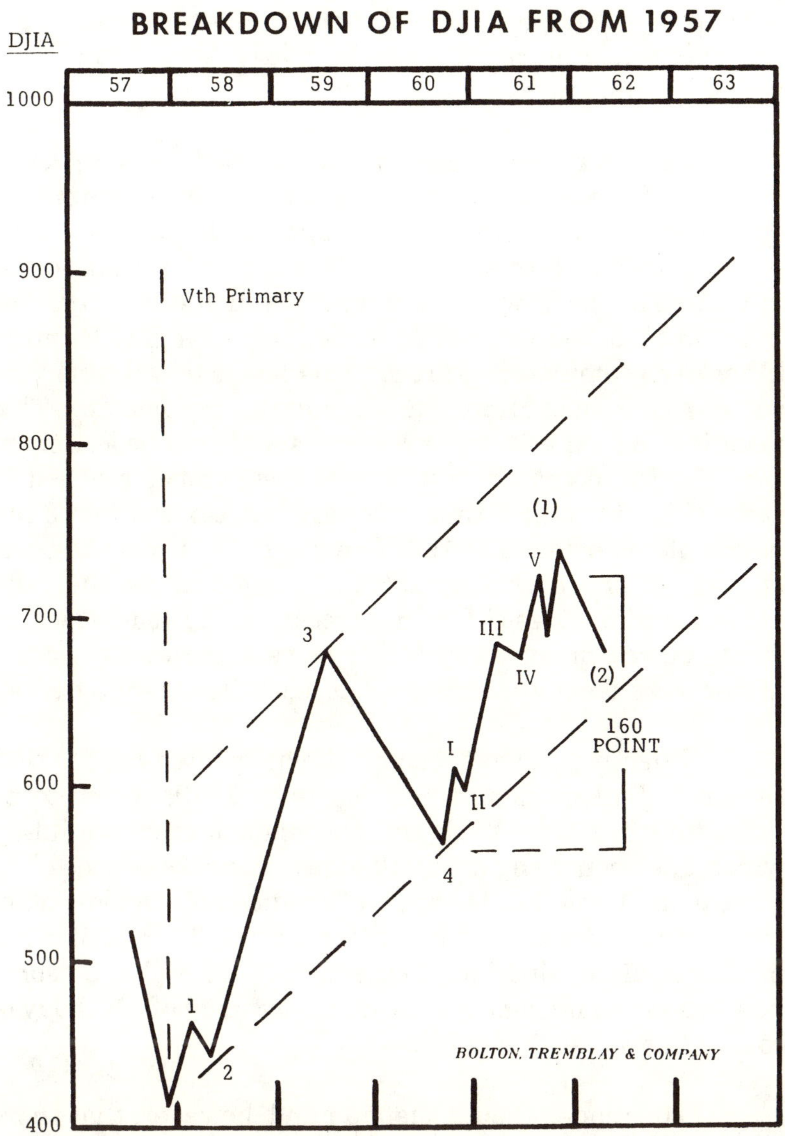

1962 or early 1963. Now it appears that the whole process of completing Intermediate 5 of Primary V of Cycle 1 is still well in the future.

(It is perhaps not out of line in this connection that the whole business cycle, which should perhaps have been completed by early 1962 as viewed from the turn-around in late

1960, is now being complained about and its termination put off indefinitely as current results (early April 1962) seem rather disappointing.)

The chart herewith provides some further perspective on the *fifth wave*. We start this chart with the beginning of Primary V. (For comparison, see updated Figure 48, on the previous chart). If this whole analysis is valid, the market as measured by the Dow Jones Industrials should not break the 1949-53-57 base line *until* Intermediate wave 5 of Primary V has been completed. Further, this seems to call for a very substantial rise in Minor wave 3 (now due to come up). This is indicated by the fact that Minor 3 should not be less than, say, 150-165 points from whatever low point is reached in early 1962. In point of time, it is hard to see how Minor 3 can be completed before late 1962 or early 1963. From the point of view of the economy, 1963 is suggested as the next recession in business. Given a recession in 1963-64, which would be accompanied by Minor wave 4, we would look to Minor wave 5 not appearing till at least the 1964-65 period.

Effectively, what seems to be happening here is that the great bull market, which began in 1949, seems to be extending in time. With the tremendous credit build-up which has been going on on all sides, this makes sense. At some point, Cycle 1 (1949 to date) should end in a blow-off of major dimensions. What will cause this? Will it be a multilateral devaluation of currencies? Or will it be some new era in the nuclear age as yet undreamed of? Nobody of course knows, at this point.

The reader should keep in mind, however, that there is not only one way that the Elliott Wave cycle can go, as many times waves expand or correct in accordance with local political and economic conditions. While we view the credit build-up as conducive to the projections suggested below, we would also bring your attention to Chapter XI of the 1960 *Elliott Wave Principle*, and in particular to the alternative charts shown in Figures 49, 50 and 51. While we feel that the basic pattern of Figure 49 is more likely, we cannot entirely throw out the possibility that Figure 51 could be correct.[2] The key at this point is whether the basic long-term trend line from 1949 will be decisively broken on the downside in 1962.[3]

April 27th, 1962

FOOTNOTES

1 Bolton's conclusion *is* warranted, given his larger view that the Supercycle began in 1949, although it causes him here to abandon his earlier conclusion that 1962 would contain a crash. His second best count is that the fifth Intermediate is over.

2 As indeed it is.

3 This, in effect, was Bolton's "stop" on his opinion, which was triggered a couple of weeks later at a comfortably high level. Though his opinion was a rare error, the requirements of the Wave Principle kept damage to a minimum.

THE ELLIOTT WAVE PRINCIPLE OF STOCK MARKET BEHAVIOR

ADDENDUM TO

THE 1962 SUPPLEMENT

The Bolton-Tremblay

BANK CREDIT ANALYST

A. Hamilton Bolton, editor-in-chief

THE ELLIOTT WAVE PRINCIPLE OF STOCK MARKET BEHAVIOR 1962 ADDENDUM

May 28th, 1962

Last month, as is usual at this time of year, we issued the annual 1962 Elliott Wave Principle Supplement. Events since, terminating in several market downside climaxes, suggest the desirability of an addendum to this supplement in order to trace the rather stunning developments made clear by market action since the first of May.

Subscribers should keep in mind the fact often reiterated that the Elliott Wave Principle is not a forecasting device. It can, however, be used to advantage by investors to keep them out of trouble. It can often prevent selling at the wrong time, for instance, and can forestall "following the crowd." It may be appropriate, therefore, to take up the story of the waves from the point that we left off in late April.

WHAT THE 1962 SUPPLEMENT SAID

Following the wave pattern from 1949, which is the last important bull market starting point of Cyclical (and probably Super Cyclical) dimensions, we have traced the Dow Jones Industrial Average to illustrate the principle throughout, through four or five waves in the upward direction. Thus,

Primary I: June 1949 to September 1951
(5 Intermediate waves) 160 to 275

Primary II: Sept. 1951 to Sept. 1953
(3 Intermediate waves down)
275 to 255

Note that the peak of the second wave, which terminated in January 1952, was higher than the terminus of Primary I, i.e., 295 vs. 275. This is known as an "unorthodox" top formation and is quite prevalent, having happened in 1929 and 1946, to name only two other important tops.

Primary III: Sept. 1953 to April 1956
(5 Intermediate waves up)
255 to 522

Primary IV: April 1956 to December 1957
(3 Intermediate waves down)
522 to 419

Primary V: December 1957 to date
419 to ?

This wave should be in five waves, of which we calculated four had been realized and we were now in the fifth and final wave. The breakdown of the fifth Primary was suggested as likely to be as follows:

Intermediate 1: Early 1958 - 420 to about 455
(see Figure 48 in the 1960 edition of the book, *The Elliott Wave Principle — A Critical Appraisal*)

Intermediate 2: 455 to 435

Intermediate 3: 435 to 685 in mid-July 1959

Intermediate 4: 685 to 565 in October 1960

Intermediate 5: 565 to date.

It can be seen that as the Cycle advanced, the waves tended to spread out so that by the time we got into the fifth Primary in December 1957, Intermediate waves were practically as big as Primary waves of the earlier part of the Cycle.

FIFTH WAVE OF THE FIFTH WAVE

The period from October 1960 (565) to date was also assumed to develop into 5 waves, as it has to under Elliott's rules. Further, because of the fact that the 5-wave pattern which terminated in August 1961 at approximately 725 was so little above the termination of Intermediate wave 3 in July 1959 at 685 approximately, it was assumed that this was only wave 1 of a total of 5 to be seen. By the very nature of these waves, it would therefore be highly unlikely that the final bull market top could be reached prior to the mid-1960s, allowing the necessary time factor. This was the *assumption* till recently.

This interpretation now seems unlikely and must be considered suspect for the following reasons:

(a) The correction of the 5 wave "Minor" from October 1960 to August 1961 at recent market levels has cut back 100% of the rise. This suggests that it is not a simple correction, but the first wave of a series of corrective waves.

(b) The long-term trend line on semi-log paper which is drawn through the 1949 and 1953 bottoms was decisively broken recently when the Dow Jones tumbled through the 640 level. This was pointed out in the 1962 Supplement as a possible key factor, although it is not pure Elliott.

Neither of these in and of themselves, nor together, in accordance with any Elliott rules, prove that the wave from October 1960 to August 1961 was necessarily the complete fifth wave of the fifth wave," but they do lend a suspicion that this may be so. The clincher, however, is (c) below, assuming of course, that our interpretation is correct at this point, which we will discuss in greater detail below.

(c) The correction of the 5 wave up (Oct. 1960 to Aug. 1961) is clearly a 3-wave affair, and is what is known as a *flat*, i.e., 3 down, 3 up, 5 down.

The first 3 down ran from August 1961 to January 1962; the second 3 up ran to mid-March 1962, and the final 5 down ran from March 15th to date. However, this final 5 wave pattern became *extended*, and one of Elliott's rules in this connection is known as *double retracement*. (See Chapter VI of the 1960 edition of *The Elliott Wave Principle*.) This rule is very important, as it tells us a great deal about the probable character of the market to come, and as such should be quite a test of the whole Elliott theory.

EXTENSIONS AND DOUBLE RETRACEMENT

Extensions on the downside are rare. Extensions only come in waves of 5 sub-waves, never in 3-type waves. The rule that Elliott formulated was that if a fifth wave (of any degree) gets extended, after completion of that extension the market will turn around and retrace one hundred percent (or more) of the extended wave,[1] and after that, at some point later will double retrace what it has previously single retraced. Let us look at this through stylized diagrams.

Note that Elliott said that double retracement was indicated only in the case where the fifth wave became extended, not the first or third wave of a 5-wave pattern. However, he did make clear that these retracements and double retracements would later fit into conventional over-

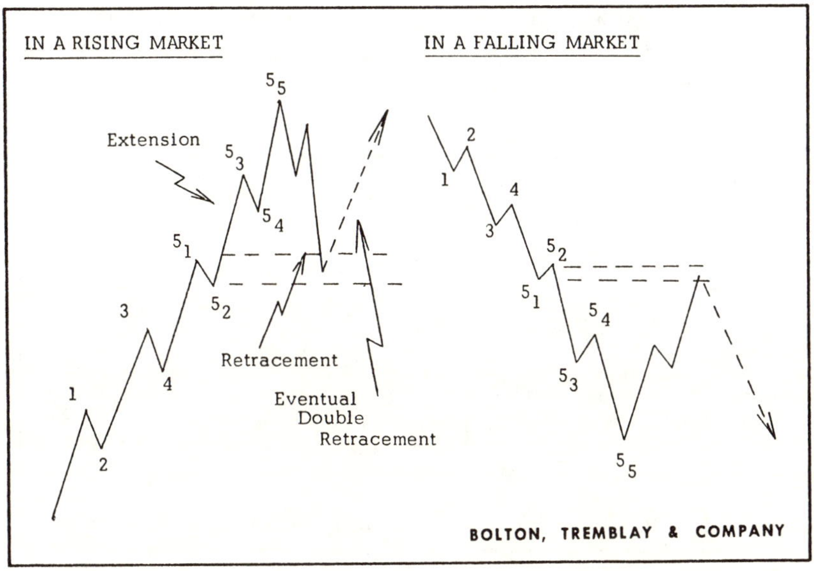

all patterns, i.e., it would not be a question of getting a couple of extra wave patterns which could conveniently be added as a sort of hiatus between two sets of waves, i.e., extra waves to be disregarded with the Elliott count starting anew after such hiatus. Conventional wave patterns would remain.

Let us now look at the current market.

NORMAL CORRECTION TILL APRIL

The October 1960 to August 1961 market can be conveniently analyzed as five waves up. Let us forget whether these five waves are Minor or Intermediate in character. Five up waves call for a 3-wave correction. Such correction normally will retrace one third to two thirds of the advance, but there is no Elliott law which says that the correction has to conform to any specific percentage pull-back. In the postwar period, however, due to the wartime inflation factor, corrections have been even less than one third, and never until 1962 as high as 50%.

The pattern of the correction from August 1961 is clearly one of a *flat* rather than a *zigzag*. A *flat* is a 3-3-5 affair; a *zigzag* is a 5-3-5 affair, as follows:

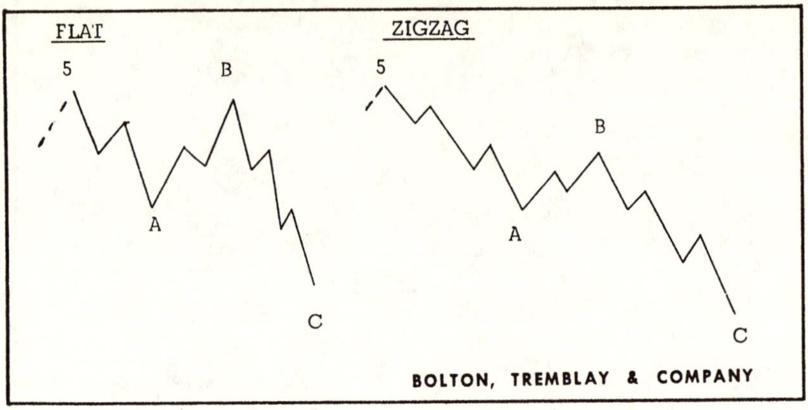

The pattern since mid-1961 cannot be broken down into a 5-3-5 or zigzag pattern.

Both *flats* and *zigzags* are a 3-wave correction in the form of A, B, C as indicated. In a flat, however, wave "B" tends to come back close to (a little under or a little above) the previous end of the fifth wave, whereas in a zigzag, wave "B" is usually considerably lower.

The analysis of the flat correction from August 1961 is shown in the next chart. As we went to press on the 1962 Supplement, the correction from August was proceeding in a completely normal manner, and in fact the third wave of the correction was developing as a normal 5 wave down, and under ordinary conditions should have terminated at 659 in the Industrials. In fact, it did not.

Whatever may be the reasons, the fifth wave of the final wave of the flat correction extended, and we have had so far four additional waves in a normal downside channel.

(Ed. Note: It is no part of Elliott theory to say that the most recent of these down waves has produced in some ways

A PERFECT DOWNWARD EXTENSION ?

HOURLY DOW-JONES IND.
March 15, 1962 Onward

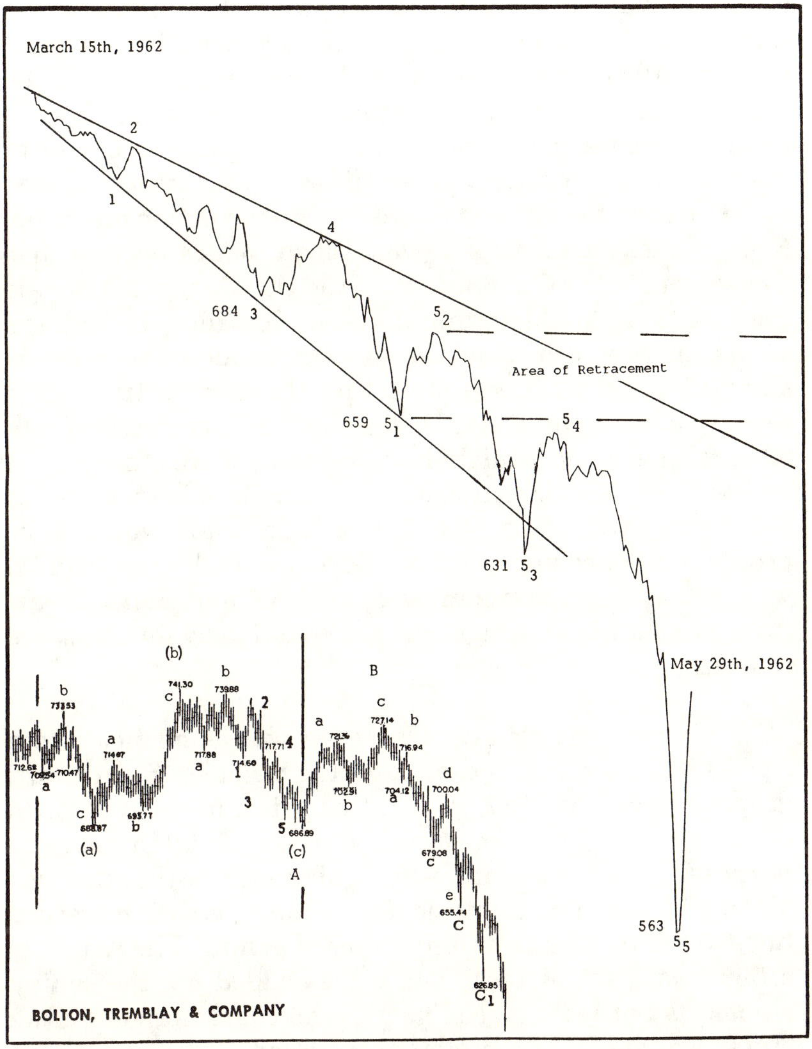

one of the most oversold market climaxes of recorded history. While this is of no moment in the Elliott context, it does lend weight to the proposition of probable *retracement* in the weeks or months ahead.)

Analysis of the hourly Dow Jones Industrials from

March 15th to date is also shown on the chart.

This chart indicates both the value and the limitation of Elliott Wave theory. It had been clear for many months that a correction of the rise from October 1960 to mid-summer 1961 was in store, and accordingly it could be assumed that this would take place in three waves. Everything, therefore, in the spring of 1962 was going according to plan. Various ways such as trend lines, resistance levels, etc., could be used to estimate how deep the correction might be. Most of these assessments would lead to a conviction that somewhere in the 650-680 level of the Dow Jones Industrials the reaction should terminate. For instance, in Elliott's terms, in view of the subnormal amplitude of corrections since 1949 (albeit it was clear that these corrections were tending as time went on to be deeper), a 38% correction (100-62, a Fibonacci ratio) might have been considered "par for the course." Such a correction of the 177 point advance (564 to 741 intra-day) in the Dow Jones Industrials would have produced a bench mark of 674. (Ed. note: Such a target (675) was actually proposed in late 1961 in our *Bank Credit Analyst* as a likely target, but not consciously for the same reasons.)

Such a target in general terms was being met in late April 1962 when the market, after the Kennedy-Steel affair, dropped to 659 on May 1st. At this point, five waves down could be counted from the mid-March top. To all intents and purposes, Elliott wave analysts would conclude that this was about "it." It could be noticed, for instance, how the Average hugged the trend line around exposed points. The Kennedy affair was "past history," the waves added up, the selling climax had at least a good part of the characteristics of an "Intermediate-type" completed correction, and it would have been normal and reasonable for the correction to stop here. In fact, it did not. "Why" will perhaps not be known except in retrospect.

Instead, a series of additional down waves were added after the completion of the orthodox 5-wave down from March 1962. In doing so, these "extended" the fifth wave of the 5-wave down from March 1962, and broke the long-term trend line which joined the 1949 and 1953 bottoms when approximately 640 was violated in recent days. And they thereby set up a condition which calls under Elliott's rules for a "double retracement."

Elliott formulated his "double retracement" theory in terms of bull moves rather than bear moves. It may rightly be questioned, therefore, whether he needed to formulate the "double" retracement. Why not simply "retracement," and let the future take care of itself? There is no answer to this except to say that he made a great point that there had to be (and was) in each case a retracement and then a double retracement back again. In fact, he mentioned a number of such cases, which we may note here.

EXTENSIONS IN PAST HISTORY

Elliott only notes two downward extensions in past history. The first was in the down leg of the September-November 1929 market, which was retraced in the spring of 1930 and double retraced thereafter. The second was in the fall of 1937, near the bottom in October, which was double retraced immediately. In each of these two cases, the market later went to new lows, but not necessarily immediately.

Elliott stated that he had not discovered any rules which would tell him when an extension would take place.

WHAT OF NOW?

Let us return to the present. We had five waves up from October 1960 to August 1961. As we analyzed this in the 1962 Supplement, this was probably the first of five waves of the "fifth wave of the fifth wave." It also conceivably could be the whole of the "fifth wave of the fifth wave." This would be rather an unusual interpretation, particularly as such a fifth wave of all the rise from 1949 came nowhere near touching the upper parallel of the channel of stock prices from 1949 to date. But because of the extensiveness of the 3-wave correction from August 1961, which has now retraced all the rise since October 1960, and the fact that the third wave of this correction has apparently extended, thus calling for a double retracement, which will undoubtedly take much time and produce considerable amplitude (probably 100 odd points up, say, and another 100 points down just as rough guide lines), it does seem rather unlikely that we can have the wave from October 1960 to August 1961 simply as the first of 5 with four more to come at this stage of the investment cycle. Logic suggests that this is too large a correction to be simply a wave 2 type setback.

GREAT BEAR MARKET AHEAD?

It seems to us that the main message of the breakthrough of the 1949-53 trend line is not that a great bear market lies immediately ahead. On the contrary, the present level of the market suggests that we will have a very large pullback which will probably take the market over the next few months to back up close to a duplication more or less of the old highs, followed possibly later by even higher highs. Let us look at the overall perspective. There would appear to be only three possible long-term interpretations. The first says the new Super Cycle began in 1932, the second (Elliott's before he died) in 1942 the third (ours) in 1949.

Interpretation (A) had a deep wave II (1937 to 1942, a 50% decline), and consequently could expect a deep wave IV. But at this juncture, wave IV is nowhere near in sight. The subdivisions of wave III have been all subnormal, hence such should be the expectation for the fourth wave thereof, which we now take as starting in 1961.

Interpretation (B), which we have ruled out on technical grounds alone, but which continues nevertheless to

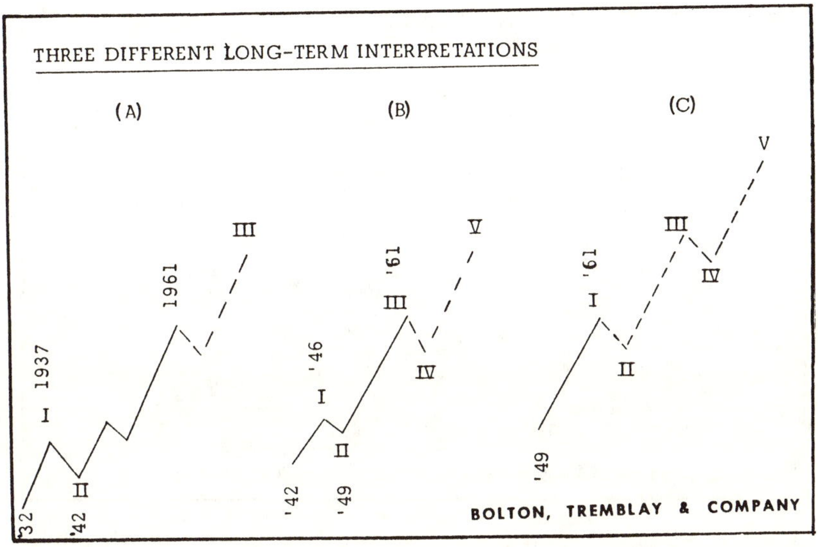

THREE DIFFERENT LONG-TERM INTERPRETATIONS

rear its ugly head, has a smaller wave II, as befits the inflationary environment of World War II to date, running an approximate 25% correction from 1946 to 1949. Wave IV also should be shallow since the whole Cycle from 1942 was a *thrust* out of a triangle. See Appendix "B" of the 1960 edition of *The Elliott Wave Principle*, published by our firm.

We have to face facts and not dwell in idle dream land. When the fifth wave of the part of the correction which began in March 1962 extended, it suggested an important message. This was that we should now be in for an extended "trading market" bounded probably by about 575 or lower on the downside and 740 or higher on the upside, the first part of which is the wave from August 1961, which is currently being completed.

Nobody, of course, at this point knows the future. However, if we have now begun a correction of the whole advance from 1949, it may last for several years, and in all probability will be an *irregular* correction. It will have to be in the form of three waves, but because of the slant in the form of three waves from 1961 to mid-1962, it inevitably must take the form of a *flat*, not a *zigzag*. Because of the way

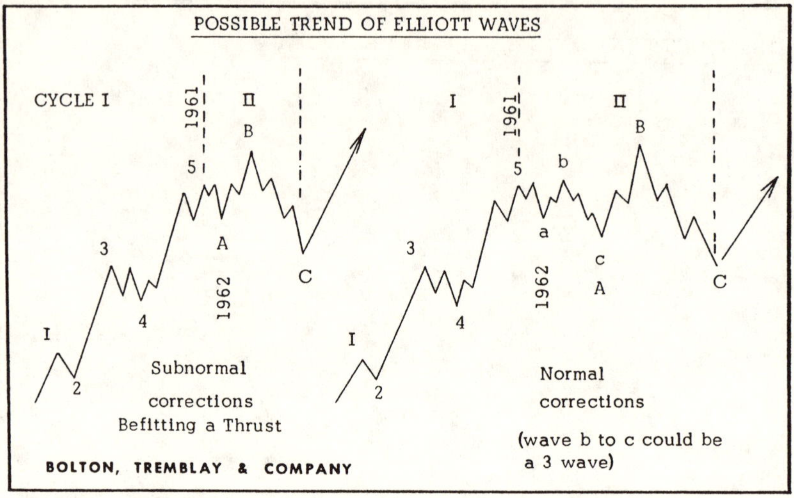

that all through the 1950s, corrective waves have tended to retrace their first downward legs in the second wave, and in most cases go on to new highs, we can still expect new highs in the averages before the final bear market begins. To give some idea of what to expect, let us put down in chart form two possible combinations. These are not the only possible combinations, however.

Interpretation (C) is also a *thrust*, with its base in 1949, in distinction to 1942, also being the aftermath of a (21-year) triangle. It has been truly a series of sharp upward waves followed by subnormal corrections, and fits entirely into the concept of a thrust. Wave II should be no exception. The probable pattern suggested by the completion of Cycle I from 1949 is one of a shallow Cycle wave II, which might, at most, probably retrace 40% of the rise from 160 in the Average in 1949 to any future top, and which might actually be limited to as low as a 25% setback.

CONCLUSIONS

(1) It is possible now that the *orthodox top* of the 1949 stock market to date occurred in 1961.

Factors in favor are:

(a) Breaking of trend line
(b) Two thirds correction of last wave
(c) Downward extension and implications of double retracement.

Against:

(d) Mouse-like character of fifth wave, 1960-61
(e) Doesn't fit into a Fibonacci time period, i.e., 12 years instead of 13, say. (But neither did the 1921-28 market, which took 7 instead of 8 years.)

(2) The first wave of the correction is now about over. In view of the type of waves (a *flat* rather than a *zigzag*), it would be folly to sell the market at this point, since the second part of the *flat* correction is bound to bring the market back much closer to the old 1961 highs.

(3) We could be entering a series of broad and swift trading areas in which the amplitudes of rises and declines will be much greater than in the whole period since 1949.[2] This calls for different techniques in investments, and places perhaps a premium on investment timing. It will also be a strong test of individual and professional investment management.

(4) Purchases made at the present time should work out extremely satisfactorily.

FOOTNOTES

[1] This rule was more accurately stated in *The Elliott Wave Principle — A Critical Appraisal.*

[2] This sentence well describes the next twenty years.

THE ELLIOTT WAVE PRINCIPLE OF STOCK MARKET BEHAVIOR

1963

A SUPPLEMENT TO

The Bolton-Tremblay

BANK CREDIT ANALYST

A. Hamilton Bolton

THE ELLIOTT WAVE PRINCIPLE OF STOCK MARKET BEHAVIOR 1963 SUPPLEMENT

INTRODUCTION

Since 1952, Bolton, Tremblay & Company have been interpreting Elliott's Wave Principle in the light of hindsight. It has been an invigorating experience. In 1960, the editor arranged to have published *The Elliott Wave Principle — A Critical Appraisal*. This book is still available from the publishers. Therein will be found the basic principles upon which Elliott built his theory. In the book and in the annual supplements, no attempt has been made to "improve" upon Elliott. It was pointed out, however, that as we moved further and further away from the last terminal date, i.e., mid-June 1949, the Principle by force of circumstances would be faced inevitably with more and more rival interpretations. It was for this reason that we have written continually that any interpretation of Elliott which attempts at this point to make a forecast must from now on be considered relatively tentative. We need only to remind ourselves of what happened in 1962 to show that even the so-called expert can be off-base. We quote the last paragraph of last year's "Introduction":

> "...Finally, a word of warning is necessary. The Elliott Wave Principle has had an excellent record in the postwar years. At no time has it been possible to proclaim the imminence of a major bear market. This

> position is now changing. In Elliott parlance, we appear to be well into the "fifth wave of the fifth wave." While the sky is currently apparently the limit, a day of atonement is probably due sometime in the not-too-distant future. When it arrives, nevertheless, we expect it will come from considerably higher levels."

If we had left out the last sentence, our record would have been considerably better so far as forecasting by Elliott was concerned. However, we have repeatedly deplored any attempt to make a precise and perfect forecast using Elliott's principles. The general trend can often be determined with considerable accuracy, but the details often escape except in retrospect. For instance, in the 1962 Supplement it was clearly indicated that we were in the fifth Primary from 1949, which started in late 1957, and further that we were in the fifth Intermediate of the fifth Primary, which latter started in the fall of 1960. Given no other background information, it does seem clear now in retrospect that we should have interpreted the fifth Intermediate of the fifth Primary and, therefore, the whole Cycle wave from 1949, as completed in August 1961. Instead, we suggested in the diagrams that the fifth Intermediate was only completing its first of five waves. By so doing, we proved the "caveat" which has run through all our annual Supplements and the 1960 *Critical Appraisal*, which is that it does not pay to be too sure about anything.

The key factor proved to be as mentioned in the last sentence of last year's analysis: "The key at this point is whether the basic long-term trend line from 1949 will be decisively broken on the downside in 1962."

In other words, had this trend line not been broken decisively in 1962 (a decisive penetration meant going down to about 640 or lower, as measured by the Dow Jones Industrials), there is reason to believe that the ultimate course would have been to continue another four waves in

Intermediate 5 of Primary V of the Cycle commencing in mid-1949. Unfortunately, this was not to be, and the sad but true facts are now apparent in retrospect that the great orthodox bull market of Cycle dimensions plodded to its finish in the summer of 1961, and thus technically we are in a bear market of Cycle dimensions from that date on and will probably continue in such an Elliott type bear market for a number of years to come.

Does this mean immediate (1963) new lows in the averages and in stock prices generally? If we relied solely on Elliott's Wave Principle, there would be no way of knowing. In fact, however, there are technically so many alternatives, having decided that August 1961 was the Orthodox Top of the 1949-61 Cycle wave, that each student will have to puzzle it out for himself. Some of these alternatives, as we shall find, can pretty well be eliminated on the basis of what has happened since June 1962, but others, strictly according to Elliott, without recourse to other studies such as money and credit, must be admitted as possibilities. This Supplement to Elliott, then, will point out: (a) various possibilities assuming that our interpretation that August 1961 was the true orthodox bull market top is correct; (b) one other possibility which may mean that the Cycle from 1949 is not yet technically completed, and (c) some other thoughts on the whole wave theories of the Elliott school.

A. Hamilton Bolton
May 1963

THE ELLIOTT WAVE THEORY

It is some three years now since *The Elliott Wave Principle — A Critical Appraisal* was published. It may be appropriate, therefore, to set out Elliott's basic thinking in some detail. Elliott actually wrote very little about the Wave Principle that is still extant. Two monographs, one in 1939 and one in 1946, a series of articles in *The Financial World* in the summer of 1939, and certain Interpretive and Forecasting Letters to, we would judge, a small band of subscribers, are all that remain. Only part of this literature is actually in the hands of the editor, and what is missing are *The Financial World* articles, which certainly could be found from the files of that publishing company, and certain Forecasting Letters in the period 1940 to 1945.

Elliott thought he had developed a very simple forecasting principle. Two things led him to that conclusion. First, only from 1928 was there available a "high-low close" type of market record and, secondly, the pattern from 1929 through 1938, when he was writing his first monograph, was relatively non-complex in wave pattern development.

For past history, Elliott depended on two basic indices: (1) the Dow Jones Industrial Average back to 1897, and (2) the Axe-Houghton Industrial Stock Price Average back to 1854. This latter was certainly a hodge-podge, yet who is to say that it is less representative than the later Cowles Commission Index of Stock Prices from 1871 built upon the Standard & Poor's formula (inherent in S&P's Industrial Index from 1926 to date), to which the Cowles Index has been linked?

At some future date, we hope to do a detailed comparison of these two indices: the Axe-Houghton from 1854 to date and the Cowles Commission 1871 to date. The latter has been carried back even further to 1831 by the Cleveland Trust Company by obtaining records of rails, banks and canal stocks. Further, it is not generally known that the Dow

Jones Industrials themselves, which go back only to 1897, have been worked back to the 1870s by the Federal Reserve Bank of New York.

From these varied sources of stock prices, it is clear that it should not be too difficult to find almost any starting point for a wave theory. Elliott used what was available to him — the Axe-Houghton Index — and started his wave from its lowest point: that of the famous depression of 1857. (It is rather interesting that the later Cowles Commission, Cleveland Trust series did not reach its lowest ebb until the depression of the '70s, and in particular the year 1877.)

We point out these anomalies in order to make our readers cognizant of the fact that we are not really dealing, in connection with the Elliott Wave Principle, with a science, but simply a *tendency*. It is so easy to overlook a detailed study of the past and spend spurious hours studying the intricate movements of the present as if everything were up to now, or at least the recent past, absolutely accounted for. Let us keep in mind, therefore, that we *are* dealing only with a *tendency* and not an incontrovertible scientific fact.

It is our opinion that the Elliott Wave Principle cannot be proven with the data at Elliott's disposal, but that it has so many interesting features to it that a pattern of stock market behavior can be delineated. Since 1953, for instance, we have been publicly interpreting Elliott's wave theories in a series of annual bulletins. Our intention has been to continue Elliott's thinking, not to develop a new theory. The facts are that as we re-read these interpretations (despite their faults), we realize that Elliott's principles, and vision perhaps, have been fundamentally correct (from complete unconcern about market levels in 1953-54 with the Dow Jones Industrials flirting with the 250-300 level to increasing distrust but no desire yet to throw in the sponge as we progress through the 700 level in the same average). Appendix "A" carries extracts from our annual reviews since the initial commentary in February 1953, with some appropriate footnotes based on retrospect.[1]

BASIC WAVE SEQUENCES

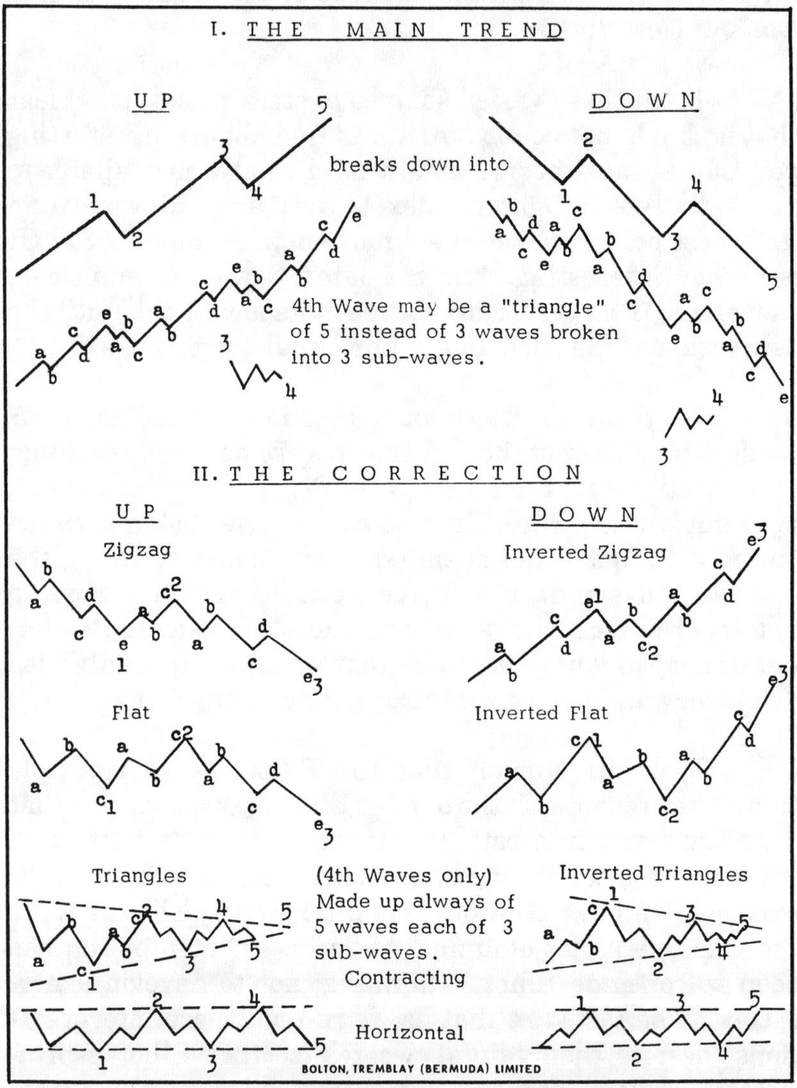

This chart is taken from the 1960 edition of *The Elliott Wave Principle — A Critical Appraisal.*

Elliott's basic theory is fairly simple. Bull markets develop into 5-wave patterns: three waves in the direction of the main trend (i.e., upward) interspersed with two corrective patterns. This type of pattern is shown in the chart herewith of "Basic Wave Sequences." Each 5-wave upward pattern is then "corrected" by a 3-wave sequence. From this 3-wave sequence, another 5-wave upward pattern develops.

When one breaks down the 5-wave pattern of an Elliott bull market, one finds that the upward waves (1, 3 and 5) subdivide into five smaller waves each, whereas the two waves in between (2 and 4) subdivide usually into three smaller subdivisions.

While the major waves in the direction of the trend (i.e., waves 1, 3 and 5) are simple in that they subdivide into 5's of a lower order or degree, all sorts of complications and complexities arise in the so-called corrective waves. These can become any of the following (and probably many more besides):

Zigzags	three's subdivided into 5-3-5;
Flats	three's subdivided into 3-3-5;
Double threes	three's subdivided into 3-3-3-3-3-3-3;
Triangle	five's subdivided into 3-3-3-3-3.

Corrections in bear markets, i.e., rallies in basic Elliott bear markets, are inverted forms of the above: inverted zigzags, inverted flats, inverted double or triple threes and inverted triangles.

There is no doubt that corrective waves are by far the most difficult to interpret. They seem to adjust themselves to economic and political events. For instance, a glance at Figures 1 and 2 herewith indicate the difficulty of interpretation.

Figure 1 depicts a simple and relatively normal correction of a 5-wave bull market. At point "0", however, in Figure 1, one can assume (correctly or incorrectly) that the bear market is over. But under Elliott's rules, there is absolutely no way of knowing for sure, although there may be one or two clues.

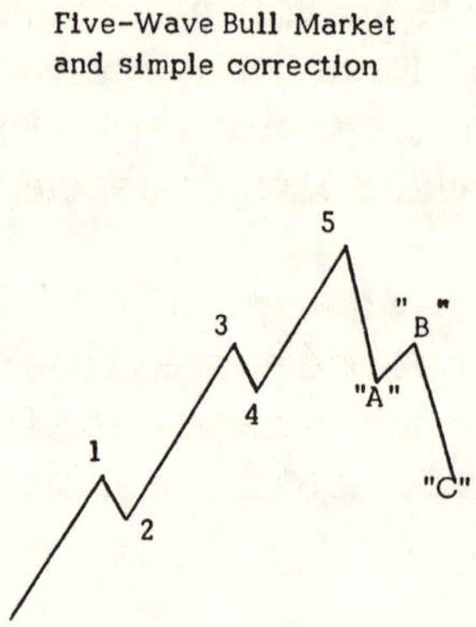

Figure 1

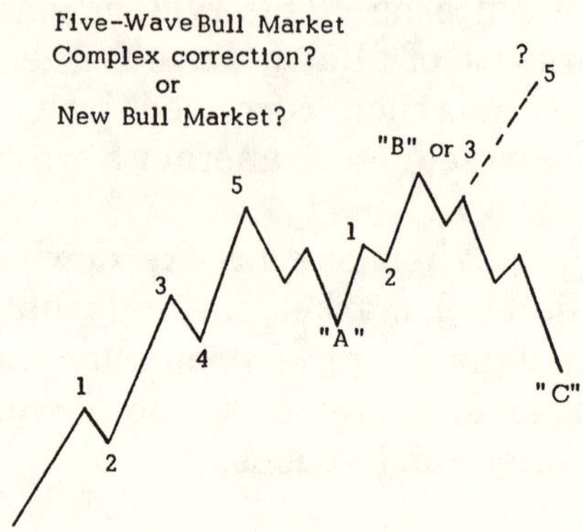

Figure 2

Assume we have arrived at wave "C" in Figure 1. This will be indicated usually by a 5-wave down from "B" to "C." (If the wave from "B" to "C" cannot be counted a 5-wave down, it is extremely suspect as the end of the bear market.) Now, what happens here is most important. If a clear-cut 5-wave up develops, it is probably the indication of a new bull market. But everything must be in reasonable perspective. A 5-wave up if only 10 points magnitude cannot be considered in the same league as a "BC" wave (Figure 1) of 100 points. Such a 5-wave up would only be a subwave, and therefore, of doubtful interpretive value. But three of such five waves up in a 5-3-5-3-5 sequence from "A" to "B", say, as in Figure 2, would be enough to indicate the probability of a major bull market developing.

Now, an Elliott bull market is one thing, and a traditional bull market is (or may be) something else again. In Figure 2, the "A" to "B" is part of an Elliott bear market, "A"-"B"-"C", but in ordinary terms it is probably a major bull market. The problem does not particularly rise until "B" (in Figure 2) is being reached. At this point, there is no clear Elliott answer. Is the whole wave from "A" (Figure 2) going to complete itself at "B" in an inverted 3, or, is "A" to "B" just three waves of a new bull market from "A" which will end in a 5 up rather than a 3?

Again, Elliott has no answer to this conundrum.[2] For example, a further alternative is given herewith in Figure 3.

Point 5 (5) in Figure 3 represents the end of a long bull market (let us say similar to 1949-61) in which 5 is the end of the last of five waves and (5) is the end of the whole series. If we were only dealing with a correction of waves 1, 2, 3, 4, 5, then at point C (A), we would expect that the bear market was over. But point C (A) only takes, say, a year versus a bull market of, say, 12 years. Common sense says that no bull market of 12-year duration is going to be corrected in one year. It just does not happen that way.[3] The correction is likely to take several years, not one. Now, supposing the pattern develops as in Figure 3. From C (A), a five wave up takes place to "a" (1), but a 3-wave correction to (2) and then another 5-wave up to "c" (3). At this point, as in Figure 2, a major bear market can develop in five waves down to new lows below point C in Figure 3. But it may not, and there is little in orthodox Elliott that will tell us whether it is going to or not. Instead of "B" developing in 5 waves down to "C," as in Figure 2, terminal "c" (3) A in Figure 3 can develop upward after the corrective wave B "d" (4) - Figure 3 - to (B) C "e" 5![4]

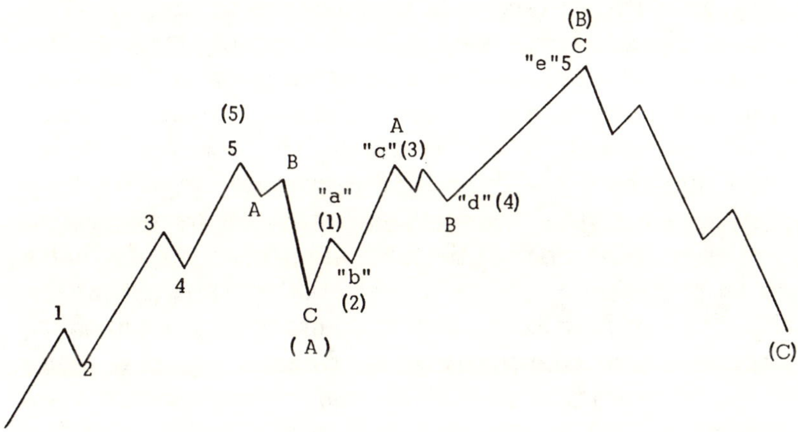

Figure 3

If anyone thinks that Elliott is the "be-all-end-all" of stock market forecasting, let him now recant!

Let us now look again at Figure 3. The point 5 (5) is established as the end of a long bull market. (In modern parlance we place 5 (5) as August 1961, in relation to the long bull market of 1949-61). Assuming corrective phase from 5 (5) to C (A), which we place as June 26th, 1962, what goes on since this time? At this point, by reference to Elliott, *nobody knows*. Let us assume for the sake of argument that the pattern (A) to (B) is going to develop (Figure 3). (We need not point out that if pattern "A" to "B" of Figure 2 is what is going to happen, then it is clear that we need to be actively selling this market at this time, but unfortunately Elliott gives us no major clues, except in retrospect.) Pattern (A) to (B) in Figure 3 can be judged as a 3-wave pattern (inverted correction) A to B to C, *or* it can be considered a 5-wave pattern (1) to (2) to (3) to (4) to (5).[5] The only rule which distinguishes a 3-wave from a 5-wave in such a context is that in a 5-wave pattern, wave (4) must not go lower than the top of wave (1). But this does not prove it is necessarily a 5-wave, but only that if the (4) wave drops below the top of wave (1), it is not a 5-wave.

This little exercise is perhaps one of futility. Why bother? The answer is, why indeed? Our only purpose here is to highlight the flexibility of interpretation at almost any point, but particularly in the consideration of corrective waves. In the next section, we develop the *orthodox* interpretation that the Cycle from 1949 terminated in 1961, to be followed by a several-year correction in three parts, the first of which terminated in June 1962 and the second of which is now in progress. Our own thinking at present is that this second phase of the Elliott bear market is still probably fairly young, and that eventually point (B) as in Figure 3 should put the market into new high ground (by more than a nose), as registered by our leading stock market averages. Is (A) to (B) in Figure 3 a 3 or a 5? If we accept the orthodox interpretation, it should be a 3. But what if we accept the alternative interpretation of one of Elliott's original collaborators,[6] that the whole period from the 1956 top to the 1962 bottom is an irregular and highly inflationary corrective wave? In this case, we might well conclude that the new bull market, which this commentator agrees started at the end of June 1962, should run its course in five rather than three waves. If the pattern developing should follow that of Figure 3, it is clear that Mr. X's interpretation of five waves up, and that of Figure 3, will find themselves completely in agreement.

To attempt to describe the basis of the Elliott Wave theory in a few lines is, of course, ridiculous. Anyone who has ever worked at it will realize how tentative it is. Our own opinion, as we said, is that it is a *tendency* rather than a principle.[7]

We would suggest to our readers a review of Chapter XII of *The Elliott Wave Principle — A Critical Appraisal.* This was written in the spring of 1960 and has not, therefore, the benefit of three years of further hindsight. But the pattern suggested therein seems reasonably accurate. It tends, we believe, to vindicate Elliott so far as his broad principles are concerned. The top suggested in late 1960, or early 1961, seems to have been completed in the summer of 1961. The 15% correction anticipated became much more than that, of course, amounting to over 25%. The presumption was made in the penultimate paragraph that because of the theory of *thrust* since 1949, to quote, "the 522 mark in the DJIA would be about as low as one could expect the market to go."

As a *tentative* type of forecast, this, as usual, proved to be somewhat off the mark,[8] but by not too far a margin considering the imponderability of the future 1960-style. So much has happened since that time. Khrushchev attended, in September 1960, the United Nations and pounded the desk with his shoe in a fit of rage. (There seems little doubt that he planned to put a man in space at this time but that it failed, the first such event happening only in April 1961.) The bull market commencing in late October 1960 became truncated in the over-the-counter frenzy of the spring of 1961. The steel impasse of April 1962 provided a background for the psychological bear market of April-May-June 1962. The Dow Jones Industrials on an intraday basis did reach a low of 524, "about as low as one could reasonably expect the market to go." Objectively, this 524 mark in the Dow Jones Industrials looks like a barrier that will not, within the next few years, and perhaps ever, be surpassed on the downside.[9]

THE 1962 BEAR MARKET AND BEYOND

According to our interpretation of Elliott's Wave Principle, the postwar bull market, commencing in 1949 of Cycle dimensions and beginning a Super Cycle of five such Cycles, the first Cycle came to an orthodox top in August 1961. The Cycle was 12 years in length and close to 144 months (a Fibonacci number of the mathematical summation series).

According to this interpretation, we are now in the second Cycle of this Super Cycle of five waves and will probably remain so for several years. This corrective Cycle should take the form of three Primary waves, starting from the August 1961 top, and it is our estimate that the *first* of these waves of Primary significance was completed at the end of June 1962, in the form of 3 waves down.

The breakdown of the five Primaries of the postwar Cycle bull market 1949-61 is given in the next chart, showing the breakdown of Primaries and Intermediates (the next lower degree below Primaries) since 1949.

BREAKDOWN OF DJIA FROM 1949

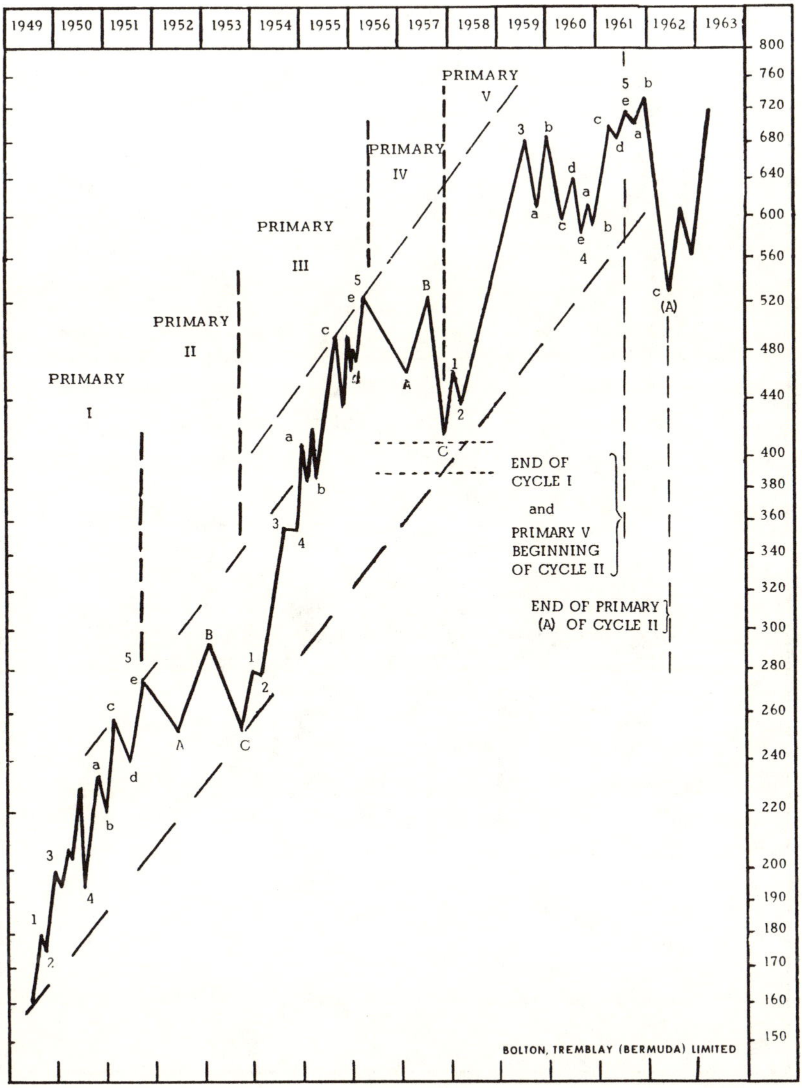

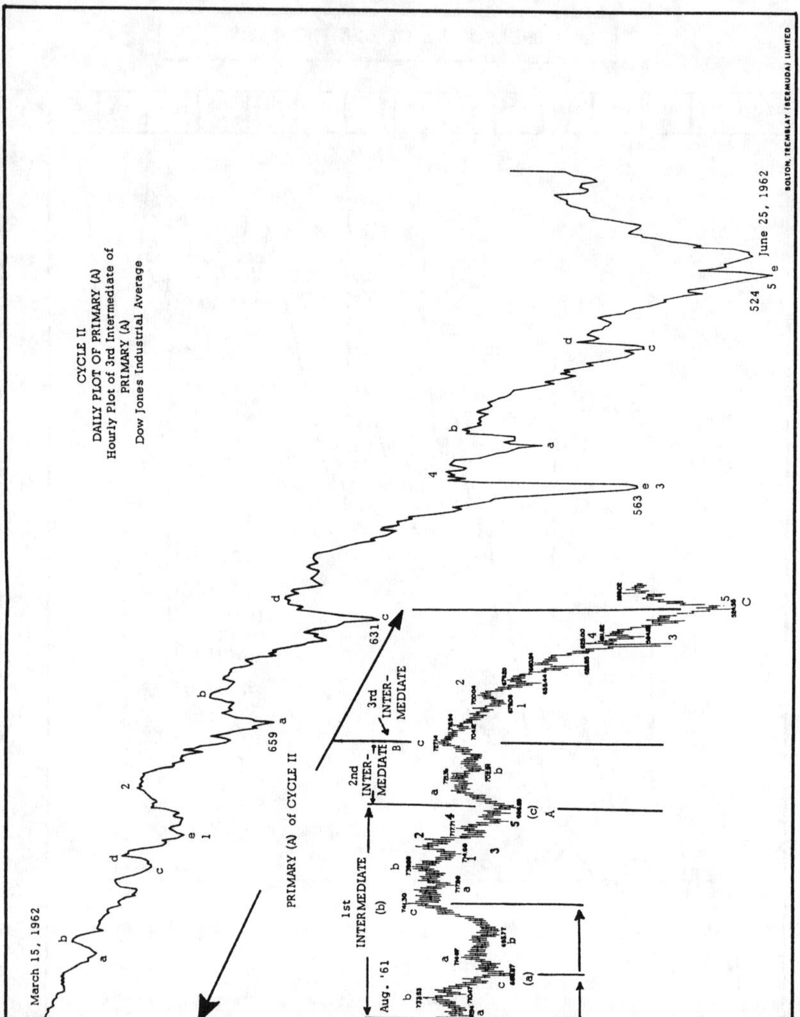

PRIMARY (A) OF CYCLE II

According to our count, Primary (A) of Cycle II was completed in all respects in late June 1962. This took the form of three waves (rather than five) of Intermediate degree, to be labelled A, B and C. This type of correction is known as a flat, and takes the form of Figure 4 herewith.

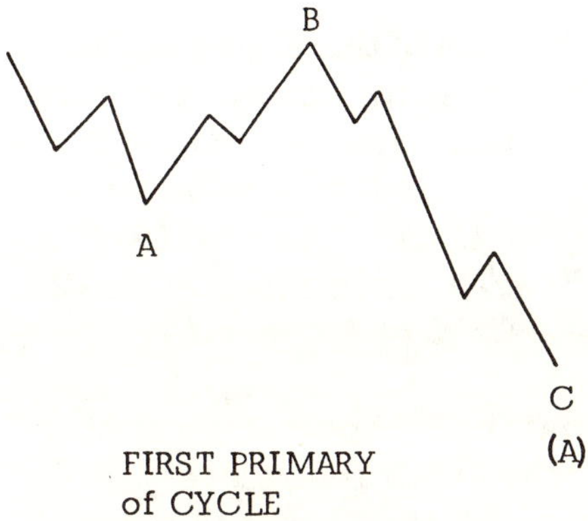

Figure 4

The daily plot of the three Intermediates making up Primary (A) is given for the Dow Jones Industrials in the chart on the preceding page. It will be noted that the first Intermediate is a 3-subwave pattern in the form on the chart of (a), (b) and (c). This sets the key to the type of wave Primary (A) will be. Had the first Intermediate been a 5-wave down instead of a 3, it would have indicated a probable 5-wave Primary (A) rather than a 3. And this would have implied a Cycle II in the form of a downward zigzag as indicated in Figure 5 herewith, made up of Primaries (A), (B) and (C).

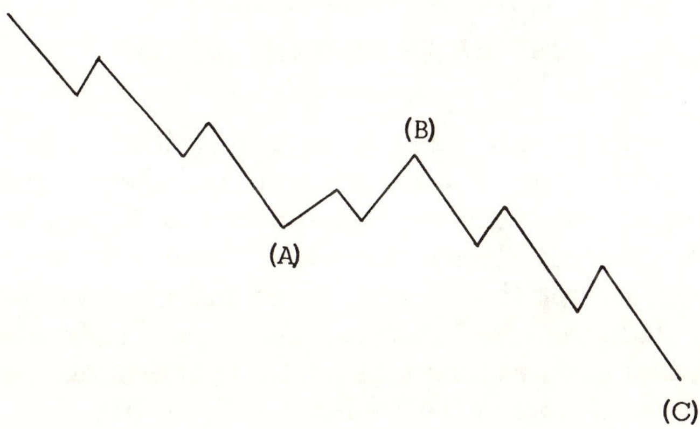

Figure 5

In fast moving markets, Elliott used to recommend plotting hourly averages, and this has been done for the third Intermediate of Primary (A) of Cycle II in the same chart as the daily averages of the whole Primary.

The implications of a three-wave (3-3-5) Primary down are that the formation will probably take the shape of a "flat" in the next higher degree (Cycle) and certainly not a "zigzag."

Primary (A) being in the form of three Intermediates calls for Primary (B) also to be in three Intermediates. *It also calls for a return to at least not much below the old high (733) of August 1961, and at most Primary (B) may be very much higher than the orthodox top of Cycle I (August 1961) as happened, for instance, in 1929.* (See, for example, Figure 26, *The Elliott Wave Principle — A Critical Appraisal.*)

It is clear, therefore, that the first part of the implications has currently been matched with the recovery of the market to over 720 from its low of 524 and that therefore it could be that Primary (B) is now coming to a close. It could also be that what may look like the completion of Primary (B) in three waves from June 1962 may well be only the completion of *Intermediate A of Primary (B)* (see Figure 3).

ALTERNATION SUGGESTS IRREGULAR PRIMARY (B) TOP

As we have noted in the section entitled, "The Elliott Wave Theory," the whole of Primary (B) could spread out into an *irregular* second wave as happened in 1929, after the orthodox top took place in late 1928. There is no sure way of knowing, except that it may be so indicated by Elliott's theory of *alternation.* Elliott said that wave patterns including regular and irregular tops tended to alternate. (See *The Elliott Wave Principle*, 1960 edition.) Since 1919, major tops at approximately 8-10 year intervals have alternated between *regular* and *irregular* formations, as follows:

1919	Regular
1929	Irregular
1937	Regular
1946	Irregular
1956	Regular
1964-65(?)	Irregular (?)

One other aspect of Elliott which suggests that Primary (B) may move on to new highs in the form of three Intermediates (of which we are only now getting near the termination of Intermediate A) is the time element involved. *It does not seem logical to expect Cycle II to be completed, say, in two-three years* (which is what is implied if Primary (B) is now near its end, and Primary (C), a bear swing to below the June low of 524, is about to commence in the next month or so) *when Cycle I took twelve years, from 1949 to 1961, to be completed.*

But apart from this thinking, there is little in Elliott to give us a clue as to the duration of the current bull market that began in early July 1962 and which we have labelled Primary (B).

(Bank Credit studies and other long range technical studies suggest that the bull market which commenced last summer is still in its infancy, but these can only strengthen and possibly eventually confirm the two points of light which Elliott throws on the strength and duration of the Primary (B) bull market.)

Taking all factors together, then, including Elliott, money and credit, and other technical factors, we are of the opinion that so far we are only in Intermediate A of Primary (B), that this will be followed by Intermediate B of a corrective nature (three Minor waves) and that some time later in 1963, or possibly early in 1964, Intermediate C (this time in five waves up), will commence, which at its completion will terminate Primary (B). Maybe this last Intermediate will be the one which will push the Dow Jones Industrials through 900, as has been anticipated to happen by some of the more long-term bullish analysts in the last few years (Figure 3).

ALTERNATIVE SOLUTIONS

Not all Wave Principle analysts agree entirely with the various long and short term analyses promulgated by this interpreter. This is a healthy trend. The more disagreement we have, the less chance there is for the general public successfully to use the Elliott Principle for correct forecasting. We know that once a tool becomes too successful, it creates the conditions in the market place whereby in the future it will fail. The more failures along the route, the better will the tool be for those who read it right. This is really an extension of Humphrey Neill's Theory of Contrary Opinion.

We have pointed out in *The Elliott Wave Principle* (1960 edition) that as we get further from any terminal date, the more open to alternative interpretations becomes the wave theory. Examples of variance may be seen in that while we have in recent years taken 1949 as the last major terminal point for the commencement of a new Super Cycle, others take 1932. Yet, again, some analysts feel that 1942 is the date and that we must pay a lot of attention to "failures." Failures basically are waves which do not complete in trend channels what they are supposed to.[10]

FAILURE IN 1962?

Some analysts[11] feel that the real bottom of the 1962 bear market was in October, culminated by the 5-wave down pattern from the August 1962 high. The count that we have used ends up at the bottom in June, not October, but it is possible to count out the July-August rise as a 3 followed by a final 5 down which "fails" to go into new low ground. Some indices actually did go to new lows in October. Failures on the downside indicate great strength in the opposite direction, and certainly the market, since the Cuban "failure," if such it was, has been extraordinarily strong.

"THE FIFTH STARTED IN JUNE 1962"

One commentator who has done a great deal of work over the years feels that the famous fifth wave did not end in 1961, but began only in June 1962. To arrive at this interesting result, he places the top of Primary III as we do in 1956, with all which follows from then to June 1962 as an irregular Primary IV,[12] thus leaving the door open for Primary V to commence in mid-1962. This is an off-beat interpretation, but one which can be technically justified. If correct, it, too, implies tremendous strength for Primary V, with the ultimate probability of anywhere from 900-1200 in the Dow Jones Industrials.[13]

FOOTNOTES

[1] Quoted substantially at the end of this book.

[2] Actually, there are many clues. The two main ones are slope and breadth. "B" waves in larger degrees are almost always less steep than would be expected of a third wave. They also almost always display worse, rather than better, breadth as compared to the previous impulse wave of the same degree.

[3] Sometimes it does, as in 1929-1932.

[4] As per Footnote 2 of Chapter X in *The Elliott Wave Principle — A Critical Appraisal*, Bolton should amend this

example to make wave (B) a double zigzag, adding an "e" - "f" - "g" after wave "d".

[5] See Footnote 2 of Chapter X of *The Elliott Wave Principle — A Critical Appraisal.*

[6] I.e., Charles J. Collins, who apparently wished to stay anonymous at this time. See 1966 Supplement.

[7] Bolton has said this often, but I would say that the Principle is a *principle* of human social behavior that has a *strong tendency* to be repeated in the price movement of stock averages.

[8] His limit was precisely correct to 2 Dow points.

[9] Less than a year after the event, Bolton made a prediction that has stood so far for thirty years.

[10] A "failure" is a specific thing: a truncated fifth wave, i.e., one that does not exceed the end of wave three.

[11] A. J. Frost caught this "Cuban Crisis" low, which ended with a clear "five" down, while Hammy was away in Greece.

[12] This is a bogus interpretation. To get the correct count, change "1956" to "1959." "June 1962" may also be changed to "October 1962."

[13] This Supplement contained an Appendix which is printed in this volume at the end of *The Elliott Wave Principle — A Critical Appraisal.*

THE ELLIOTT WAVE PRINCIPLE OF STOCK MARKET BEHAVIOR

1964

A SUPPLEMENT TO

The Bolton-Tremblay

BANK CREDIT ANALYST

A. Hamilton Bolton, editor-in-chief

THE ELLIOTT WAVE PRINCIPLE OF STOCK MARKET BEHAVIOR 1964 SUPPLEMENT

THE PATTERN OF THE INDUSTRIALS

Current Position

Now that the Dow Jones Industrials have passed 800, the 1962 bear market seems less of an aberration. People are probably gradually getting used to it, and are adapting themselves increasingly to the new era bull market theory which was, to say the least, slightly broken in mid-1962.

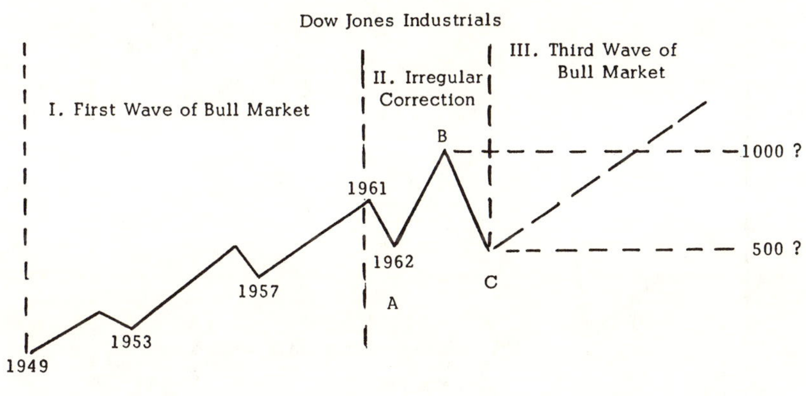

Once the long trend line of the lows from 1949 was shattered in the spring of 1962 (when the Dow Jones Industrials broke to about 540 from their then all-time high of about 740), it became apparent that the *orthodox Elliott bull market* had terminated and that the downward leg 1961-62

was the first wave of a major correction of the whole advance in stock prices from 1949. Events of the last two years tend to confirm that we are now in the upwave of a gigantic correction of the whole 1949-61 rise. This is diagrammed herewith in the broad pattern of stock prices as measured by the Dow Jones Industrial Average.

Background

The only reasonably complete and currently available study on the Elliott Wave Principle was published in 1960 by your editor. It explained and carried forward R. N. Elliott's basic theories, without attempting either to improve or change his tenets.

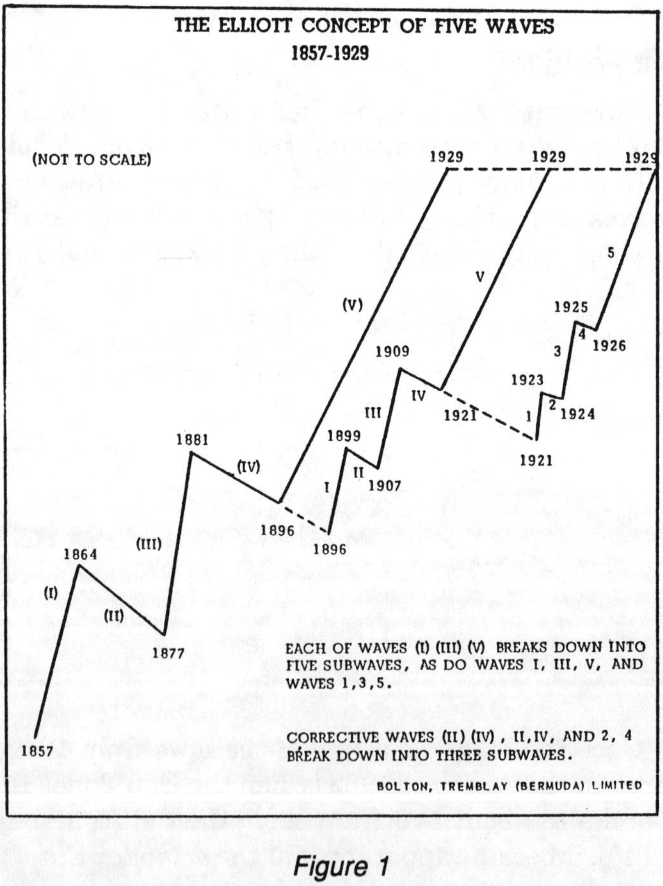

Figure 1

The basic Elliott concept is that major bull markets develop in five waves. This concept is illustrated by the preceding chart, from the aforementioned book.

From 1929 to 1949, there developed a corrective pattern in a huge 21-year triangle. This is illustrated in a further chart, Figure 46, from the same book, shown on the next page.

Since the publication of Figure 46 four years ago, it appears that the pattern of the bull market since 1949 has been modified slightly. This pattern suggested that the top of wave 5 of the bull market would probably not terminate much below 1000 in the Dow Jones Industrials. However, the downside break-out in 1962 clearly indicated a foreshortened *orthodox* bull market terminating in the 700s, only in August 1961.

Instead, therefore, of the fifth wave from 1949 being completed around the 1000 level, it now appears that an *irregular* correction is presently in force. Such corrections are far from rare, and in fact, in the context of a *thrust* out of the 21-year triangle apex in 1949, should have been an anticipated type of move.

Secondary Confirmation

The principle of *alternation* which Elliott developed seems to confirm the probability of an *irregular* top developing. Major tops tend to develop regular and irregular characteristics in alternate time cycles. Thus, 1919 was a *regular* top, whereas 1929 was *irregular*. A regular top means one in which the fifth wave clearly stands out in historical perspective as the highest point reached. An irregular top indicates that the second wave of the correction (the B wave of the ABC corrective formation) goes higher than the termination of the *orthodox* top (i.e., the top of the fifth wave).

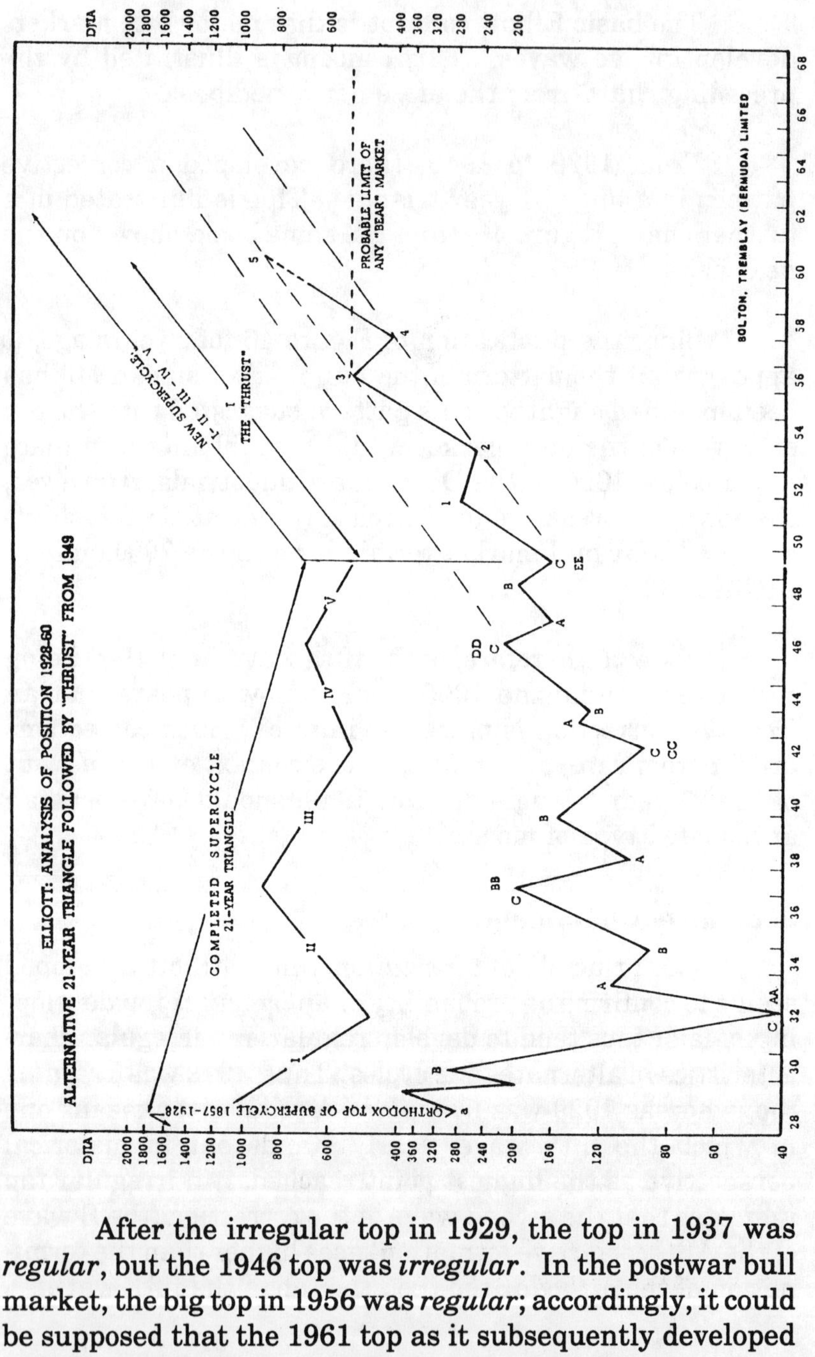

After the irregular top in 1929, the top in 1937 was *regular*, but the 1946 top was *irregular*. In the postwar bull market, the big top in 1956 was *regular*; accordingly, it could be supposed that the 1961 top as it subsequently developed would be *irregular*, and this appears to be the case.

How High?

There is no sure way of knowing from Elliott theory how high the Dow Jones Industrials will go from bottom in 1949 to irregular top (wave B of ABC correction) in the 1960s. However, in Chapter IX of *The Elliott Wave Principle — A Critical Appraisal*, the relationship of Elliott theory to the Fibonacci number series is developed. The following quotation, written long before the Industrial Average had ever crossed 700, may be of interest:

> "Should the 1949 market to date adhere to this formula, then the advance from 1949 to 1956 (361 points in the DJIA) should be complete when 583 points (161.8% of 361 points) have been added to the 1957 low of 416, or a total of 999 DJIA."
>
> "Alternatively, 361 over 416 would call for 777 in the DJIA."

Since we are now well past the 777 level, it looks as if 1000 in the Averages could be our next major target.

How Low Thereafter?

This chart suggested in 1960 that the probable limit of any subsequent bear market would be the 1956-57 top of 522 in the Dow Jones Industrials. Actually, the 1962 wave A of the major correction later got down on an intra-day basis to 525, thus tending to confirm our projection.

The basis of the projection was that in a *thrust* out of a long triangle, such as has happened since 1949, the wave corrections should tend to be substandard. Thus, the full correction is not likely significantly to break below the top of the third wave up of the whole orthodox bull market. This third wave up was completed in 1956 at 522 in the Average.

It should be noted, however, that since 1962 there have been four splits in Dow Jones stocks. By the construction of this average, a split tends to put a higher floor than heretofore under the average. This is because when a stock like Chrysler is split 2 for 1 while selling in the 90s, it then takes its place in the averages at about 45. In old prices, should it drop from 90 to 45, in new prices the drop would only be from 45 to 22 1/2. Thus, other things being equal, the DJIA would not go back to where it was when the stock was at 45. Thus, today, after 4 splits since 1962, should the DJIA return to 525, it would mean that the market as a whole as measured by these 30 stocks would be significantly lower than when last in 1962 at the 525 level.[1] It could well be, then, that in any subsequent bear market, 525 will not be seen again.

The Current Wave Pattern

Herewith we reprint the chart from our Addendum to last year's Supplement, dated November 11th, 1963.[2] This was a couple of weeks before the assassination of President Kennedy.

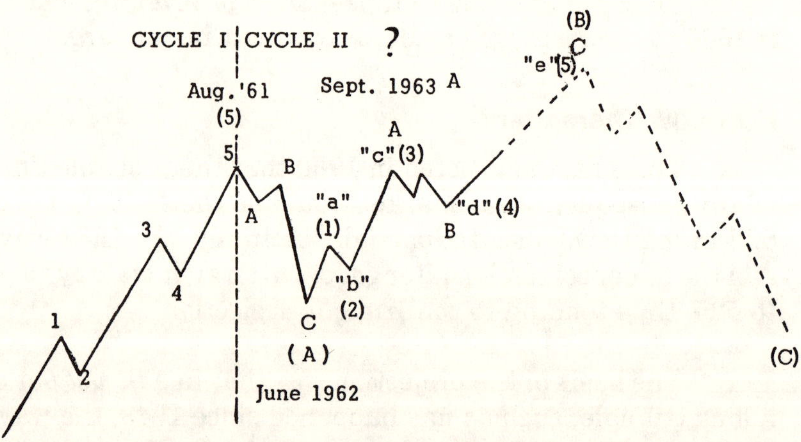

At the moment, our guess is that wave A was completed as indicated in September 1963, and that wave B was completed at the end of November. If this is true, we are now in wave C, which, when completed, will end the bigger wave

(B) of the (A)(B)(C) formation since the orthodox top in August 1961.

There is no way of knowing how long this wave may extend out in time, but other indications as above suggest that we are probably in the last 20% of the Industrial Average rise. Within this framework, however, there may still be room for considerable capital appreciation before the main trend turns down.

WHAT ABOUT THE RAILS?

For years, the Rails have been of little interest except as speculative vehicles. Recent changes in the "political" atmosphere suggest that they may again be becoming "investments."

DOW-JONES RAIL AVERAGE

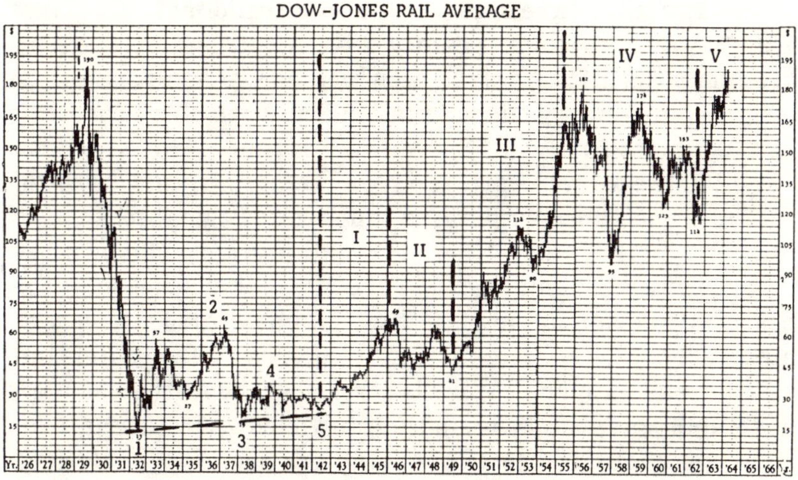

The rail picture from a chart point of view has always been confusing. However, the chart herewith, taken from the M. C. Horsey & Company "Stock Picture," may perhaps be one sound interpretation. Unlike the Industrials, the Rails appear to have completed their triangle in 13 years (instead of 21 years) in mid-1942. From here, we have the first big wave up (I) in five waves to 1946, followed by a zigzag correction to 1949. Wave III carries up to an orthodox top in 1955, and a very irregular triangle formation appears to run from 1955 through to 1962. The fifth wave (V) appears now to be in progress, but is probably nowhere near completed.

An alternative count might be to consider the correction to wave III (i.e., wave IV) as completed in late 1957. In this case, 1957-59 would probably be wave 1, 1959-62 wave 2, and 1962 to date wave 3 of the final wave V. In this case, too, the rails would appear to have a good way to go.

THE TIMING OF GROUPS

Group Waves Do Not Coincide

Edmund Tabell, Director of Institutional Research of Walston & Company, recently gave a talk before the San Francisco Security Analysts in which he was kind enough to refer to our work on the Elliott Theory. (See also "The Case for Technical Analysis," by Messrs. Edmund and Anthony Tabell in the March-April 1964 *Financial Analysts Journal.)* At the same time, he pointed out a very logical method of interpreting Elliott in the major bull market, which in the various averages ran from 1949 to 1961 (as discussed at the beginning of this Review). This was that while the Average made a 5-wave upward pattern from 1949 to 1961, and that all that has happened since is corrective, nevertheless various important groups made their 5-waves up from whatever base was made in the 1947-49 period, some up to 1956-57 (chemicals, oils, etc.), some up to 1959 (steels, etc.), some up to 1961 (electronics, etc.) and some up to 1963-64 (automobiles probably, etc.). Thus, while the average pattern came out in 1961, with various groups topping before and after, the spread between the highs of various groups was very wide, and it could well be, too, that certain groups such as the Rails have not yet reached their 5-wave upward objectives.

The graphs of individual stocks that follow, with comments beside each, represent a selection of well-known stocks from the stock book mentioned above and indicate fairly clear examples of the 5-wave pattern, particularly. It will also be noted how in many cases the relative action of the particular stock (its price related to the S & P average) also often goes through clear-cut Elliott patterns, and in some cases, this is useful in deciding the degree of the wave pattern when the stock pattern itself may appear marginal.

Edmund Tabell's interpretation of the group action suggests that many of the groups which topped out in 1956, 1957 or 1959 probably had completed their initial downtrends in three waves by 1960 or 1962, and were ready for either a new bull market, or perhaps more probably a major B wave up, to be followed later by the final C wave down. Just as the averages from time to time will go through simple followed by complex types of corrections, so some stocks and groups could be expected to correct either simply (or in a short time period), or to react in a more complex fashion. To know which type of correction to expect is certainly not an easy task. However, generally speaking, where the corrective waves, say, from 1959 to 1962 were clearly in the form of a 5-wave down (provided, however, that this was not a C wave of an irregular A-B-C formation), this would imply a further corrective formation consisting of a 3-wave pattern up, and thereafter a continuance of the decline in a third wave down of 5-wave dimensions. This sort of action would normally take several more years. Examples of this sort are also mentioned in the individual charts shown.

HOW ABOUT INDIVIDUAL STOCKS?

It is a curious fact that it is harder to reconcile the Elliott Wave Principle to individual stocks than it is to the "market as a whole," as indicated by leading stock market averages.[3] It is probably this factor which mitigates against a more extensive use of the Wave Principle in technical market analysis of individual companies.

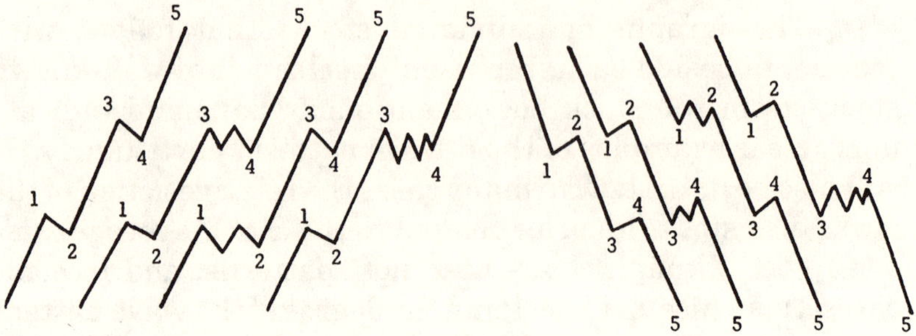

The Five-Wave Characteristic

Four versions of this pattern are given for each direction in the diagram above. These are not the only possibilities, but do comprise probably 90% of the cases where a 5-wave pattern exists. The main characteristic to watch for is the fact that for this pattern to be valid, wave 4 must not overlap wave 1. The moment this happens (unless it is purely momentary for a small bit), it is necessary to recount the waves, and from this recount it often appears that another wave is added.

In the 1960 edition of *The Elliott Wave Principle — A Critical Appraisal*, your editor wrote a short chapter (XV) on the subject, "Is Elliott Applicable to Individual Stocks?" In this chapter, the following quotations may be of interest four years later.

> "Perhaps the most significant use of Elliott in individual stocks is the appearance of the *five-wave* pattern. The author has found that when one sees a clear-cut 5-wave pattern developing and being completed, one is almost sure that it is the end of this move. This can be useful, particularly in preventing investment in a stock which is *well advanced in its fifth wave*."

Two examples were given of the possible use of the Elliott's five wave principle, picked at random. These were Figure 53 of Libbey-Owens-Ford Glass and Figure 54 of Admiral Corp., taken from charts then current by Securities Research Corporation of Boston, Mass.

The reader should bear in mind that there was no attempt on our part to forecast what the future held for Libbey-Owens-Ford and Admiral Corp.; rather, what was suggested was that the odds seemed to be that L-O-F had completed by mid-1959 a *major five-wave Elliott bull market* (see reproduction below), having risen from 11 in late 1948 to 77 in 1959. Each of the odd-numbered waves could be counted into five sub-waves, and in particular, the last wave from late 1957 to mid-1959 looked very regular. Of course, there always was the possibility of an "extension" of the rise in the last wave into a 9-up, but with the break-out downside to the low 60s at the time this chart was plotted, this seemed unlikely.

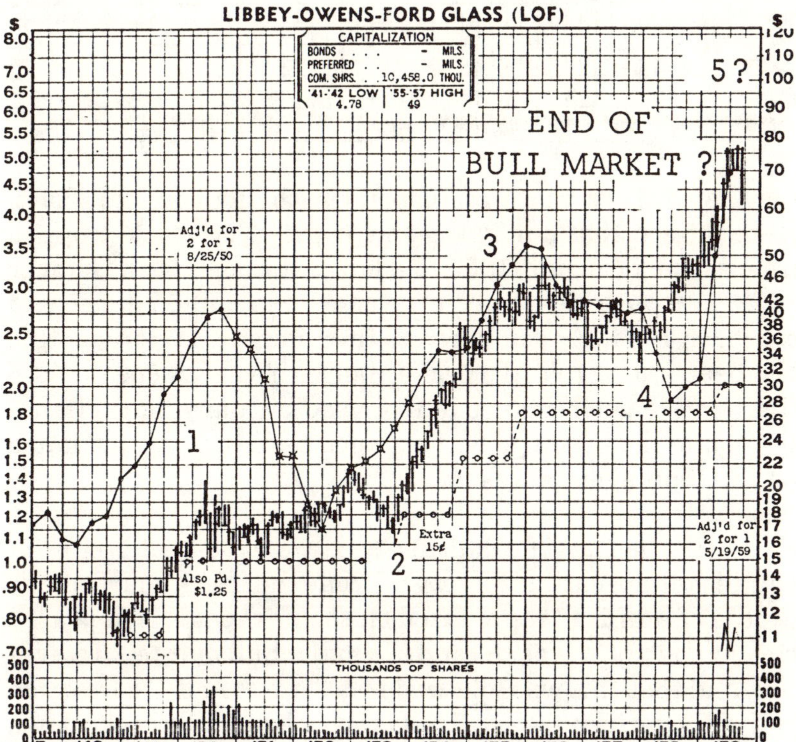

Let us look and see what happened over the next four and a half years. We now bring an up-to-date chart of the same stock from the same source. We have numbered only

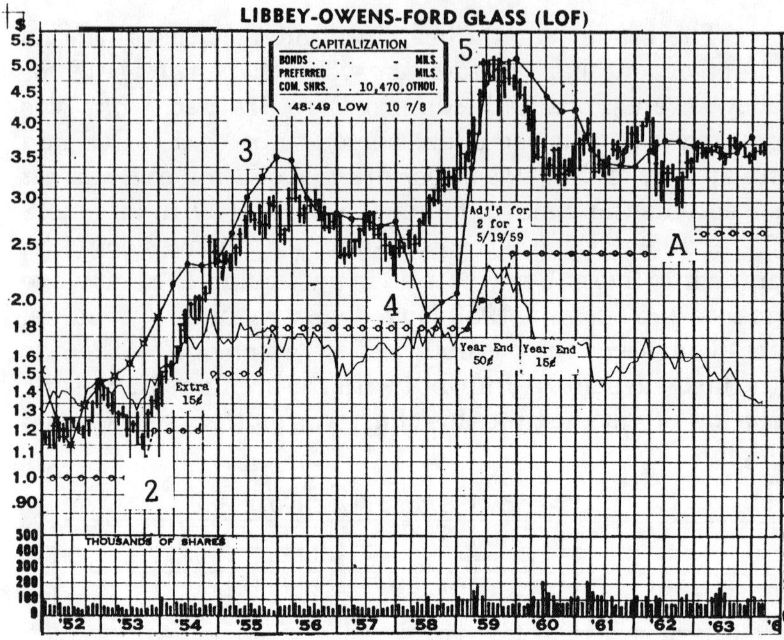

the last 5-wave up to correspond with the original chart. Here we see that our guess was right. The stock dropped from about 77 in mid-1959 to a low just under 44 in October 1962, and has recovered on the chart to about 55 at the end of March 1964. As compared to the Industrial Average, this has been a poor relative performance. Yet at the peak, both the relative performance (a tool used by many market analysts) and the earnings performance were turning in a much better than average result.

In the case of Admiral Corp., we have a different but equally illuminating history. From the 1960 chart of the profile of Admiral, reproduced on the next page, it appeared clearly that 1950 was the end of a major bull market (5 waves up), and that this was followed by a 3-wave A-B-C correction of the *flat* variety (3-3-5). The C wave also clearly broke down into a 5-wave down without irregularity, indicating as shown on the chart a *major bear market completed.* From this point started what was interpreted as a *first leg of new bull market completed* again in the period 1957 to 1959, with the stock rising from 6 1/2 to 29 in a very clear-cut 5-wave pattern.

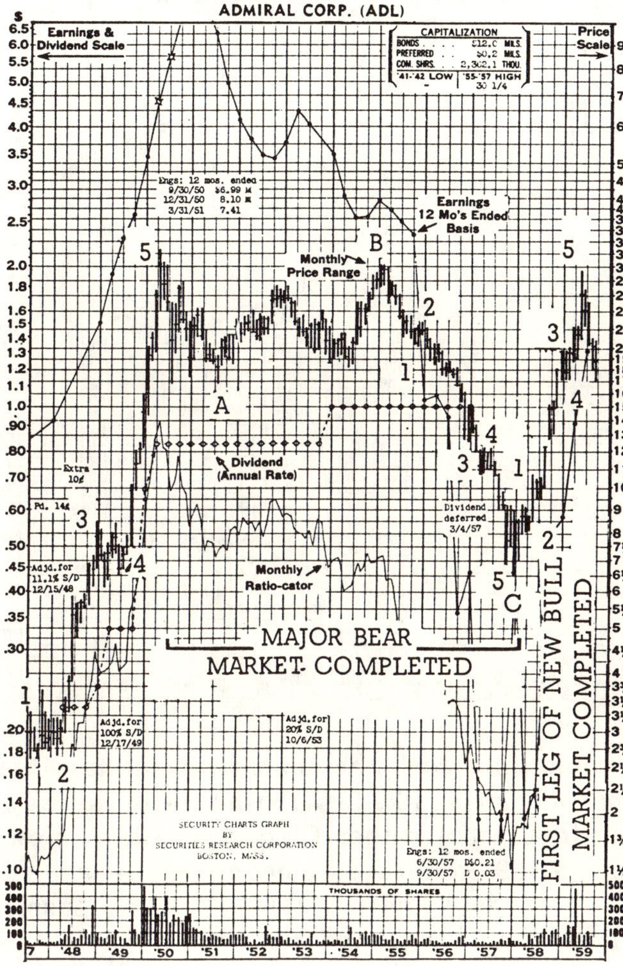

Here again, the break-out on the downside suggested that there would be no extension, and that a correction to the whole 1957-59 new first bull market wave would get under way.

Again, as in the case of L-O-F, we bring the case history up-to-date (see next page). Note the bear market which got under way. From the peak in 1959, we have till October 1962 what looks like a *flat* correction (3-3-5), which can be marked a-b-c. Wave c breaks down clearly again into 5, leaving little doubt that this was the end of the move, and

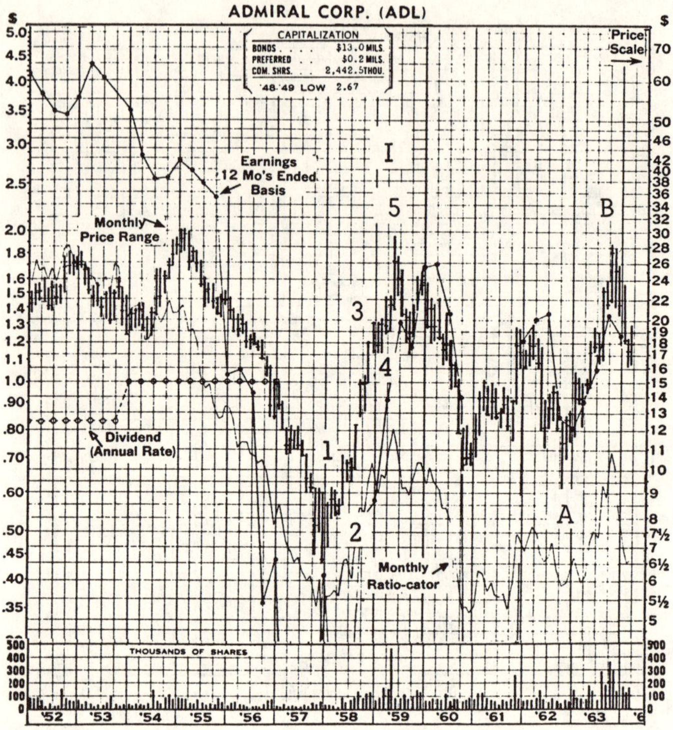

in close conformity with the general market in 1961-62, except that this stock, like L-O-F, was one of the laggards, bottoming in October rather than June 1962. However, unlike in 1957-59, Admiral does not appear to have made a 5 up from 1962 to date, and in fact this wave looks suspiciously like an inverted *flat* in a 3-3-5 formation. If so, then we will find that Admiral is still continuing in a corrective phase from the 1959 peak and is not yet ready to start the second bull market (which is usually the most dynamic) in Elliott's terms from 1957. We have accordingly marked 1962 as only wave A of the correction, with wave B as having terminated in late 1963.

Again, we wish to reiterate that these are not forecasts, but only odds-on tendencies, a current reading of both charts which simply suggests that these are not likely to be the winners for the balance of post-war bull market.

In concluding this discussion of the two case histories, it is well to repeat that in individual stocks, what is useful in Elliott wave theory is the *five wave* pattern, not the three-wave one. This is because the 5-wave pattern is seen far less often, and the 3-wave pattern lends itself to too many varieties which often become so elongated in time that there is no way of knowing when they end. Time and again (but nevertheless only in a minority of stock patterns), a 5-wave pattern appears. Almost always, this 5-wave pattern is the end of that particular move, when related to its degree.

From the current edition of the Security Research Corporation's 3-Trend Cycle-Graphs, we have selected a number of charts which show up the 5-wave tendency with short comments and numberings on our part. These are discussed in the Appendix to this study.

CONCLUSION

The history of individual stocks is often too short and too variegated to be certain that Elliott Wave Principle tendencies will show up when wanted. Further, averages represent a long and basically inflationary view of equities over time. As stocks lose favor, they are often replaced in such averages as the Dow Jones Industrials. This gives a long term record which can then be fitted into the broad Elliott theory that first was built up on averages before it was applied to individual issues.

In our view, its individual use is strictly limited in value, yet the examples above and in the Appendix do suggest that it is possible to outline a pattern in behavior for certain stocks. Certainly, the examples given, which represent only a small percentage of the total stocks shown in the chart service mentioned, provide some extra hooks upon which to hang one's hat. At certain junctures in each stock, the Elliott theory, particularly in its 5-wave concept, can add that grain of assurance or hesitation when other methods of analysis, either technical or fundamental, agree or disagree.

As to the market as a whole (which many people say does not exist, but which actually is available to investors through the use of open or closed-end investment funds), Elliott provides a philosophy which has a certain merit. For instance, at the present time, it would appear that a logical expectation of a level for the Dow Jones Industrials before wave B is completed would be somewhere in the area of 1000. This assumes that the current expansion in due time will run its course and that we do not immediately embark upon an all-out currency (monetary) inflation of the hyper type, or that we do not enter into a ruinous world-war, which would produce the same result.[4]

Putting a time period and price level on the termination is always difficult and dangerous. We have seen how the Elliott patterns tend to spread out to accommodate themselves to political and economic events. Our guess, though, would be that wave B above could well be completed within the next 12 to 24 months. For reasons explained in *The Elliott Wave Principle — A Critical Appraisal* (1960 edition), stock prices are not likely to drop below 525 under any conditions in the foreseeable future, and in the case where economic difficulties provide their attempted solution through conscious monetary manipulation, it could happen that wave C will not necessarily reach the low level seen in wave A in 1962.

Individual stock charts are reproduced by the kind permission of Securities Research Corp., 211 Congress Street, Boston, Mass.

April 27, 1964

APPENDIX

ELLIOTT NOTES ON SELECTED STOCK PATTERNS

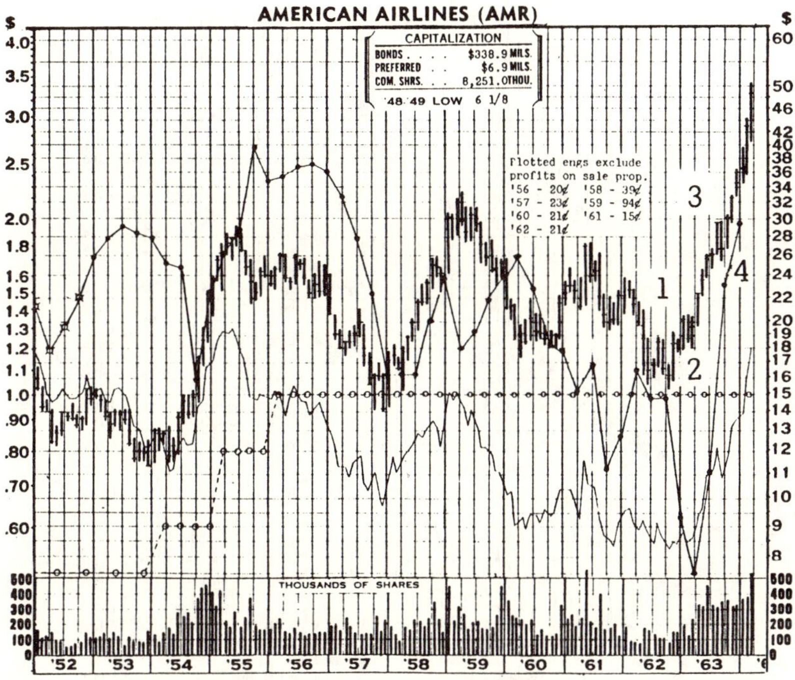

American Airlines — An example of a stock (and group) which has apparently taken off. The 1961-62 down move appears to be a "5 down," thus setting the stage for this advance of probably major proportions. Thus, everything from the 1946 high (not shown on the chart) is probably a correction of the major war-time bull market. Is it too late to invest in airlines and AMR? From an Intermediate point of view, probably yes, since we seem to be in the 5th Minor up since the low of October 1962, but if this is a valid new starting point in October 1962, then there is lots of room for expansion in the 1960s. (See also Delta Airlines.)

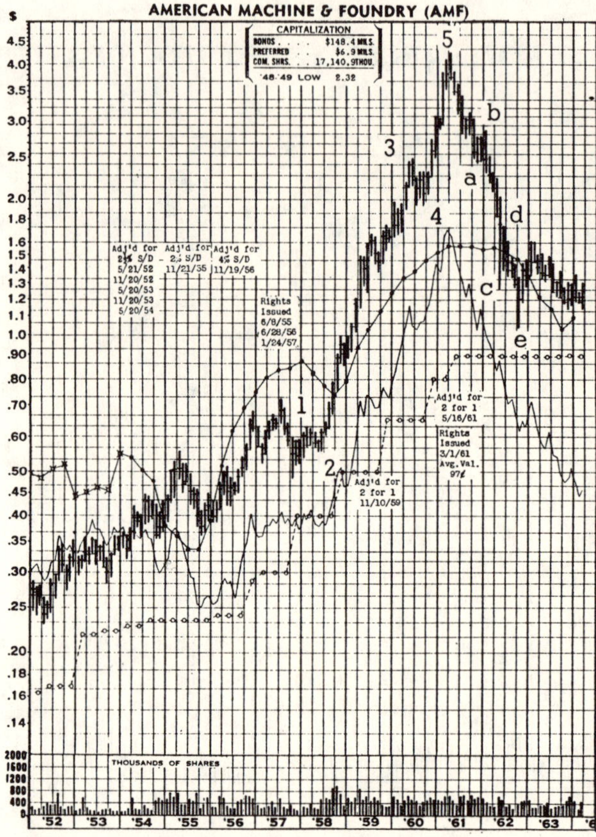

American Machine & Foundry — Here is the tragic aftermath of a great "growth stock" of the 1957-61 period. When patterns are unclear, it helps sometimes to look at a sister company of which we would judge that Brunswick Corp. (see below) would qualify. From 1954, Brunswick has five waves up to its fantastic high of over 70 in 1961. We calculate that the last of the five waves broke down into a 9 up. Since the peak, we seem in Brunswick and hence, probably in AMF, to be in a "5 down." Five waves down of this kind are usually only the first A wave of a basic bear market unless they arise out of an irregular top, which does not appear to apply to either AMF or BC. Any interest in either of these stocks would now seem to be reserved for the alert trading type.

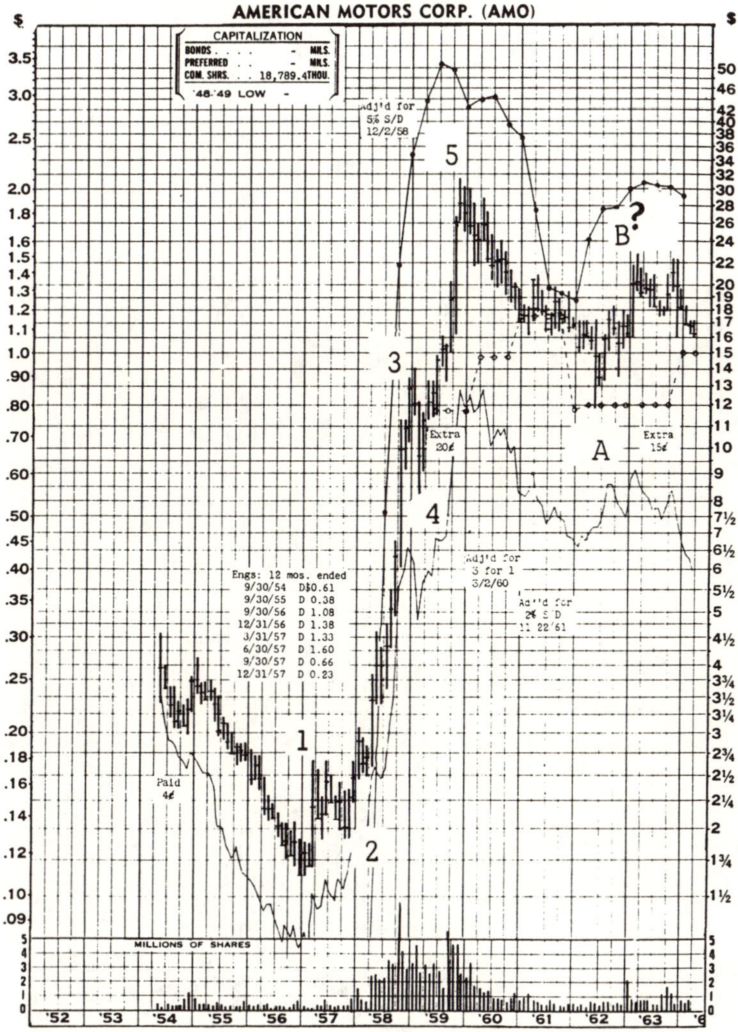

American Motors — Has been in a basic Elliott bear market since 1959. After a clear "5-wave up" from late 1956, all we can assume is that the 1962 low represented the bottom of wave A (the first, in other words, of three), and that probably the early 1963 peak was the termination of wave B.

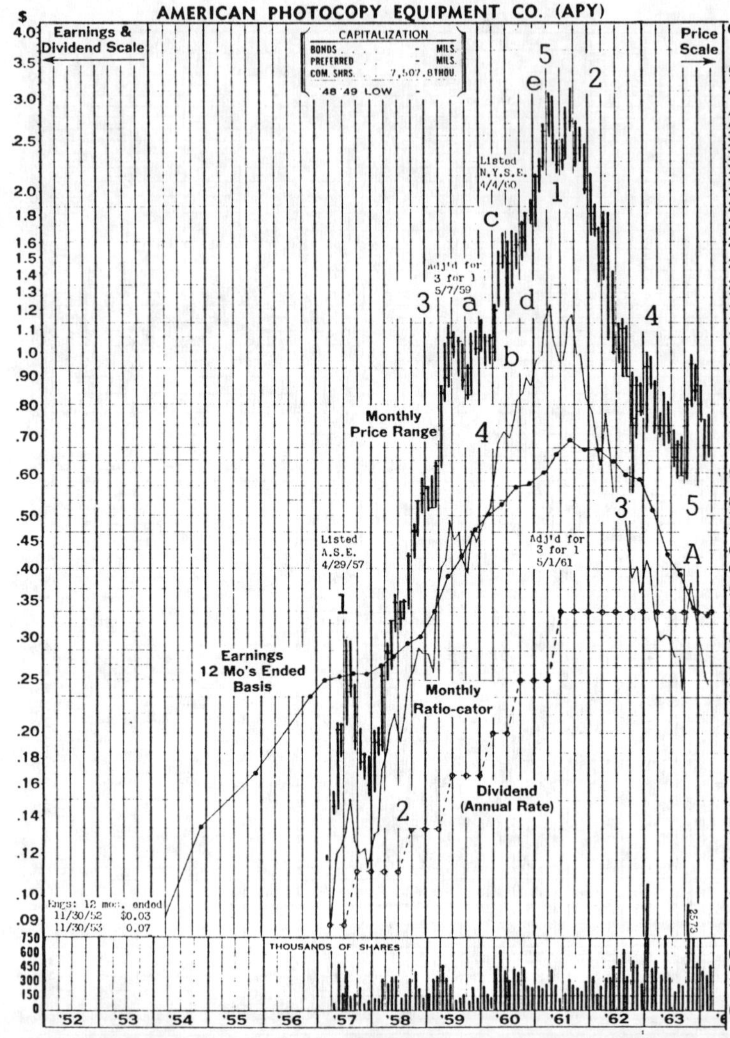

American Photocopy — Another example of a stock of great "growth" promise in the 1957-61 period. There may be some legitimate doubts as to the proper count in this stock. We assume that the 5-wave down from early 1961 is completed in late 1963. If so, there are trading possibilities, but little else. This stock, from an Elliott point of view, has "had it."

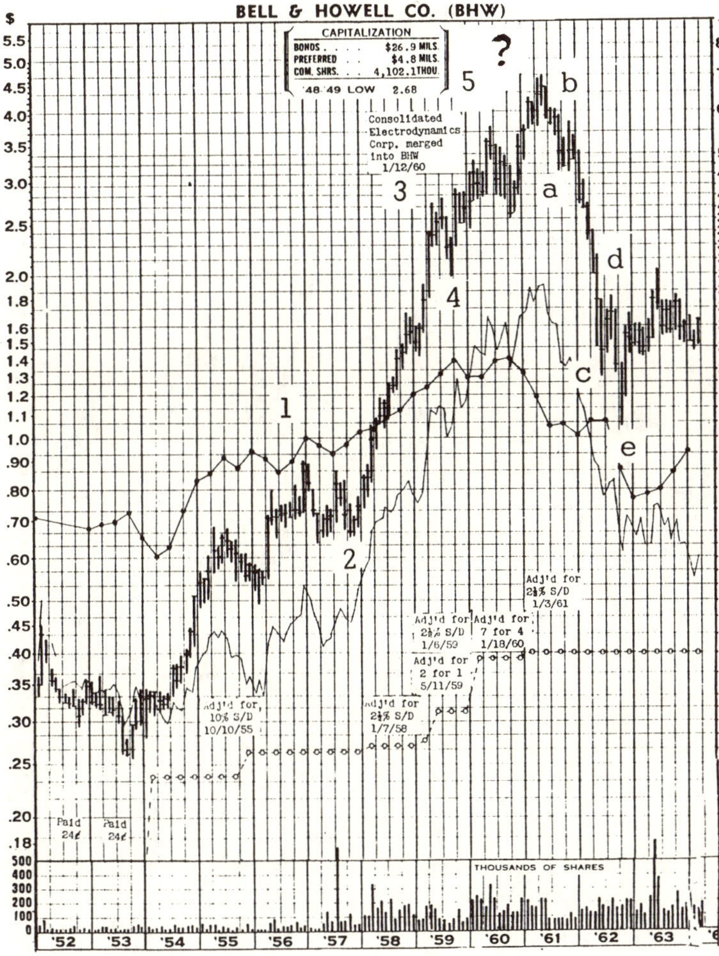

Bell & Howell — Another stock in a basic Elliott bear market. From 1961 to late 1962, we have a typical "5-wave down." It is interesting to note how many of the great favorites of 1958-61 have developed this pattern. See, for instance, the charts American Machine & Foundry, American Photocopy, Brunswick, Cenco, IBM, Korvette, Polaroid and Zenith.

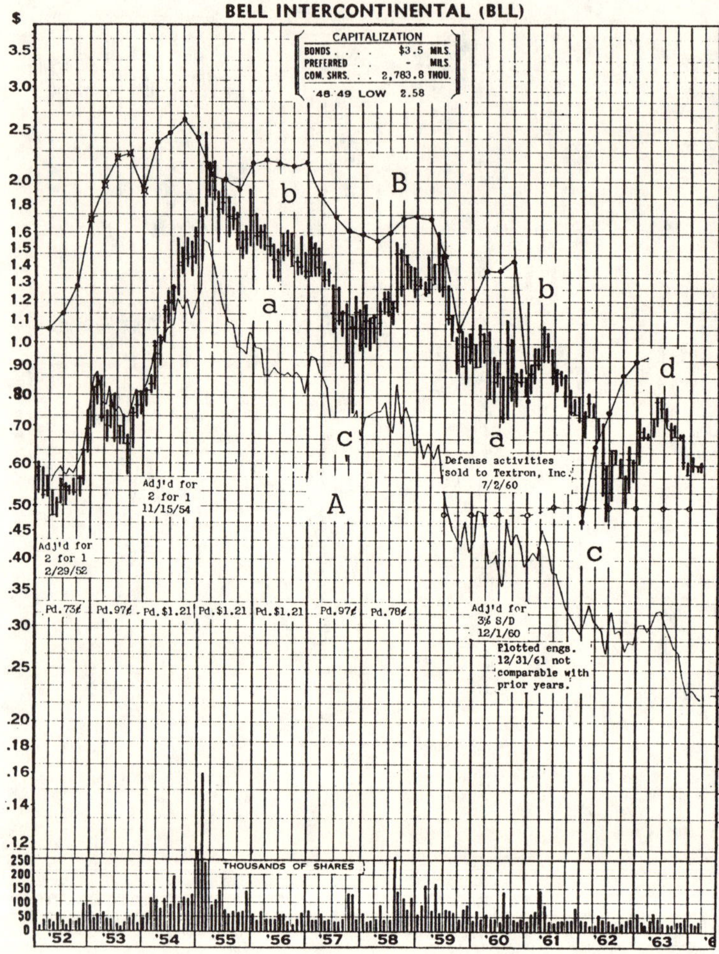

Bell Intercontinental — This is a long bear market in Elliott terms, from early 1955. (Incidentally, it disproves the point that a bull market never is consummated on maximum volume.) It may well be in its last Intermediate leg downward. Incidentally, this pattern illustrates some of Elliott's tenets. Wave A is divided into 3 waves (a-b-c). This is not known, however, at the time, but only afterwards, when peak B goes considerably higher than Intermediate wave a. Wave C is probably projecting in a "5 down" (a-b-c-d-e), of which all but e have yet to appear. How long it will take to clear up this already 9-year old bear market is anybody's guess.

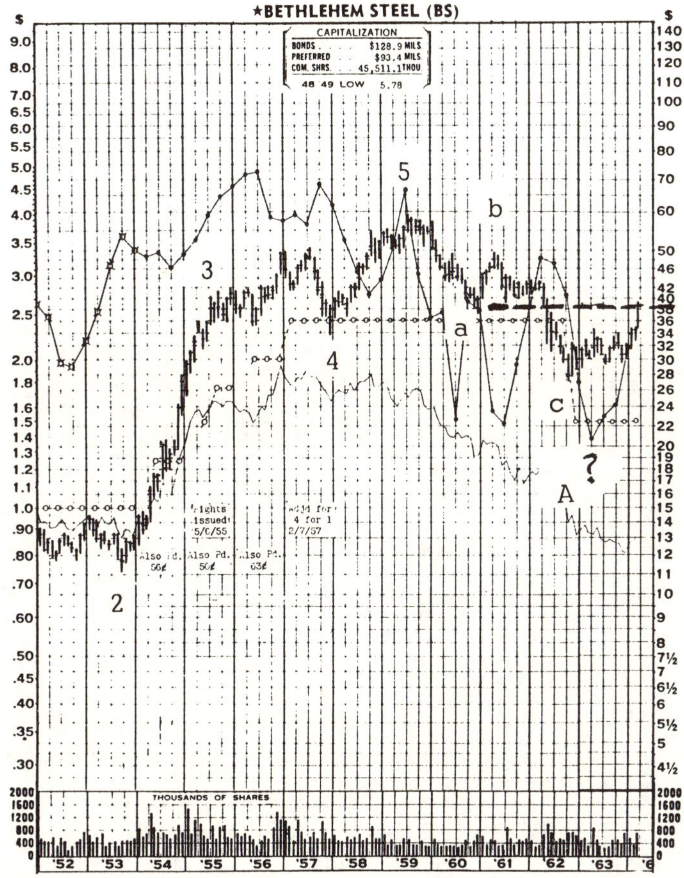

Bethlehem Steel — BS is typical of many steels. See also Lukens, illustrated here. It would appear from the 1959 peak that we have only seen 3 of a "5 down" pattern, but this could be a problem, and suggests one of the basic difficulties of the Elliott forecaster. If the current upswing carries BS appreciably higher than the low of 1961, i.e., say, to the high of 1961 around 50, Elliott fanciers will conclude that the October 1962 in the steel stocks generally is wave A of a basic bear market that began in mid-1959. Either way (assuming a "5 down" from 1959 or assuming only a "3 down"), the investor, if he pays any attention to Elliott, will be looking for an "out" long before the old highs of 1959 are reached. Elliott says they will not be, for a long, long time.

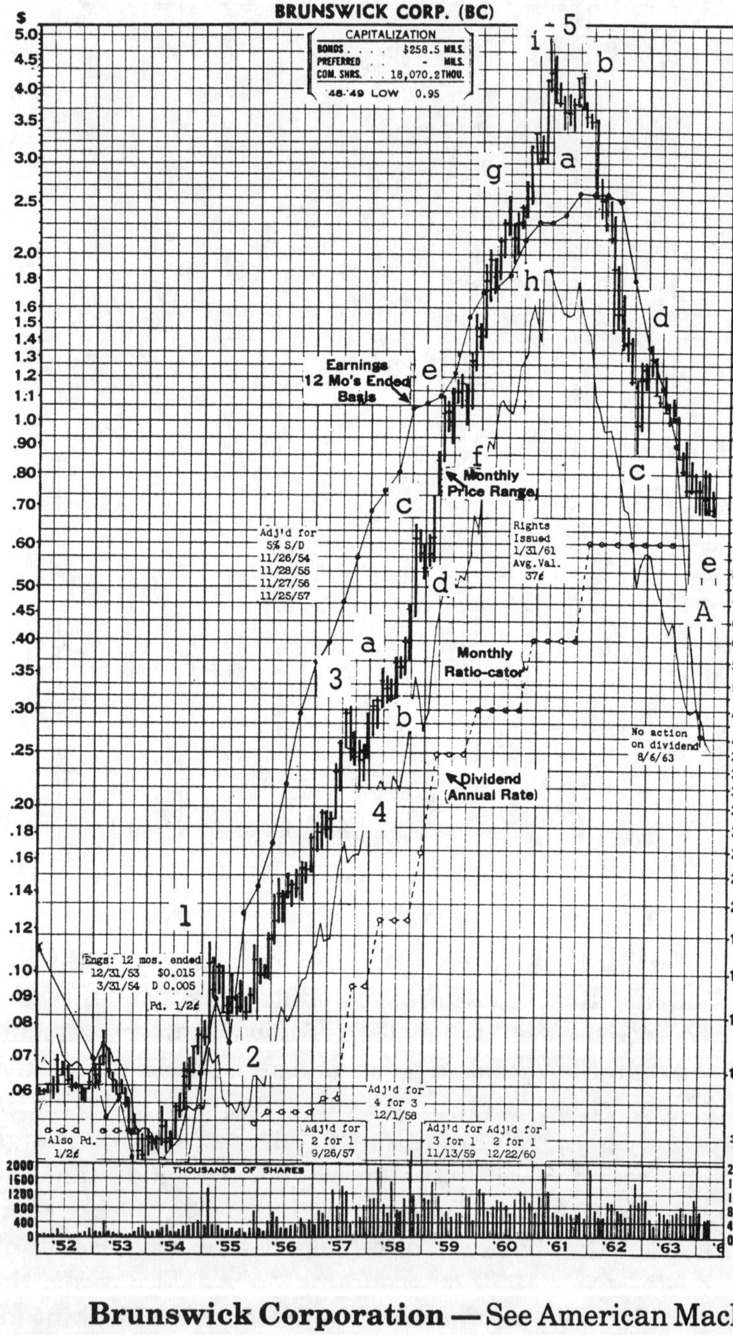

Brunswick Corporation — See American Machine & Foundry.

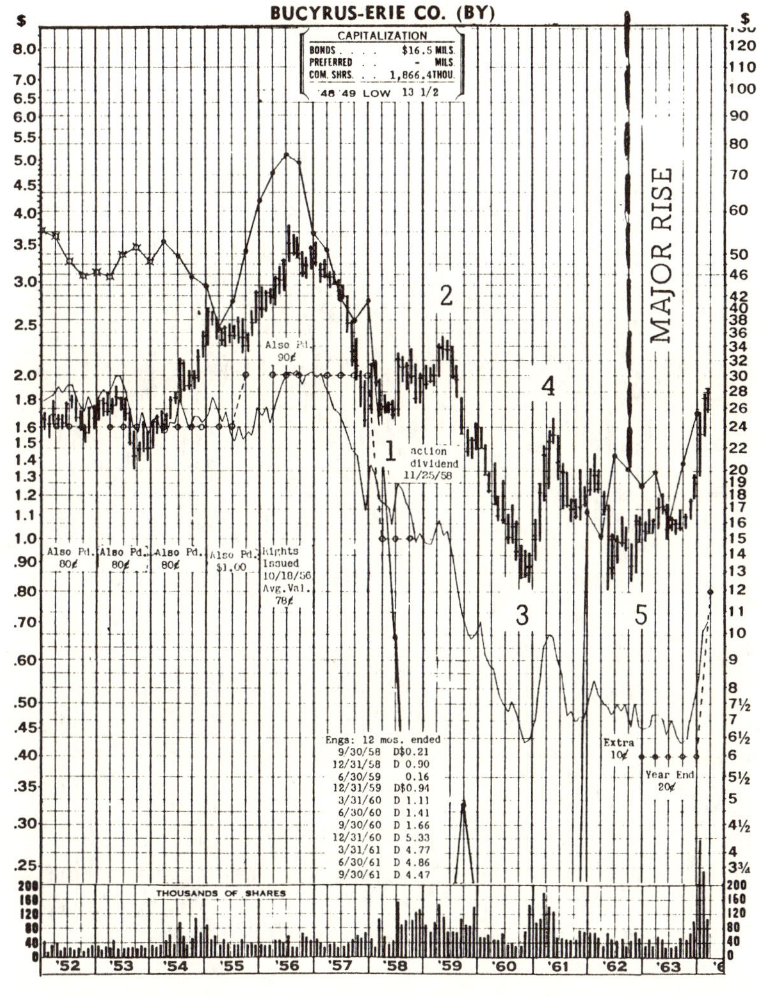

Bucyrus-Erie Co. — In a basic bear market since 1956, as of October 1962 this company appears to have started a new high bull market. On this basis, it would appear that BY has traced three out of five Intermediate waves. Thus, 1962 could be the beginning of a major reversal, in Elliott's terms.

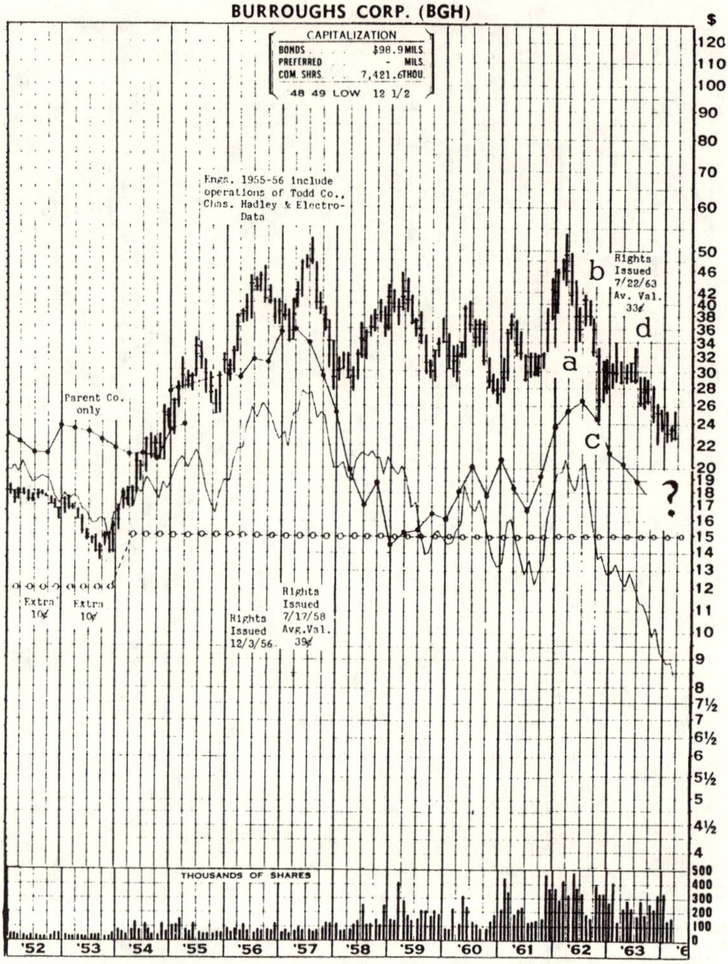

Burroughs — A confused picture. All that can be said is that if the 1957 high is the end of the previous bull market, all that has happened since is corrective, a series of 3's up to the early 1962 top. Since then, we appear to have the development of a "5 down." Nothing in earnings or relative performance suggests that it is over yet, but who knows? Five down-waves have a habit of creating a new base for at least a sizeable (50% or more) correction.

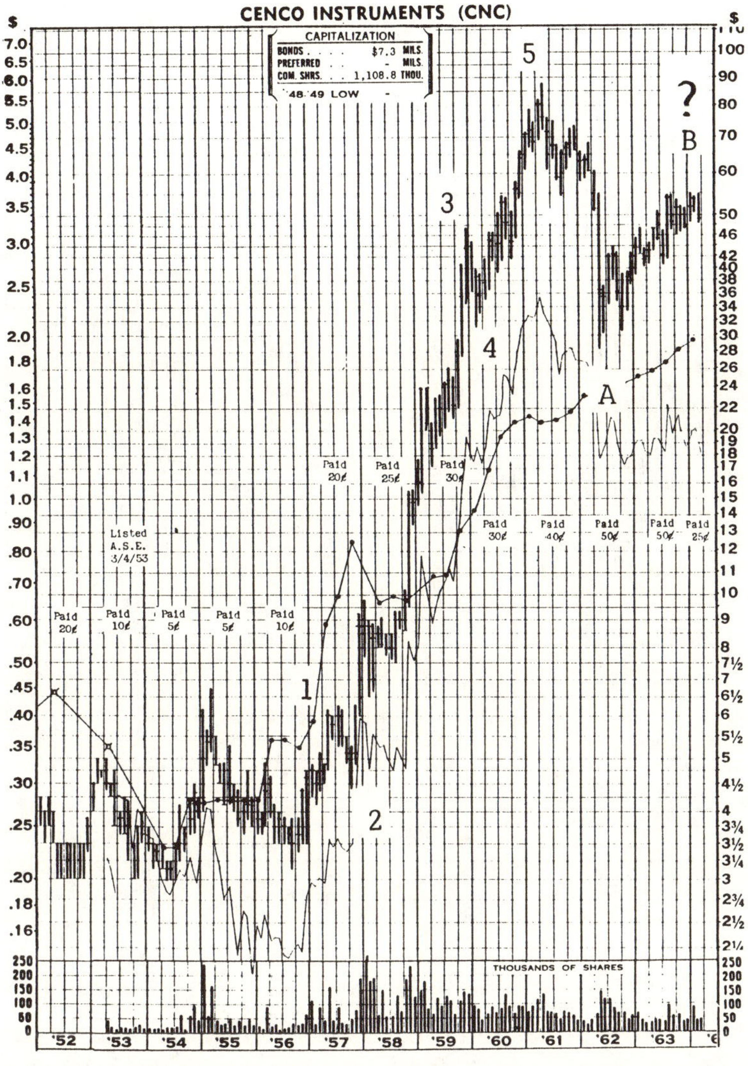

Cenco Instruments — Another "growth stock" which has deceived a number of people. The peak in 1961 looks like the end of the road. The bottom in 1962 looks like an a-b-c A bottom. The rise in 1963-64 looks like a typical B wave. All told, Elliott suggests that pearls are available elsewhere.

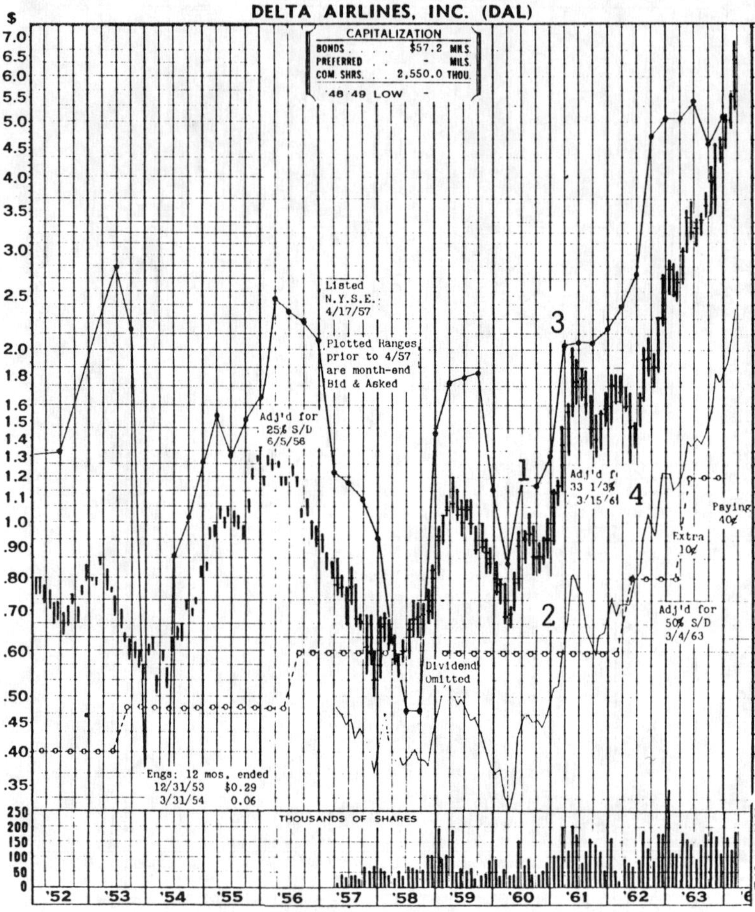

Delta — See American Airlines. Far advanced in the fifth wave from early 1960, consequently treacherous for investment at this time.

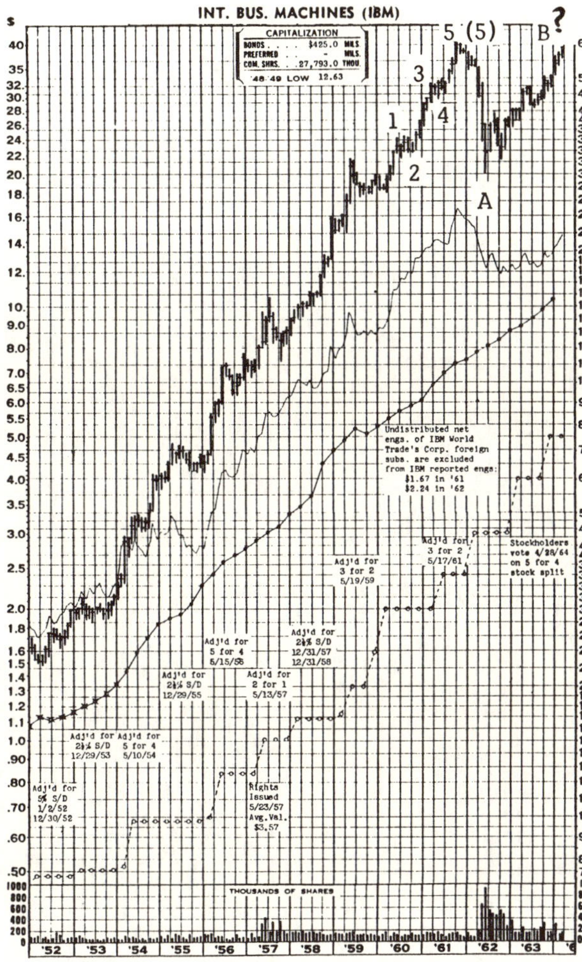

IBM — Here is the classic. Someone in Wall Street said that IBM had ceased to be a growth stock: it had become a religion. The count is difficult, but quite clearly, early 1960 to late 1961 is a typical "5-up" from which came a major downside break out. This late 1961 top looks like the end. We would classify the 1961-62 down move as wave A, with currently wave B in progress. Often wave B in growth stocks such as IBM, Minneapolis Honeywell, etc., run somewhat higher than the orthodox top, but this should not be allowed to confuse. After B should come C, which is downward.

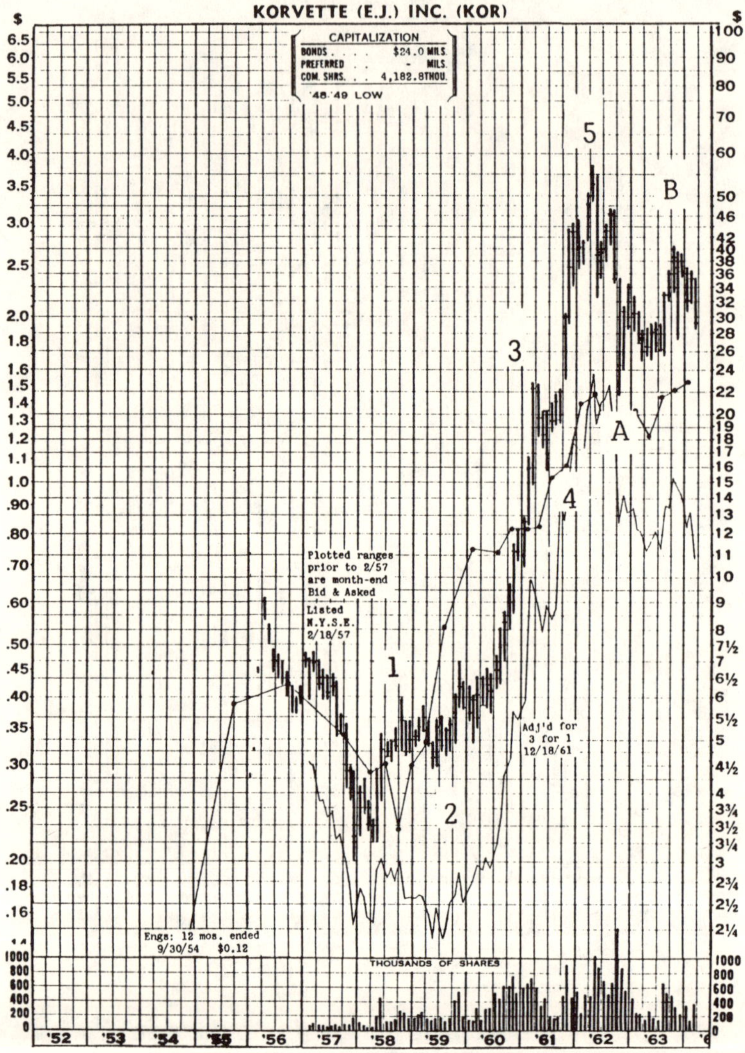

Korvette — This is a real classic in the type of "growth" stocks so popular in the 1958-61 era. Five waves up from late 1957, right from the bottom. All that has happened since 1962 is in the context of a major Elliott bear market. Wave B will probably be followed by the inevitable wave C.

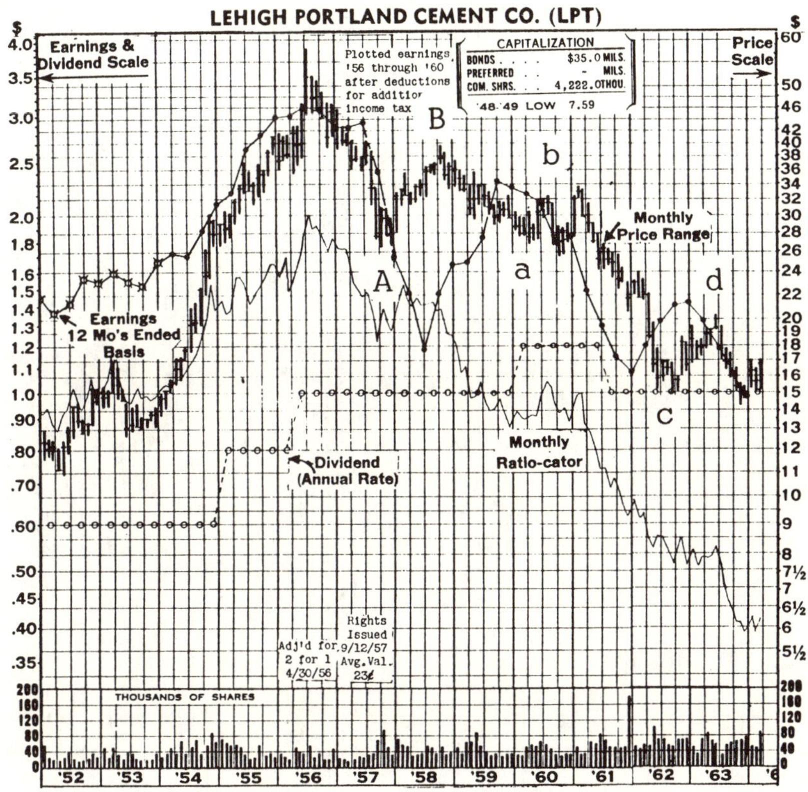

Lehigh Portland Cement — The pattern since 1956 is that of a major Elliott bear market. Of the 3-3-5 type (a flat), it would appear that LPT is close to at least an important intermediate and possibly a major bottom.

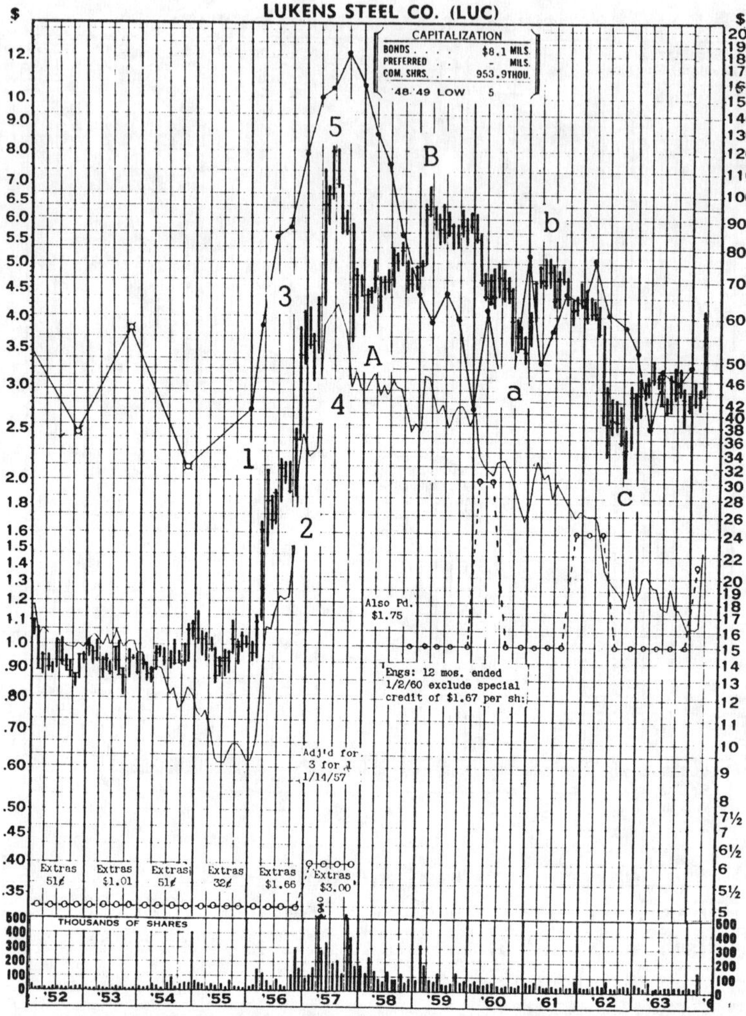

Lukens Steel — Lukens is typical of the steels individually, and as a group. See, for instance, Bethlehem. But there is an anomaly here. The 1957 high (two years before the average steel stock high) seems to have developed into an ABC, the C wave of which should be a five down. This seems to be developing, except that wave d has already gone above the low point of wave a, which it should not do under strict Elliott theory. So the pattern is in the air. But if the other stocks such as Bethlehem are a key, we would consider the present pattern as dubious.

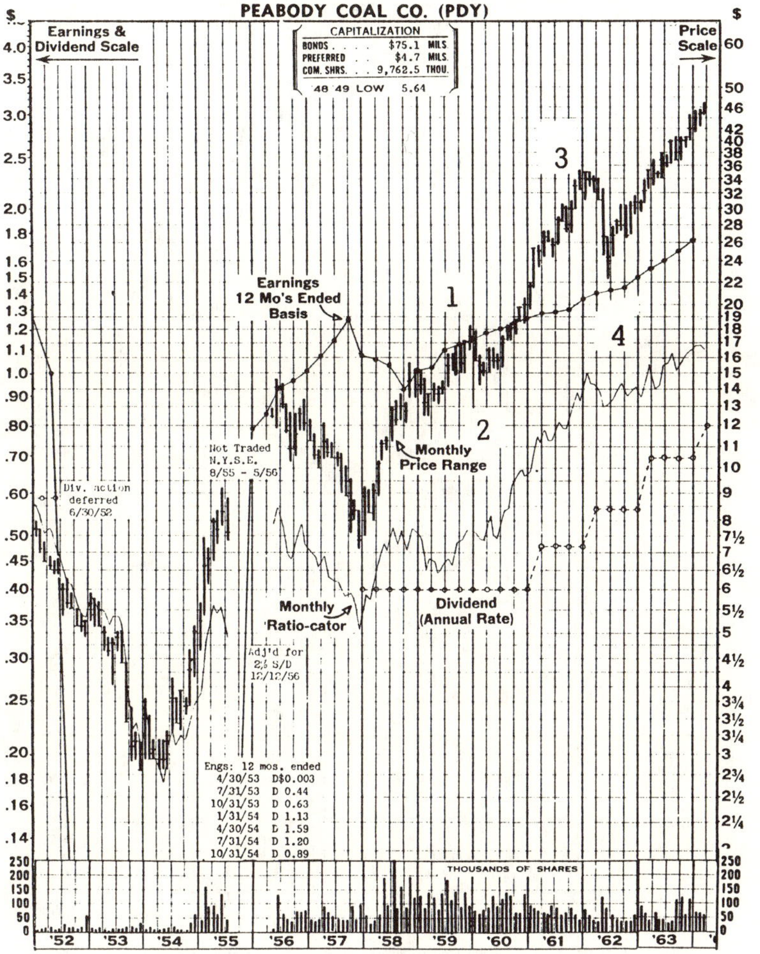

Peabody Coal Co. — After the major upwave from 1954 to 1956, another upward wave started in 1957. It appears to be well on into its fifth wave, and therefore suspect. Assuming that 1954 is the start of five upward waves of which the third will be completed in the current stock market cycle, the future is bright, but in the meantime, any proper correction of a stock wave which has run from about 7 to about 50 is bound to be painful. Accordingly, we'll wait this one out.

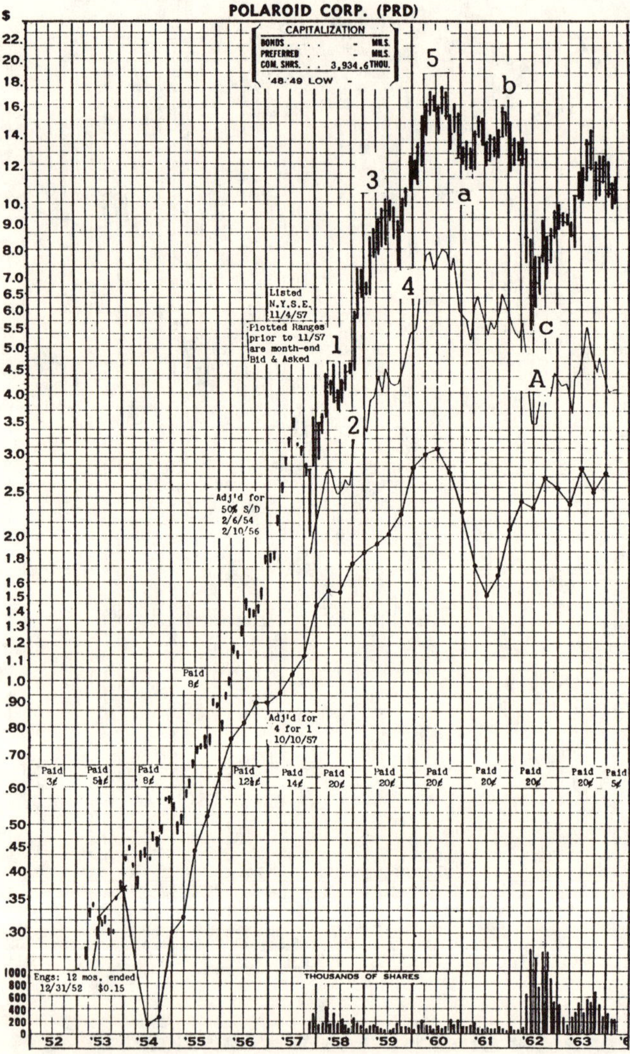

Polaroid — Another classic "growth" stock, which in Elliott's terms has obviously "had it." The period 1960-62 qualifies as a three wave correction, but this is probably only the first down wave of a bigger three wave correction. From 1960 to date looks like a large flat (3-3-5), of which we have had the first 3, and probably the second 3 (upwards). The balance remains to be seen, but it offers little long-term bull encouragement.

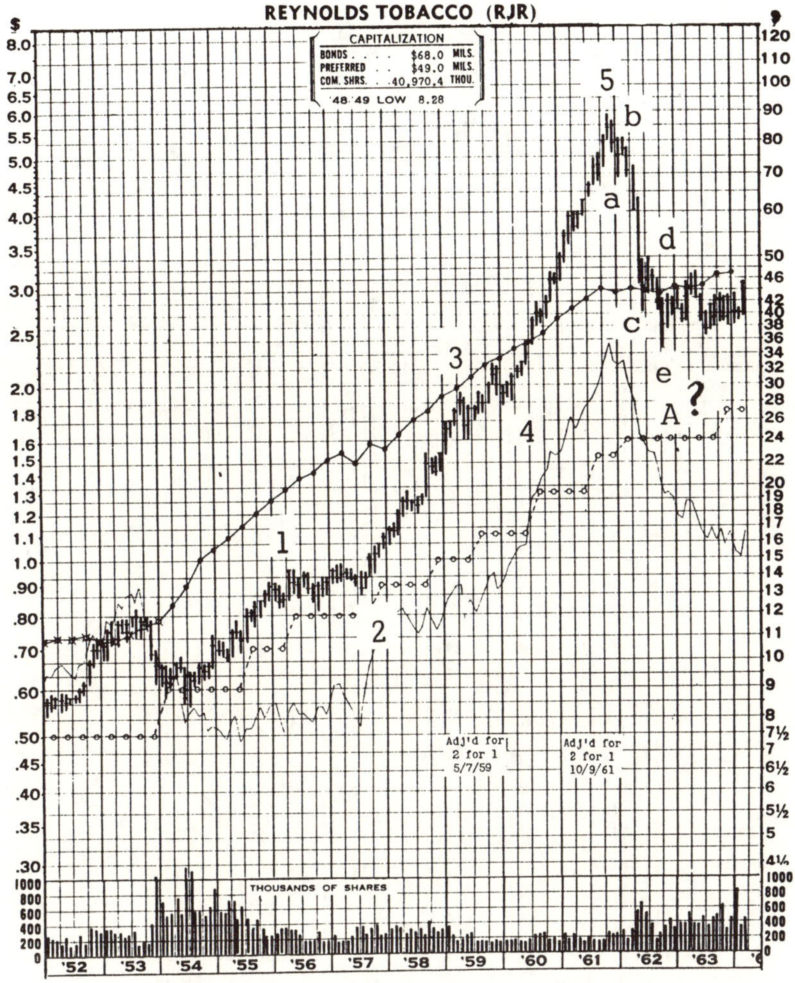

Reynolds Tobacco — This is an enigma. What looks like a "5-wave up" from 1954 (1-2-3-4-5) has been translated into an immediate "5-wave down" (a-b-c-d-e). From this has developed a side-wise movement, which could mean anything. It suggests, however, a limited potential on the upside until the pattern clarifies.

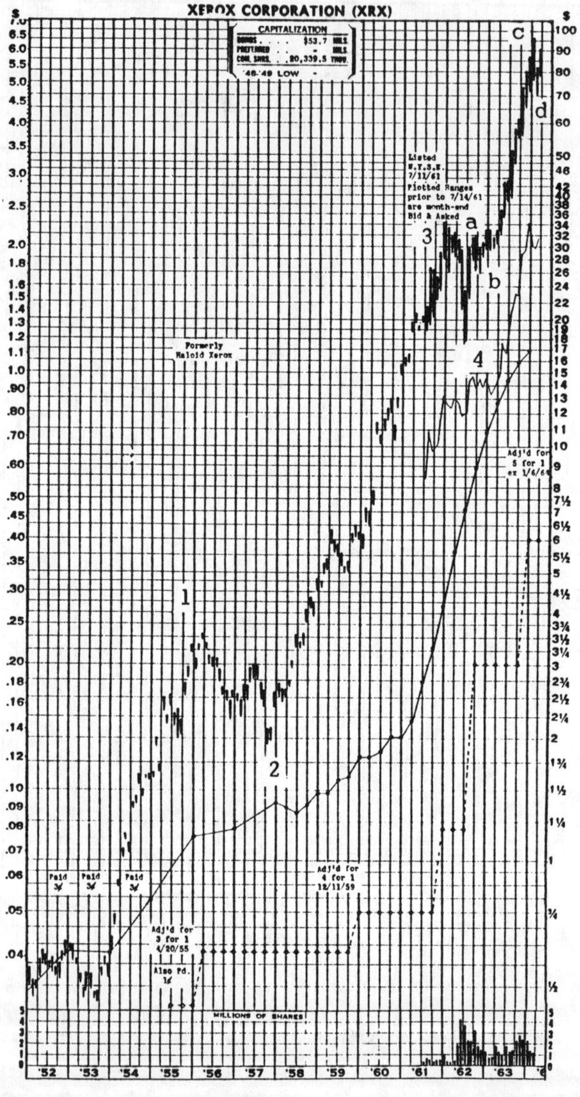

Xerox — Another classic, and difficult to define. It looks like we are well on in wave 5, but that it is not yet quite completed. Wave 5 appears to have started in mid-1962, and is now well advanced, probably having completed sub-wave c. At all events, this looks "chancy" as a new purchase at these levels. The pattern, however, points up the difficulty of defining the waves in a high-flying stock.

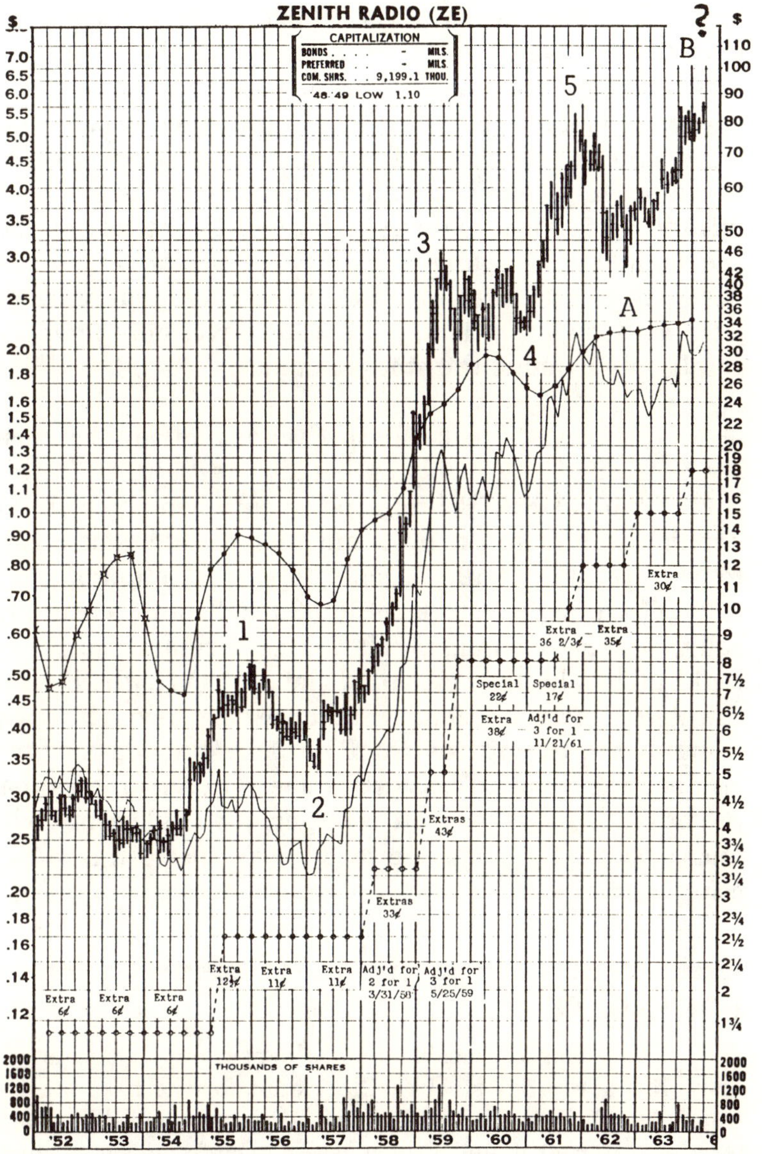

Zenith — Another classic "growth" stock. The orthodox top appears to be in 1961 (as in so many of these types of stocks), from which a "5-wave down" developed into October 1962. This we classify as A of the long-term correction. Wave B is now in progress, we assume, and as in so many other ones, it appears to hit new high ground. From an Elliott point of view, this type of pattern should be avoided.

The fascination of the Elliott Wave Principle is not with the 3-wave pattern, but rather with the 5-wave up or down. A number of old-time technicians have suggested that one should forget about the 5-wave pattern and concentrate solely on the 3-wave, since the latter is far more prevalent. It is a matter of opinion. Elliott certainly did a lot of writing from time to time to explain his 5-3-5-3-5. Yet, we think that the sample of company stock market charts demonstrated herewith will do much to indicate that there is definitely a 5-wave pattern, even though these examples only represent a small proportion of the stocks listed.

Of what value is Elliott so far as individual securities are concerned? Probably on balance very little. However, there are occasions (Polaroid, perhaps) when a stock has had a major decline in which the question of judgment arises as to what level it should be sold. The completion of a major wave down (as in Polaroid 1960-62) calls almost automatically, despite earnings, relative performance, etc., for a build-up to a broadly calculable level. This is the B wave of the A-B-C combination. But once this level is reached (roughly the 180-220 level in Polaroid), the odds of a further rise become less and less attractive. On a long-term basis, the bull market is over. It is better, it would seem, to be in stocks where the major upward 5-wave pattern is yet to be completed.

FOOTNOTES

[1] This discussion makes sense only if one is of the opinion that *certain* stocks will account for the bear market to come. The DJIA as a whole is no more or less vulnerable to decline (or rise) after stock splits, because the Dow's divisor is changed simultaneously. The weighting merely shifts to higher priced components.

[2] This is the only document missing from our collection, so it is nice that Bolton reproduces this chart, which was probably the focus of that document.

[3] If the Wave Principle governs mass emotional psychology, then this "curious fact" is exactly what one should expect.

[4] The bullish position of the Supercycle precluded both of these events.

THE ELLIOTT WAVE PRINCIPLE OF STOCK MARKET BEHAVIOR

1965

A SUPPLEMENT TO

The Bolton-Tremblay

BANK CREDIT ANALYST

A. Hamilton Bolton, editor-in-chief

THE ELLIOTT WAVE PRINCIPLE OF STOCK MARKET BEHAVIOR 1965 SUPPLEMENT

ELLIOTT IN A NUTSHELL

Background Information

The Elliott Wave Principle was little known only a few years ago. Due primarily to our continuous annual supplements published every year since 1953 in the spring of the year, it has become, if not a household word, at least a recognized stock market theory.

Elliott's writings are all out of print, with the exception of his 1939 articles in the *Financial World.*[1] In addition to the *Financial World* articles, which give a pretty thorough resume of all that Elliott knew about the Wave Principle at least up to that time, he wrote two monographs: *The Wave Principle* (1938) and *Nature's Law* (1946), both published privately.

Up until 1960, there was no thorough study of Elliott theory. In 1959, however, your editor decided to put together a full-fledged and critical book. This was published in 1960 under the title, *The Elliott Wave Principle - A Critical Appraisal.*

A further study of Elliott, based on all he wrote during his lifetime, has appeared in Arthur A. Merrill's 1964 edition of *Behavior of Prices on Wall Street.*

What is the Principle?

Elliott postulated, based on a study of stock market averages since 1854 (using the Axe-Houghton stock average, which was then the only one available, and the Dow Industrials since 1897), that the movement of stocks could always be classified into waves which could be subdivided into smaller waves on the basis of a recurring principle. This was the phenomenon illustrated by the following diagram:

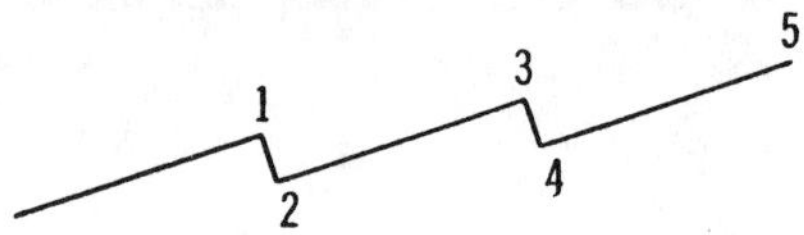

From this, it can be seen that a wave breaks down into five subwaves, with subwaves 1, 3 and 5 in the direction of the whole wave and subwaves 2 and 4 acting as temporary corrections.

Elliott then hypothesized that each subwave within the main wave should break down into a fixed number of sub-subwaves. Accordingly, he studied empirically market fluctuations and found that, in the pattern above, sub-waves 1, 3 and 5 would again break down into five smaller waves. This is illustrated herewith:

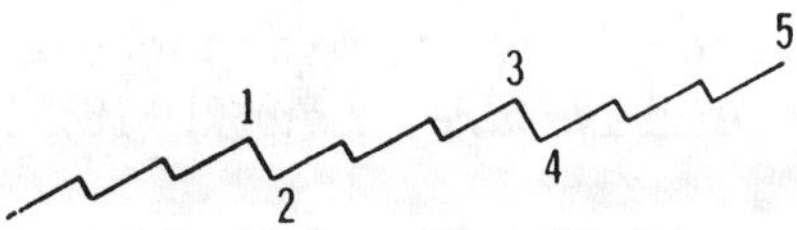

Finally, the sub-subwaves mentioned above would also themselves break down into further groups of five sub-sub-subwaves, as indicated:

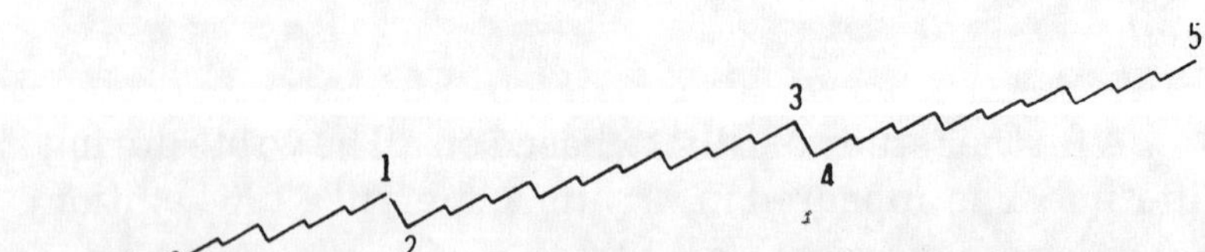

What about the corrective waves (i.e., waves 2 and 4)? These, according to Elliott, could (almost) always be broken down into three subwaves. In theory, these subwaves should break down into 5-3-5 patterns known as "zigzags," as shown herewith:

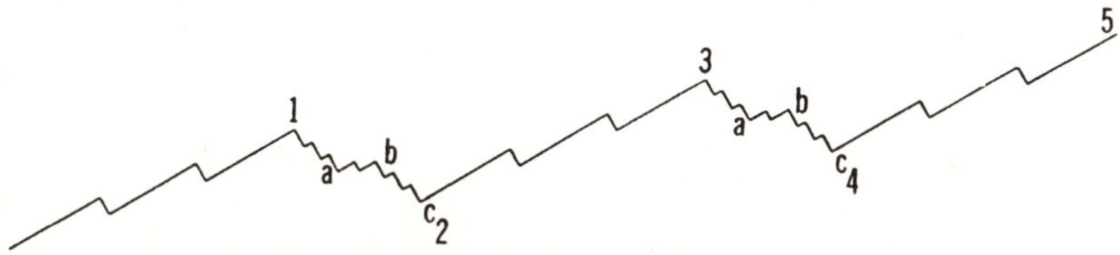

In practice, however, Elliott soon found that it was impossible to make this theoretical corrective wave pattern "work" when he came to actual movements. Consequently, he had to analyze these market movements and come up with variations. The variations that he came up with are shown on the following page. (All these diagrams are taken from the series of twelve articles by Elliott which the *Financial World* published in 1939, referred to at the beginning of this Supplement.)

It becomes plain that corrective waves are much less predictable than waves in the direction of the main trend. In later writings, Elliott developed even more complicated corrections, with the result that while one can usually (after the event) fit a known type of corrective wave into what has happened, it becomes extremely difficult, if not impossible, to do so at the time the wave is actually progressing through time, i.e., to know in advance which type of corrective wave will follow.

So much for the broad principle, which can be studied in greater depth with the help of the various publications noted.

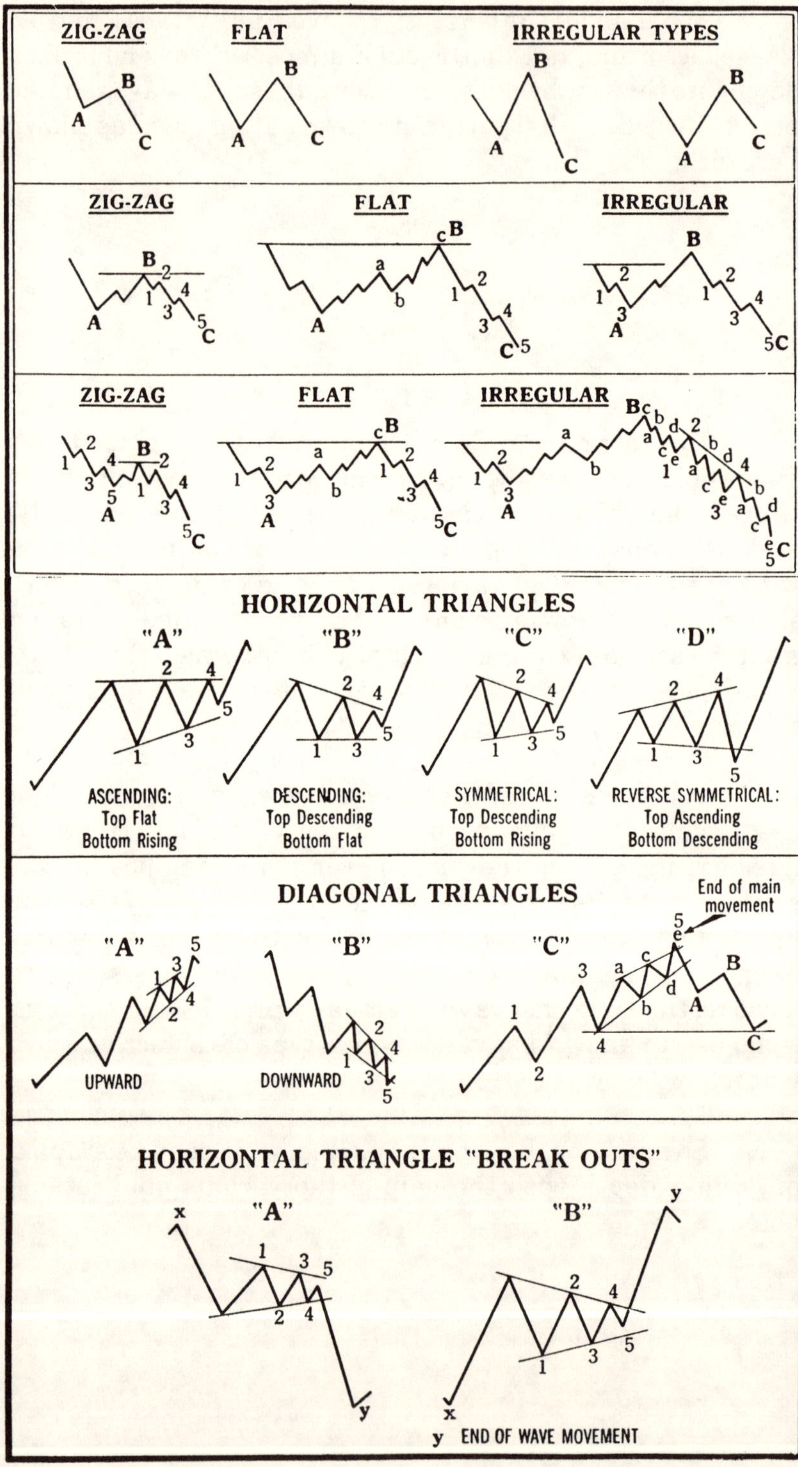
ZIG-ZAG
FLAT
IRREGULAR TYPES
ZIG-ZAG
FLAT
IRREGULAR
ZIG-ZAG
FLAT
IRREGULAR
HORIZONTAL TRIANGLES
"A"
"B"
"C"
"D"
ASCENDING:
Top Flat
Bottom Rising
DESCENDING:
Top Descending
Bottom Flat
SYMMETRICAL:
Top Descending
Bottom Rising
REVERSE SYMMETRICAL:
Top Ascending
Bottom Descending
DIAGONAL TRIANGLES
"A"
"B"
"C"
End of main movement
UPWARD
DOWNWARD
HORIZONTAL TRIANGLE "BREAK OUTS"
"A"
"B"
y END OF WAVE MOVEMENT

THE ELLIOTT PRINCIPLE AND THE HISTORY OF THE STOCK MARKET

As 1854 was the earliest date of calculation of a stock market average then available, Elliott examined the record up to 1929 and found that from 1857 to 1929, he could divide the history into five large waves, and that each of the subwaves seemed also to fit into the pattern, etc. Actually, the data available were not really sufficiently precise to be sure of this, but at least it appeared to make sense. Each of the three waves in the direction of the trend could be broken down into five subwaves, and each of the two intervening waves became rather complicated families of three subwaves.

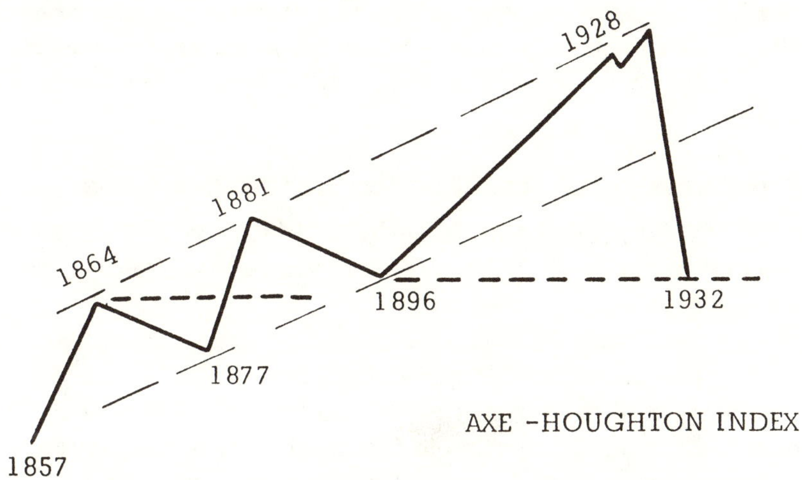

The chart above (from the author's *The Elliott Wave Principle - A Critical Appraisal,* 1960 edition) shows how this was calculated and what it looked like.

Usually, in the last generation, bull markets have been long in both time and amplitude, and bear markets (or Elliott corrections) short. In the period from 1857, however, to the orthodox top of the market in November 1928, except after 1896, bull markets tended to be shorter in time than the corrections which followed them, as the preceding chart shows.

Bull Market	1857-64	7 years
Bear Market	1864-77	13 years
Bull Market	1877-8	14 years
Bear Market	1881-96	15 years
Bull Market	1896-1928	32 years

One logical explanation of this was the fact that prior to the Federal Reserve Act of 1913, the United States did not have a flexible monetary system. Thus, as business expanded after a depression, the demand for funds became so high that stock market credit began to get out of reach. Something had to give and, of course, it had to be collateral borrowings rather than self-liquidating business borrowings. At any event, by 1921 at the latest, the pattern of more rapidly expanding and longer bull markets and shorter bear markets began to appear and have generally (despite 1929-32, which some analysts feel was a full and complete correction of the whole 1857-1929 super bull market) been the rule since.

The Correction of the 1857-1928 Grand Super Cycle

Elliott called this series of five bull market waves a Grand Super Cycle. Each of the five waves was thus a Super Cycle.

The correction of the Grand Super Cycle would be another Grand Super Cycle. It could be in three waves, or possibly in triangular form in five waves. This latter type of correction presumably only comes in the fourth wave. At least, Elliott never found triangle waves other than in the fourth wave formation.

Three views have been expressed as to the terminal point of the Grand Super Cycle correction.

Early Elliott	1932
Later Elliott (after 1942)	1942
Bolton (after 1949)	1949

The first is a 3-wave affair. The latter two are triangles (5 waves).

Each has its points in favor and against. The first is very short in time, only three years to correct 72 years of bull market. The second is reasonable, except that technically one of the triangle waves does not break down properly. The third is technically correct in all waves, is long enough, but puts the starting point of the new Grand Super Cycle rather high (161 Dow Jones Industrials) in relation to the 1932 low (41), or the 1942 low (92).

Either one of these points can be used as a starting point for the third Grand Super Cycle since 1857. Naturally, we favor 1949 as a starting point because it is technically correct and we invented it! But we cannot claim that Elliott would have agreed.

In *The Elliott Wave Principle — A Critical Appraisal,* we showed how two of these interpretations were probably getting into gear. Figure 47 of that publication is reprinted on the next page. What was marked 196-? when published in 1960 has now been resolved as terminating in 1961.

What is marked as the termination of II could conceivably have terminated in June 1962, although here again such an interpretation suffers from the same fault as the 1929-32 wave interpretation as a correction of 1857-1928: too short in time.

We have favored the interpretation that the down wave of 1961-62 was only the first of three waves of which we are still in only the second, i.e., an A-B-C affair.

We recognized the probability in 1962 that if we had this A-B-C type of correction, wave B would go well beyond the orthodox top of the 1949-61 bull market. An interesting aside is one of the conclusions from the Addendum to the 1962 Supplement, dated May 28, 1962: "Purchases made at the present time should work out extremely satisfactorily." Regardless of conclusions by other technical or fundamental authors, this Elliott interpretation shows the value of keeping an eye at all times on this technical market principle.

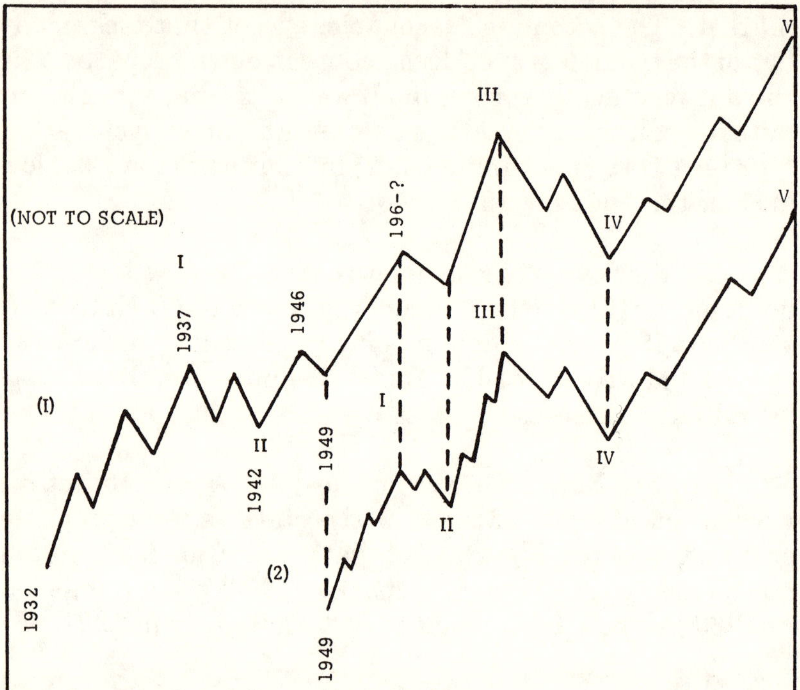

TWO BASIC INTERPRETATIONS:

(1) NEW SUPERCYCLE BEGINS 1932
(2) NEW SUPERCYCLE BEGINS 1949

AND AN EXPLANATION OF HOW THEY COULD GET INTO GEAR WITH EACH OTHER IN THE 3rd, 4th and 5th WAVES.

BOLTON, TREMBLAY (BERMUDA) LIMITED

THE BULL MARKET SINCE 1962

Last year in our Elliott Supplement, we published a hypothetically probable course of the bull market in chart form. This outline chart is reproduced herewith. What it added up to was that we were probably only halfway through the remaining part of the bull market since the Kennedy assassination in November 1963.

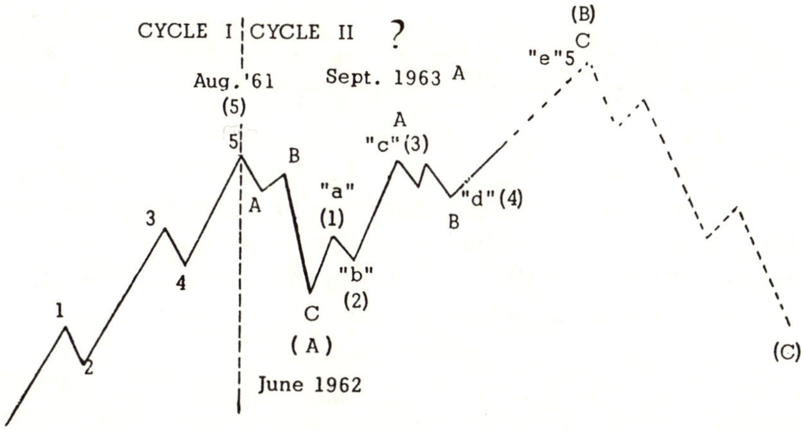

This now requires some modification of the numbering because of the subnormal character of the correction throughout 1963, 1964 and 1965-to-date.

The character of the market since the June 1962 bottom, and in particular in the third wave, which started with the Cuban crisis in late October, now gives us the distinct impression that we are seeing a remarkable *extension.*

The figure herewith, from the *Financial World* articles, shows how waves can extend, and this particular extension pattern seems to be very akin to what has been happening since the Cuban crisis.

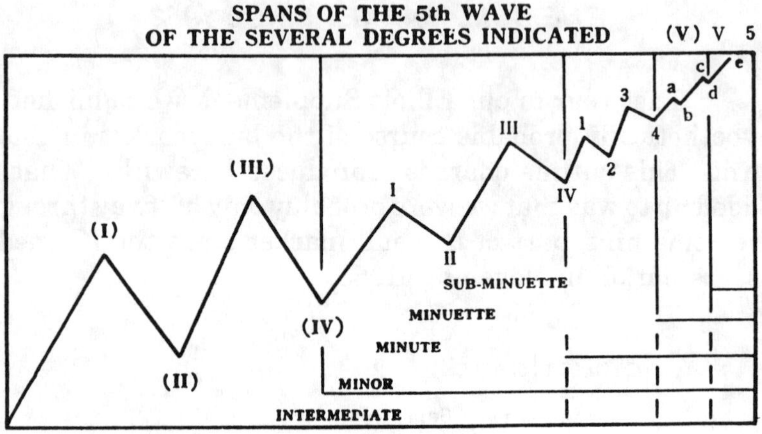

The chart below, from R. W. Mansfield's Stock Chart Service, gives our interpretation of the numbering of waves since 1961. This numbering is, of course, tentative, but it would look to us as if the waves began a series of successive extensions of lower degree at the end of wave IV.[2]

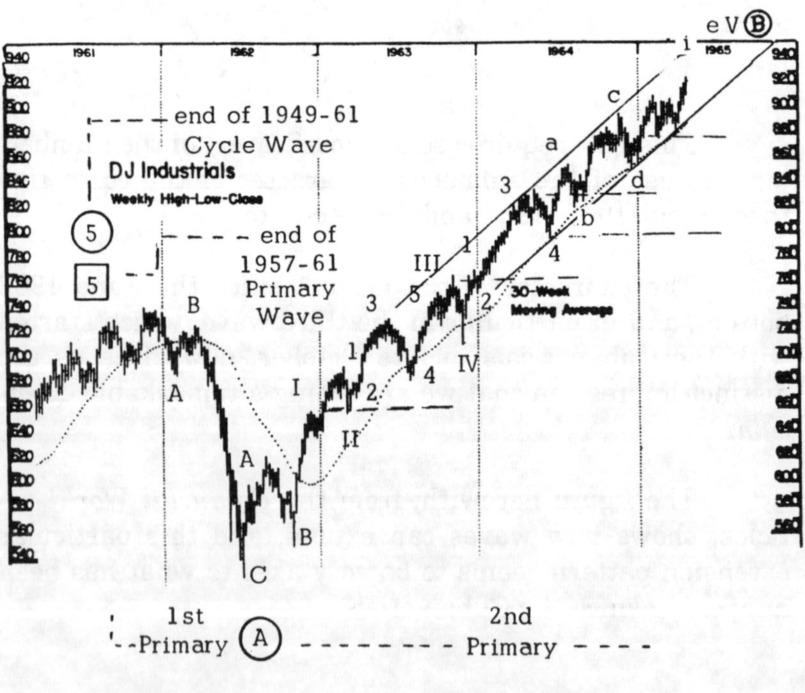

Elliott's comment on extensions included the following points:

> (1) "In an extension, the length (and degree) of the wave becomes much longer than normal. It may occur as a part of wave 1 or 3, but is usually a part of wave 5 of the main movement."[3]
>
> (2) "Of the normal five waves, the fifth vibration is usually the largest and most dynamic of the series, thus becoming in effect an extension of an extension."[3]
>
> (3) "The completion of the normal or first five waves of an extension *is never the end of the cyclical movement,* but does constitute a distinct warning that the end of the bull cycle is approaching, as only two more broad waves (one down and one up) would fully reflect the maximum force of the bull market."

If our wave V, which commenced with the Kennedy assassination in November 1963, is being extended (actually an extension of an extension), then it may still have some way to go. One characteristic that Elliott pointed to was that extensions often pushed upwards through "channels" around the waves, and that this was a sign to look for.

As can be seen by the successive numbering of the waves and sub-waves, we still do not appear to have completed i of e of V of Ⓑ. And, of course, even the tentative wave marked i on the preceding chart can itself start to extend again.

The number of waves of all degrees starting from the Cuban crisis so far totals 17. If wave V is extending also, as we think, then the completion of i plus ii, iii, iv and v would total 21 waves, a sound Elliott (Fibonacci) number.

One further rule that Elliott used was that extensions were always double-retraced, once by a downward movement and later by an upward movement. Thus, if the series of extensions started in wave III, the market at some point in the future would return to about the top of wave I, or around 660. Alternatively, the extensions of wave V only should return to the top of wave III, or about 760 in the averages. Similarly, the extension of 5 of wave V should come back to somewhere near the top of 3, or about 820. Again, the extension of wave e of wave 5 of wave V calls for coming back to at least the approximate 885 level. And so on.

There is, however, apparently no particular time limit for these returns to lower levels, but presumably they will be done after wave Ⓑ is completed and wave Ⓒ gets under way.

To conclude this discussion of the current bull market, we may summarize a few points:

(1) The wave since the Cuban crisis is extending.

(2) The extensions are not complete yet.

(3) The last extension of an extension will be a typical 5-wave formation.

(4) Look for a possible upside breakout over the upper channel line.

(5) Or, any break down through the lower channel line which also breaks through the top of the third wave or bottom of the fourth wave of any degree will probably be a clear indication that the whole wave from October 1962 is over.

(6) Thereafter, look for a possible come-back to above the end of the final extension of the fifth wave before the big bear market begins.

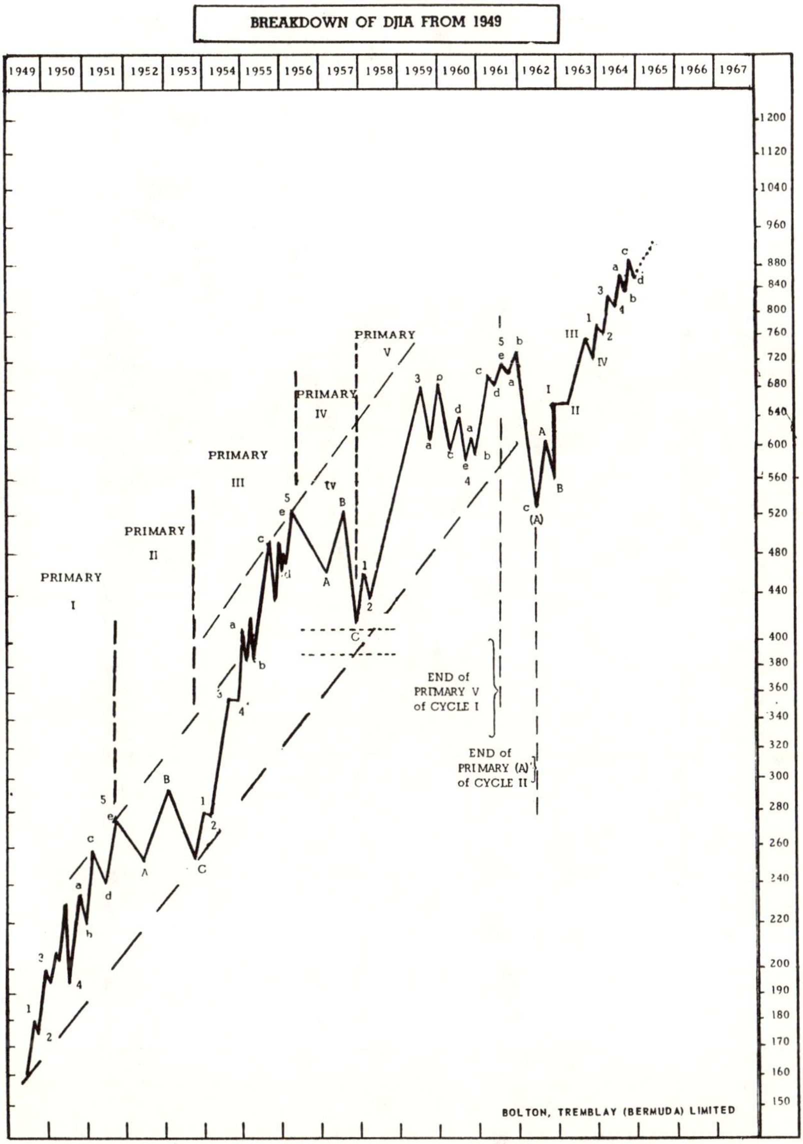

The chart above shows our detailed breakdown of the Dow Jones industrials from 1949-to-date, as published each year.

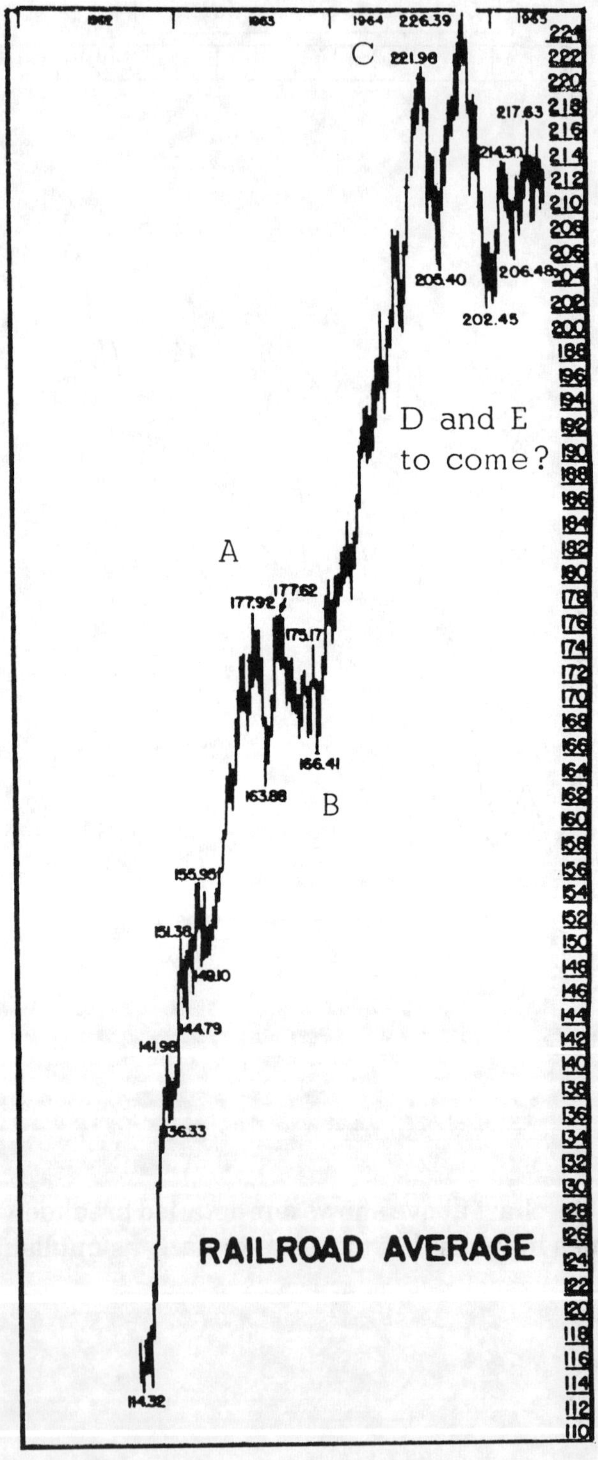
1962
1963
1964
1965
226.39
C
221.98
217.63
214.30
205.40
206.48
202.45
D and E
to come?
A
177.92
177.62
175.17
163.88
166.41
B
155.95
151.38
149.10
144.79
141.98
136.33
RAILROAD AVERAGE
114.32

WHAT ABOUT THE RAILS?

In the preceding chart, from R. W. Mansfield's Service, we tentatively put some numbers on the main waves. It would appear to be completing, or have completed, wave four (or D) of V, which began in 1962. The chances are, therefore, that the Rail average will go to new highs before the present bull market is over.

Last year's diagram of the broad picture of the Rails is repeated below. According to this analysis, the Super Cycle began in 1942, and we have been in wave V since the lows of 1962.

DOW-JONES RAIL AVERAGE

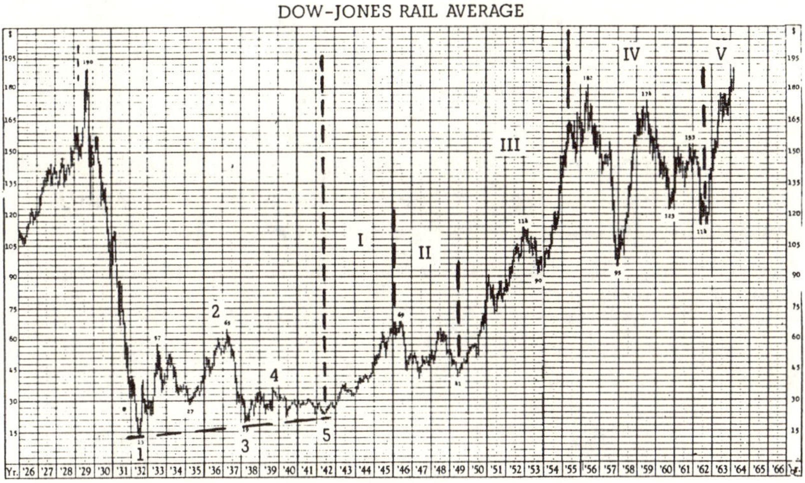

Source: M. C. Horsey Chart Book (1)

THOSE INDIVIDUAL STOCKS

We commented last year on the fact that it was more difficult to apply Elliott to individual stocks than to the market as a whole. The main feature of value in Elliott is his five-wave proposition in the direction of the main trend.

Last year, we published as an appendix a number of charts of individual stocks that were to illustrate the 5-wave principle, which is that in individual stocks, if you can see a clear-cut 5-wave pattern, you can be reasonably sure that you are at the end of the move of that degree. The 5-wave pattern is given in the diagram below. Spotting this in individual stocks can be quite rewarding, either on the upside or on the downside.

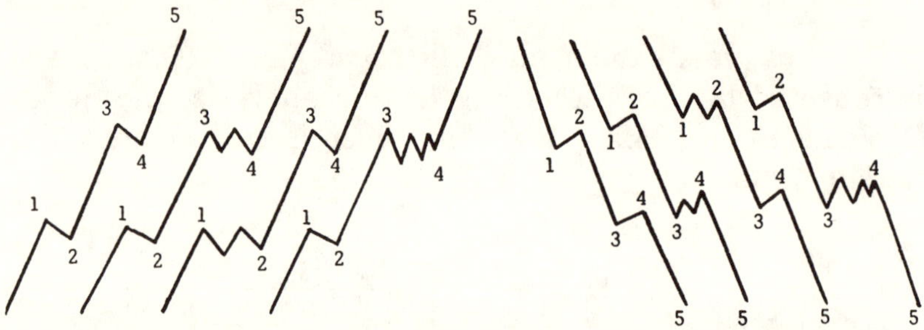

It is not our intention in this issue of the Elliott Supplement to give a great number of further examples of the 5-wave principle. In many cases, they are difficult to find. In some cases, however, we seemed to see the 5-wave pattern developing, but felt that it was not yet completed. A typical example is that of Xerox, which is certainly many people's growth favorite.

Xerox

Last year, we theorized that Xerox was then in its fifth wave since 1953. However, we felt that only three of the five waves might have been completed. We called it "chancy" as a new purchase. Actually at 90, in retrospect, the risks were not great. It appears now, however, that wave d has been completed, and we are along in wave e, which eventually will wind up the bigger wave 5. Usually, when one gets a short first wave "a" and a very long third wave "c", the fifth wave, "e", tends to be somewhat comparable in size to the "a" wave. Thus, we would now conclude that Xerox at 130 would be more "chancy" than last year. Interesting, too, is the fact that while earning power continues to climb, relative action has flattened right out. This may indicate a loss of market momentum.

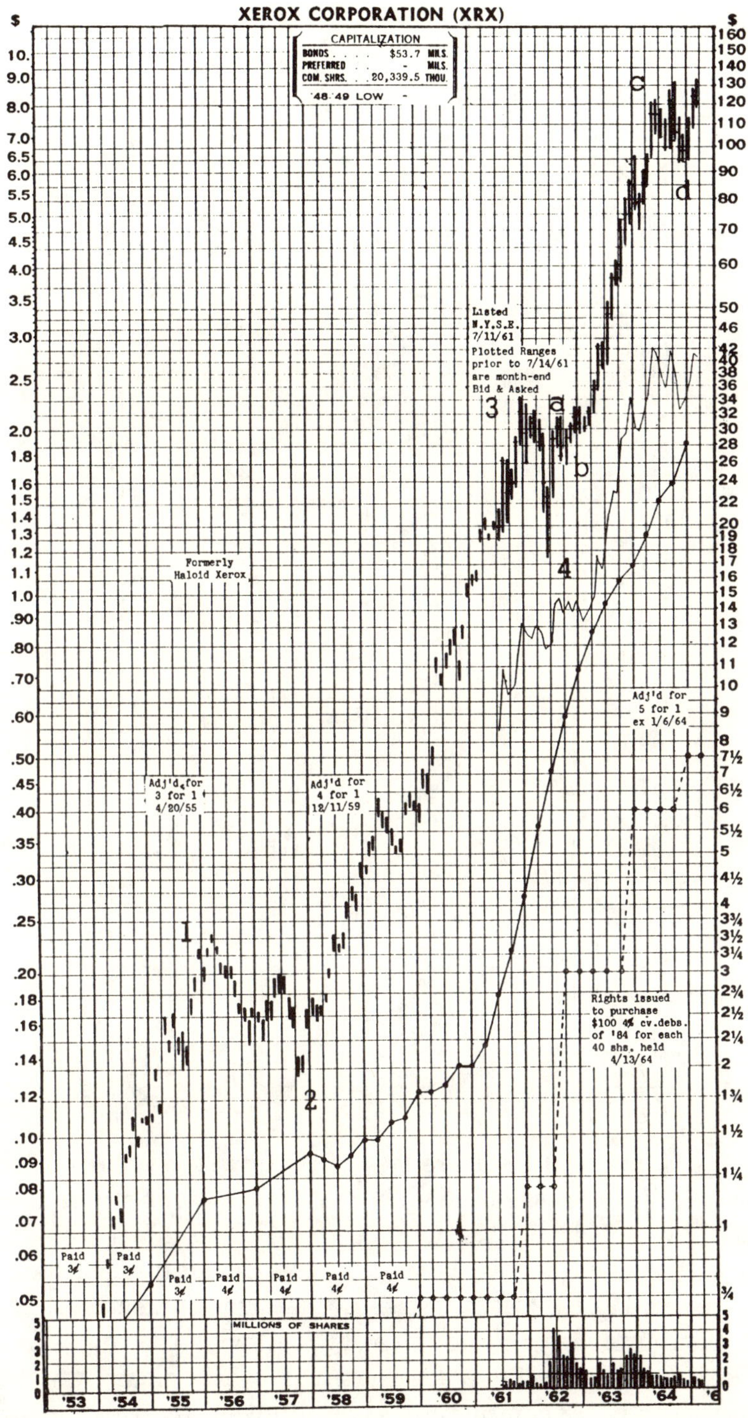
XEROX CORPORATION (XRX)
CAPITALIZATION
BONDS $53.7 MILS.
PREFERRED - MILS.
COM. SHRS. 20,339.5 THOU.
'48-'49 LOW -
Listed N.Y.S.E. 7/11/61
Plotted Ranges prior to 7/14/61 are month-end Bid & Asked
Formerly Haloid Xerox
Adj'd for 3 for 1 4/20/55
Adj'd for 4 for 1 12/11/59
Adj'd for 5 for 1 ex 1/6/64
Rights issued to purchase $100 4% cv.debs. of '84 for each 40 shs. held 4/13/64
Paid 3¢
Paid 3¢
Paid 3¢
Paid 4¢
Paid 4¢
Paid 4¢
Paid 4¢
MILLIONS OF SHARES
'53 '54 '55 '56 '57 '58 '59 '60 '61 '62 '63 '64

IBM

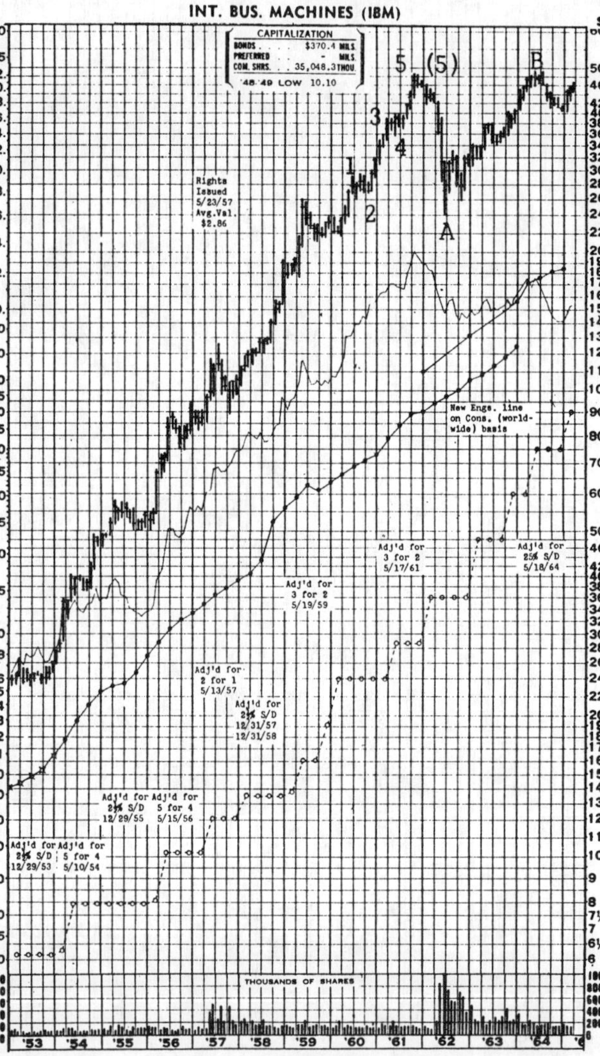

Xerox and IBM are two of the great favorites of the Street. We expressed the view that the postwar bull market in IBM was over in 1961, when the stock had clearly finished the fifth wave of the larger 5-wave formation, the 50% decline in 1961-62 being wave A of a large correction. This analysis probably did not sit very well with the majority of investors, but the facts are that it is pretty clear now that wave B may be completed, to be followed by a downward wave C.

What's happening here? Earnings are still rising, but, it would appear, at a slightly slower rate. Relative action is quite uninteresting. Obviously, the mass of investors is now gradually revising its idea of what multiplier the earning power should have. A few years ago, it was 60 times; now it is only 35 times. If earnings flatten out at all markedly, the multiplier (price-earnings ratio) could decline some more. Sacred cows can be dangerous.

Vendo Company

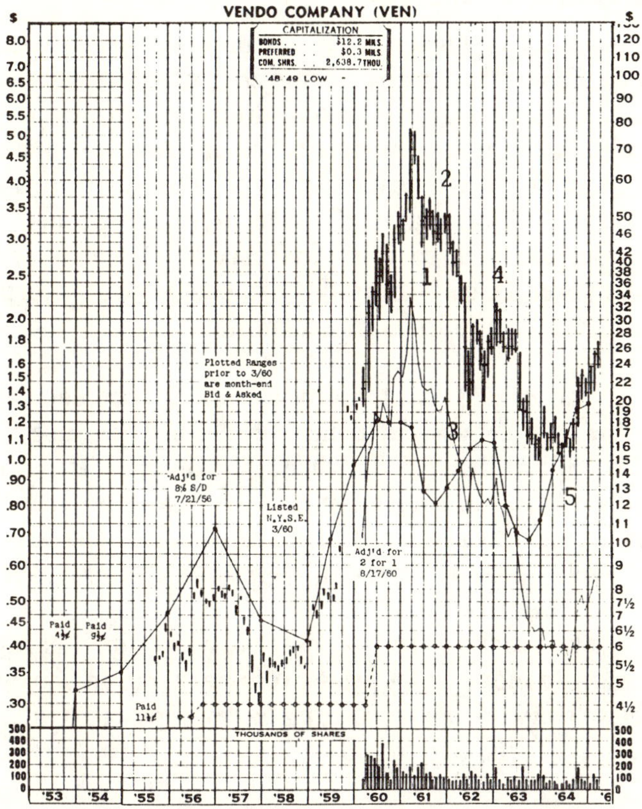

As an example of a stock which has gone through an extreme bear market (76 to 14 in four years), Vendo Co. is typical of its industry. A high flyer which would have been extremely difficult to analyze on a count basis in the rise from

1958 to 1961, and symbolic of so many of the over-touted so-called growth stocks, Vendo shows a pretty clear-cut 5-wave down pattern, which terminated at 14 in 1964. Since then, there appears to be a minor 5-wave up developing. Earnings trends are favorable, as is relative action. This could be the first leg of a new bull market of some size.

FURTHER RAMBLINGS ON ELLIOTT

Making Elliott Scientific?

As all of us know, investment is an art and not a science. There are many people that can estimate earnings reasonably correctly in an expanding economic cycle. Not too many, however, can measure the impact in advance of a change in the business cycle. The Elliott Wave Principle started with the averages. Only later, and much less successfully, was it applied to individual stocks. It even appears that in many broad cases, individual stocks do not conform to any rigid Elliott Wave Principle formula.

The reason that many stocks do not seem to have recognizable Elliott patterns is probably because the company itself is neither going through a phase of expansion nor one of contraction. With a broad average, however, there is always a secular rise around which the business and investment cycle operates, caused by growth and/or inflation.

The stocks with the fastest growth in earning power will usually move up in price. It is here and in the opposites (those with long-term declining earning power) that the best 5-wave patterns are found.

Can we make Elliott scientific? The answer in individual stocks is certainly no. A stock like General Motors does not have and never has had a pattern like Chrysler. Each has its own individuality.

An average, by its nature, has a much better chance of being orthodox, i.e., of conforming to a visible and somewhat predictable pattern.

Arthur Merrill, in his book *Behavior of Prices on Wall Street,* has taken all waves and subwaves from 1928 to early 1963, and has classified them by size as follows:

Over 80%	I, II, III, etc.
Over 40%	A, B, C, etc.
Over 20%	1, 2, 3, etc.
Over 10%	a, b, c, etc.

Under this count, 1928 to 1932 broke down into A-B-C. So did 1932-37 (A-B-C). So did 1937-42 (A-B-C). But 1942 to date has only produced an A, with 1961-62 not being deep enough to produce a B. None of these fits in too well with Elliott's own counts. For instance, from 1928-32 (Elliott's first Grand Super Cycle before he revised his count in favor of 1928-42), Merrill measures as follows:

One wave over 80% in amplitude,
Three waves over 40% in amplitude,
Eleven waves over 20% in amplitude,
Fifty-seven waves over 10% in amplitude.

From 1932 to 1937, the situation was as follows:

One wave over 80% in amplitude,
Three waves over 40% in amplitude,
Seven waves over 20% in amplitude,
Thirty-nine waves over 10% in amplitude.

From 1937 to 1942, the score was:

One wave over 80% in amplitude,
Three waves over 40% in amplitude,
Five waves over 20% in amplitude,
Thirty-one waves over 10% in amplitude.

From 1942, the count comes out as follows, directly up-to-date:

> One wave over 80% in amplitude,
> One wave over 40% in amplitude,
> Eleven waves over 20% in amplitude,
> Thirty-seven waves over 10% in amplitude.

It is clear that while the highest degrees fit Elliott numbers (perhaps by coincidence), the next degrees down of 11, 7, 5 and 11 are *not* Elliott numbers, except one, and the lowest degrees of 57, 39, 31 and 37 bear the relation to Elliott wave totals. (Elliott's wave divisions fit the Fibonacci mathematical time series of 1, 1, 2, 3, 5, 8, 13, 21, 34, 55, 89, 144, etc. See *The Elliott Wave Principle — A Critical Appraisal.)*

Now, there is no particular reason why we should use classifications such as 80%, 40%, 20% and 10%. These are purely arbitrary. Perhaps we should look for precision in determining what are Elliott waves by sticking to percentages which are akin to the Fibonacci numbers themselves. Instead of 80%, 40%, 20% and 10%, perhaps we ought to use 144%, 89%, 55%, 34%, 21%, 13%, 8% and 5%.

This type of research we have not yet done, but should it prove that the number of waves of various Fibonacci percentages fell into Fibonacci numbers, we would have a formidable additional tool to use in making Elliott interpretation more precise, at least in handling averages.

But would this help us with individual stocks? Perhaps. We might find some stocks which operate in a pattern of main moves made in accordance with a certain Fibonacci percentage, say 55%, and corrective moves being according to a smaller Fibonacci percentage, such as 13% or 8%. Once a pattern was found in a stock over a generation, let us say, it would be an assumption that it should continue, unless, of course, there was a drastic change in the company's outlook. As a corollary, a change in the numbers might be a signal of an underlying change in the insides (management, etc.) of the corporation.

This certainly is food for thought among those who wish to make the Wave Principle more useful.

Extensions

If we are correct in thinking that we are seeing a vast extension in Elliott terms in wave V of the market since the Cuban crisis, it seems also possible that we are seeing, or have seen, extensions in individual securities.

Many of the high flyers of the 1959-61 "growth stock" market appear to have had extensions. These are what other technicians might call stilt formations. Take Brunswick Corporation, depicted in the next chart. It is perhaps a perfect example of what happens to an extended stock.

Elliott was not 100% clear as to where a stock should come back to, but it is somewhere between the top of the third wave and the bottom of the fourth wave before the extension. Last year, we published our analysis of Brunswick, and on the up-to-date chart we have put this in without change, except that the 5-wave down from 1961 is now clearly numbered.

In this case, the extension started at point d in wave 5. If there had been no extension in this wave, the top of wave (5) would have ended at e. But here it continued on to f, g, h, and i, thus spreading the wave e into five further waves.

According to Elliott's rules, one would expect the stock to revert to the beginning area of the extension, i.e., to between c and d, and, in effect, this is exactly the area at which the 5-wave down was completed in late 1964.

Then one had an indication, additional to the downside count, that Brunswick around 8-10 would turn around in an important way.

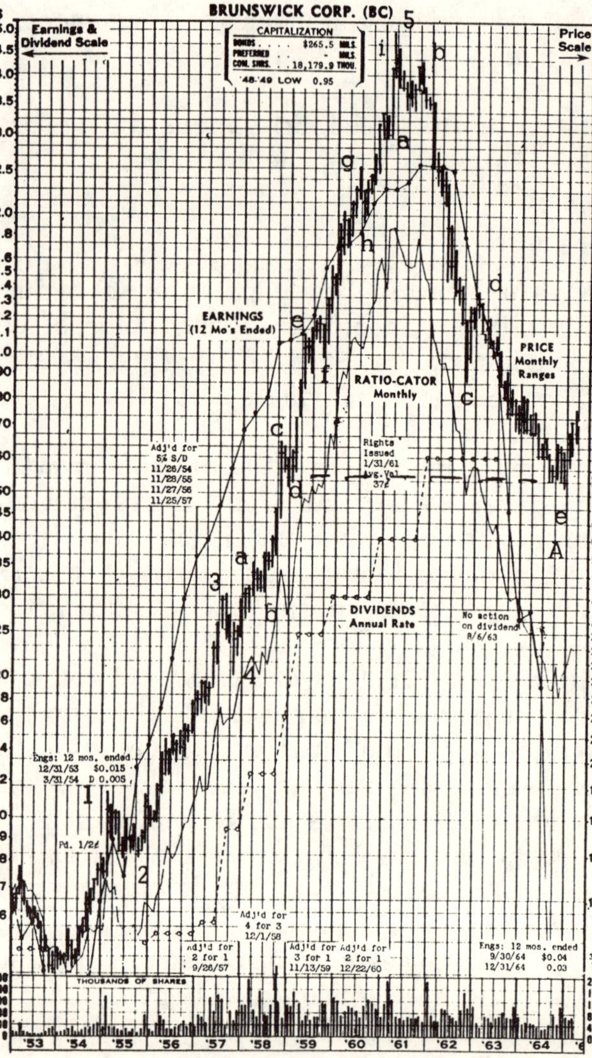

Elliott used to say that if one had an extension in any of waves 1, 3 or 5, one would not have an extension in any other. This remains to be proved, we feel. In other words, if Brunswick extended in the fifth wave in 1960-61, its final bottom will be in the 8-10 area, as recently reached. However, if it is possible to have a normal first wave up, a third wave which is made up of five sizeable waves rather than normal in size, and a fifth wave which breaks down into nine sizeable waves, as might seem to be the case in Brunswick (say), we might argue that when Brunswick completed its fifth wave down in late 1964, it did not necessarily complete its final bear market. In fact, the 5-wave down pattern from 1961-64 really suggests that this is only wave A of the bear market, as we noted in our last year's analysis that we are now in a B (3-sub-wave) upside correction, and that in due course we will have another 5-wave down to complete the C.

If Brunswick can keep above 8 or so in future years, this may well prove Elliott's theory. At present, it is sometimes difficult to know what is an extension and what is simply a spreading out of waves.

The application of this to the general market picture seems to be as follows. In the normal case, wave V should have been completed at point a in mid-1964. [See bottom chart on page 326.] Thus, it began its extension at point 4. From no matter what top, then, that the market finally makes, we would expect the next major downward wave to fulfill its implication by falling to the 800-820 level in the Dow Jones Industrials. Let us say for the sake of argument that the Dow finally gets to well over 1000. The ensuing decline should stop at least temporarily around the 800-820 level.

This could be an interesting test of one of Elliott's theories.

Double Retracement

Elliott's double retracement theory is harder to justify. In the normal case, if the third wave of a correction (A-B-C) takes the market back to the beginning of the extension, this is fine, for the next wave will carry up and through the old highs. But what happens if the A wave goes back to the right spot, as in Brunswick, and this is a 5-wave down, implying a zigzag (rather unusual) correction? If it is a zigzag, how can wave C stop at the bottom of wave A or higher?[4]

These are some of the riddles to which Elliott did not live long enough to give us his answers, as in many other fields.

Relative Performance

Relative performance charts are used by a number of technical students. They measure the relationship of a stock's price trend to that of the averages. If the curve of this ratio rises, it means the stock is doing better than the market. If it declines, the contrary is indicated.

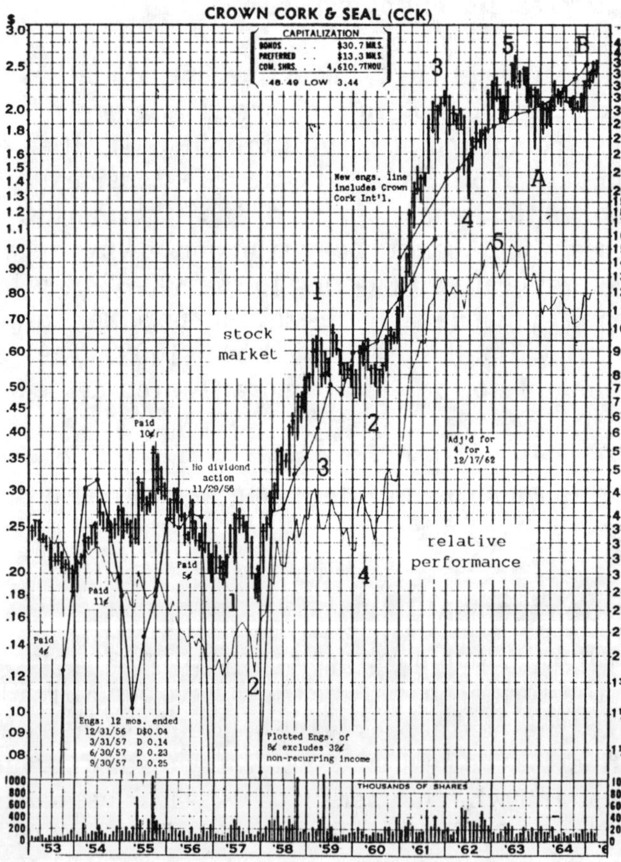

A further refinement, however, is to attempt to apply an Elliott analysis not only to the stock price trend, but also to the relative performance curve.

An example of the use of this might be the case of Crown Cork and Seal, depicted here.

The normal 5-wave up appears to have run from late 1957 to mid-1963. What has happened since the orthodox top at close to 40 looks like a part of the correction of that major advance. The top of wave B could exceed the orthodox top, but it should not be considered the first wave of a new bull market until much more work is done.

Similarly, it is interesting that the relative performance curve started its 5-wave move in early 1957 before actual price bottomed out, and reached its peak in late 1962, well before the final orthodox top in price in mid-1963.

Many other examples can be found in the chart books, where watching the waves in the relative performance curves can help judgment as to the wave count in the stock itself.

CONCLUSION

1. The object of these Elliott supplements has never been to make a flat prediction. When we are as far up in a major bull market as we obviously are at present, there will tend to be many and varied interpretations.

2. Elliott, like Dow Theory, can only be entirely effective in hindsight. It has some advantages, however, over Dow Theory in that it does not depend on a confirmation of two averages or prices. Again, it often prevents a whip-saw such as happened to most Dow Theorists in the 1961-62-63 stock market. To show how this happens, consider the diagram on the next page.

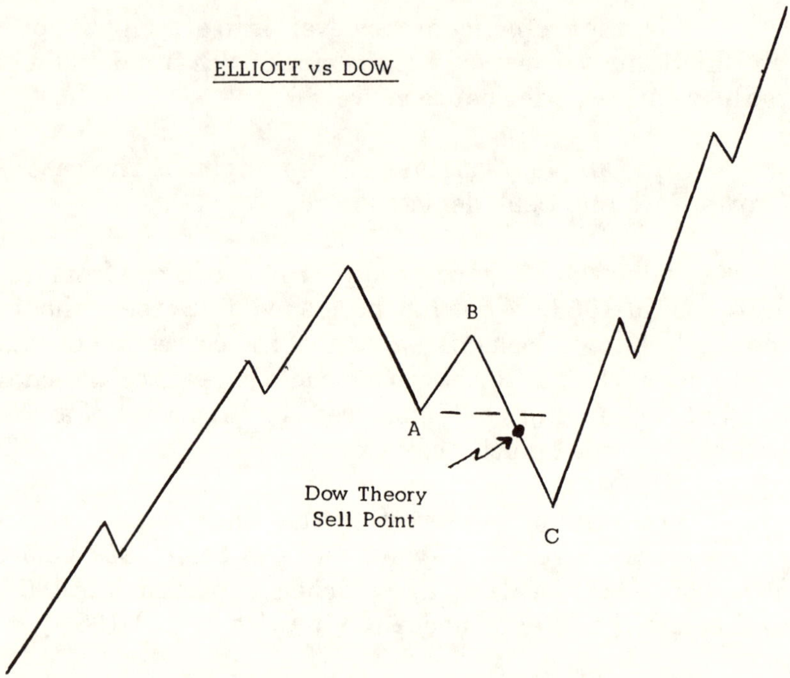

Just at the point that the Dow bear signal is given, the wave C is progressing normally. From B to C under Elliott will almost invariably be a 5-wave down. Of course, it may extend to 9 waves, but if it does, the automatic retracement will give an "out" for any seller better than the "Dow Theory sell point" under any conditions. If the C wave is normal, the new bull market 5-wave up will not produce enough correction to allow the Dow Theorists to get back in. They will be awaiting the "testing" of the old lows, which practically never comes.

Elliott and Dow, however, can be complementary. If a Dow signal is given way down after the top, the Elliott count should be studied closely. In past history, Dow sell signals have been most effective when the second corrective wave was a long one, as in 1929, 1937 and 1962. It is least effective in other markets such as 1953, 1957, etc., where by the time the signal was given, the market on Elliott's counts was close to downside completion.

3. It may be time to try to dissect Elliott on a more scientific basis. The main problem is that once one commences to do so, what comes up is not Elliott, but an entirely new wave theory. Maybe at this juncture of the great postwar bull market, this might not be a bad idea.

In the meantime, as the bull market progresses toward its ultimate top, it may be wise to keep a sharp lookout for stocks which appear to be remaining out of 5-waves-up.

May 6, 1965

FOOTNOTES

[1] BCA Publications had just reprinted these articles in pamphlet form, with a green cover.

[2] The liftoff from 1962 is better counted as a series of at least four first and second waves of decreasing degree.

[3] Although fifth waves *can* extend, the third is usually the extended wave.

[4] The larger extension of wave 5 began at point b in 1958, so Brunswick *should* fall lower, as per Bolton's wave labeling. As it turned out, Brunswick did indeed fall lower, completing an ABC bear market in 1966 at a price of 6, not quite to the beginning of the extension.

From the July 1965 Edition of
THE BANK CREDIT ANALYST

Elliott's Waves

Ordinarily, we do not comment on the Wave Principle between annual supplements. The current juncture is so interesting, however, that it deserves a note. Please see the updated graph of the Industrials. It is our view that on May 14th, they completed in all details their orthodox top. We had prejudged in our Annual Supplement two months ago that:

(1) the 1949-61 Cycle wave was complete in August 1961,

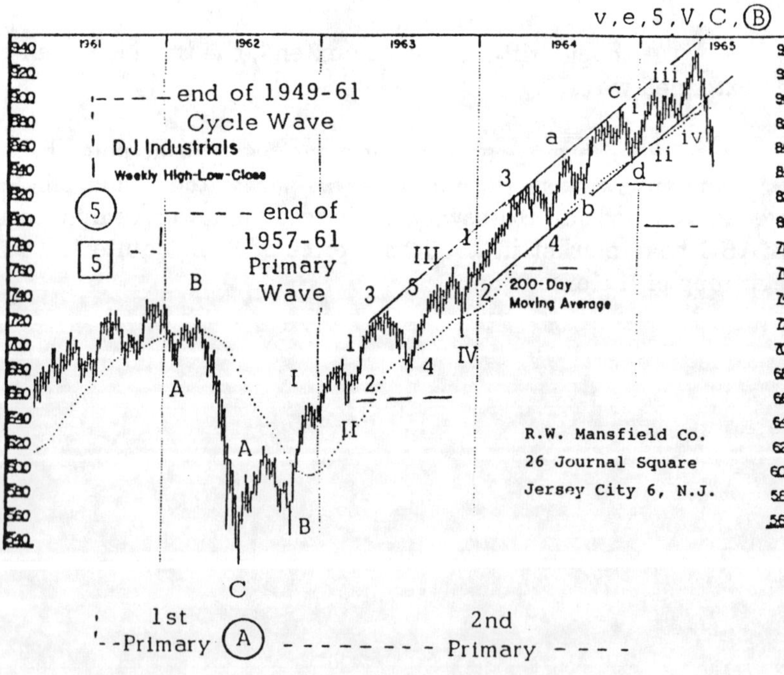

(2) that August 1961 to June 1962 was wave Ⓐ of Cycle II,
(3) that June 1962 to ? would be wave Ⓑ of Cycle II, and that this would be an irregular ABC formation with C starting at the Cuban Crisis in October 1962.

Of the C wave, as the diagram shows, we had completed four waves (I, II, III and IV), and were in the fifth wave V. Of wave V, we had completed 1, 2, 3 and 4, and were in 5. Of 5, we had completed a, b, c, and d and were in e. Of e, it now appears we completed i, ii, ii, iv and v on May 14th, thus at the same time completing e, 5, V, C, and Ⓑ. Note the break-out downside from the channel at about 906.

Technically, in Elliott terms, the bull market is over. However, because of the successive extensions of fifth waves starting with V, going on to 5, going on to e, going on to v, we have to bring in the principle of double-retracement. The market should go back and retrace to the beginning of the extension. The last extension was i, ii, iii, iv, v; consequently, the market should retrace back to between point c and d, which is already accomplished. The second retracement is a, b, c, d and e, or back to somewhere between 3 and 4 (roughly the 800-830 level). From either one of these areas, a double-retracement should take place, i.e., first coming down, then going up again. And, it is possible that we may have to retrace back to wave IV, or in the area between 750 and 710.

Of interest, too, is the down wave from May 14. This has already itself extended on the down side. The $64 question now is whether Elliott's dictum is correct, as given in paragraph (3) on page 11 of "The Elliott Wave Principle of Stock Market Behavior — 1965 Supplement", i.e.: "The completion of the normal or first five waves of an extension *is never the end of the cyclical movement*, but does constitute a distinct warning that the bull cycle is approaching an end, as only two more broad waves (one down and one up) would fully reflect the maximum force of the bull market...." If so, then the Dow Industrials are going to, after whatever level they stop at here, return to the old high of around 944.

Conclusion

A firm test of the 850-860 level has now been made, and it has failed. In view of this last minute development, we think that the chances of new highs in the averages are well less than 50-50. Breaking the 850 level looks like real trouble, with successive possible turning levels in the 800-830[1] level and again in the 710-750 level. Either of these would make it almost impossible to see new bull market peaks in view of the unfavorable monetary background.

June 28, 1965

FOOTNOTES

1 The hourly low occurred at 835.54 on June 29.

Montreal
February 11, 1966

Mr. Charles J. Collins
Investment Counsel, Inc.
800 Buhl Building
Detroit, Michigan 48226

Dear Joe:

This year, as usual around the end of April, we will be preparing our usual Elliott review. It occurred to me that maybe you would like to expose your views in the form of perhaps a guest editorial. This might be very appropriate as I feel that your count from June 1962 to date may well be very valid. My own, as you know, came out with May 14th, 1965 as a perfect 5-up from Cuba with a number of extensions. If this had been all we would have had a 1-2-3 from June 1962. But in the context of what has happened since, and keeping in mind any distinction between "extended" waves, which only can come in the last of the waves (because of the correction factor involved), and "elongated" waves, which often take place in a middle wave and are not corrected in the same way as "extended" waves, I feel that probably what has been going on since June 1965 is the 5th wave of a 5-up from June 1962.

In this context perhaps your idea of 1956-1962 irregular correction makes quite a bit of sense, and how this fits into the bigger 1949-pattern and the bigger still 1942-pattern, let alone the gigantic (in your count) 1932-pattern, might be of particular interest at present as the 5-wave 1962 to date (if that is what it is) pattern approaches its climax.

......page 2

Page 2.

This is a rather unusual request, and maybe you would prefer to skip it, but in the interests of a better knowledge of Elliott I am sure your views would be appreciated. If you decide to do this let me know whether you want it under your own name or unanimously.

Any copy you might care to write would be re-submitted to you for a final check to make sure that your ideas were faithfully projected.

If you are away, as I hope you are at this messy time of year, perhaps your secretary will be kind enough to forward this on to you. In any case, please give my very best regards to your good wife. Tony and I often talk of our one or two good times together.

Very best regards,

A.H. Bolton

AHB/th

EIGHT HUNDRED
BUHL BUILDING
DETROIT, MICHIGAN 48226

March 28, 1966

Dear Hamilton:

I am now back in Detroit and shall start working on the memorandum you wished, which I understand should be in your hands not later than April 20th. If there is any change in this deadline, please advise me. I, also, want to thank you for the copy of the Japanese edition of the Wave Principle, also, for your very generous notation on the flyleaf. It will make an interesting and unique edition to my library.

Regards,

C J Collins
ag

A. Hamilton Bolton, Esq.
Bolton, Tremblay & Company
1245 Sherbrooke St., West
Montreal 25, Canada

Charles J. Collins

1934

1934

1946

1980s

THE ELLIOTT WAVE PRINCIPLE OF STOCK MARKET BEHAVIOR

1966

——— *A SUPPLEMENT TO* ———

The Bolton-Tremblay

BANK CREDIT ANALYST

A. Hamilton Bolton, editor-in-chief

THE ELLIOTT WAVE PRINCIPLE OF STOCK MARKET BEHAVIOR 1966 SUPPLEMENT

INTRODUCTION

Last year in our Elliott Supplement, we published a hypothetically probable course of the bull market in chart form. This outline chart is reproduced herewith. What it added up to was that we were probably only halfway through the remaining part of the bull market since the Kennedy assassination in November 1963.

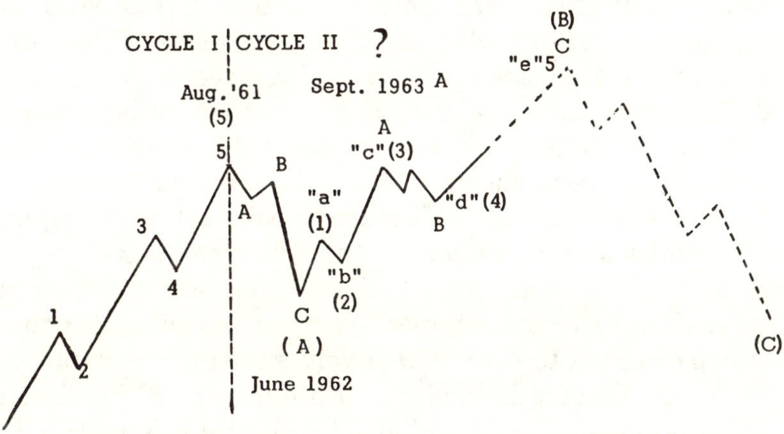

This count now requires some modification of the numbering because of the subnormal character of the correction throughout 1963, 1964 and 1965-to-date. This problem is tackled in this Supplement, as always, however, with the recognition that Elliott Wave theory is never final except in historical retrospect.

Your editor is particularly fortunate in this Supplement in having prevailed upon Charles J. Collins to contribute his views of where we are in the Elliott cycle, as well as in documenting his own very considerable part in the testing and formulation of the Elliott Wave Principle when it first appeared in 1939.[1] In fact, as he says, he wrote Elliott's first book for him, and if one is fortunate enough to have both the first book (1939) and Elliott's later *Nature's Law* (1946), one cannot but be impressed with the clarity and precision of the presentation of the first as compared to the diffuseness (albeit interspersed with fascinating, if esoteric, ideas) of the second.

It is suggested that Collins' interpretation later in this Supplement be studied. Its simplicity of presentation will appeal.

Mr. Collins has always been a proponent of the theory that Grand Super Cycle wave 5[2] commenced in 1932, not 1942 as Elliott later thought, nor in 1949 as your editor has espoused. In our 1960 book, we documented his ideas anonymously in some detail. Actually, it seems to make little difference as a practical matter whether one makes a case for 1932 or for 1949 (or for that matter 1942, although technically, as has been shown in *The Elliott Wave Principle — A Critical Appraisal*, the 1942 starting point is highly suspect). The differences can be seen in the following diagram, which is in broad outline only. Charles Collins' use of 1932 as the start of the fifth Grand Super Cycle (comparable to the third, which ran from 1857 to 1929) involves the consideration that wave (III) thereof probably is terminating in 1966. Elliott's 1942 date presumably will also be terminating in 1966[3] as the end of Super Cycle (I), if one accepts the count that Collins has placed on wave (III) as a 5-wave up made up of the following Cycle waves:

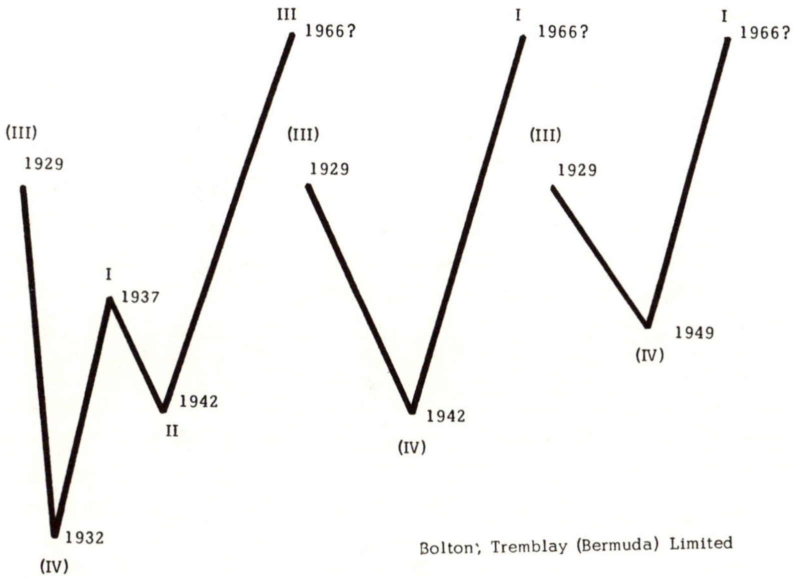

Figure 1

Cycle	I	1942-46
	II	1946-49
	III	1949-56
	IV	1956-62
	V	1962-66, making up Super Cycle (III).

The novelty of Mr. Collins' interpretation is in his large correction 1956-62,[4] which, however, can be correctly counted in detail without violating any of Elliott's basic principles.

Developments in 1965 point clearly now to the probability that there have been five waves up since the low in June 1962, and that this runs counter to your editor's view of probabilities that there would be only three waves up (in a larger unorthodox A-B-C formation with the B top much higher than the 1961 peak, and the C wave duplicating the A wave at around 500 at some point in the future). The basic differences between our 1965 and prior count and what now appears as a more logical count can be seen in the diagram herewith.

As of May 1965, it appeared that three waves up (the last from the Cuban Crisis in October 1962 being an extended wave, as outlined in the 1965 Supplement and further documented as completed as of May 14th in the July issue of *The Bank Credit Analyst*) had made up the

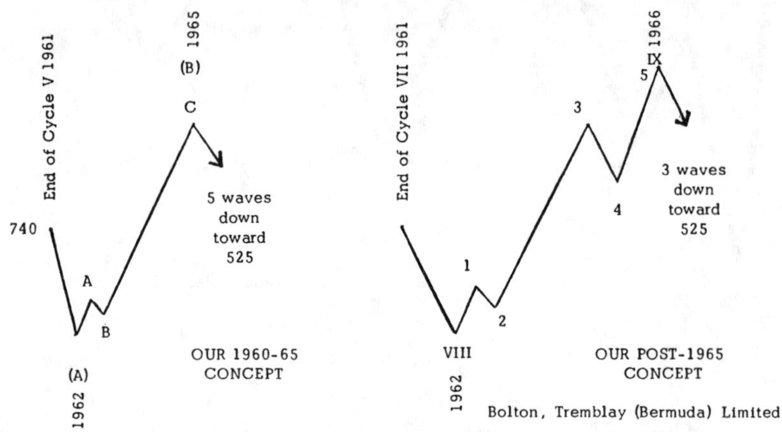

Figure 2

inverse corrective wave B, and that this was the end of the move. Subsequent events, however, clearly indicated that June 1965-January 1966 was another supplemental wave made up of five smaller waves up. Thus, we have to face the probability that we completed a major five wave upward pattern of Cycle degree in January 1966, and we need, therefore, to fit this into a larger pattern.

HOW ELLIOTT LOOKS TO US TODAY

The problem may be defined as follows. If June 1965 to January 1966 is Primary 5 of the Cycle wave from 1962 to 1966, then can we fit this into a pattern which with 1949 as a starting point gives us a 5-wave sequence of Cycle waves?

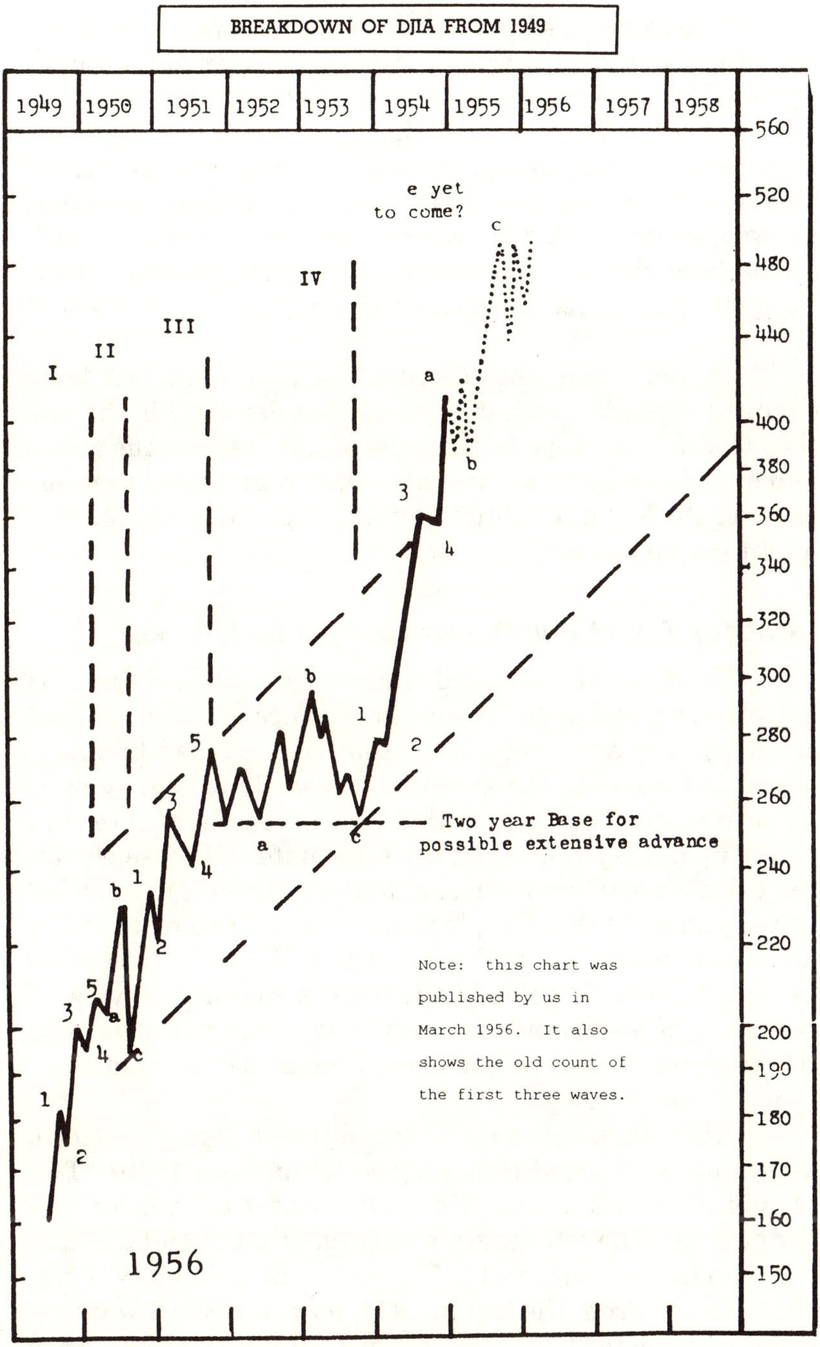
BREAKDOWN OF DJIA FROM 1949
1949
1950
1951
1952
1953
1954
1955
1956
1957
1958
560
520
480
440
400
380
360
340
320
300
280
260
240
220
200
190
180
170
160
150
e yet
to come?
I
II
III
IV
Two year Base for
possible extensive advance
Note: this chart was
published by us in
March 1956. It also
shows the old count of
the first three waves.
1956

Figure 3

The key to this is the breakdown of the 1949-56 Cycle wave, which in Collins' interpretation is Cycle wave III of Super Cycle (III). In order to break this down into five Primary waves, one has to go back to the count which we employed prior to 1958 in analyzing the Wave Principle at that time. The preceding diagram, taken from our 1956 Supplement, shows how we counted the waves from 1949 to come out with a completed five up. (Intermediate e in that cycle closed out in April 1956 at 520 in the averages.)

At any rate, this count (which we used but later changed when the 1958-59 cycle got under way) is the one that Collins has kept to throughout the intervening years and explains why he felt (in talks with your editor) that our count of 1957-61 as the final wave of the postwar bull market might not be correct.

Orthodox Top of Bull Market Likely in Early 1966

Be that as it may (and readers are reminded that it is not always possible to be sure in advance of what the real count is), it is now pretty clear that we have had five fully completed waves in the average up from June 1962, just as it became clear last summer that we had completed three full waves up in May 1965 from the same date. Of these waves, the third wave (Cuban crisis to May 1965) was an extended wave. (Later in this Supplement, we will have more to say about extensions and will suggest that it may be necessary to modify Elliott's rules about them somewhat in view of certain logic which indicates that they need not always be retraced, but this need not concern us at the moment.)

How then can this be fitted into a logical pattern, assuming we started Super Cycle (I) in June 1949? Two possibilities exist, and each is documented in the accompanying graphs. The left diagram suggests that 1949-56 is a 5-wave up in accordance with Collins' count and our own pre-1958 count. From the low in 1957, however, the 5-wave up from 1957 to 1961 and the 5-wave up from 1962 to 1966 would constitute extensions of the 5th wave from 1953 to 1956.

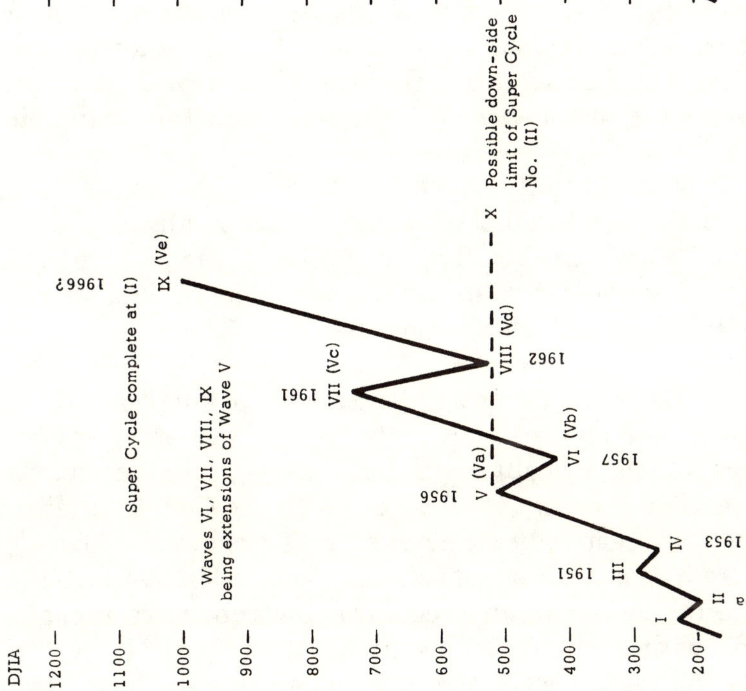

Figure 4

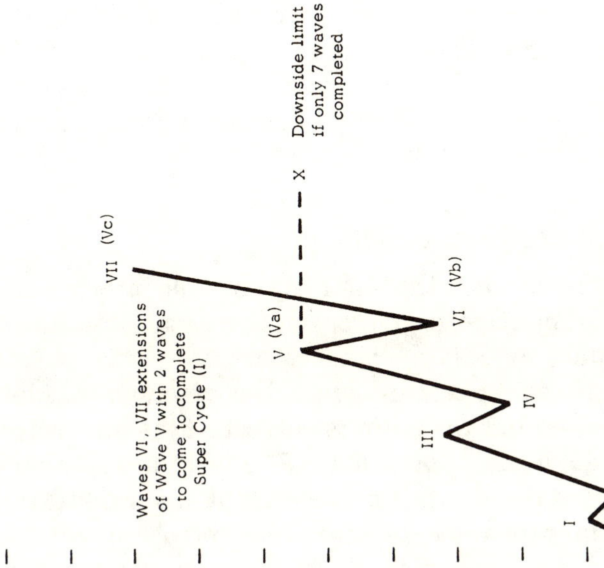

Bolton, Tremblay (Bermuda) Limited

Figure 5

The right diagram, however, shows another possibility, which does not fit in so well with Collins' interpretation, but which might conceivably be correct. This calls for a completion of wave VII in January 1966 to be followed by wave VIII, which should have a downside limit of about 740 (being the top of wave V).

Importance of 740 level DJIA

It is to be noted that in these possible interpretations, there is an objective in one case of around 525 and in the other around 740. It is clear, therefore, that while we cannot at this point say for certain which is correct, we will be able to say that the left diagram is correct, if, as and when the market breaks the approximate 740 level in the averages, because one of Elliott's basic rules is that in a series of 5-wave type bull markets and extensions (as contrasted with 3 wave corrections), the correction of any wave should not go below the top of the previous wave but one. Thus, the correction of a wave 4 should not drop below the top of wave 1, or of wave 6 below the top of wave 3, if the wave structure is to hold.

This is vitally important, since it gives us two downside bench marks for the market correction ahead, the first being 740, which should not be broken if the pattern of the right diagram is to rule, and the second being 525, which is the 1956 top and, by coincidence, the 1962 low.

What makes the left diagram the possibly more likely pattern — apart from the economic and monetary environment which logically calls for a very important market correction — is that (a) it agrees with the Collins' interpretation in practically all details, (b) it produces a downside figure which is the same as that suggested in our post-1962 bulletins calling for an irregular A-B-C type correction after 1961, with the top of B much higher than the 1961 top of 741 to be followed by a C wave which should have a floor around 525 in view of the "thrust" characteristics (caused undoubtedly by successive spurts of monetary inflation) of the post-1949 Super Cycle bull market.

Collins suggests (and this seems logical) that we will probably have a bear market in three stages, i.e., an A, B and C wave, with a possible objective around the 740 level for A, a retracement upwards of part or all of the decline from what the top level is, and a C wave bottom around 525.[5] Obviously, such a pattern fits in with Collins' basic 1932-66 Super Cycle waves (I), (II), (III) pattern and our own 1949-66 Super Cycle wave I pattern, but does not fit in with the alternative pattern suggested in the right diagram.

One further note is worth mentioning. A glance at both diagrams shows that corrective waves are getting deeper and deeper as the bull market continues. Thus, in the left diagram, the corrective wave II was very minor in relation to I, that of IV greater but still minor, that of VI more important, and that of VIII was maximum as it could have been to still keep the bull market pattern intact. This suggests, but does not yet prove, that the next corrective wave will be greater still, in which case it may very easily break the 740 level, particularly as it is clearly reinforced, as the 1962 correction was not, by a well-nigh untenable economic and monetary background.

This, then, is the basic probability as we see it. Collins' Cycle wave V of Super Cycle wave (III) (1942-66) terminating early this year, or our Cycle wave IX (wave V extended into five further waves) terminating at the same time, to be followed by Collins' Super Cycle wave (IV) and our Super Cycle wave (II), which should, reasonably, parallel each other. As an outside chance, we have the third possibility that the Super Cycle is not yet complete, in which case the 740 level in the DJIA will not be broken, and the ultimate top could be anywhere in the stratosphere, say from 1300-1800 in the Dow Industrials. We will not be able to say which is correct until 740 is tested, if, as and when.

In case the student of Elliott interpretation should consider the above somewhat equivocating, we would like to point out what we said in our 1960 Elliott book:

> "Elliott is *not an exact science*. It never will be. The two great *terminal dates* of the century are obviously 1929 and 1932. We are getting further away from them. If the implications of Elliott that we have discussed come to pass, there will be a much greater interest in interpreting Elliott. New students will try their hand at it. There won't be any one expert, but several, just as today there are several Dow Theory experts, some of whom do not agree with one another."

The Recent Waves in Detail

The July 1965 issue of *The Bank Credit Analyst* documented the wave count up to May 14th, 1965 pointing out that three waves in all details were complete from the June 1962 bottom to the May 1965 top. The chart of the way we counted these out is reprinted below from that issue. The

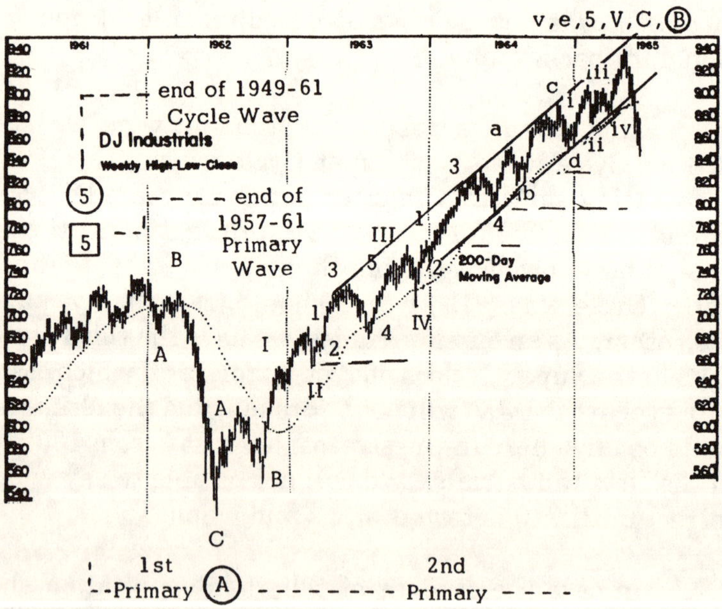

Source: R. W. Mansfield Co.,
26 Journal Square, Jersey City 6, N.J.

Figure 6

third wave of this series extended from June 1964 (the point marked a on the chart).

Bringing the story more up-to-date, we publish herewith a chart of the whole movement from 1962 to a recent date. This chart is from the service put out by Worden & Worden, Inc., Suite 322, Bayview Bldg., Fort Lauderdale, Florida, and printed by permission. It is a unique chart in that it is twice weekly instead of weekly, and accordingly gets in more frequent small waves which make up the pattern than is possible from a weekly chart. We have not bothered to fill the details of all the waves up to May 14th, 1965, as these are given in the previous diagram.

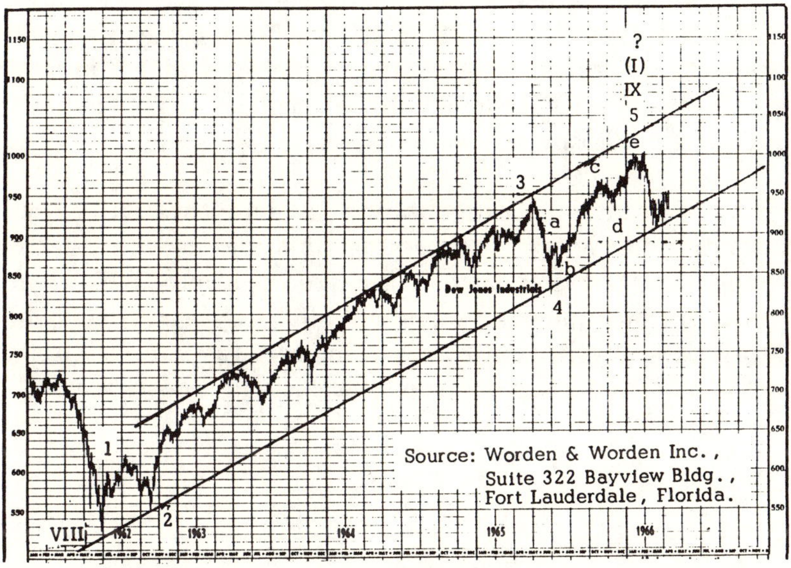

Figure 7

The aftermath of the May 1965 top at the point marked 3 now classifies as a completed 5 up of various degrees shown respectively as e (Intermediate), 5 (Primary), IX (Cycle) and I (Super Cycle) under our count.

Collins, however, points out the possibility that what we have labeled as c, d and e, may only be wave c (ending in November 1965) followed by a 3-wave irregular A-B-C type correction completed in March, thus making this latter point only d instead of the end of the first downward wave of a new Cycle. Factors in favor of this latter interpretation are (a) the fact that wave termination at e, 5, IX, (I) did not hit the upper parallel of the rise, (b) that so far the down wave from January 1966 stops short of the point a (about 890 DJIA), which it should not break if wave e, 5, IX, (I) is not yet complete, and (c) that the lower rising trend parallel was met but not broken, thereby giving the implication that the whole wave from June 1962 is still intact.

In our opinion, it is too early yet to tell from what has happened since March 1966 as to whether the market is developing 5-upward-wave characteristics, which it must do if the January 1966 top is not the orthodox top, or is developing only a 3-upward-wave pattern.

To conclude, Elliott students should watch particularly the 890 level in the Industrials and secondarily the rising lower trend line, which is currently around 915-20 and by the end of June will be at about 935. Any break decisively below these levels would be tantamount to an admission that the back of the Primary from last June had been broken.

ELLIOTT'S WAVE PRINCIPLE

by

Charles J. Collins

How I Knew Elliott

Knowing of my early acquaintance with R. N. Elliott, Hamilton Bolton, whom, aside from his outstanding position in the field of monetary analysis, I consider Elliott's most capable interpreter, has asked me to contribute an article expressing my views on the wave movement over recent years for his 1966 Elliott review.

Before beginning such discussion, it might be of interest, now that Elliott's Wave Principle has attracted such a wide following among students of the stock market, to mention how I became acquainted with Elliott. In 1934, and for some years previous, I was editing a weekly investment bulletin that went out nationally, this in conjunction with a personal investment supervisory service. As must be common to all who publish investment services, I received frequent letters and personal calls from individuals who had developed "infallible" methods or systems for forecasting the stock market. My usual reply was that the individual go on record with me over a market cycle, after which I would determine whether I cared to investigate the matter in detail. In most instances, at some point in the cycle, the system went haywire and correspondence died on the vine.

Elliott was one of three notable exceptions. He wrote me from California in late 1934 that a bull market had begun and would carry for some distance. He also proposed that I look into his method. I followed with the usual request that he go on record for a period. In March 1935, the Dow Rail Average crashed under its 1934 low, accompanied by an eleven per cent break in the Industrial Average. Having recent memories of 1929-1932, this development scared the lights out of the investment public. On the bottom day for the Industrial Average, the Rails having leveled off four days previously, I received a late evening telegram from Elliott in which, as was always his way, he *dogmatically* affirmed that the break was over and that another leg of the bull market was beginning. This break, looking back, was Primary wave 2 of the Cycle movement then under way under Elliott's Wave Principle, although at the time, I had no idea as to his method. In any event, the market advanced dramatically over the next two months and, impressed by Elliott's dogmatism and accuracy, I invited him to be my house guest in the East where I might then go over his method with him.

Elliott accepted the invitation and we spent several days going thoroughly into his system. He was an American citizen, but stated he had been a telegraph operator down in Mexico[6] when a malady[7] forced him back to California where, for two or three years, about all he could do was to sit on his front porch and nurse his trouble. For want of anything to keep his mind occupied, he began from scratch to study the stock market. In due course, the Wave Principle was thus evolved.

Elliott, who was just then trying his wings, wanted me to take him into my organization. I explained to him that we could not use his method exclusively, as it was not, and could not be, our practice to base our decisions on any single approach. However, I was instrumental in securing him risk capital in New York City for supervision, and from that point forward he acquired a series of accounts and commenced the issuance of interpretative letters. Later, still feeling under obligation to Elliott for fully disclosing his method to me, I wrote his first monograph, *The Wave Principle*, which was later supplemented by *Nature's Law*, a more comprehensive document prepared by Elliott in which to the framework of *The Wave Principle* he added many philosophical points, including reference to Fibonacci's Summation Series, all of which were related to his basic premise. We remained friends and correspondents until his death.

My Views of Where We Stand Today

As to my views on the wave movement, to fully clarify where we seem to be at the present time (11th April, 1966), it will be necessary to pick up the market, as reflected by the Dow Industrials, from the 1932 low point. I say this for the reason that, in my opinion, the 1929-1932 stock market decline, while falling short from a time standpoint, was of sufficient intensity to correct the Grand Supercycle wave which Elliott dated from 1857 to the orthodox top in 1928. Such being the case, I assume that a new Grand Supercycle wave had its commencement from the 1932 bottom.

Elliott dated Grand Supercycle wave 1 as running from 1800[8] to 1850; 2, from 1850 to 1857; 3, from 1857 to 1928. The succeeding drastic correction (1928-1932) would thus, under my count, be Grand Supercycle wave 4, meaning that the advancing price level from 1932 to its conclusion years hence will constitute Grand Supercycle wave 5. A comparison of the time intervals of Grand Supercycle waves 3 and 5 (to date), as broken into the smaller Supercycle components, follows:

Grand Supercycle Wave 3

	Supercycle		Years
Wave 1	1857-1864		7
Wave 2	1864-1877		13
Wave 3	1877-1881		4
Wave 4	1881-1896		15
Wave 5	1896-1928		32
		Total	71

Grand Supercycle Wave 5

	Supercycle	Years
Wave 1	1932-1937	5
Wave 2	1937-1942	5
Wave 3	1942-1966 ?	24

The longest Supercycle wave in Grand Supercycle wave 3 was the fifth, running 32 years; it may prove that the longest Supercycle wave in Grand Supercycle wave 5 will be wave 3.

The Grand Supercycle wave now under way, as applies to other such waves of the same category, will naturally break down into successively lesser wave formations, namely, Supercycle waves as shown in the tabulation above; Cycle waves, or so-called bull and bear markets; and, for the monthly, weekly and daily swings, Primary, Intermediate and Minor waves.

In the count of Grand Supercycle wave 5 from 1932, I find, as shown above, that two Supercycle waves have been completed and a third may have completed in January 1966 or, if not (see subsequent discussion), then it is in process of completion. These Supercycle waves are illustrated in Chart I.

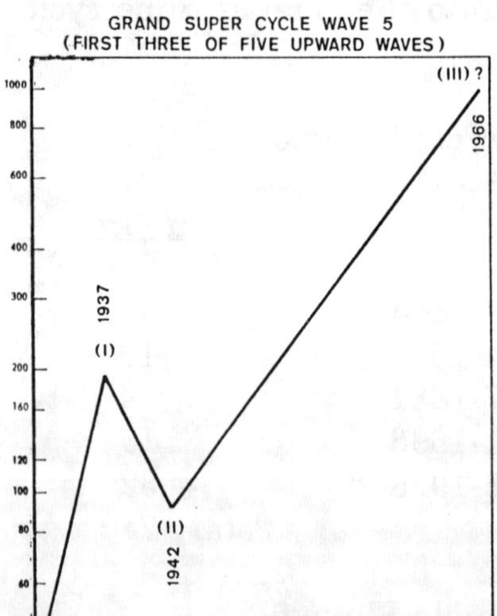

Chart I

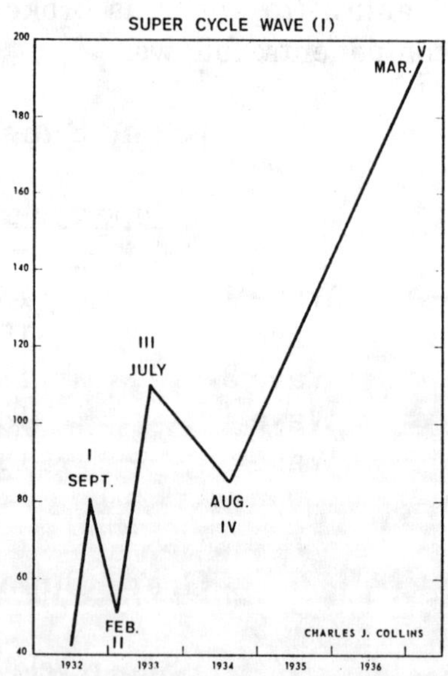

Chart II

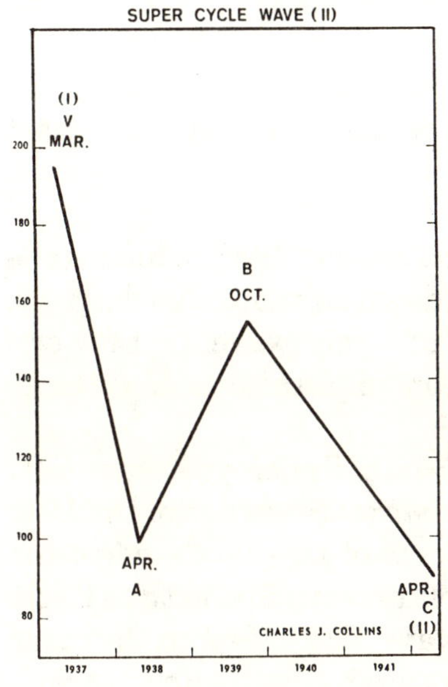

Chart III

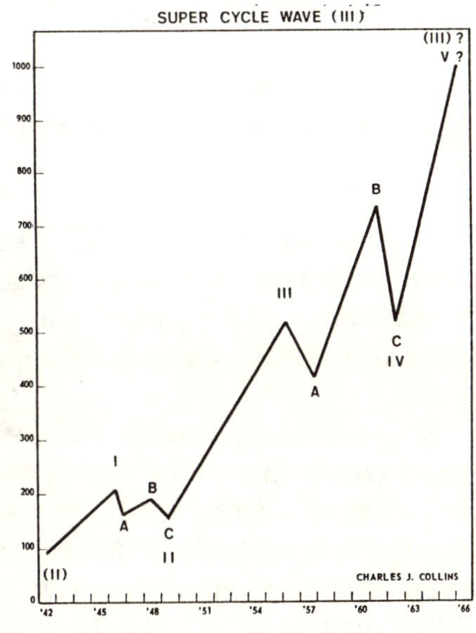

Chart IV

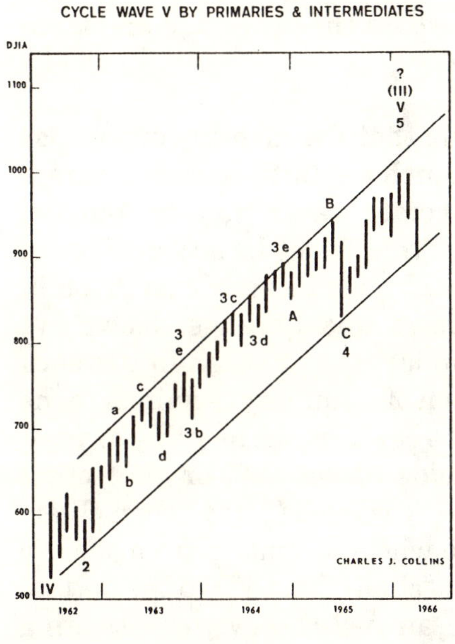

Chart V

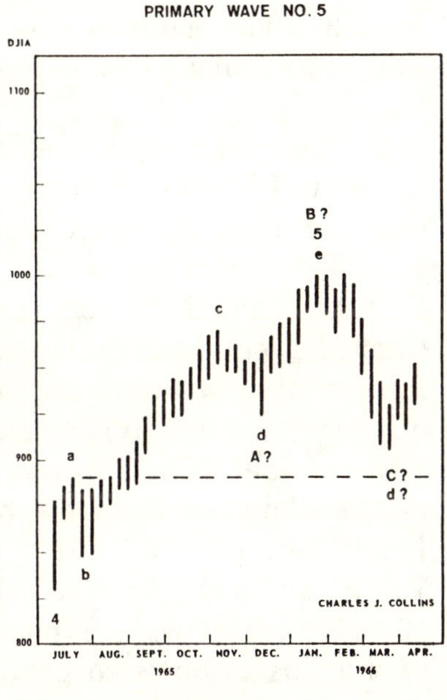

Chart VI

Supercycle wave (I) was classical, being broken into five distinct Cycle waves, as shown in Chart II.

Then, as concerns Supercycle wave (II), again we see the classical cyclical three wave pattern, as shown in Chart III.

Supercycle wave (III), beginning in 1942, which is the wave of current interest, I break down as shown in Chart IV. Incidentally, the upward slant of Cycle wave IV between 1956 and 1962 carries inflationary implications.

Cyclical wave V (1962-1966?) of Supercycle wave (III) is shown in Chart V by giving the *monthly swings* of the Dow Industrials. Since Primary wave 3 of this Cycle wave extended, it would appear that Primary wave 5 (and thus Cycle wave V as well as Supercycle wave III) ended in January 1966, as the market has subsequently developed a downthrust. Those who might argue that such a downswing constitutes wave 2 of an extension of wave 5 are faced with Elliott's dictum that an extension can occur in any one of waves 1, 3 or 5, but never in more than one. The extension in Primary wave 3, under Elliott's rule, would thus preclude an extension in Primary wave 5.

It is, of course, possible that the monthly swings, as shown in Chart V, hide too much detail to permit accurate interpretation of the Intermediate waves that, in toto, develop into a Primary wave. If this thesis be accepted, then Primary wave 5 of Cycle wave V (see Chart V), as given in Chart VI on a basis of the Dow's weekly range, shows five Intermediate waves to the January top, thus tending to back up the preceding interpretation of a January terminus to the Supercycle and Cycle waves, as based on the monthly swings. But, so long as the Dow holds above 890, or the top of Intermediate wave 1 of Primary wave 5 (point "a" on Chart VI), it can be argued that the whole formation from the top of Intermediate wave 3 (point "c" on Chart VI) to the bottom of the correction is to prove an A-B-C wave, constituting

Intermediate wave 4, leaving Intermediate wave 5 as now in process. The fact that the January 1966 peak failed to approach or exceed the upper trend line or parallel as shown on Chart V, and the lack of the wide public excesses that should normally accompany the peak to a Supercycle wave, would seem to lend some support to such viewpoint.*

If it be assumed that the orthodox top to Cycle wave V was registered in January or (see above paragraph) is in near process of being established, there are a number of inferences that follow. First, the correction that ensues would constitute Supercycle wave (IV) and thus should normally be more extensive in time and/or depth than any of the corrections occurring between 1942 and 1966, or during the course of Supercycle wave (III). Second, such Supercycle wave (IV) should be followed by Supercycle wave (V) carrying stock prices materially above levels so far registered.

Third, and of more immediate interest, it will be recalled that Cycle wave III (see Chart IV) ending in 1956 registered an orthodox top; that is, there was no subsequent early swing into new high ground.[9] Under Elliott's rule of alternation, an early irregular top into new high ground would not be inconsistent with the wind up of Cycle wave V.

---

* Ed. Note: In other words, while it looks at the moment as if the fifth wave of Cycle Wave V from 1962 (and consequently the fifth of the fifth wave of Super Cycle Wave III from 1942) did end in an orthodox way without extensions in January 1966, there is still a chance that the whole movement from the November 1965 top to the March 1966 bottom was an irregular 3 wave correction, leaving room for a final fifth up wave of Primary No. 5 to be taking place now from the March 1966 bottom. This is why the 890 level in the Industrials is so important. If it is broken, then the fifth Primary under this count will have dropped below the top of the first Primary in mid-July and will thus nullify this interpretation as possible. To break 890 also involves breaking the lower trend line of Chart V, which in itself should be a fairly clear indication that the move was really over in January 1966.

Lastly, the third wave of Cycle wave V (see Chart V) extended. Elliott states that an extension will be retraced twice. Such being the case, this would call for the "C" wave of the Supercycle wave (IV) that will follow Supercycle wave (III) (see Chart I), as a corrective move, to carry back at least to 770-710 on the Dow, in other words, to the approximate area within which the extension of Primary wave 3 began (see points 3 and 3b on Chart V). The decline could carry further, however, under Elliott's rule that the correction of a wave should normally carry back to around the terminal point of the fourth wave of the five lesser waves that characterized the swing. The terminal point of the fourth cycle wave to Supercycle wave 3 (see Chart IV) was established in 1962 at 524 on the Dow. Purely as a speculation, might not the "A" wave of Supercycle wave (IV) carry to the 770-710 area; the "C" wave to around the lower 524 point; with a sizable intervening "B" wave?

Elliott placed the terminus of Grand Supercycle wave (IV) not in 1932 as I have in this discussion, but in 1942. He based this on a triangular formation developed by the Dow between 1929 and 1942. To those who prefer Elliott's count to the 1932 terminus, and there certainly is some cogency to Elliott's viewpoint, there need be no confusion so far as the foregoing remarks are concerned. It merely will be necessary to reclassify the Supercycle swing from 1942 to 1966(?) (see Charts I and IV) as (I) rather than (III), and the correction to follow as Supercycle wave (II) rather than (IV). The significance of this reclassification greatly extends into the future, both in time and price, Grand Supercycle wave (V).[*]

---

[*]Ed. Note: Nor is there any conflict here with the editor's thought that 1928-49 is a gigantic 21-year triangle from which started Grand Super Cycle wave 5. The year 1949 takes the place of 1932 or 1942, and the Super Cycle wave from 1949 to 1966(?) becomes classified as (I) instead of (III).

One concluding word. Students of Elliott's wave principle know that retrospective measurement of the stock market's swings always proves easier than concurrent counting. Thus, the foregoing enumeration is not dogmatically given. As the future unrolls, the diagnosis may be subjected to revision.

Charles J. Collins
April 11, 1966

AREAS FOR FURTHER EXPLORATION

Now that the Elliott theory is getting better known, there have been a number of forecasters who have attempted to use it, in some cases with success. Further, it is often possible blithely to assume that a certain wave formation has 5-wave characteristics when, in actual fact, it does not. This in itself leads to certain suppositions which, when examined in detail, fail to stand up to Elliott's test. Then again, are we sure that Elliott's wave formations themselves are correct? Since his early days, we seem to have developed a great and growing number of complications, all of which may be put down as exceptions, or at least unusual aspects of the basic principle.[10] Generally speaking, we can classify these areas of ambiguity as falling in three general areas:

a. Wave Formations
b. Problems in Amplitude
c. The Time Factor

We cannot possibly cover all the problems in the wave formation or count, but it does seem important to spend some time on a number of things that worry us all in the Elliott picture. Accordingly, we propose to bring up some questions without necessarily being able to provide any final answers.

Amplitude and Wave Formations

Problems in amplitude and in wave formations are among the most difficult in the whole Elliott approach. One would think that it would be possible to apply some sort of a percentage rule to the waves to determine whether a correction is of one degree, or of the next smaller or larger. Attempts have been made along these lines without much success. Arthur Merrill, in *Behavior of Prices on Wall Street*, has analyzed all waves in terms of set percentages such as 5%, 10%, 20% and 40% swings. What happens, however, is that the numbers of waves resulting no longer bear the Elliott relationship of 5-3-5, etc., which is based on the

Fibonacci summation series. Perhaps the percentages chosen are too arbitrary and unrelated to the basic summation series themselves; suffice it to say, however, that we have not been able to apply a particular set of percentages representative of Cycle, Primary, Intermediate and Minor waves, in Elliott's context, which will enable us to know that a particular wave formation is progressing without doubt in a certain direction and to a logical end. As we have seen in our discussion of the wave context since 1949, this fortunately does not matter too much when we are attempting to forecast the larger formations. It does matter, however, in the context of Elliott's Intermediate and smaller wave formations.

Extensions

No subject in Elliott is more intriguing than that of extensions. According to Elliott, extensions may appear in any one of the three impulses of the 5-wave formation, but more often in the fifth wave. Practically all of Elliott's writing on extensions was based on experience in a fifth wave. According to Elliott, extensions occur only in new territory of the current cycle, and are retraced twice. His diagrams point this out. This is a fifth wave extension and seems to be completely logical.

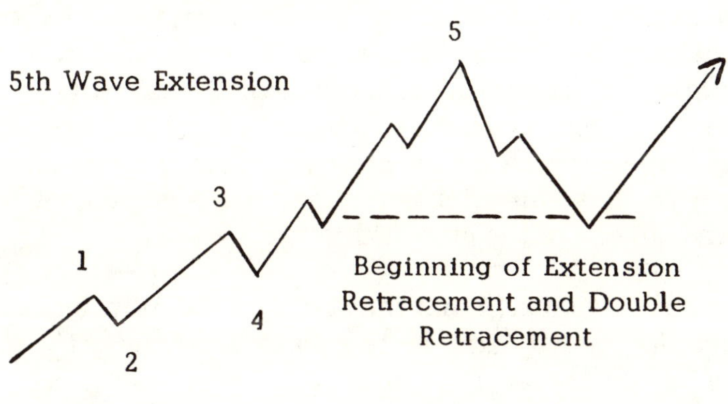

However, when one tries to apply the same reasoning to first and third wave extensions, one becomes completely bogged down.

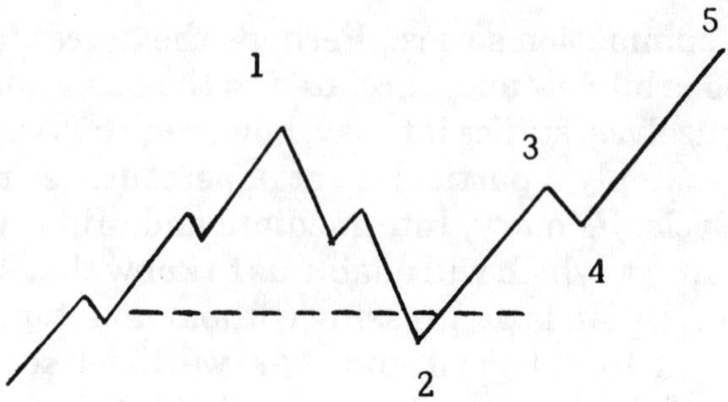

1st Wave Extension and Retracement

For instance, here is a diagram of a first wave extension. The first wave extends as indicated, and therefore, according to Elliott, has to be double retraced, which happens in waves 2, 3, 4 and 5. However, this is no longer a legitimate 5-wave formation. For one thing, it does not look like a 5. Further, Elliott says that wave 4 must not fall below the top of wave 1, which it must in the type of movement above.[11] Considering such a wave formation in the context of a 5-wave up seems to this writer a twisting of facts without any particular benefit. The whole formation would much more logically be thought of as a 3 up rather than a 5 up - an inverse corrective wave rather than a wave in the direction of the main movement.

Similarly, one can consider a doubly retraced third wave extension. The diagram herewith shows what logically would happen if double retracement takes place. Here again, the pattern looks corrective. Barring an extension in the fifth wave, this latter is practically bound to end up lower than wave three[12], which makes no sense. Elliott, however, says that if you have an extension in any wave, you do not have another in one of the other three main waves.

The conclusion that the writer accordingly comes to is that *while one may experience extensions in any of the three main impulse waves, up or down, it is only extensions in a fifth which are double retraced.*

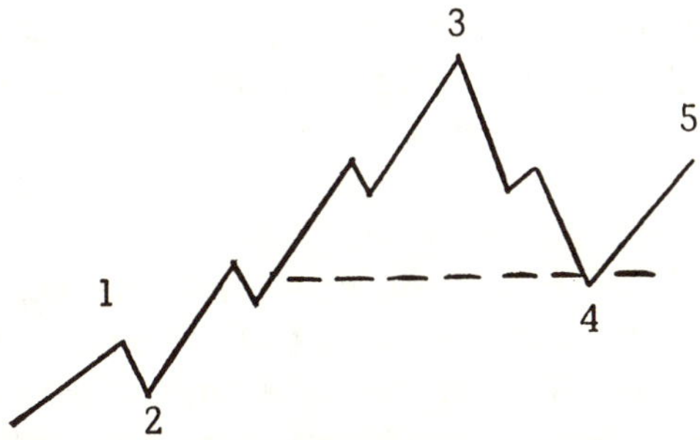

3rd Wave Extension and
Retracement

Assuming that this principle is valid, it helps to explain a number of things. Thus, take the 5-wave up from June 1962 to January 1966. The third wave of this from October 1962 to May 1965 was definitely an extended wave under our count. (See the first diagram in the section entitled, "The Recent Wave in Detail.") The fifth wave of wave V is extended. The point of extension is at point a after wave 4. Point a is approximately 850 in the DJIA. Point b is approximately 820. In actual fact, the market double-retraced this when it dropped to 835 in June 1965 and then went on to new highs. However, this was only a retracement of Intermediate degree. Actually, the whole wave V can be considered an extension, in which case the double retracement rule called for a return to between points 1 and 2, or to about 760. This did not happen, and consequently we may conclude that because this is a third wave extension, there is no law which says that this must be retraced. Note the difference here. The fifth wave of the third larger wave extended. It was of Intermediate degree, and was doubly retraced. In addition to that, the whole third wave of larger degree (October 1962-May 1965) appears also to have extended. It is this latter, because it is *not* a fifth wave, which does not appear to need double retracing. It may happen in a later wave cycle unrelated to the particular cycle under consideration, but it does not appear that it has to be retraced in the next contiguous cycle, which is certainly what is implied by Elliott's rules.

Collins has another count for wave 3 of the five wave formation, 1962-66. It may be appropriate, therefore, to look at his count, which is somewhat different, for he, too, has an extension in the third wave. (See Chart V). His third wave begins to extend at the point marked 3e. Thus, under Elliott's double retracement rule, the retracement would have to bring the market back to between 3e and 3B, or between 770 and 710. Because of a different count, Collins' wave 4 does not get followed by an extended fifth wave, thus proving Elliott's point that of the five waves of the same degree, only one will extend. According to our interpretation of Elliott's rules, wave 4 should have gone much lower, i.e., into the 770-710 area. There would seem to be little logic in suggesting that such a double retracement could await another completely different set of cycles outside of the 5-wave upward pattern that we are currently discussing, i.e., in this case, 1962-1966. If we can allow a rule, for instance, which says that sometime in the future the market should retrace the October 1962-May 1965 extension, we have added nothing to the Wave Principle and have perhaps decreased overall its usefulness. Further, the writer has seen many first and third wave extensions of various degrees which have occurred since 1932 which have never as yet been retraced, let alone doubly retraced.

As a practical matter, therefore, we propose to look at extensions as candidates for retracement only if they are fifth wave extensions and only to the degree that the retracements come within the context of the next larger wave and its immediate neighbor.

Under this principle, and specifically in relation to the 5-wave up from 1962, our Intermediate fifth wave in Primary 3 of Cycle V was doubly retraced because it was a fifth wave. However, the extension of Primary 3 itself was not, because it was not. Primary 3 having extended, Primary 5 (June 1965 to January 1966?) will not. This means that either Primary 5 was complete in January 1966, or that only Intermediate 4 of Primary 5 has been completed as of mid-

March, and Intermediate 5 is now underway (the wave formation is not yet clear enough to be sure of this yet). So we have to leave it at that.

Alternation

Does alternation have anything to say at present? Alternation applies to many facets of wave theory.

Corrective Waves

In a 5-wave movement, there are two intervening corrective waves. Alternation suggests that if the first (wave 2) is a "zigzag" (5-3-5), the second (wave 4) will be a "flat" (3-3-5). In actual fact, it is our experience that "flats" outnumber "zigzags" by a large measure. In fact, in larger formations, the "zigzags" are practically unknown in our experience.[13] Thus, alternation does *not* appear to be a factor in types of corrective waves, except that often if wave 2 is simple (or complex), wave 4 will be complex (or simple).

Tops

Tops are said to alternate between *regular* and *irregular*. Regular tops are those in which the end of the fifth wave is higher than the end of the second wave (wave B) of the correction. Irregular tops imply the top of wave B being higher than the top of the fifth wave which preceded it.

The problem of alternation is one of degree. Mr. Collins points out that according to his analysis, the last major top was in 1956. This was regular,[14] therefore there is a possibility that this one will be irregular. Thus, of his Cycle waves in Super Cycle (III), he has the following:

Cycle I	May 1942-May 1946	Irregular
Cycle II	1946-49	
Cycle III	June 1949-April 1956	Regular
Cycle IV	1956-62	
Cycle V	June 1962-January 1966	Irregular?

This alternation implies that even if January 1966 is the orthodox top of the fifth Primary of the fifth Cycle since 1962, there is a possibility (perhaps a probability) that there will be an irregular A-B-C type wave coming up which will call for a wave B top higher than the end of the fifth wave. A diagram of this is shown herewith. Since wave 5 ended up at about 1000 in the DJIA, this implies that we will see a close of wave B at a higher figure than this.[15]

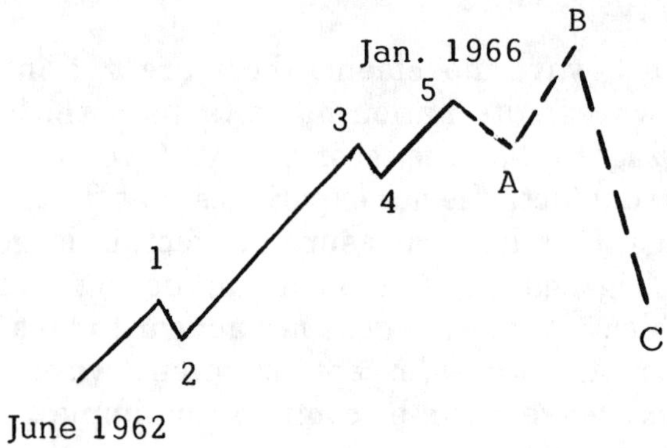

On the other hand, the count that we espouse, whereby from 1949 to date we have seen 9 waves, of which waves VI, VII, VIII and IX are extensions of wave V from 1953 to 1956, has the exact opposite implications.

Wave	I	June '49-June '50	Regular
	II		
	III	July '50-Sept. '51	Irregular
	IV		
	V	Sept. '53-Apr. '56	Regular
	VI		
	VII	Oct. '57-Aug. '61	Irregular
	VIII		
	IX	June '62-Jan. '66	Regular?

So here we have a conflict of view. Our count suggests a regular top, i.e., one in which the upward wave of the following correction will fall short of the final wave of the fifth bull market phase.

The results of this analysis are therefore not conclusive.

Wave Lengths

Alternation is also expected to take place in the length of waves, and in particular in the size of corrections. Logically, corrective wave 2 should be shorter in time and probably in amplitude than corrective wave 4. In practice, it does not always seem to work out this way. In the bull market from 1921 to 1929, for instance, the first correction (1923) was considerably greater in time and amplitude than the second correction in 1926. In the 1949-66 bull market (see Figure 4), corrective wave II in our count was short, corrective waves IV and VI were about the same length in time, and corrective wave VIII was shorter than either IV or VI.

In Collins' wave (III), the 1946-49 correction lasted three years and that of 1956-62 about six years, thus following a normal pattern.

What can we look for from 1966 on? Using Collins' analysis as a base, we have had three Super Cycles to date. The timing was as follows:

Super Cycle I	1932-1937		5 years
Super Cycle II	1937-1942		5 years
Super Cycle III	1942-1966		24 years
		Total:	34 years

Normally, one could expect a longer Super Cycle IV than Cycle II, but as we have seen, we often have a shorter time in wave 4 than in wave 2. It could be, therefore, that Super Cycle IV could be over in less than five years, say, three years or even two as a possibility. One economic reason for this might be the probability of a more active monetary and fiscal policy in an inflationary direction than was experienced in the 1937-42 period, even though the latter part of that period did see a very active increase in the nation's money supply.

At any event, the principle of alternation still seems to be highly nebulous, and we doubt that analysts have in it anything really tangible upon which to hang their hats.

Numbers of Waves and the Fibonacci Series

Elliott claimed in *Nature's Law* (1946) that he had found the basis of the Wave Principle to be the Fibonacci number series. We have documented this fairly thoroughly in the 1960 edition of *The Elliott Wave Principle*, particularly in Chapter IX. The Fibonacci numbers series is as follows:

1, 1, 2, 3, 5, 8, 13, 21, 34, 55, 89, 144, 233, 377, etc.,

each number being the total of the two numbers behind it. This in itself is not significant, since one can put together all sorts of series of this kind. What is significant is that, after the initial few, each number is 0.618 times the one above and 1.618 times the one below. This series has therefore arithmetic characteristics and geometric or logarithmic characteristics. It also combines square root aspects in that each number is related to the one before by the formula $(\sqrt{5}+1)/2$ and to the one above by the formula $(\sqrt{5}-1)/2$.

If one counts out Elliott's theoretical waves, one gets 5+3+5+3+5, or 21, which is one of the series. If each 5 is broken down into 5+3+5+3+5 smaller waves, and if each 3 is broken down into 5+3+5 (or 13) small waves, and if all these are totalled, the result is 89 waves, or one of the numbers. And if one goes through the same process for the 3 corrective waves, one comes up with a grand total of 144 waves (which also happens to be 12 squared).

The catch is that in a stock market cycle (a bull market, for instance), one never gets 89 waves. Instead, one of the corrective waves, or both, maybe, instead of having 5+3+5 waves will have 3+3+5 waves, or only 11. Consequently, the perfect theory bogs down.[16]

So not only are we unable to determine in advance the amplitude of the waves, but we do not know how many there are going to be. Possibly the introduction of extensions is supposed to bring the wave numbers up to the required total, but if so, nobody has found a way of predicting when they are due to come along.

In concluding these remarks on wave formations and amplitude, we would point out that Elliott was convinced he could make stock market forecasting a science. Instead, it appears that it still ends up as an art.

Relative Amplitudes of Waves

Elliott was intrigued by the Fibonacci relation of 1.618 and 0.618. He made 61.8% a central part of his measuring mechanism so far as the averages were concerned. Thus, he showed how the first three waves of the 1921 to 1928 bull market wave were exactly equal to 62% of the final wave. Also, he showed that the 1937 bull market went up in points 62% of the amount in points that it lost from the spring of 1930 to the summer of 1932. Also, that the 1937-38 bear market took back 62% of the rise from 1932-37, and so on.

Trying a hand at a similar projection in 1960 while writing the book on Elliott, your editor took the number of points from 194.9 to 1956 (522 less 161, or 361 points). If the waves from 1949 to 1956 should equal 61.8% of the final wave from the 1957 bottom of 416, then we should add another 583 points to the bull market *orthodox* top, which brings us up to the figure 999 as a point at which to look for the orthodox top. By coincidence, it would appear, our count of the 5th Primary of the IXth Cycle wave (Vth Cycle wave extended) in January 1966 came out on the nose (995) at this figure.

Another coincidence, too, is the fact that the 1929 high of 381, if multiplied by 1.618, gives a figure of 618 points, which, if added to the 1929 high, also produces a figure of 999. Thus, we have at least two bench marks at 999 indicating that this level is particularly significant. But we have to keep in mind that this 999 may be only the "orthodox" top, just as in 1928 the orthodox top was 299 followed by the final B type top of 381 in September 1929.

The trouble is that these coincidences are rarely predictable in advance, owing particularly to the fact that the Elliott wave theory has no firm grounding in time.

The Fibonacci Numbers

That the Fibonacci summation series has an important bearing in nature and natural phenomena is well established. Flower petals, for instance, come in 5's, 13's, 21's, 34's, etc. Why this should be is not known. The more one studies the Fibonacci series, the more one becomes amazed at the combinations, percentages, etc. Just as there are no two other numbers, except 2, which when added together and multiplied together give the same answer, so too there is no series of numbers which produces so many coincidences as the Fibonacci series. Each number is 61.8% of the next higher and 161.8% of the next lower. Each number is 261.8% of the second lower number. Each number divided into the second number above goes twice, with a leftover of the exact number below (e.g., 21 goes into 55 twice with 13 left over). The numbers are all related to each other by a factor of the square root of 5. The ratio .618 when squared equals .382, which is itself the reciprocal of .618 (1 minus .618 equals .382).

Two further "discoveries" were made recently by your editor.

Each number multiplied by 7 bears a relationship to the nearest number below in the summation series such that the difference becomes another summation series.

Fibonacci Numbers	34	55	89	144	233	377	610
7 multiplied by 4th lower no.	35	56	91	147	238	385	623
Difference	+1	+1	+2	+3	+5	+8	+13

Similarly, the Fibonacci series when multiplied by 11 is short of the fifth higher number by differences which make up a new Fibonacci series.[17]

Fibonacci numbers	89	144	233	377	610	987	1597
11 multiplied by 5th lower	88	143	231	374	605	979	1584
Difference	-1	-1	-2	-3	-5	-8	-13

All of this is interesting, of course, but not particularly instructive from a stock market forecasting point of view. That people are thinking in terms of the Fibonacci series as a possible timing device seems clear, yet nobody apparently has been able to build a system which will lead to future prediction. An interesting example of 7 times the Fibonacci numbers being used in counting time in the stock market appears in a letter to *Cycles* magazine April 1966 by Dudley Castle, in which he arranges the S&P 425 Industrials on a square root scale and in intervals of seven months highs and lows. His major turning points often come out at 7 times Fibonacci intervals, but no method appears available to tell in advance whether one is to expect highs or lows. Its interest, therefore, is somewhat academic.

A much more elaborate system of cyclical timing based on the Fibonacci principle has been developed by Thomas E. Frey of the First National Bank of San Diego. It appeared in the September 1964 issue of *Cycles*, and is worth investigating for a thorough understanding of how various time cycles (each .618 of the one next to it) combine to make important peaks and troughs. It is interesting to note, for instance, that by far the largest number of cycles troughed in mid-1932. Of 120 cycles making up the system developed by Frey of a length of from about 1 month to 100 years, 82% of them troughed in 1932. Other important troughs according to his analysis in the current century are the spring of 1921 and the late fall of 1967. No other periods appear to have a comparable number of coincidental cycle bottoms.

These, then, are the areas for future research. Is there a method of being sure of wave formations either in advance or as they develop? Is there a consistent rule of alternation? What happens with extensions? Can amplitude be measured, given a set of early bench marks? Is there a timing device built into the Fibonacci numbers that can be valuable in the stock market? How can we develop Elliott's theories to make them more useful to the day-to-day investor? All these and many other questions so far have defied an answer. Our knowledge in other fields of science is increasing by leaps and bounds; it seems a shame that comparable progress cannot be made in analyzing the behavioral aspects of stock prices.

THE RAILS AND INDIVIDUAL STOCK PATTERNS

Theoretically, the Wave Principle should apply to other averages than the Industrials, and to individual stocks. In practice, it is only rarely that a picture is clear.[18] Further, there are practical dangers in trying to apply the principle to the highflyers, because, typically, even one Primary wave may go through a price rise of several hundred percent. Intermediate moves, therefore, can fluctuate widely, causing all kinds of whipsaws if one's nerves are not of steel.

What about the Rails?

Last year, we came to the conclusion that we were in the fifth Cycle wave up from the 1942 bottom. According to our diagram at that time, repeated herewith updated, the Cycle waves from 1942 were as follows:

Cycle Wave	I	1942-1946
	II	1946-1949
	III	1949-1955
	IV	1955-1962
	V	1962-1966?

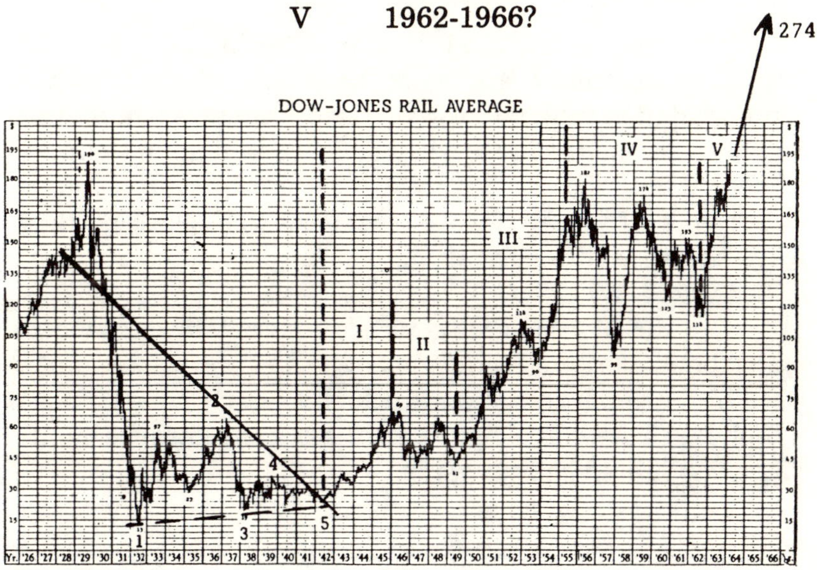

Source: M. C. Horsey & Company, 37 Wall Street, New York 10005.

In early 1965, the Rails appeared to be completing Primary 4 by December 1964 and to be poised, ready for Primary 5. However, a supplemental cycle came along in May-June 1965 which meant that Primary 4 was not actually completed till July 1965 at 185 in the Average. It appears that Primary 5 got under way, running from 185 to a peak of 274 in February 1966.

The next chart, from R. W. Mansfield, in our opinion, shows the strong probability that Primary 5 from July 1965 was completed in February 1966. The last Minor wave from December 1965 to February 1966 may have been an extension, in which case we may expect a double retracement, of which the first part has already been accomplished in March 1966.

According to our count, therefore, it appears that the Super Cycle from 1942 is technically completed, with Primary 5 of Cycle V ending in February 1966. This top seems to coincide with the Super Cycle top of the Industrials.

Individual Stocks

The way to use the Elliott Wave Principle is to make sure that purchases are made in stocks which have not completed their major 5 wave pattern. Conversely, it is often dangerous to invest in stocks, which are well up in their 5th waves. Many times, however, it is next to impossible to decide where the wave formation is, in which case the Elliott wave theory is of no use at all.

In our last issue, we pointed to one or two areas where major bear markets had obviously taken place. Examples were in the vending stocks, which had clearly gone through a 3-phase (5 wave) wringer and might, therefore, be candidates for limited capital gains.

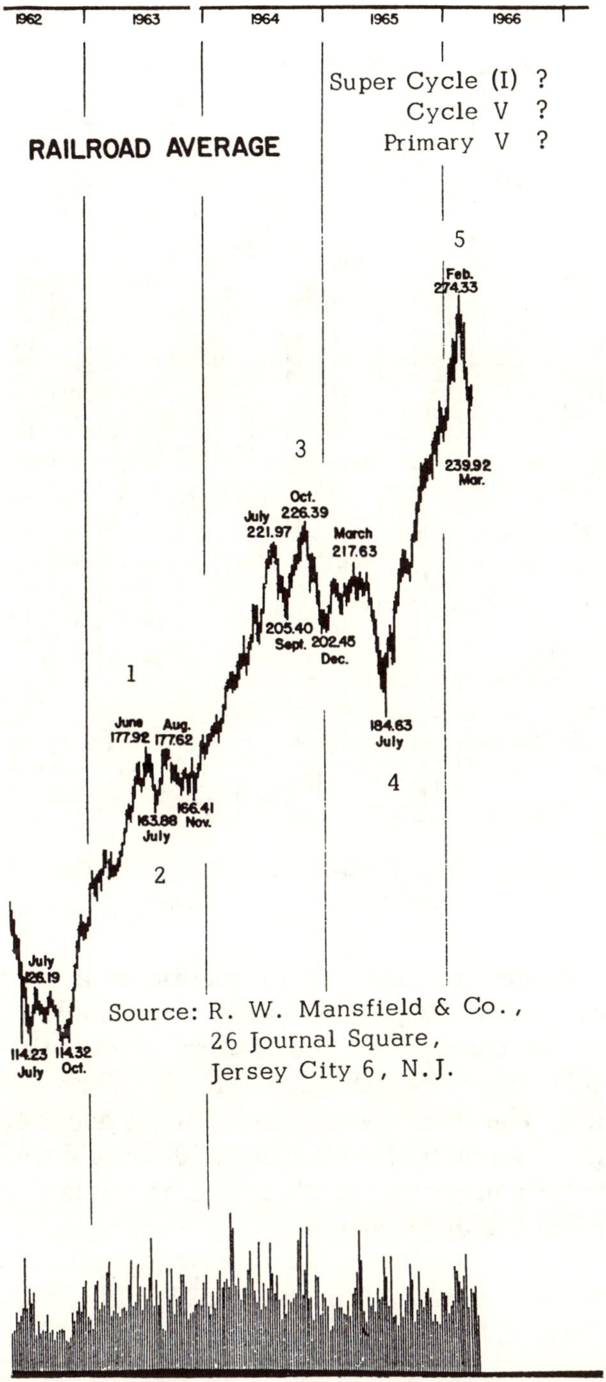
1962
1963
1964
1965
1966
Super Cycle (I) ?
Cycle V ?
Primary V ?
RAILROAD AVERAGE
5
Feb.
274.33
239.92
Mar.
3
Oct.
226.39
July
221.97
March
217.63
205.40
Sept.
202.45
Dec.
1
June
177.92
Aug.
177.62
184.63
July
4
166.41
Nov.
163.88
July
2
July
126.19
114.23
July
114.32
Oct.
Source: R. W. Mansfield & Co.,
26 Journal Square,
Jersey City 6, N.J.

Vendo Company

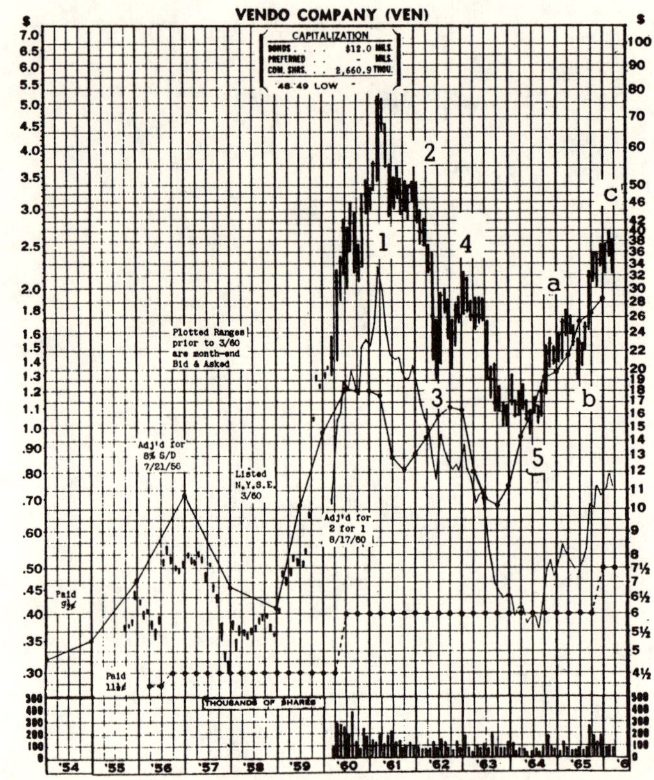

Source: Securities Research Corp., 211 Congress St., Boston, Mass.

Specifically, this stock was mentioned at the time its price was around 25 as indicating a probable new bull market. The chart shows the pattern. From mid-1964 to early 1965, the stock exhibited a 5 up. Then followed a correction. The third wave moved it up to about 40, and a correction is again under way. Mid-1964 could well be the beginning of a major bull market, with an immediate target in wave 3 of the upper 40s.[19]

IBM

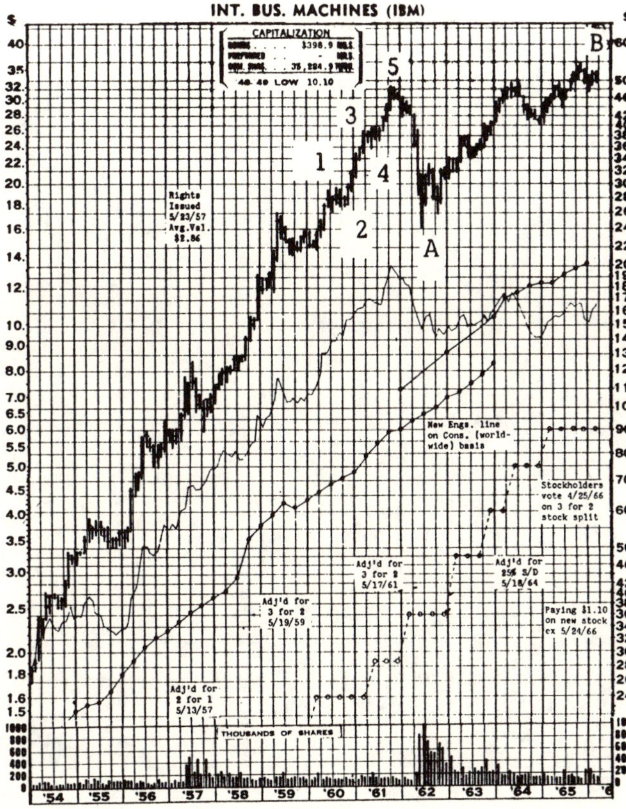

IBM has been a bone of great contention. In everybody's book, it is the great growth stock of the century. Yet the Elliott count shows a 5 wave top in 1961. Since then, the relative action has been much less than average, which means that most stocks since 1961 have done better for the investor. The chart shows that the shareholder today is not too much better off than he was at the peak in 1961, and certainly he would have done better in the majority of other stocks. It may still be that we can classify 1962 to date as a 5 up instead of a 3, but at the present time there should be little incentive to follow this one up, especially as the rate of earnings gain is diminishing. We continue to classify this as an A-B-C situation with the stock hitting its head against B.

Continental Air Lines

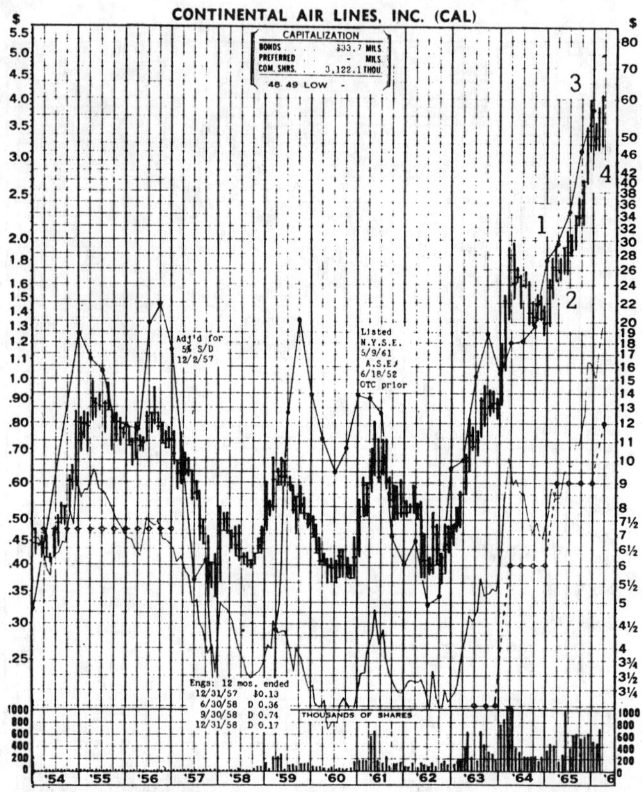

What about the airlines? Patterns are not too clear, except to say that all are in extended waves. One chart that does not yet appear finished is Continental. After hitting a low in late 1964, a new upward pattern developed. Going right through the May-June 1965 decline, the stock has been rising steadily until the year end. The correction in early 1966 appears to be only wave 4, and implies in due course a 5th wave, which may well take the stock off the page.

Finance Stocks

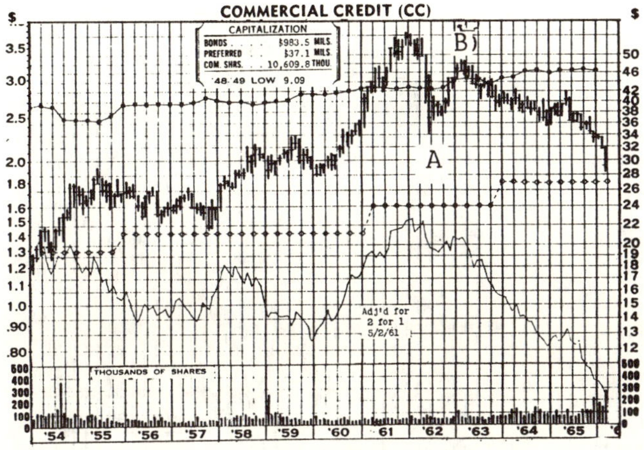

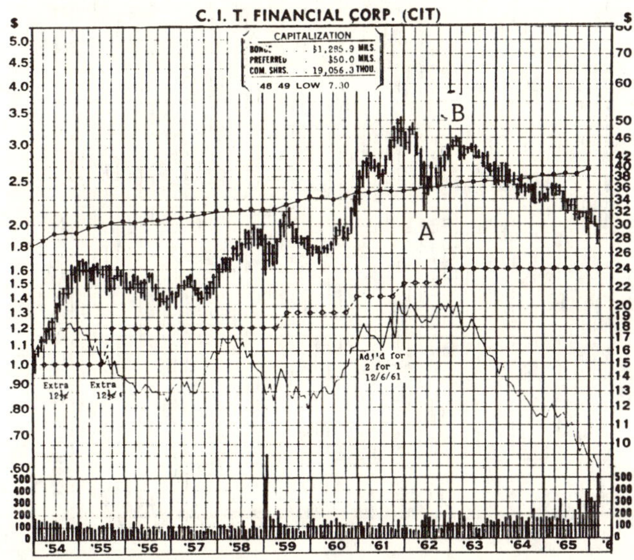

Commercial Credit and C.I.T. Financial are obvious examples of stocks suffering from tight money, in theory. Yet both companies' earnings have continued to expand. Here, then, is a basic revaluation by the public of the price/earnings multiplier. At some point or other, both these stocks will become good value. It would appear that they are well down in the third corrective wave. Not necessarily candidates to be bought now, they should be thoroughly watched over the next few months.

Bristol Myers

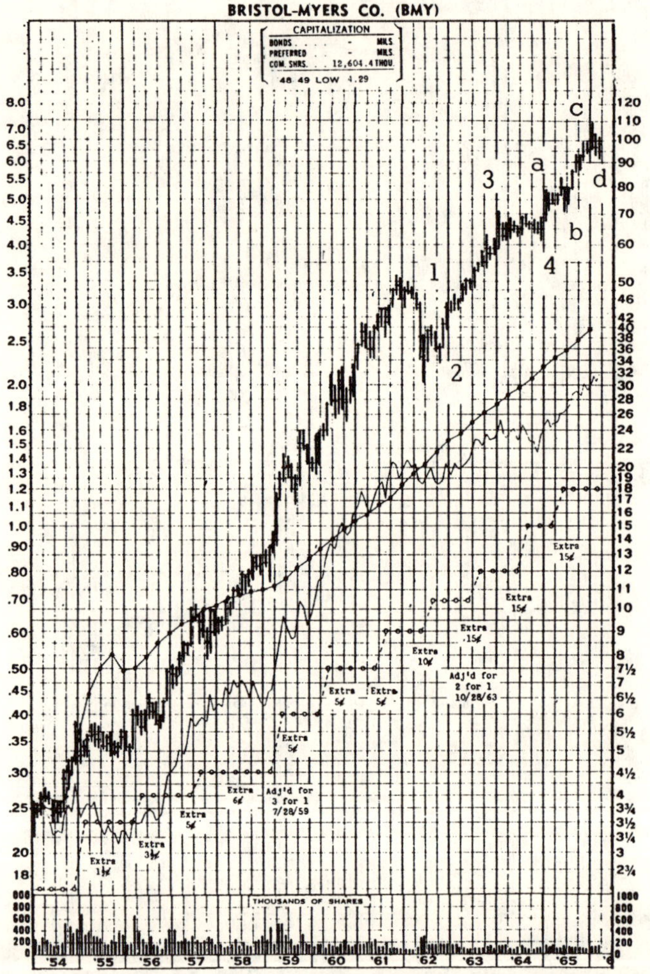

Bristol Myers is a growth stock which has always had something going for it, including constantly expanding earnings. Since 1962, there are clearly three upward phases, with the fifth wave starting in late 1964. However, in the last wave it seems reasonably clear that there have only been so far four phases. The fifth wave of the fifth wave would appear still to be in the future.

Zenith Radio

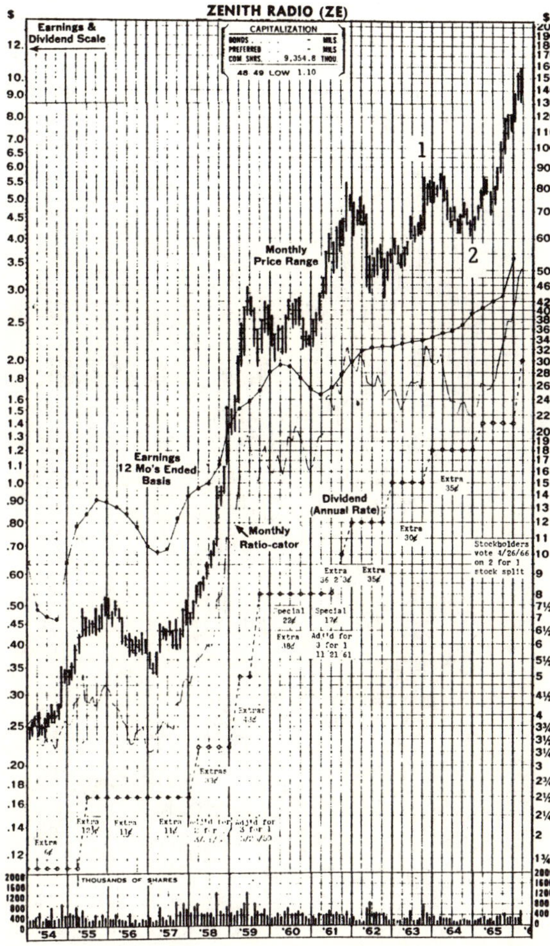

Is Zenith in its fifth wave up from December 1964 or only in its third? We do not know. However, 1962 seems to have been a major starting point from the Elliott point of view. Thus, what we have had so far is a Primary 1 and 2 followed by Primary 3, either still in force or due to close out. Given the possibilities, it would appear that there is a good chance that no major bear market in this stock will take place. The odds favor wave 5 of wave 3 being ahead, but in any event, the odds also favor a bigger wave 3 being in due course followed by waves 4 and 5 at higher levels.

Xerox

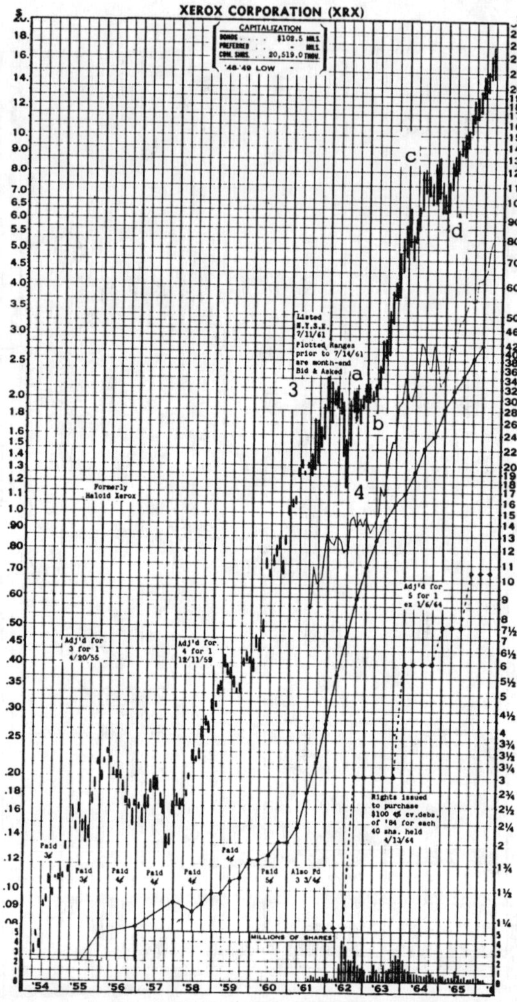

A year ago and 100 points lower, the stock appeared to be in its final wave, but only barely begun in it. Today, and 100 points higher, it is still in its fifth wave. This kind of stock has terrific momentum up to the point that its earnings begin to suffer. Investors should realize with this one that they are on a roller coaster. When it completes its pattern and breaks out, it can bring quick and substantial losses. In the mean-time, there is no indication that the pattern is through.

Ed. Note: We are deeply indebted to Worden & Worden Inc., Ste. 322 Bayview Bldg., Fort Lauderdale, Florida; M.C. Horsey & Co., 3 Wall St., New York 10005; R.W. Mansfield & Co., 26 Journal Square, Jersey City 6, N.J.; and Securities Research Co., 211 Congress St., Boston, for permission to use their charts in this study.

FOOTNOTES

1 Actually 1938.

2 Collins throughout uses wave terminology that is one degree larger than convention. His "Cycles" are Primaries, etc. In this supplement, Bolton shifts his degrees accordingly, probably so as not to confuse a new reader. However, in a personal conversation, Collins told me that when he refers to "Grand Super Cycle wave five," he means Grand Super Cycle *subwave* five, which is of Super Cycle degree.

3 It is a remarkable, if not stunning, observation that for the current dollar Dow, for which Collins' count is correct, a substantial new high is ultimately required, and was achieved in the 1980s, while under the two triangle interpretations, which are correct *only* for the constant dollar Dow, the *final* top is indeed occurring in 1966! Regardless, both Bolton and Collins have recognized a *major top* within weeks of its occurrence.

4 Reflecting Bolton's discomfort, this is Collins' only error, as the correction is far better counted as occurring from 1959 to 1962, and the preceding rise from 1949 to 1959.

5 This is a near perfect description of the market's upcoming path from 1966 to 1974. After the 1966 drop, A. J. Frost computed the final hourly low to be 572, which was met to the dollar at 572.20 in December 1974. See the 1970 Supplement to *The Bank Credit Analyst* in *The Complete Elliott Wave Writings of A. J. Frost* (New Classics Library).

6 Actually he had been appointed by the U.S. Secretary of State to be the chief accountant for the nation of Nicaragua, and was later the chief accountant for the railroad system of Guatemala. For a thorough biography of R. N. Elliott, see *The Major Works of R. N. Elliott* (New Classics Library).

[7] A severe case of parasitic anemia that nearly killed him.

[8] Actually, Elliott, without price data, presumed the start of Grand Supercycle wave 1 as being near 1776 or 1800, a good range for a guess. Data shows the low in 1784.

[9] Collins (and later Bolton as well) refers to this as a regular top, despite the fact that Collins' count labels the "B" wave that follows as peaking *much* (too much, in fact) higher than the fifth. Collins says that the "B" wave was not an "*early* swing into new high ground," so that is probably their criterion for a non-orthodox, i.e., irregular, top.

[10] While this discussion is useful, Bolton's own history shows that he encountered trouble only when *breaking* a rule formulated by Elliott, such as in calling 1928-1949 a triangle.

[11] This is not a "must," as this better drawing shows. Nevertheless, his point that the overall look is that of a "three" is still valid.

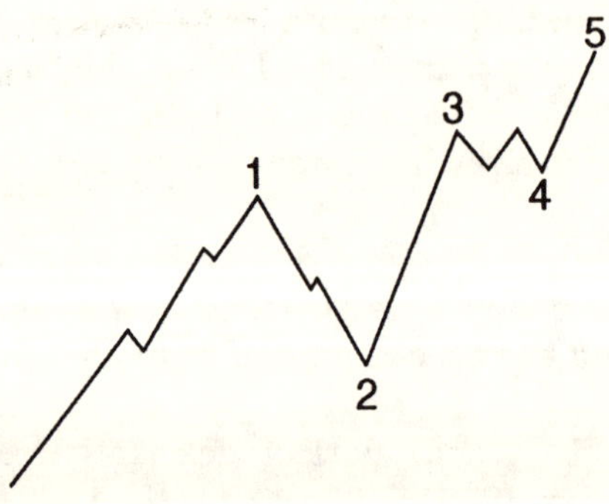

[12] I.e., if waves 5 and 1 are approximately equal in length, as is normal.

[13] Degree makes no difference whatsoever. Both 1929-1932 and 1937-1942 were zigzags. So, apparently, was 1720-1784!

[14] See Footnote 9.

[15] This indeed came to pass at the 1973 high, but not for the reason Collins gives. The 1966-1974 correction was "flat" because the 1937-1942 correction was a zigzag, i.e., Cycle wave IV alternated with Cycle wave II.

[16] The triangle, totaling 15 subwaves, balances the flat, which has 11. The average is still 13.

[17] Seven and eleven are part of a new sequence of numbers related by the Fibonacci ratio. The next number, 18, yields the same results. Any number used as a multiplier will yield differences that produce a sequence of numbers that are related by the Fibonacci ratio, though only certain numbers yield differences that are Fibonacci numbers.

[18] The Industrials are *the* socially accepted barometer of the stock market, and as such, engages the emotions of investors like no other.

[19] Bolton's analysis appears bullish, but the chart's wave count is bearish.

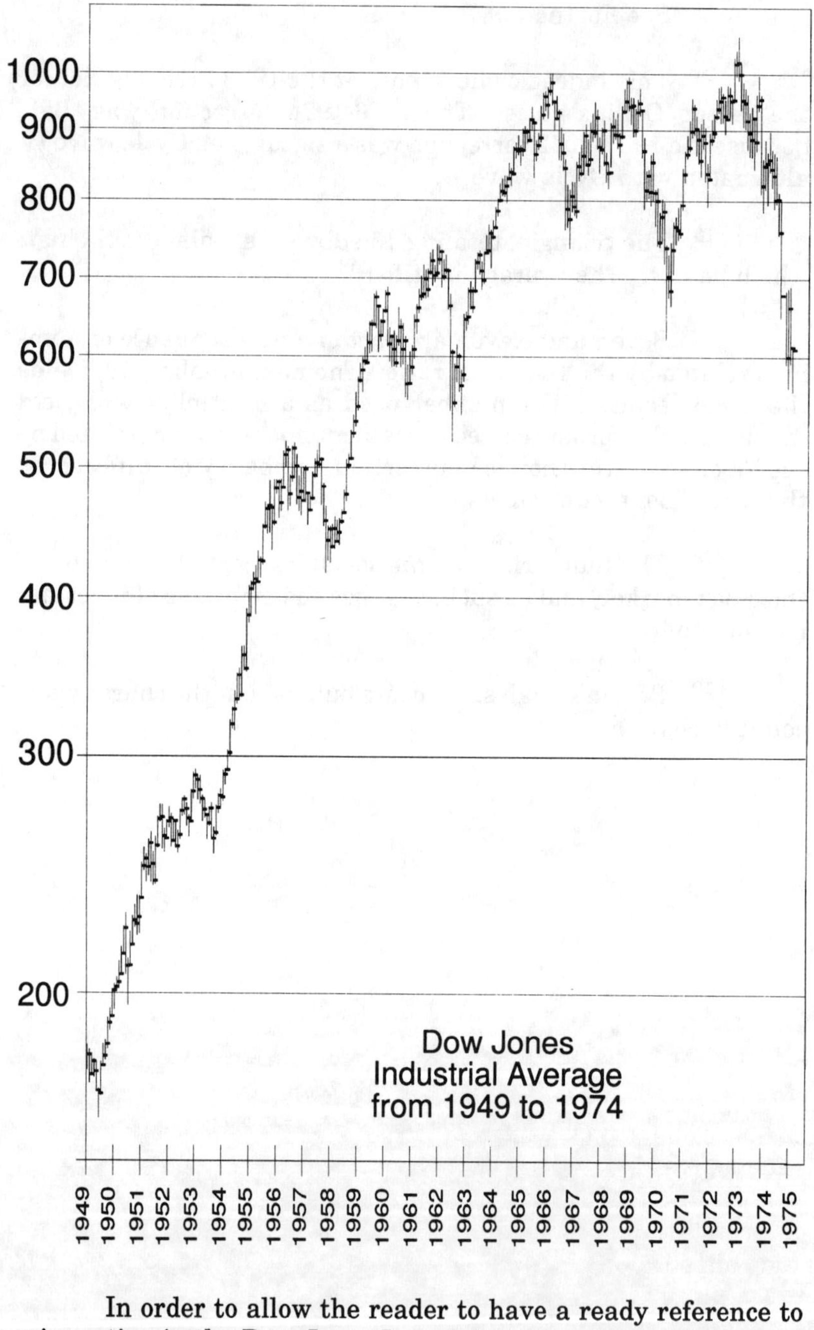

In order to allow the reader to have a ready reference to price action in the Dow Jones Industrial Average over the entire period of the BCA's Elliott Wave forecasts, we have included the above chart.

THE VALUE OF THE WAVE PRINCIPLE IN RETROSPECT

EXTRACTS FROM PREVIOUS ANNUAL "ELLIOTT" REVIEWS, 1953 TO 1966

In order to point out in retrospect the usefulness of Elliott as an investment concept, we quote herewith paragraphs from each of the issues published by us at approximate annual intervals. These issues, of course, were written without the benefit of today's hindsight; they represented opinions expressed as to the likely direction of stock prices, and in the earlier period as to the likely bottom areas to be expected.

"While the market seems historically high, and a great deal of current comment is emphasizing this point, *it may well be that current levels generally are on the low side for some years to come."*

February 1953
Dow Jones Industrials 284

"The Intermediate wave that started in September 1953 has all the ear-marks of similar waves starting in 1935, 1942 and 1949. Thus, when this first wave is completed, we should see four other waves before the fifth Primary closes out, which close-out would terminate the first Cycle wave from 1949. Obviously, if this interpretation is correct, there is lots of time and bullish amplitude ahead."

April 1954
Dow Jones Industrials 319

"Any consolidation should be from considerably higher levels."

March 1955
Dow Jones Industrials 410

"The general bullish prediction of basic Elliott theory is still intact."

March 1956
Dow Jones Industrials 490

"The new bull wave which started in 1949 is of tidal proportions. It will be interrupted from time to time, but corrections will tend to be subnormal. With the prospect of perhaps 1000 DJIA in the early '60s, there need be no excess of long term pessimism."

April 1957
Dow Jones Industrials 486

"We are still in the corrective wave from 1956, though the 'Elliott' outlook is not too bearish for the next year or two, and ultimately we should push up to new highs way above the levels of 1956."

April 1958
Dow Jones Industrials 453

"We are now well along in Primary wave V, which will complete the Cycle wave from 1949."

March 1959
Dow Jones Industrials 602

"We have not yet seen the final phase of the great 1949—? bull market. The advance from 1949 should be completed when 583 points have been added to the 1957 low of 416, or a total of 999 DJIA."

May 1960
Dow Jones Industrials 620

"We are now well entrenched in the fifth wave. This should be a period of great activity and speculation, and may well be followed by an important market crash. A logical area to expect the bottom of the ensuing bear market would be about the 520 level."

May 1961
Dow Jones Industrials 692

"The key at this point is whether the basic long-term trend line from 1949 will be decisively broken on the downside in 1962."*

*It was. (Ed.)

April 1962
Dow Jones Industrials 680

"The first wave of the correction is now about over. Purchases made at the present time should work out extremely satisfactorily."

May 1962
Dow Jones Industrials 577

"A new bull market started at the end of June, 1962. Eventually wave (B) should put the market into new high ground, by more than a nose. The 524 mark in the Dow Jones Industrials looks like a barrier that will not, within the next few years, and perhaps ever, be surpassed on the downside."

May 1963
Dow Jones Industrials 720

"It looks as if 1000 in the Average could be our next major target."

April 1964
Dow Jones Industrials 812

"The wave since the Cuban Crisis [1962] is extending; the extensions are not complete yet."

May 1965
Dow Jones Industrials 934

"It is now pretty clear that we have had five fully completed waves in the Averages up from June 1962. We have to face the probability that we completed *a major five wave upward pattern of Cycle degree* in January 1966. This gives us two downside bench marks for the market correction ahead, the first being 740 and the second being 525. Collins suggests that we will probably have a bear market in three stages, i.e., an A, a B and a C wave, with a possible objective around the 740 level for A, a retracement upwards of part or all of the decline, and a C wave bottom around 525."

April 1966
Dow Jones Industrials 942

THE *Bolton-Tremblay*

BANK CREDIT ANALYST

WHAT IT IS

The Bank Credit Analyst is a privately circulated *monthly barometer* of the long term economic trends and broad business conditions for *Investments of all types:* inventories and capital outlays as well as stocks and bonds. Its raw materials are the complex banking and credit statistics published weekly and monthly by the Federal Reserve System, U.S.A.'s central bank.

UNDERLYING PRINCIPLE

An expanding economy creates a favorable climate for investments in general whereas a contracting economy does the opposite. The most effective gauge of economic expansion or contraction is the Flow of Money (and Credit) — the life-blood of the economy and the common denominator of all business transactions. The information is comprehensive, accurate and — unlike most data from other sources — very quickly available, which allows the weekly charting of the Nation's economic health for *Investment Planning and Timing:*

> "Money and Credit provide the one denominator common to all economic activity. If we attempt to compare trends in carloadings with trends in personal income, GNP, wages or steel production, we run into considerable difficulties as to appropriate weighting. The problem becomes considerably simplified when it is realized that all activity takes place in current dollars. Since we want to get to know about the whole economy as quickly as possible, we don't want to have to take each little segment measured in units of no comparable standard, and then have to try to arrive at the whole from the diverse parts.
>
> "The only alternative (and a particularly attractive one) is to study the whole flow of money and credit, and from this study decide what the trend is going to be. Fortunately we have the data on a relatively precise and timely basis from the condition statements of the banking system. We get the broad picture without having to make a number of suppositions with regard to the parts."

TOOLS

Our Editor-in-Chief, A. Hamilton Bolton, and our money-minded research staff have pioneered in this Money and Credit Approach to Investments. The analytical techniques which they devised and over the years perfected are unique. The main tools used are the Composite Equity Index and the Composite Bank Credit Barometer. These basic indices and the many others which supplement them are described in our new 100-page handbook "Introduction to Bank Credit Analysis".

In addition to the analysis of the F. R. statistics, The Bank Credit Analyst comments technical studies of the stock market itself. Breadth, momentum, short interest and stock market credit are all under continuous study. This is truly a combination of *Research with Judgment*, resulting in lucid and straightforward analytical appraisals of the investment weather.

FOR BUSINESS INVESTMENTS

As an *economic barometer* The Bank Credit Analyst has been most helpful to businessmen and industrialists in the establishment of long-range policies and planning in general. This category of subscribers depend on The Bank Credit Analyst for the advanced signal that will tell them whether the economy is strengthening or weakening, so that they may safely increase or decrease their *inventories* and make intelligent plans concerning long-term *capital expenditures.*

FOR SECURITIES INVESTMENTS

The Money and Credit Approach to *securities investments* has had an enviable record since publication of The Bank Credit Analyst. For instance, it has correctly delineated the important buying areas of 1949, 1953, 1958 and 1960, and has pointed out in advance the danger zones of 1951, 1956 and 1959. More recently, bank credit analysis was called upon to play a different, though nonetheless important role, in helping subscribers keep a cool head during the 1962 market break which it immediately labelled as essentially psychological in nature, therefore temporary. Markets have since been approaching their previous high levels.

EDITORS — The Bank Credit Analyst is edited by Bolton, Tremblay & Company, Investment Consultants, 1245 Sherbrooke St. West, MONTREAL 25, CANADA. Registered with the Securities and Exchange Commission, Washington, D.C. — A. Hamilton Bolton, B.A. (McGill), M.B.A. (Harvard), Editor-in-Chief.

PUBLISHERS — The Bank Credit Analyst is published monthly and all rights are reserved by Bolton, Tremblay (Bermuda) Limited, P. O. Box 498, HAMILTON, BERMUDA.

DISTRIBUTORS — The Bank Credit Analyst is distributed by B.C.A. Distributors Ltd., 1245 Sherbrooke St. West, MONTREAL 25, CANADA. Subscription rates are $100. for twelve months, air mail, to any part of the world ($60. for six months). Tax-deductible in U.S.A.

EIGHT HUNDRED
BUHL BUILDING
DETROIT 26, MICHIGAN

May 4, 1966

Dear Hamilton:

Received the 25 brochures and appreciate your friendly references to my work with Elliott's theory.

It seems to me that you have made an excellent presentation of the subject, and I am glad that our respected viewpoints are now synchronized.

Sorry, but I am not attending the New York convention.

Regards,

C J Collins
ag

Hamilton Bolton, Esq.
Bolton, Tremblay & Company
1245 Sherbrooke Street W.
Montreal 25, Canada

Montreal
June 2nd, 1966

Mr. Robert A. Warren
President
R. W. Redman Company Inc.
580-610 Providence Highway
Dedham, Massachusetts

Dear Bob:

You may think you have problems in letter-writing. How about me? Yours of April 10th still is unanswered.

As to tape recorder, we have available at speeds 3 3/4 and 7 1/2.

You are right that I have been putting more study into the longer range cycles to try to prove or disprove their validity. Hence my feeling that we may be entering a 3-year rocky period.

Your assignment at Virginia sounds interesting, but I have not seen any headlines to the effect that they lynched you yet.

There seems to be little vogue these days for studies in timing. It is becoming a lost art I would gather. Your lecture outlines would be valuable, and who knows, maybe the next phase will re-emphasize its importance.

I couldn't care less about what the orthodox proponents of the status quo have to say. But one has to make sure that one is not characterized as a complete crackpot. This involves weaving the current "in" thinking into a pattern whereby one can logically become an iconoclast. It becomes a sort of investment 6th column philosophy! I'd be glad to hear from you at your leisure.

Best regards,

AHB/th

A. H. Bolton

March 29, 1967

Mr. C. J. Collins
Eight Hundred
Buhl Building
Detroit, Michigan 48226

Dear Joe,

I have your letter to Mr. Korn, and appreciate the opportunity to reply. I think in general I agree with your thinking and definitely feel that February to October 1966 was 5 waves down, which of course, makes it rather unique. The overlap that you speak of is however very small and is only in the intraday figures which, as you know, are not made at one time but are the highest or lowest quotations for the stocks at any time during the day. Since the hourly figures have been available I have used them rather than the full range, and on this basis I don't think there was any overlap.

Thus it would appear we had a 5-down. Further the way I counted the waves, I gave the 4th wave to the period from the bottom in May to July 7th. (I think. I haven't any material with me as I am en route at this moment between Bermuda and New York). This series of waves looks like a 4th wave triangle to me, and leads up to a very clear-cut 5th wave down to October 10th, as I see it. Now a 5 wave down of this size is really unique, I think, and I wonder what it means. It does not necessarily preclude a big comeback from wave B but it does suggest the implication that wave B would not go back as high as a wave B starting from a 3 wave down. The biggest 5 wave down I know (except of course 1930-32) was 1937. Here wave B in 1938 recovered 62% of the decline. (Inside the 1937-38 wave too, wave 2, after a 5 down from March to June 1937, recovered some 80-90% of wave 1, but this is not strictly comparable.) Sixty-two per cent of the decline would bring us up to about 900-910, which is the point at which the down wave from February 1966 broke the 1962-66 trend line. I would judge that this is the area at which (despite the pressures there will be to play along further] we should all be out of everything we don't want to hold through the drought.

Page 2.

Anent 62%, this is of course the Fibonacci ratio and I am quite impressed with how often recoveries and setbacks of this size seem to work out as well as the reciprocal 38%. These are of course close to Dow's original 3/8ths and 5/8ths as well as Hamilton's 2/3rds and 1/3rd. For instance, the intermediate from the November high 1966 to end December was very close to 38% of the October-November rise of around 80-85 points.

This brings me to another point. Some of us are not satisfied with a lot of Elliott, due to its imprecision and, accordingly, would like to "improve" on wave theory taking the best of Elliott and adjusting it to much more rigid analysis. Among those who feel this way (apart from me) is Bob Warren whom you may know. He spent many years at Keystone, where he was in charge of special research, and is now retired but keenly interested in Elliott as well as all other investment lore. Also, I might mention Arthur Merrill whose "Behavior of Prices on Wall Street" available from him for $8.35 you should get if you don't have it.

Bob Warren's idea is to get together a small group of Elliott buffs to try and codify and otherwise set up a real wave theory which will not be subject to the myriad of interpretations and minutiae which can well change a given major interpretation because of a small minor quibble about a wave formation. I heartily endorse the idea, and to make this more concrete I suggest such a group might well meet on the occasion of Humphrey Neill's Contrary Opinion Forum this fall in Vermont (always the last weekend in September or 1st and 2nd October). This forum starts Thursday evening, works Friday up to noon Saturday. The Elliott group c uld stay on and work Saturday afternoon and part or all day Sunday after the Forum. It would give us all an interest in setting a fixed date (plus the fact that Humphrey's Forum is always worthwhile). I would suggest however that if this is agreeable we do not publicize the same to anyone except our own group or otherwise we will be inundated with various "students" who will want to get in the act. My list of buffs is by no means complete but tentatively I would like to see:

Bob Warren
Joe Collins
Arthur Merrill
Jack Frost (ex associate of mine, now in Ottawa, Canada)
Paul Dysart of Louisville, Kentucky
Jeff Drew

Page 3.

Any other names will be gratefully received. We can then choose and pick but the initial group should not be too large.

Prior to the meeting, by mail we should try to decide an agenda of what we hope to accomplish, with a list of materials requirements. A small budget for photocopying could be set up as some may not have access to Elliott's major works, "The Wave Principle"1938, Nature's Law, 1945. Financial world articles, etc... Also, certain of the group may want to table other material.

And so, in principle, would you be willing to join such a group with such an objective ? Because of my organization, I can do quite a lot to keep the ball rolling, but I undoubtedly will need a good deal of help.

Please let me hear from you at your earliest convenience. If your answer as a keen Elliotter, is positive, I can go ahead from there.

Best regards,

A. H. Bolton

AHB/cc

Editor's Note: Bolton died one week later.

August 1993

MEMORANDUM TO
ROBERT R. PRECHTER, JR. CMT

The Nicholas Molodovsky Award was presented to A. Hamilton Bolton posthumously in 1987 by the Financial Analysts Federation. It reads,

> *"This award is presented periodically only to those individuals who have made outstanding contributions of such significance as to change the direction of the profession and to raise it to higher standards of accomplishment. It was established to honor Nicholas Molodovsky, one of the profession's outstanding scholars and the first recipient of the award."*

Since that date, there have been eight recipients, with A. Hamilton Bolton being the fifth. The award was received by Dominic Doluhy, Mr. Bolton's brother, on behalf of the Bolton family during a meeting of the Montreal Society of Financial Analysts. I made the presentation of the award in my capacity then as Vice Chair of the Financial Analysts Federation. A. Hamilton Bolton was Chairman of the Federation in 1959-1960 when the organization was called the National Federation of Financial Analysts Societies.

Cordially,

Bernadette B. Murphy, CMT
Past President of FAF, 1988-1989